Edinburgh University Library

Books may be recalled for return earlier than due if so you will be contacted by e-mail or letter.

Due Date	Due Date	Due Date

Gender, Politics, and Democracy

Gender, Politics, and Democracy

WOMEN'S SUFFRAGE IN CHINA

Louise Edwards

STANFORD UNIVERSITY PRESS

STANFORD, CALIFORNIA

Stanford University Press
Stanford, California

Printed in the United States of America on acid-free, archival-quality paper

Library of Congress Cataloging-in-Publication Data

Edwards, Louise P.
  Gender, politics, and democracy : women's suffrage in China / Louise Edwards.
      p. cm.
  Includes bibliographical references and index.
  ISBN 978-0-8047-5688-4 (cloth : alk. paper)
  1. Women--Suffrage--China--History--20th century. 2. Women in politics--China--History--20th century. 3. Feminism--China--History--20th century. I. Title.
  JQ1518.E39 2008
  324.6'230951--dc22   2007029133
Typeset by Bruce Lundquist in 10.5/14 Adobe Garamond

For my parents,
Howard Charles Edwards (Ted)
Sonia Elizabeth Edwards (née Lee)

Contents

Figures

Acknowledgments

New Zealand children learn early in their education that in 1893 their homeland was the first self-governing country to award women the vote. Moreover, the franchise extended to both Maori and Pakeha women simultaneously. Around a century later, women occupied the two top government positions: Helen Clark and Jenny Shipley as prime ministers, and Catherine Tizard and Silvia Cartwright as governors general. Women's early and continuing success in political leadership is a matter of some considerable pride in Aotearoa New Zealand.

As one of those New Zealand schoolchildren, I progressed through schools in Otara, Otahuhu, and Opotiki and the women suffragists continued to draw my attention. I rather liked the idea of women from the "olden days" standing up to be heard. I was in awe of their strength, bravery, and organizational skill. And I was amazed that they coordinated their movement with "sister suffragettes" from all parts of the world—including China. As an adult, my fascination continued, and when I learned that nothing had been written on the Chinese women I set myself that very task.

This book has taken a very long time to write, and my debts of gratitude are many. The research took place while I worked variously at the University of Queensland, Australian Catholic University, Australian National University, and the University of Technology, Sydney. Colleagues and students in each of these institutions have contributed much to the ongoing pleasure I have in writing and learning. Librarians and archivists in Beijing, Shanghai, Hong Kong, Taipei, Canberra, Brisbane, Melbourne, and Sydney have been remarkable in their enthusiasm for tracking down sources. The Australian Research Council provided funding for the project, enabling me to travel to libraries and find time to write. Stanford University Press's team of Muriel Bell, Kirsten Oster, Joa Suorez, Mary Barbosa, and Mariana Raykov as well as Kathryn Bernhardt and another anonymous reader for the press have been invaluable in improving the manuscript as it underwent the many revision and editing processes. To all of these people and institutions, I owe enormous thanks.

On a personal note, my friends and family in New Zealand and Australia provided many welcome distractions and much needed support over the years. You are too numerous to list individually, and here I will make particular mention only of my family. My strong, brave, and highly organized Kiwi sisters, Debbie, Kate, and Nicola, show me that the spirit of the suffragists of the 1890s continues to thrive in New Zealand today. My Aussie son and daughter, Chris and Alex Louie, are a constant source of joy, jokes, and common sense. My husband, Kam Louie, has managed two decades of life with a wannabe suffragette with untold patience. And finally my greatest debt is to my parents, Ted and Sonia, to whom this book is dedicated. You provided me with life, then filled it with love and laughter, and showed me the value of courage and resilience. Thank you.

Sydney, 2006

Gender, Politics, and Democracy

Introduction

In March 1912 a group of over sixty women's suffrage activists stormed the parliament of the new Republic of China in Nanjing demanding the right to vote and stand for election. They smashed windows, chanted slogans, and scuffled with security guards while the male parliamentarians who inherited the mantle of rule dismissed women's claims to full, equal, enfranchised citizenship in Asia's first republic. Nine years later, in March of 1921, another women's suffrage group marched into the provincial parliament of the southern region of Guangdong to press the case for political equality with men in their provincial constitution. Conservative male legislators hurled ink boxes and chairs at the women, rendering one petitioner unconscious and leaving several others with cuts and bruises. Clearly, the prospect of Chinese women voting and standing for election on an equal basis with men generated considerable tension and anxiety among the political elite of early Republican China.

The persistence and vigor of the women's suffrage campaigns eventually produced the longed-for success. Within a few years of the Guangzhou incident, the constitutions of several important provinces provided women equality with men in political rights, and women were elected to provincial legislatures. By 1936 a national constitution guaranteeing women equality had been drafted and waited only for the election of a National Assembly for ratification. A decade later, in 1946, the women's suffrage activists won a guaranteed minimum 10 percent quota of seats for women. Despite this impressive record of feminist success in China, little is known about the Chinese women's suffrage movement. The women that led the campaigns from the 1900s to the 1940s had apparently slid into the recesses of history—their courage, vision, and initiative forgotten.

The women's suffrage campaign was but one part of the vibrant women's movement in China in the first half of the twentieth century. For the women involved, winning the franchise was deemed the key to simultaneously redressing past injustices and confirming women's rightful place in the present political arena in order that potential future injustices could be prevented. Other women's groups focused on winning improvements in wages and conditions for women workers, and yet others still aimed to link women's activism with philanthropy and welfare or family reform. Women in these various groups collaborated and contributed to each other's campaigns because women activists in China soon came to conceive of women as a group with a unity of interests and political needs. However, the activists that took winning the suffrage as their prime focus regarded formal political power as the ultimate guarantee of all other rights. Improved work conditions and wages for women and effecting family and marriage reform that expanded women's rights were all seen to be dependent upon women gaining representation in formal legislative processes, according to the suffrage activists. They believed that women politicians could best defend women's rights.

Through narrating the story of the women suffragists' campaigns, this current volume demonstrates that over the course of the first five decades of the twentieth century China's feminists moved pragmatically between arguments based on women's inherent equality with men and those based on women's difference from men. In China, arguments for suffrage rights that invoked the logic of the "essential and fundamental equality of human beings regardless of sex" appeared as frequently as those that invoked the logic of the "essential and fundamental differences between the sexes." These twin logics were not regarded as diametrically opposing tools, as was often presumed in Western feminist writings of the late 1980s and 1990s, and neither did they cause schisms in the movement as a whole. In the hands of China's feminists, both became strategic tools of fluctuating efficacy depending on the particularities of the historical moment. Thus, China's suffrage feminists mobilized "equality arguments" and "difference arguments" at distinct times within their campaigns. Difference arguments initially were important in building a notion of women's collective political interests and later became powerful tools for winning special quotas for women in legislative bodies. Equality arguments were at first fundamental to the destruction of long-standing notions of women's lack of independent personhood—a view that deemed political participation unnecessary for women as individuals. Later the equality arguments came to underscore campaigns for legal reforms on matters of winning equal access to education, property, and divorce. Pragmatic goal orientation typified the Chinese suffrage movement during the first half of the twentieth century rather than theoretical purity.

This book explores the evolution of this feminist-activist pragmatism and in so doing suggests that anxieties among contemporary feminist theorists about the relative merits of one argument or the other may be less pressing if one takes a historical view.[1] Both "equality" and "difference" are useful arguments, depending on one's specific political goal in relation to the given historical and cultural context.

Significantly, China's suffragists mobilized both arguments within the premise of women's collective disadvantage as a group. Until the end of the nineteenth century, recognition of women's lower status as a group compared to men did not translate into recognition of the potential political utility of this consciousness. From the first decade of the twentieth century the expansion of the women's movement created a collective notion of women as human beings that deserved identification outside clan or familial relationships.[2] The feminists' propounding of women's unity of disadvantage created just such a political category that over the course of the decades under consideration became increasingly publicly accepted. Whether women as a political category were equal or different from men was less important than the underlying premise that women were identifiable as a discrete and disadvantaged political group. And, as a recognized political group, they pressed convincing arguments for political representation.

Women's collective identity as a disadvantaged political group was framed not only in contrast to men as a presumed politically advantaged group, but also in connection to the key political signifier of the time—the nation. Consciousness of women's politicized collectivity was central to rhetoric of national strengthening from the 1898 Reform Movement onward. Indeed, nationalism and feminism emerged almost simultaneously in China, and as a consequence much scholarly attention has been devoted to untangling the connections between the two.[3] Sometimes this "untangling project" was driven by the search for a pure feminist tradition and other times by the desire to deny the existence of this very same feminism. Yet the pragmatism of the suffrage activists points to a new perspective on our understandings about the connection between nationalism and feminism in China.

In an attempt to find a path between the search for a pure feminist tradition or the denial of one, one current scholarly perspective on these twin forces presents an intimate relation between nationalism and feminism. For example, Peter Zarrow stated, "feminists generally argued their case for the equality of women in China while accepting a discourse dominated by nationalist concerns."[4] Wang Zheng argued, "women wove the two lines of argument—national strengthening and equal rights—into a single thread: national strengthening required women's equal participation in all spheres."[5] While emphasizing the intimacy of the connections between feminism and nationalism, even this kind of scholarship tends to reify a static conception of both feminism and nationalism. As will become clear through the chronological development of the chapters to follow, neither feminism nor nationalism connoted the same theoretical perspective or activist position across the entire five decades.

The commonplace use of the term "nationalism" in current literature homogenizes a diverse range of positions, beliefs, expectations, and actions.[6] Just as Chinese feminism incorporated arguments based on both equality and difference, Chinese nationalism embraced apparently contradictory sentiments of nativism and internationalism. Depending on the dominant political voice at each particular historical juncture, Chinese nationalism has assumed many diverse forms including anti-Manchu Han chauvinism, anti-imperialist Marxism, and anticommunist radicalism as well as national salvation, nation building, and national defense. China's feminists found the flexibility of the meanings encapsulated in "nationalism" extremely useful since they were able to invoke multiple different qualities within the broad category of nationalism as it suited their cause. However, from the mid-1920s onward, as the political situation in China concentrated power in the hands of two major political parties—the Chinese Communist Party, or CCP (*Gongchandang*) and the Nationalists (*Guomindang*)—the feminists' flexibility to mobilize around the term "nationalism" diminished as one or the other party wrought supreme control over its meaning. Nonetheless, nationalism was contested throughout the decades, and feminism's connection to it evolved pragmatically at each point of contestation.

Declaring that China's feminists were always also nationalists does little to illuminate their political positions, actions, or arguments given the fluctuations in meanings of *nationalism* over the course of the five decades in question. As the women's suffrage movement in China explored gendered notions of political citizenship they invoked these ever-fluctuating conceptions of nationalism and national benefit as it suited their particular goals. Multiple versions of patriotism and nationalism were variously safe havens, useful tools, and firmly held beliefs at different times over the course of the decades of struggle for women's franchise in China. Dismantling the commonplace assumption that there was one, unitary nationalism, with identical political characteristics and utility across the entire period is crucial to understanding the nature of Chinese feminism, as we will see below.

WHO WERE THE SUFFRAGISTS?

Throughout this volume, readers will be introduced to a host of individual suffrage activists and will come to appreciate the evolution of the movement's membership over the course of the decades under exploration. Starting with a narrow elite the movement broadened to include both middle- and working-class women by the mid-1920s. The diversification of the women's suffrage movement mirrors that of China's politically active population as a whole. While the membership increasingly drew from a broader cross-section of society, the leaders of the suffrage movement filled the ranks of China's expanding professional class. Suffrage leaders comprise China's first women school principals, university presidents, doctors, journalists, and lawyers. They sought political power to extend the scope for women in China's public spaces and naturally went on to form the core of China's first women politicians and party leaders.

As Chapter Two shows, women active in seeking equal political rights with men during the years immediately before and after the 1911 revolution were comparatively wealthy and were overwhelmingly privileged with education, first in their family homes and later as students in Japan. For the most part these women were free of marital responsibilities—being variously unmarried, widowed, or separated.[7] Without family or clan restrictions, these first suffrage activists crafted political identities for themselves as women that were both public and antagonistic. They fought in formal military battles and served as spies and assassins as part of the movement to build a Chinese democratic republic—without which they would have no suffrage rights. They wrote articles and gave speeches at rallies demanding their audience to recognize the necessity of improving women's rights and status. The early suffragists' freedom from financial and marital constraints along with their privileged access to education was central to expanding awareness about the possibility of women's political consciousness and group activism. Their success was evident in the growth of the women's movement in later decades.

The women leading the movement from the 1920s onward were typically educated in China or the USA rather than Japan and grew more concerned about their potential to represent women as a constituency. At this time we see the full power of the collective consciousness of women's unity of disadvantage coming into effect. In the public spaces created by their women political leaders through the 1920s, 1930s, and 1940s, a wider variety of women were active in a broader range of political spheres—women from all walks of life with a full range of political perspectives appeared in the public arena. Communists and Nationalists joined forces to campaign for expanded women's political space, making effective use of their now well-developed sense of women's collective identity and the power of its politicized lobby. Since the 1920s, as a result of the sustained efforts of the suffrage activists, women voted and were elected to formal political positions in villages, cities, and provinces to a range of different assemblies, parliaments, and councils.

Rather than being a brief spark of "bourgeois feminism," the discussion to follow shows that women's suffrage activism in China was a sustained campaign, where activists of one generation passed information, tactics, and energy on to the next, oftentimes across political party divides. The increasingly common public appearance of individual women in high-level political roles signified the importance of women's suffrage to the overall status of women in China. These women advocated changes to fundamental social and economic structures in their espousal of an explicit agenda for increasing women's power and influence relative to men. Regardless of an individual woman's perspective on the preferred political system, the public appearance of women leaders in advocacy roles on behalf of women as a collectivity increasingly ensured that no political party could ignore the question of women's status and role in society.

As the following section argues, there are strong and pressing reasons for an enhanced appreciation of the history of the women's suffrage movement. Above and beyond its significance to the Chinese women's movement as a whole, the suffrage movement had important impacts on the broader Chinese political scene.

WHY EXPLORE THE CHINESE SUFFRAGE MOVEMENT?

This suffrage movement warrants wider attention for a number of reasons—not least because the women involved deserve recognition for their struggles and successes in reshaping China's political terrain. A deeper understanding of the history of this movement contributes to our expanding knowledge of China's gendered political landscape and the history of women's suffrage at a global level. The suffrage movement also reveals the complex reformulations of Chinese notions of political legitimacy that took place in the transition from monarchy to democracy (albeit fragile) during these decades. It uncovers the fraught search for publicly recognized political legitimacy that accompanied the transition from a government structured around monarch-appointed literati bureaucrats to popularly elected legislators. The women suffragists' public contestation of the centuries-old assumption that formal political power was embodied in the male form undermined many attempts by male legislators to assert legitimacy for assemblies that did not include women in the post-monarchy political order. Parliaments and senates that excluded women, the suffragists declared, were illegitimate and unrepresentative structures.

The women's suffrage movement shows us the manner in which the anxiety about China's weakened international standing made these new, male-only political structures vulnerable to attack. The women argued that a "modern" nation, such as China aspired to become, included women as full and equal political citizens. They invoked examples of "advanced" nations around the world to which China's current parliaments were unfavorably compared. By presenting women's suffrage as an emblem of modernity, the activists played on China's new leaders' longing for international respect. In this regard the story of the suffragists provides evidence of the manner in which China's leaders grappled with the impact of globalization on China's domestic politics in their oftentimes defensive assertion of China's integrity and equality within the "brotherhood" of nations.[8]

The story of the suffragists' campaigns also shows how women complicated the long-standing Confucian premise that formal education legitimized access to political power. This was a system that was open only to men, and for centuries Chinese governments drew learned men into their bureaucracies through formal examinations on philosophy and literature. Mastery of this knowledge was deemed to demonstrate virtue, which in turn legitimized a man's exercise of bureaucratic power. In the first half of the twentieth century, women suffragists uncoupled this naturalized connection between men and political power through demonstrations of women's literacy, erudition, and eloquence and their participation in formal, examinable education. Rather than challenge the link between education and access to power, the women activists promoted women's participation in the education system. They agreed that educational attainment was an important marker of the right to wield political power and then demonstrated that women could be as expert in learning as men once they won access to the same education system.

Simultaneously they transformed gendered customs of politics by carving a space for women in public affairs. Their sustained and often controversial public political actions gradually dismantled customary prohibitions restricting "good" women's public presence. Previously, isolation in the domestic sphere signified a woman's high moral standing, yet over the course of the first half of the twentieth century a "good" woman increasingly was conceived as a politically aware and politically active woman. This shift impacted directly on family politics and national politics as well as on gendered codes of personal virtue.

Histories of women suffrage in China also promote further knowledge of China's long-term, continuing, and evolving engagement with democracy and democratic principles. The first half of the twentieth century is routinely dismissed as a period of political and military chaos, yet as this book reveals, the vibrancy of the democratic activism grew from the extensive, albeit often flawed, political structures in place. Frank Dikötter presents a convincing case that governance in these decades "displayed considerable elements of continuity in terms of political vision, administrative practice or government personnel" and that the politically engaged population experienced openness to new ideas and the world "as global flows fostered an unprecedented degree of diversity."[9] The campaigns of the women's suffrage activists in engaging with governments and bureaucracies and in eliciting support and tactics from their global sister suffragists support Dikötter's view. The history of democratic activism in China has long been captive to disputes between pro- and anti-Marxist positions that have variously decried the corruption of the republican governments or the repression of the CCP governments.

This history of democratic activism in China is a hotly contested and evolving process—the changing reception of the histories of the women's suffrage campaigns provides new insights into this phenomenon. Until the last decade, historians from the People's Republic of China (PRC) had routinely dismissed the women's suffrage campaign as a marginal bourgeois movement, yet a new interest in histories of women's suffrage is emerging there, no doubt inspired by increasing democratization in China itself.[10] In such scholarship, the CCP's role in harnessing and leading the women's suffrage movement toward their democratic goals is newly celebrated as China's ruling party seeks to inscribe its machinery with democratic historical roots.

The several decades of feminist campaigning for suffrage rights also provides strong evidence for a political voice in China outside of the CCP and the Nationalists. The dominance of these two major political parties in the histories of this period has obscured those struggles that worked within, around, and between these two groupings—including a sometimes antagonistic feminist movement. Moreover, it reveals that women developed a clear feminist agenda that cut across party, nation, or class loyalties as they invoked their collective identity as women and moreover sustained this through several decades of activism.

The significance of the Chinese movement on international women's suffrage studies is equally important, though largely unknown. China's feminist activists became fully informed about international developments over the course of their fifty-year engagement, and the international suffrage movement similarly publicized progress reports on the Chinese suffrage movement. However, today English-language scholarship on women's suffrage would lead one to suspect that little occurred outside of the Western world or its direct colonies. Many comprehensive, detailed studies on women's suffrage have been published for the anglophone world of Britain, USA, Australia, and New Zealand alone. But no similarly comprehensive studies on non-Western case studies have appeared. As Carole Pateman observed in 1994, "We know remarkably little about how women won the vote around the world. . . . How important are cultural differences, or difference in political regimes?"[11]

Important attempts to redress the Anglocentrism of the suffrage histories include the pathbreaking 1994 volume by Daley and Nolan that included Pateman's challenge. More recently, in 2000, Fletcher, Mayhall, and Levine contributed to the internationalization of suffrage histories with a volume titled *Women's Suffrage in the British Empire*—an exploration of suffrage struggles in countries linked by common colonial history.[12] In the same year DuBois and Cherny edited a special issue of *Pacific Historical Review* dedicated to exploring the histories of women's suffrage in nine separate nations bordering the Pacific Ocean.[13] Mina Roces and I followed this with the publication of *Women's Suffrage in Asia* in 2004 in order to present the diversity of women's engagement with formal politics in several key nations in Asia.[14] This current volume contributes to the lengthy process of filling the lacunae Pateman identified by providing a comprehensive overview of the history of the campaign for women's suffrage in China—one of the world's most enduring cultural and political entities.

The China case study is important for providing a breadth to our understandings of women's involvement in the development of democratic institutions in the international context for a range of reasons. China provides a window into the functioning of women's suffrage movements in a cultural system that evolved, prospered, and declined outside of the Judeo-Christian sphere and in different philosophical traditions from those that produced the Enlightenment and evolutionism. It provides insights into the manner in which suffrage movements intersect and interact with nationalist or anticolonial struggles in countries where the very concept of a discrete, politically unified nation was fraught with uncertainty. National identity and citizenship were hotly contested concepts for that large section of the world living ostensibly in their own lands but effectively with European domination of their economies and policies. We can learn from the China case how women utilized and exploited that ambiguity to further their specific goals.

Finally, the China case study demonstrates that there are many points of confluence between the Western and the non-Western women's suffrage struggle. The inspiration gained by suffrage activists from the experiences of their sisters around the globe cannot be underestimated. Conversely, the arguments deployed by opponents to women's suffrage are startlingly similar across the decades and among cultures. Biological determinism and gendered essentialism underpin the arguments presented by opponents to suffrage from around the globe.

SCARCITY OF SCHOLARSHIP ON
THE "CHINESE SUFFRAGETTES"

A complex matrix of Chinese and international factors coalesced to inhibit scholarship on Chinese women as political activists lobbying for their rights as citizens. Some of these factors mirror reasons given for an earlier paucity of Western interest in Western woman's suffrage struggles, but others are specific to the Chinese case.

Ellen Carol DuBois argues that Western academic studies of the suffrage movements around the world were hindered by the notion that a narrow elite with conservative political tendencies dominated women's suffrage struggles.[15] Academic trends in the 1960s and 1970s encouraged research into nonelite histories and ordinary people's lives. The suffragists were an unfashionable subject matter in this milieu. Similarly, in her analysis of the trends in historical writing on women's suffrage, Sandra Stanley Holton confirmed DuBois's point about academic fashions. She notes that in scholarship on the topic there was tension between the "constitutionalist" school writing prior to the end of the nineteenth century and the "militant" school writing for the bulk of the twentieth century. Holton argues that the former histories have been largely ignored in part because of the "measured tone" they adopted relative to the latter's more revolutionary flavor.[16]

An excellent example of the impact of this trend to favor revolutionary histories on China studies is provided by Roxanne Witke's 1973 statement that "the women suffragists were among the more articulate factions of urban intellectuals, and their public appeal was narrow if not divisive." She continues by describing the suffrage movement's calls for working women to join their movement as "fatuous . . . given the elitist scope of their concerns."[17] Chinese historians in the PRC have also tended to dismiss the women's suffrage movement as an affair of "bourgeois" conservative and elite women. Suffrage was overlooked because it was erroneously regarded as an institutional reform rather than a social movement wherein the suffragist "set out to redefine and recreate, by political means, the sexual culture" of their nations.[18] Marxist historical method, favored above all other methods in the PRC since 1949, has prioritized worker and peasant struggles and glossed over the broader women's movement as a dead-end battle for gender equality rather than full liberation. As China's foremost scholar of women's studies, Li Xiaojiang, wrote: "Just as the political slogan of 'equality' that originated with the bourgeoisie can also include equality between men and women, so it was a socialist revolution opposed to a feminism of women's rights [bourgeois feminism] that brought women political liberation. This is not just an opinion but historical fact."[19] Suffrage struggles are given only passing mention in the standard texts of Chinese women's history published in China itself and are often described as being ineffective until coming under CCP guidance.[20]

Yet, the narrative of the experiences of Chinese women activists provided below supports DuBois's assertion that it is inaccurate to dismiss women's suffrage as a "conservative, right-of-center" cause.[21] As will be clear throughout the book, Chinese suffragists maintained delicate and complex relationships with both the left and the right and proved to be effective political lobbyists in rapidly changing conditions. Dismissing the relevance of a movement on the basis of its elite origins conceals the deeper political motivations, including the historically strong opposition to "bourgeois parliamentarianism" and feminism more generally on the part of socialist and communist movements internationally.

The barriers inhibiting Western scholarly analysis on China's women's suffrage movement also include factors specific to China and her place in the world. Western academia, for the most part, had previously drawn heavily on an Orientalist tradition that posited China as a nation where despots ruled over an acquiescent and passive population. The existence of politically active women did not tally with this version of China. Indeed, the early women's suffrage movement in the West developed an Orientalist epistemology to argue its case in the 1860s and 1870s. Rendall reveals that from this evolutionist perspective women's suffrage was a higher point in the ladder of social and cultural development to which all civilized nations of the world would aspire.[22] To provide the explicit comparison necessary in evolutionist rhetoric, the "passive, oppressed, and ignorant" state of non-Western women was invoked as evidence that nations of progress and advancement were moving in a linear fashion toward full democratic rights for women. Women in the "barbarous East" were constructed as benchmarks, immobile and homogenous, from which Western women's advancement could be monitored. Movement in the benchmark casts the schema into chaos. In her 1912 visit to China, the eminent American suffragist Carrie Chapman Catt devoted considerable space in her reports of the journey to proving that women were actually in China's parliament. She visited the legislature in Guangzhou to see these women with her own eyes in order to counter widespread American disbelief of China's advanced status on women's rights.[23]

So disruptive were reports of progress in women's political rights in these "backward" nations that humiliating international comparisons were invoked to shame legislators into political reform. In 1918 one Washington-based suffrage journal, *The Suffragist*, pressed its cause in an article titled "In Heathen Lands," stating (not altogether accurately): "Equal suffrage has now been established in almost every country in Europe. However, in Africa, China, the United States and the Fiji Islands it is still considered that woman's sphere is in the home."[24] In 1919 the same journal revealed the tensions provoked in "civilized nations" by movement in the "benchmarks of backwardness," declaring "women are reaching out to lift up their sex, in such countries as China and Japan, where womankind is yet considered scarcely better than the animals of the field—using the influence of their increasing power to an advantage which ultimately will break the shackles from the wrists of enslaved womanhood the round world over."[25]

As we will see in the following chapters, Chinese women rejected the role they had been assigned in the evolutionary ladder. They perceived themselves to be mothers and daughters of one of the greatest world civilizations, albeit temporarily weakened, and accordingly took their lessons from nations that they regarded as being of similar stature. Imitating the success for women's suffrage in New Zealand and Australia, where women won the franchise in 1893 and 1902 respectively (before China's suffrage activists were organizing), carried far less force as an argument for women's suffrage in China than success in more prestigious colonizing powers like Britain, USA, and Germany. Women in these nations won the franchise in 1918, 1920, and 1918, respectively, enhancing the Chinese women's suffrage campaign considerably through their recognized prestige and power internationally.[26]

Another reason advanced to explain the privileging of histories of Western women's activism on suffrage issues has been our scholarly preference for unity and closure.[27] Work on women's suffrage has prioritized consistently the year that universal womanhood suffrage was won. This perspective posits a unified, linear path between the poles of "no female franchise" and "female franchise." Such clear lines are not possible in nations emerging from colonial rule, civil war, or external invasion and whose social fabric was fragmented by economic chaos during the period when women's suffrage was advocated.[28] In countries like China, where the political and military situation led to frequent changes in the structures of governance, the women's suffrage campaigners took multiple paths and made complex and astute allegiances to survive the rapid shifts. It is commonplace to see the dates of women's suffrage victories in various states of the USA or Australia listed separately in chronologies or overviews. Similar recognition of diversity and partiality in non-Western nations is urgently needed if we are to break the Orientalist practice of homogenizing and generalizing the non-Western experience. It is crucial to avoid dismissing the victories of women suffrage activists simply because there is less unity in the narrative than we are accustomed to or feel comfortable reading.

The absence of distinct and fixed political boundaries and geographic borders in nations extricating themselves from colonial or economic imperialism has also tended to make the women's suffrage campaigns appear less "authentic" because they are often intermingled in myriad ways with broader democratic, Marxist, or national independence struggles. In the case of China, explorations of the history of the women's movement in the early twentieth century have been retarded by the view that feminism was purely a tool for furthering nationalist or democratic ends used specifically by women. In 1942 Song Qingling (1893–1981), wife of the Republic of China's founding father, Sun Yat-sen, declared: "From the very start, our women fought not under the banner of a barren feminism but as part and parcel of the democratic movement as a whole."[29] Similarly, Roxanne Witke wrote in 1973: "A remarkable trait of politically motivated Chinese women was that the most avant-garde would not be arrested at the feminist stage of struggle for suffrage and women's rights."[30] The movement for women's equal political rights to men is often summarily dismissed as merely feminism and therefore inconsequential to the real struggle.

A further reason for the paucity of work on women's suffrage internationally, including in China, emerged from the overwhelming acceptance of the "rightness" of women's equal access to political and electoral powers as the twentieth century progressed. Diverse political interest groups sought to claim credit for the suffrage success once it was won. In her pioneering work on women's suffrage, Patricia Grimshaw noted in 1972 that research on the Western experience was inhibited initially by the common perception that women were granted suffrage rights without the existence of a sustained campaign (you cannot research a movement that did not exist).[31] Governments around the globe have been enthusiastic promoters of their own agency and foresight in "giving" women the vote. Grimshaw's work on New Zealand was the first to reveal this tendency, and later scholars have found similar patterns elsewhere.[32] The suffrage campaigners' lengthy struggle to persuade their government of the necessity and rightness of the cause is less prominent or even denied in the various national narratives, and only since the 1970s have scholars, led by Grimshaw's work, redressed this misconception.

Historiography and popularly circulating stories of nationhood in both China and Taiwan have certainly supported this type of abbreviated history of women's access to voting rights. Popular perceptions are that Chinese women did not struggle to win the right to vote. Instead, enlightened and paternalistic governments granted it to them—the Nationalist Party in the case of the Republic of China (ROC) on Taiwan, and the Chinese Communist Party in the case of the PRC. Women's agency was denied in the case of China just as it had been in the histories of the early New Zealand victory outlined by Grimshaw. Li Ziyun, an expert on women's writing in contemporary China, reflected the general perception of how Chinese women won the vote. In 1994 she wrote, "New China [post-1949] made provisions for women's political, economic and legal rights. With one flourish of the pen, Chinese women acquired the right to vote, something their sisters in the West had spent decades even centuries fighting for."[33] The Chinese political consciousness, reflected by Li, thus acknowledges the struggles of Western women while blithely denying the existence of indigenous Chinese activism on the issue. Ch'ien Tuan-sheng's seminal work on China's political history described the 1946–47 constitution under which Taiwan was ruled for many subsequent years, as encouraging women's reluctant interest in politics. Of the set minimum quotas for women, Ch'ien wrote, "the reference to women is intended to give them stimulus to seek elective offices."[34] In fact, as will become clear in the chapters to follow, many women lobbied long and hard to win the special quotas, and many more before them had campaigned seriously for the chance to vote and stand for parliament.

In the histories of both the PRC and the ROC on Taiwan, the narrative of female activists' agency and male governments' reactive acquiescence is consistently ignored. Neither the CCP or the Nationalist Party have been at pains to dispel these myths since neither has been enthusiastic about encouraging the excavation of histories of democratic movements until very recently. Both governments have legitimized their rule on the basis of a putative unified popular mandate that stems from benevolent paternalism rather than a democratic electoral process. Popularization of the histories of groups that proposed alternative versions of the origins of the two systems would have undermined the supposed unity of the masses. At best, both parties claimed that the authentic women's movement of the nation was subsumed into their respective Women's Affairs bureaus. These bureaus served often to constrain women's activism within the broad party agenda, but they also afforded women powerful negotiating positions.[35] Moreover, as will become clear in the chapters that follow, there were women who deliberately remained independent of the two main parties and who remained effective lobbyists for women precisely because they were not constrained by rigid party discipline.

Since 1949 improvement in the position of women in China has been a major public relations success for the CCP government internationally. Much work of considerable importance has been achieved in the PRC promulgating and implementing policies that have enhanced the status of women in the ensuing years. These successes were achieved without the existence of a separate feminist lobby group. The official rhetoric is that the CCP through its women's wing, the All-China Women's Federation (ACWF), obviates the need for an independent women's movement by pre-empting women's concerns.[36] Part of the story that "the CCP knows best" on women's issues includes the teleological narrative: before 1949, in the feudal past, Chinese women were abject slaves suffering under the cruel and harsh Confucian family and clan structures; after 1949, the CCP legislated and educated the masses to halt these oppressive practices.[37] Discussion of the presence of an independent women's organization that sought to fight against these very privations, or the existence of a government and legal system that could be and was lobbied on behalf of women during the period of the Nationalist government, undermines somewhat the horrific "before 1949" stories. Moreover, recent scholarship by Susan Mann and Dorothy Ko on the varied lives of women in the Ming and Qing has demonstrated that the picture of unmitigated misery in "feudal China" is far from accurate.[38]

The excellent albeit scarce scholarship on the history of the Chinese women's movement during the years prior to 1949 has for these and other reasons focused primarily on women in the communist movement or women workers. In the PRC in particular, these two groups of women have been projected as the heroes of the twentieth century women's movement at the expense of the contribution of middle-class or elite women who promoted democratic-constitutional government. The full mosaic of women's contribution to social and political development in the first half of the twentieth century requires academic scholarship on multiple perspectives. In this respect this current volume will contribute to the field opened by the dynamic and pathbreaking work of Christina Gilmartin, Kathryn Bernhardt, Gail Hershatter, Wang Zheng, and Emily Honig.[39]

SUFFRAGE OR PARTICIPATION IN POLITICS?

In the PRC today there is considerable concern about the falling rate of women's participation in formal politics since the lifting of the protective quotas for women in the late 1980s. In all discussions about this trend the phrase used is *funü canzheng* or "women's participation in politics." The identical term, *canzheng,* was used to describe the campaign that sought to win equal political franchise for women prior to the establishment of the PRC in 1949. Indeed, a cursory glance at this volume's bibliography reveals that magazine and newspaper articles routinely append *canzheng* to a range of terms for women (*nüzi, funü, nü, nüxing*). Yet I have translated this term as "suffrage" rather than "participation in politics" or "involvement in politics." This choice requires a brief explanation.

Tani Barlow has already provided a detailed discussion of the evolution of the terms for "women" in her 2004 book, *The Question of Women in Chinese Feminism,* revealing the changing political connotations of these words in relation to feminist identity. The term *canzheng* is also problematic, albeit to a far less complex degree, in its connotational evolution. In contemporary PRC usage *canzheng* does not signify "suffrage"—the legal right to vote and stand for election—but rather to the actual participation in formal politics. Specifically, it refers to participation in the PRC government bodies and the CCP-authorized departments, committees, and mass organizations. It is invoked in numerous volumes and articles espousing the importance of increasing the involvement of women in PRC politics and of overcoming obstacles to this improved quality and quantity of participation.[40] In the ROC on Taiwan a broader conceptualization of the term has come into use—including not only participation in formal politics and electoral processes but also the informal activities of participation in public rallies, lobby groups, and public speaking.[41] Actions that aim to influence government in any way at all are included in this broader ROC understanding of *canzheng.*

Yet in the first half of the twentieth century, the period covered by this book, *canzheng* meant "suffrage"—it centered on the twin rights to vote and to stand for election associated with the full political franchise of full citizens. The women active at this time linked their campaigns with the international women's suffrage movement and clearly adopted the term *canzheng* as equivalence for "suffrage." For example, the International Women's Suffrage Association (IWSA) was routinely translated as *Wanguo nüzi canzheng hui* during the decades in question. PRC historians of early Republican

China, aware of the potential for misunderstanding, often declare their definitions. For example, Wu Shuzhen wrote on the first page of her article on the Chinese suffrage movement: "The women's suffrage movement is women's struggle to win the right to participate in government."[42] Such attention to definitions was unnecessary in the commentaries written prior to 1949. Accordingly, throughout this volume I have adopted the term "suffrage" when translating pre-1949 references to *canzheng*.

Moreover, the division between informal politics and formal politics current today was irrelevant in China during the first half of the twentieth century. The two processes were inextricably linked. At this time women activists and radicals asserted their right to practice informal politics, lobbying and parading, and pamphleteering and rallying, simply by "doing."[43] Their campaign for the right to access formal political rights equal to their fathers, brothers, and sons manifested all the traits we currently associate with informal politics. Indeed, much energy was expended mobilizing increasing numbers of women to participate in social, economic, military, and family politics in order to demonstrate the fitness and capability of their sex to access formal political power in the public realm.

BUILDING EQUALITY INTO THE CONSTITUTION

The chapters to follow reveal that the women's suffrage activists were intent on effecting constitutional change. They believed that if women's equality with men were embedded within a national or provincial constitution, their rights would be assured. Their trust in the protection afforded by a constitution was not unique at this time. Belief in the notion that constitutional government and the adoption of an organic law would strengthen China and lead to good government flourished among both radicals and conservatives and men and women. During the first half of the twentieth century it gained philosophical credibility as a form of government that could be scientifically engineered and morally willed by the people to succeed. Andrew Nathan noted that the technocrats and active modernizers of China at the dawn of the twentieth century held constitutionalism as an overriding goal and "their models were the Western nations and Japan, where constitutions and national power seemed conspicuously linked."[44] Faith in constitutional government as a panacea to the political disunity that China faced during the 1920s continued, albeit in increasingly fragile forms and programs for stability were almost always framed in the context of constitutional debate. Nathan clearly demonstrates that there was a true belief that constitutionalism would save, revive, and modernize China. Edmund Fung has shown that even into the Nationalist government period in the disrupted 1930s and 1940s, "for the liberal intellectuals of the Nationalist period, democratic and constitutional change offered the best hope for a peaceful and modern China. They advocated democracy (*minzhu*) and constitutionalism throughout the period, only to find the road to democracy was blocked."[45]

Constitutionalism became a touchstone of political discussion even though it was ineffective in resolving China's vast problems. Ch'ien Tuan-sheng notes that between 1908 and 1946 China had no less than twelve constitutions, provisional constitutions, and constitutional drafts.[46] Warnings about the futility of trusting the constitutional path were frequent. For example, the 1923 Nationalist Party manifesto argued that a constitution, in itself, could not protect China from decline. The document explained that a "prerequisite of a constitution is whether the people are able to guard it. There is no use putting the cart before the horse. What is more, if the people are not organized, the existence of a constitution will not enable them to use it; and even if there are no militarists to abuse it, it will only remain a dead letter."[47]

While the bulk of China's population had no knowledge or interest in constitutional matters, the reformist intellectual and political elite section of the population considered it to be a matter of grave concern. No government with democratic pretensions, however flimsy or short lived, maintained its legitimacy without paying at least lip service to the revision of one or the other of the numerous constitutions that emerged in China during these years. The nurturing of a concept of citizenship whereby the people and the state interacted within a constitutional framework was a major concern for advocates of reform.[48]

Like the majority of China's enthusiastic reformers, China's suffragists were convinced of the rationality of this process. They had faith that a constitutional government would improve the status of women by guaranteeing equality with men by force of legislature. Accordingly, as we will see in the following chapters they committed themselves to decades of engagement with the process of constitution drafting and amending to ensure that women's interests were enshrined in any document that might emerge from the turmoil of Chinese politics during these decades.

China's women suffragists were first and foremost constitutionalists on a path committed to struggles over seemingly endless iterations of documents that sometimes masked despotism and self-interest. Nonetheless, the suffragists' repeated interventions in the provincial or national constitutional battles asserted the autonomy of the individual female as a politically, economically, and socially independent entity. Centuries of patriarchal clan and family rights to speak on behalf of women faced destruction by the simple insertion of the words "or sex" within documents that readily included provisions guaranteeing equality regardless of "race, class, or religion." The suffragists announced that it was possible for a "woman to have interests separate and distinct from those of her husband" and that a woman could "be considered an individual citizen with the rights of a distinct individual."[49]

INTERNATIONAL SISTER SUFFRAGISTS: INFLECTIONS ON THE CAUSE

The suffrage movement was well networked internationally from its inception. Women activists in China kept abreast of progress on women's enfranchisement in a host of nations around the world through the links forged with the IWSA.[50] League tables denoting "success in suffrage" ranked nations according to their progress on the issue, and these were regularly published in China's women's press. China's suffrage activists also attempted to sway their governments with pressure bought to bear directly from international delegations. During September 1912 Chinese suffrage activists hosted women from the IWSA led by Carrie Chapman Catt. Catt spoke at meetings and rallies in Nanjing, Shanghai, and Beijing, attracting further media attention to the international aspect of women's suffrage.[51] Support for the cause among China's women was demonstrated by strong attendance. One rally in Nanjing attracted over a thousand people.[52]

Yet the international women's suffrage movement was typified by the diversity of its movement as much as it was by its sisterly spirit of cooperation. Chinese suffragists created a uniquely Chinese version of suffragist internationalism, just as did their Japanese, German, Indian, and American comrades. Different religious, political, and cultural realities necessitated variation in emphasis and approach from each national women's suffrage group. As an international movement, the style and focus of the various women's suffrage campaigns necessarily carried national and cultural inflections. For example, the Chinese women's suffrage activists were not products of the Protestant churches' Women's Christian Temperance Union (WCTU), as were most women's suffrage activists in the English-speaking world. Although the WCTU did provide an institutional base for some of China's suffrage activists, for the most part there were distinct differences between the Chinese women's suffrage movement and the Western equivalent.[53] Throughout this volume, the unique characteristics of the Chinese suffrage movement will become apparent.

Unlike many of their Western counterparts, China's "suffragettes" were not regarded to be dour teetotaling moralists. Alcohol-induced domestic violence and poverty was not endemic in China as it was in Europe, America, or Australasia. The Chinese women's suffrage activists' interest in restricting the use of alcohol or, in the case of China the more common scourge of opium addiction, was marginal. Western suffrage activists throughout the English-speaking world had faced opposition from many men simply on the grounds that if women gained the right to vote, men's drinking pursuits would be curtailed. Melbourne suffragists presented the city with a public drinking fountain, a constant supply of drinking water, as a practical symbol of their antialcohol campaigns.[54] By contrast, Chinese women suffragists were considered to be dangerous and daring women who broke bounds and social norms that were perceived to have remained stable for centuries. Accusations that suffrage activists behaved in unwomanly fashions stemmed from their unconventional dress, outspoken habits, and daring freedom of movement. China's suffragists were not alluded to for their stifling, religious morals but rather for their questionable morals.[55]

There are key differences in the manifestations of radicalism in the Chinese movement when compared to the European or American version. The radical and militant wings of the British suffrage movement were not involved in formal military or antigovernment activities, unlike the Chinese suffragists in their early years. In 1911 China's suffragists were engaged in establishing and mobilizing women's armies and joined rebel groups in bombing raids on Qing government officials. During 1912 in Britain the most militant wings of the suffragists sought publicity for their cause by undertaking "a range of terrorist acts against property, such as mass window-breaking, setting fire to empty buildings and post boxes, pouring acid on golf courses and cutting telephone and telegraph wires."[56] They used their middle-class status as respectable women to scandalize through these "antisocial" acts and thereby sought to win publicity for their strength of purpose. Similarly, the radical American and British suffragists use of hunger strikes was not adopted in China. In a country such as China, with a long tradition of veneration of chaste widows who committed suicide by starving themselves to death on the passing of their husbands, hunger strikes could easily be misinterpreted. Indeed, for China's early suffragists, as well-bred women, simply appearing in public and demanding the right to be heard in public spaces was a dramatic breach of long-held customs about female modesty being manifest by women's seclusion in the home. Viewed from a global perspective, perceptions of "radicalism" clearly were determined by cultural norms.

China's suffragists challenged fundamental gendered precepts of virtue—broadly speaking, for women virtue was conceived as sexual chastity and for men as the performance of cultured learning.[57] By leaving the confines of the domestic world, earning an education, and winning access to public power, suffragists presented radical challenges to these gendered norms of virtue. Women activists increasingly claimed access to a form of virtue that rendered old patterns of virtue, earned through women's isolation from public view, redundant.[58] Yet, the significance of these actions would probably escape detection in a survey of radical feminist activism internationally.

Unlike the experience of Western suffragists in pioneering nations like Australia, New Zealand, and the Americas, the Chinese suffragist could not invoke her role as a partner in the racialized grand endeavor of forging life in a new land. The colonial settlement adventure presented women with many opportunities for partnership with men. In the colonies there were fewer white women than men, thus their voting rights were perceived to present less of a threat to the political status quo. Moreover, white women activists could more effectively define themselves as part of a ruling elite by emphasizing their difference from the colonized "natives."[59] In China during the transition from monarchy to republic, the race politics were complex. The suffragists were primarily ethnically Han, and they mobilized against the Manchu minority that had ruled as monarchs during the Qing dynasty alongside the Republican revolutionaries. The women's suffrage activists found political allies among the revolutionaries for their opposition to Manchu rule and their advocacy of Han right to rule China. Yet, this anti-Manchu sentiment was of short-lived utility to China's suffragists. Once the Manchu were defeated, China's suffragists found they were unable to credibly insinuate themselves into the legitimate "ruling group" simply by asserting Han ethnicity. The Han republic was embedded in patriarchal structures just as had been the Manchu-led monarchy. In this regard, China's suffragists were faced with the challenge of radically transforming gender relations in one of the world's most stable cultural systems.

The Chinese women's suffrage movement did not become deeply involved with other liberation movements, such as the campaign for the abolition of slavery or labor rights, as had their sisters in the USA and Europe. China's women's suffrage activists lacked clear class consciousness until the 1920s. Their early suffrage campaign focused strictly on equality between men and women. The absence of a vocal working-class or peasant political movement in China during the first two decades of the century enabled the Chinese women's suffrage movement to avoid disputes about class rights and other types of oppressed groups' rights that exercised the minds of the suffragists in the USA and Europe. In Europe, working-class men objected strongly to any compromise position that would have awarded women equality with men in franchise rights for fear that it would further inhibit the cause of universal male suffrage.[60] In China, peasant men and women were largely either without a voice or unheard by the intellectual classes until the 1930s and 1940s.[61] Both men and women political activists were, as Edmund Fung has described, "remote from the peasantry and laboring classes."[62]

The women's suffrage movement in China fought for equality with men in suffrage rights and not for universal suffrage until the mid- to late 1920s, when increasingly sophisticated and democratic ideas about political representation began to undermine the close link between education and political participation. Confucian scholars in Imperial China had for centuries earned their position in government by studying and passing exams. This tradition did not disappear overnight. The men involved in advocating the strengthening and reviving of China had the same class interests as the women's suffrage activists, and as political interests expanded to include the masses, both male and female political leaders moved together. The reformers in China, both men and women, both left and right wing, were a paternalistic middle class that inherited the notion from a centuries-old Confucian legacy that the educated had the right to rule.[63] As the chapters that follow show, numerous constitutions declared that "all" people had equal citizens' rights while simultaneously prohibiting those who could not read and write from voting. The strong link between education and political participation underpins the contradiction in these rulings.

The long-standing value placed on education as a legitimizing attribute for a bureaucratic class ensured that the Chinese women's suffrage activists emphasized advancing the cause of women's education more seriously than had Western suffrage activists. Education was a key prerequisite for participation in politics during the Qing dynasty, with bureaucrats being selected by a series of examinations. In this schema, as Susan Mann has deftly demonstrated, learned wives were expected to serve an advisory and counseling role for their husbands in their daily political or business decisions.[64] But they did not take public political roles themselves. The suffragists denaturalized the link between education and male political power with their public displays of women's education. They did not challenge the fundamental premise that education was an important prerequisite for political power, rather they asserted that women could be educated to a standard equal to that of men's, and in turn legitimately claim access to political power.

They were supported in this view by late Qing reformers like Liang Qichao. Liang had emphasized the link between education and good citizenship in the modernizing project. Zarrow notes that in Liang's view "education would enable the people to become citizens and play their full constitutional role."[65] With this cultural expectation of a link between education and access to political power, women activists in the new republic regarded access to formal education as fundamental to ensuring that women's political viewpoints be considered valid. This avenue had not been open to women in Europe, where the link between education and right to rule was less pronounced. Many of the Chinese suffrage activists were involved in the establishment of schools for girls, and yet others were involved in publishing the women's magazines and supplements that, as well as providing women with the alternative perspectives on the new social and political order, also displayed their authors' and readers' erudition.

Importantly, education also connoted virtue within the Confucian worldview. Thus, by gaining an education women suffrage activists aimed to ensure not only that they would justify their claim to share power but also that the aspersions cast on their morality, generated by their entry into the hitherto prohibited public sphere, would be undermined. This mechanism helped protect the honor of women from the urban elite but it did little to protect rural women since they lacked access to the expanding school sector. At the close of the 1940s, politically active peasant women were still derided as being little better than prostitutes. Nonetheless, the Confucian reverence for education was the moral backbone of the Chinese women's suffrage movement, just as the WCTU's Protestantism was for the Western women's suffrage movement.

Another crucial difference between the Western and Chinese suffrage movements is apparent in their different methods of mobilizing the concept of citizenship. For Chinese suffragists, citizenship was embedded within the right to participate in politics. In many Western countries citizenship had been forged with sex-specific rights and duties. Peter Zarrow's discussion on citizenship is enlightening in this regard. In France the notion of citizenship following the revolution included women—but as citizens who were deliberately excluded from politics. The British, Italian, and American national concept of citizenship was similarly gendered. According to Zarrow, "the exclusion of women may well have been an integral aspect of defining full citizenship for increasing numbers of men in the West throughout the nineteenth century."[66] In China, however, Zarrow has argued that citizenship and feminism were largely treated together as closely related problems: "The same promoters of nationalism and republicanism or citizenship were also concerned with women's rights."[67] Thus, women lobbying for political rights in China were able to argue more persuasively than their European and American sisters that as citizens they were subject to duties as well as rights, exactly the same as their fathers, brothers, and sons.

The Chinese women suffrage activists recognized the intimate link between sexual autonomy and political rights, just as their counterparts in the West had done. For example, in Britain during the 1870s and 1880s, the campaigns against prostitution and to repeal the Contagious Disease Act, whereby women were liable to random physical checks for venereal disease, explicitly linked the absence of a political voice for women and their sexual slavery.[68] In China, the suffrage activists were among the most organized and vocal women campaigners against the system of concubinage, the double standards of chastity, and the extensive prostitution industry. Many potential male supporters of the women's suffrage campaigns were repelled by the suffragists' simultaneous lobbying against concubinage, the trade in girl servants, and prostitution.

In contrast to the comparative stability in social attitudes in Europe or America, the advent of the New Culture Movement in China during the decade from 1915 created an intellectual milieu sympathetic to radical challenges to the sexual customs of the nation. The urban educated youth, both male and female, were at the very least espousing the virtues of companionate, monogamous marriages based on mutual love and decrying the horrors of the traditional parentally arranged marriage with all its misogynist accoutrements. The expanding willingness to challenge old customs among the urban population thus provided women's suffrage activists with a not entirely hostile environment within which they could challenge enmeshed sexual and political practices. China's early twentieth century "sexual revolution" was intimately linked with the women's movement for legal and political equality. Democracy, it was believed, would defend women's social, sexual, moral, and economic rights. Winning the suffrage was the first vital step in this broader campaign for democratic rights.

China's women's suffrage campaign also differed from that in other non-Western nations. As a still-sovereign nation, despite decades of political chaos spawned by aggressive European and American economic forces, China's suffragists did not have to contend with the complexities presented by direct colonial rule. In Indonesia, for example, Susan Blackburn has shown how that nation's suffrage activists faced the question of how or if to integrate with Dutch colonial women suffragists' campaigns. The role of white women colonialists in local suffrage campaigns was equally fraught in India, as Gail Pearson has revealed. Mina Roces has shown that women suffragists in the Philippines found themselves expected to support nationalist movements that threatened to disenfranchise women.[69]

Chinese suffragists, in contrast to their comrades in Japan, did not have to prove their ethnocultural purity. Yukiko Matsukawa and Kaoru Tachi wrote that in the 1930s Japan's suffragists faced charges that their suffrage activism was un-Japanese by people who believed "it would be unseemly and immoral for Japanese women to imitate Western women." Some went so far as to say women's suffrage was "against the customs of Japan."[70] Barbara Molony has explained that in the late 1930s in Japan "internationalism and suffragism fell on hard times."[71] In China up to the 1930s the pressing case for radical social and political change presented by the sorry state of the nation from the earliest years of the twentieth century ensured that appeals to "traditional Chinese" characteristics and cultural traits carried less impact. National rejuvenation in China through modernization and "Westernization" helped present women's suffrage as an emblem of national progress and a patriotic rather than treacherous act. Moreover, China's suffrage activists would all have been considered "Modern Women" or "New Women." This icon was a synecdoche for aspirations of national rejuvenation; the Modern Woman carried the burden of representing the strengthening of the Chinese nation.[72] While it was not always smooth sailing for the Modern

Woman over the first half of the twentieth century, her presumed transformative powers protected the Chinese women suffragists from the slurs their Japanese sisters confronted.

This volume explores the Chinese suffrage movement in detail within China's own historical and political context. Yet as we will see, the women involved were acutely aware of the global reach of their campaign. They conceived of themselves as one part of the international women's movement and as spokeswomen for "all the nation's women."

————

The chapters that follow trace a chronological path from the late imperial era when, politically, women were merely wives and daughters of subjects, through to the close of the 1940s when women's right to participate in politics went unchallenged. As the volume shows, the radical social and political changes that women generated in China during the first half of the twentieth century have lasting impact on women in the twenty-first century in both the PRC and the ROC. Their labors warrant broad contemporary recognition.

Chapter Two covers the period between 1898 and 1911—the last twelve years of the crumbling Qing dynasty. The chapter argues that the women's movement of this period struggled with conceptions of citizenship that were embodied by men and maleness. At this juncture citizenship was gendered male and the women wanted recognition as independent citizens, and not merely as wives or daughters of citizens. The suffragists attempted to promote a new identity—the independent woman citizen (*nü guomin*)—in an effort to carve a legitimate space for women in the political arena of a rapidly changing China. To achieve this they presented arguments that all humans were equal in every respect regardless of sex. On the basis of this equality principle the women sought full and equal political rights with men by performing a democratic, republican form of nationalism alongside men. The women activists of this time promoted the notion that educated women were equally capable of serving the nation in the political realm as men—thereby undermining the close connection between education and male access to political power that had sustained China's governance structures for centuries.

Chapter Three narrates the travails of the suffragists in the brief period between 1911 and 1913—the period of fragile republican democracy that emerged from the collapse of the Qing dynasty. It demonstrates that as a result of the failure of the new republic to grant women suffrage rights, the women activists were forced to perceive of themselves as political actors with a gendered identity and political agenda that was distinct from the men they had previously thought were their comrades-in-arms. They continued to promote the idea that women were inherently men's equals and deserving of equal treatment in all legal provisions, but they also began to enunciate more clearly a position that pronounced women's different political interests from men and did so within a sophisticated mobilization of the power of the global women's suffrage movement. In the face of explicit opposition to women's entry into the public sphere of formal politics, the suffragists of the early republic continued to press the case for the legitimacy of Chinese women's rights to political representation by women politicians.

The successful campaigns to win sex equality in suffrage rights in the provincial constitutions during the period 1919–1923 are the focus of Chapter Four. I argue that by this period the women's movement demonstrates that it is a successful social and political movement with a "gendered agenda" based on a clearly enunciated and more broadly publicly accepted notion of women's unity of disadvantage. That is, during the New Culture Movement women's collective political identity strengthened among both women activists themselves and among a broader section of the reformist political elite. Importantly, suffragists begin to take class differences into account in their political struggles. Until this period, China's women suffragists had largely ignored the problems of their working-class or peasant sisters, and equal franchise rights meant equality among men and women of the educated and privileged classes. Yet the increasing awareness of class furthered the development of the conception that women were unified as a group because of their collective disadvantage relative to men.

Chapter Five covers the period of the increasing power and influence of the two major political parties—the CCP and the Nationalist Party between 1924 and 1927. Both major parties at this time publicly espoused the principle of equality between men and women. Yet the chapter shows that the parties were concerned with ensuring that feminism did not jeopardize their political goals. Thus, the challenge for women activists was to ensure that the increasingly sophisticated party political machinery did not deploy women's rights as a bargaining chip or an optional extra. This task had to be undertaken during a period of tense cooperation between the two parties, the so-called First United Front. Committed to the constitutional process, China's suffrage activists campaigned for a National

Assembly and for women's representation for this assembly from a position of combined energies—CCP and Nationalist women joined forces with the nonaligned faction to push the women's rights cause. The chapter shows that the broad recognition of women's legitimate rights to political representation as a collectivity presented women activists with unique opportunities for influencing political mechanisms and structures in their fragile nation.

The collapse of the United Front in 1927 ushered in a period of Nationalist Party leadership of the nation known as the Nanjing Decade. The CCP was pushed into rural China, taking its affiliated women activists inland. Chapter Six reveals that despite the physical split between two major sections of the nation's politically active women, dedication to the feminist campaign was not diminished, and indeed important victories were won. The women's push for legal and constitutional changes that would guarantee equality with men was enhanced by the expansion in national institutional government structures and an expansion of popular participation in politics. The latter was enhanced by the removal of literacy as a prerequisite for voting. The chapter challenges the commonplace view that this period was devoid of feminist activism. Rather it shows that constitutional success occurred during these years with the Tutelage and Double Fifth constitutions both breaking new ground in recognizing women's equality with men at a national level. Indeed, both Nationalists and Communists had to contend with a vocal women's movement.

Chapter Seven explores the period from 1936 to 1948—the difficult years of the Japanese invasion and the brief but bloody civil war. The chapter reveals that during these tumultuous years women activists from a host of different political groupings united to successfully argue the case for protective minimum quotas for women in politics. They conceived of this joint campaigning as a result of the work of the 1920s and 1930s in establishing the notion that women had a legitimate political collective identity, distinct but equal to that of men. Sex difference was premised on a narrative that women were as a group disadvantaged and therefore required some modicum of guaranteed representation. It built upon the broad acceptance of the notion that sex equality was fundamental to a modern Chinese nation. At the same time elections were held in both CCP- and Nationalist-controlled areas, where women made significant gains for their rights to be public political actors.

Chapter Eight closes the volume with a discussion of the significance of the women's suffrage movement to China's political history and the gendered nature of national politics in China. It argues that China's suffrage campaigners fundamentally changed the connection between not only gender and politics in China but also gender and political virtue. Moreover, it presents the case that the suffrage activists, in their sustained and flexible movement, altered China's political landscape as a whole by modeling sophisticated and sustained advocacy politics within an international arena.

Anti-Qing Rebels

Conceiving Women's Citizenship, 1898–1911

China's women's rights activists at the turn of the twentieth century were aware that they were contending with both a Manchu-dominated monarchy in the Qing rule of China (1644–1912) and a Han patriarchy. Both an imperial political system and a male-centered cultural order had to be overcome for women's equality with men to be recognized in China. Moreover, women's political rights, conceived at the time as suffrage, would require the establishment of a constitutional democracy and specifically a democracy that guaranteed women's equality to men. Within this new democratic order China would have citizens and not subjects. Yet, in the narrative of citizenship of the time, women were problematic because the term "citizen" (*guomin*) was to all intents and purposes gendered male. In response to this notion, women activists elevated to the political stage the notion of "women citizens" (*nü guomin*) and called on women to aspire to this status.[1] They aimed to prove to men that women could be citizens and that their citizenship was equal with men's in every respect. To achieve this goal women political activists invoked and enacted the principle of sex equality in order to counter long-standing notions of sex difference—whereby the social roles of men and women were conceived as separate and hierarchical.

In so doing, these aspiring women citizens turned their focus to transforming the political structure of their nation. To their minds, citizens belonged to democratic republics and they hoped that proof of their equal citizenship in such a republic would derive from the quality of their participation in furthering the overthrow of the Qing monarchy. As will become clear below, the women aimed to manifest the same intellectual and physical traits of their brother citizens by working alongside them in the campaign to rejuvenate their crippled country. Their task was to close the divide between the expected different behaviors and roles of the two sexes with the ultimate goal of winning equal suffrage rights with men within a constitutional democracy.

REJUVENATING THE NATION

The Chinese nation that women sought to rejuvenate through their participation as citizens was badly in need of attention. The glorious Qing dynasty that had provided China's population with unrivalled wealth in the seventeenth century was a pale shadow of its former self in the early twentieth century. The Manchu-dominated government faced economic collapse, and the monarchy was compromised by incompetence in the face of rapidly changing political and military conditions. Humiliating defeats during the wars against the British in the 1840s and the Japanese in 1895 depleted the Qing coffers and destroyed popular faith in its leadership. Catastrophes such as the ill-conceived Boxer Rebellion of 1900, resulting in the ransacking of the national capital by a coalition of foreign powers, increased the pressure on the inept Qing monarchy to be more responsive to reform. Such internationally visible humiliations stripped Manchu rule of its few remaining shreds of legitimacy. The government announced it would move toward establishing a constitutional monarchy.

In August of 1908, the court issued its "Principles of the Constitution" and announced that China's first elected national parliament would be convened in 1917. This schedule was far too slow for many aspiring Han politicians, and after intensive lobbying the preparatory period was reduced to four years. This new time line included the promulgation of the constitution in 1912 and the convening of the parliament in 1913. While there was general agreement between the court and the advocates of reform about the timing, the years from 1908 saw the development of vibrant and increasingly confident parliamentary culture at a provincial level.[2] Ultimately, this nascent democratic spirit was to propel China along a revolutionary trajectory. As Joseph Esherick has explained, "the provincial assemblies soon established themselves as the key institution in provincial politics. The urban elite found in them a powerful platform from which to express its grievances against the government."[3] Thus, the Qing reforms, originally designed to ensure continued Manchu rule of China, ultimately nurtured opposition sentiment. Political activism increased amongst a class of wealthy and educated Han Chinese—a group that increasingly felt they had the skills to run their country without Qing supervision.

The suffrage mandated by the Qing was exclusively male and extremely limited. Voting rights, as outlined in the 1908 electoral regulations for the provincial assemblies, were granted to a small section of the male population—all those over the age of twenty-five with either the professional, educational, or property requirements stipulated. This limited franchise meant that "approximately 1.7 million men over 25—about 0.4 per cent out of a population of perhaps 400 million, representing perhaps 2 per cent of all nuclear families in the country—were registered as voters."[4] Men over the age of thirty were eligible to stand for election. Esherick describes the "complex and restrictive" electoral laws as follows:

> The electorate was composed of males over the age of 25 *sui* (24 years) who had at least a *shengyuan* degree, or a middle school education, or held an official post of the seventh rank or above for civil officials, or the fifth rank for military; owned real estate or commercial capital goods values at over $5,000; or had operated a school in their district for over three years. The requirements for candidates were the same, except that the age requirement was raised to 30 *sui* (29 years). However, a man could be disqualified for any number of moral defects: if he was untrustworthy or not upright in business, if he was "perverse and untruthful, self-serving or forcibly arbitrary," if he smoked opium, was insane, or came from an unpure family (i.e. prostitutes, actors or slaves).[5]

As Esherick notes, Western constitutionalism was to be superimposed upon a basis of Confucian morality. The difficulty for the suffragists within this merger was that women's equal political rights with men was not a universally accepted principle within either system. As we will see in the following chapter, the pattern of male-only representation and authority in parliamentlike bodies formed by these late Qing reforms was to have devastating impact on women's suffrage campaigns once China's republic was established.

The first elections for the provincial assemblies were held in 1909. The successful candidates were then eligible for election to the National Assembly. This latter body was intended to be the precursor of a national parliament with full powers to draft and pass legislation. By the end of 1909 the first stage of indirect popular participation was complete, and in October 1910 the inaugural session of the National Assembly was convened in Peking.[6] Many of the men elected were also to assume positions of authority in the republic after the collapse of the Qing dynasty in 1911. John Fincher has argued convincingly that the influence of the 1909 elections on political developments after 1911 should not be underestimated.[7] The "self-government movement," as this early parliamentary experience was called, identified local and provincial leaders who would assume prominent positions in the Republican government after the collapse of the Qing.

A major problem with the reforms was that the Qing court repeatedly ignored the opinions of these new people's representatives. The evident reluctance of the Qing dynasts to transfer any power or even take advice from the National Assembly encouraged many of the members to support the rebels advocating a total overthrow of Manchu rule. Had it not been for the alienation of the reformist elite associated with the constitutional movement and their subsequent desertion from the Qing in 1911–1912, the Manchu would probably have been given a reprieve. Thus, the desertion of the local elite who comprised the members of the provincial assemblies from 1909 was pivotal in the collapse of the Qing in 1912.

The Qing constitutional reforms made no provisions for women's participation and did not recognize women as having the "rights of a distinct individual."[8] Male kin, it was assumed, were the representatives of China's female population. Women's suffrage was simply irrelevant to many of the men contributing to these new semidemocratic institutions. In this context, women's rights activists had little cause to buttress the Qing government's provincial assemblies, and so the radicals among them turned to the anti-Qing rebels for a stage upon which to demonstrate their legitimate citizenship status and their equality with men.

The women had been mobilized to the feminist cause by the growing awareness of Western and Japanese notions of the benefits of women's education and political participation. Some of these radical women traveled to

Japan for study at the numerous women's colleges in Tokyo and while there became involved with the antimonarchist, pro-Republican groups. The most important of these anti-Qing groups was Sun Yat-sen's Revolutionary Alliance (*Tongmeng hui*), which formed in 1905. Of particular appeal to these disaffected women was the fact that equality principles were enshrined in the constitution of this rebel party and women's membership was welcomed. The Revolutionary Alliance appeared to agree that men and women were equal partners in their movement and in the republican democracy they sought to build. As we shall see later, almost all the leaders of the early women's suffrage movement were members of the Revolutionary Alliance and had been enthusiastic participants in all aspects of this rebel group's activities. The women suffrage activists put their weight and energy behind the Revolutionary Alliance in the hope that it would later serve their interests.

To reach this point of feminist consciousness, broad cultural changes had occurred among China's elite enabling the women to envisage themselves as having independent rights. How did the women activists emerge as feminists and not simply as anti-Qing rebels?

WOMEN ARE HUMANS TOO— EQUALITY AND NATURAL RIGHTS

In the late nineteenth century and early twentieth century, the European concept of natural rights (*tianfu renquan*—literally, "human rights endowed by heaven") gained credibility and popularity among China's reformist elite.[9] The notion of natural rights presented the view that liberty and equality were rights inherent to all human beings. This novel philosophical perspective gave new force to calls for political reform, and constitutional democracy was hailed as the most effective system for delivering these rights.[10] To prevent China from sinking into a state of unfitness and extinction, many reformers believed China would need to embrace the notion of the equality of all human individuals. Sex equality became central to the notion of natural rights within China, and this undermined existing notions of innate, inviolable sex differences. The circulation of the idea of natural rights and the notion that they could be defended by constitutional organic law created the space for the emergence of China's feminist movement, as both men and women saw the power of equality in effecting political reform based on representative government. Thus, sex equality rhetoric, derived from natural rights philosophy, provided Chinese women suffrage activists with a foundational platform for their campaigns throughout the 1910s, 1920s, and 1930s.

The so-called 1898 reformers, Kang Youwei, Liang Qichao, and Tan Sitong, played crucial roles in disseminating concepts of human equality through their failed but high-profile effort at reforming the Qing political structures. They regarded the improvement of the status of China's women as central to the campaign to revive China. In the 1890s, in elucidating his theories of public rights, Kang declared, "the equality of human beings is like a geometrical principle" and "all men and women have their own independent rights."[11] Wang Zheng has pointed out that Kang "not only advocated gender equality, but also placed gender issues at the center of social transformation."[12] A women's journal sponsored by the 1898 reformers and their wives and daughters, *Women's Studies News* (*Nüxue bao*) provided the platform for promoting these ideas.[13] Statements such as "men are people, but moreover women are also people" and "nature gives birth to men and women and they are born equal" featured commonly in this publication.[14]

Kang's ideas were reinforced by translations of Western works on women's rights. In the first few years of the twentieth century, works by Herbert Spencer and John Stuart Mill were translated into Chinese. Spencer's *Social Statistics* and Mill's *On the Subjection of Women* made explicit the connection between human equality and equality between the sexes.[15] There was also increasing deployment of British feminist thinking from the 1880s that invoked images of a golden age of equal rights between men and women that needed to be recovered. British radicals presented the view that the ancient Britons, at least among the elites, had equal rights between men and women in ownership of property, participation in battles, and politics.[16] Likewise China's women activists spoke in terms of "recovering" and "reinstating" women's original natural rights rather than "winning" or "gaining" new rights.

Nonetheless, the late Qing understandings of natural rights and sex equality were tempered by the view that individual rights were subordinated to one's duty to the nation. Indeed, for almost the entire stretch of the suffrage campaign in China, appeals to the restoration of women's natural rights to equality would emphasize the benefits that would accrue to China as a nation. Karl Gerth notes that this was particularly a feature of men's advocacy on improving women's status: "Male contributions to the discourse on women's emancipation from the late Qing on emphasized empowering women, alongside men, so that they might better help serve the nation; they rarely discussed the granting of intrinsic or inalienable rights."[17] Women activists, on the other hand, often spoke of their innate rights, but pointed out that through accessing these rights they would make stronger contributions to the nation.

For example, the 1898 reformers argued that changing the situation of China's women was fundamental to China's advancement. They perceived that the miserable position of Chinese women relative to men was symbolic, if not the cause, of China's weakness relative to the Western powers. The weakness of China's women represented China's national vulnerability. The logic was that China's women were letting the nation down—while they remained weak and crippled by foot binding, and ignorant, unproductive, dependent, and isolated in the domestic sphere there was no hope for the nation. Catherine Gipoulon noted that within this schema "given that the backwardness of China was due to the backwardness of its women, there could be no transformation of China without transforming the female condition."[18]

On the other hand, China's feminists reframed the concept of the problem of women's weakness by arguing that China needed to return women to their natural and original equality with men for both ethical and national purposes. One feminist group formed in 1903 declared its goals to be "to save the millions of Chinese women, to recover their resolve and their particular rights, to engender a nationalist consciousness among them."[19] The equal weighting given each of these three aspects of their mission reveals that the reinstatement of women's rights was not necessarily only a means toward a nation-building end. However, at this time China's feminists' campaigns were enhanced rather than hampered by the connection between their goals and the campaign to rejuvenate the nation. Hence, we read equally commonly of the duty women have to gain the necessary skills to shoulder citizenship responsibilities.[20] The same year, 1903, one feminist, Hu Binxia wrote, "the current weakened state of China cannot be blamed entirely on the faults of men."[21] Another prominent feminist, Chen Xiefen, explained the connection between women's rights and duties as follows:

> When men alone enjoyed rights, we could not participate, and we ceded this participation to them. And what was the reason for this? In the past, women had entirely lost their rights; they had also lost their sense of duty. Since they didn't fulfill their duties, if they had rights, those rights were bestowed on them by others—they were not rights we women ourselves had fought to obtain. And, also, if we obtained incomplete rights, then ceding them back to the givers was permissible. But today is a day when women *can* fulfill our

duty! A day when we *can* obtain our complete rights! If we don't forge ahead courageously, then it really is as men say disparagingly: "Women are slavish by nature." Therefore, if we women want to struggle alongside men, then we must first struggle to fully fulfill our duty. Then women's rights will naturally become equal![22]

If women wanted to change their status, then they needed to rise to such challenges. One male revolutionary, Jin Songcen, provided just such a program for achieving these goals.

OVERTHROW THE QING! JIN SONGCEN ON
THE QUALITIES OF WOMEN CITIZENS

The first book-length Chinese monograph conceptualizing women's equal political citizenship with men was Jin Songcen's (1874–1947) *A Tocsin for Women* (*Nü jie zhong*), which appeared in 1903.[23] Zhang Yufa described this text as comprising all the important ideas about women's issues of its time.[24] Within his radical treatise, Jin makes a direct connection between the realization of women's political rights and the overthrow of the Qing dynasty. The twentieth century, he declared prophetically, was to be the era for a revolution in women's rights.[25] *A Tocsin for Women* stands as the first Chinese manifesto advocating women's rights to participate in all aspects of a democratically elected government.

Jin Songcen's volume provides a guide for women seeking to reclaim their equal citizenship with men through nationalist activism. Indeed, *A Tocsin for Women* can be read as a manual of instruction for women on how to become directly involved in revolutionary activities and national affairs. His major concern was that women mobilize to support the overthrow of the Qing dynasty and then later contribute to the strengthening of China. This China would be one that recognized women's equal rights with men precisely because women had contributed to its construction.[26] This treatise takes as its epistemological base the proposition that men and women have inalienable natural rights to liberty and equality, outlined above. Jin explicitly acknowledged the European origins of these concepts and made repeated comparisons between the chaos in China and the power emanating from the "civilized" (*wenming*) nations of Europe. China needed to become more like the West, and Jin considered that the propagation of principles of natural rights—particularly equality between men and women—was fundamental to effecting this transformation.

For Jin, Han republicanism and equal political citizenship for women were inextricably intertwined. In the chapter devoted to women's participation in government, Jin argued that women's rights were tied to democratic government.[27] Central to Jin's treatise was his assertion that in the new republic, women will participate in all aspects of the political process by filling the full range of government posts.[28] From Jin's perspective, a parliamentary democracy would guarantee women's interests because women would have the right to full participation—as legislators and presidents, as well as voters and lobbyists. Women's political skills would develop through the broadening of the education system for girls, the expansion of opportunities for careers, the legalization of women's right to own property, and the regaining of the right to freedom in social movement.[29] Women's participation in the democratic process would inevitably result in the realization of equality between the sexes.

Jin was clearly aware of the strength of opposition to his view on women's suffrage. He lists four main reasons commonly given by opponents of women's participation in politics: (1) men are responsible for affairs external to the household while women are responsible for internal domestic affairs; any disruption to this pattern will cause a national catastrophe; (2) the qualities required of a citizen are "manly" attributes, such as the ability to make an independent decision; where this quality exists in a woman, she is the exception and not the norm; (3) women are naturally emotional and unstable; and (4) none of the nations in Europe and America have given women equal political rights.[30]

In arguing against these points, Jin notes that it is foolish to treat women as if they were children whose political views must be expressed through their husbands or fathers. Moreover, assertions about women's unstable emotional nature are irrelevant since governance is a political and not a psychological process. He argued that women's political skills would develop in concert with the educational opportunities provided. Furthermore, Jin pointed out that democracy did not require uniformity in ability and temperament from men, thus a similar diversity among women's abilities and temperaments should be expected as well. Jin regarded as fallacious the argument that women's access to political power should be restricted because historically women have never had political power. He pointed out that women have long been involved at the highest levels of government around the world and listed as evidence the various queens and empresses who had ruled independently.[31]

Jin called for women to wake themselves from a slumber of political apathy with the aim of empowering women through participating in radical politics. In the concluding section of the treatise, Jin makes an impassioned call for action: "Slaves have a slave's glory, servants have a servant's happiness, but this glory and this happiness draw not from knowledge, merely misery. But if they are encouraged to love freedom and respect equality, then men and women can unite together to create a new China."[32]

This challenge was presaged in one of the three prefaces to *A Tocsin for Women*. Lin Zongsu (1878–1944), a young student who would later go on to establish the first women's suffrage lobby group of the republican period (discussed in the following chapter), wrote: "Rights are something to be fought for; they will never be conceded. If we let Mr. Jin alone plead on behalf of women and plan for the restoration of our rights, this is the same as expecting the government peacefully to promulgate a constitution without shedding blood and overthrowing it."[33] Women increasingly saw themselves, and were seen by others, as active and equal participants in the determination of their lives, but Lin's comments also reveal that they saw their feminist struggle as independent of, albeit compatible with the anti-Qing struggle.

Indeed, women did participate in the full range of anti-Qing activities. They were determined to demonstrate that men and women were *equal* through their equal participation in the movement to establish a democracy. These early feminists were highly unusual women—they had education, money, and freedom of movement—privileges denied the overwhelming majority of their contemporaries. However, these privileges became tools for political action rather than provisions for a comfortable life. The women disregarded deeply entrenched notions of women's virtue by ignoring the scandal likely to emerge from keeping close company with nonfamily men and breaking taboos about women's involvement in public affairs. The overthrow of the Qing dynasty promised to provide China's feminists with the opportunity to promote more than just a change in the style of government. It also presented a platform for a fundamental challenge to patriarchy in toto.

ANTI-QING FEMINIST POLITICAL ACTIVITIES: WINNING CITIZENSHIP CREDENTIALS

As Jin had hoped, a host of societies and associations were formed to promote women's rights in the first decade of the century. Politically active women belonged to many groups at once and, importantly, joined the

mainstream anti-Qing groups along with the men as well. The women involved in establishing political groups during the first decade of the twentieth century took very seriously the notion that participation by women
in alternative politics would demonstrate political skill and a willingness
to sacrifice for the nation on equal terms to men. Patriotic action provided
women with a legitimate stage on which to perform their public political aspirations as equal citizens to their brothers. However, they were also
aware that women needed to mobilize other women in order to address
their sex's oppression above and beyond any national crisis. They addressed
many of the key problems for women in Chinese society: financial dependence on parents or husbands, foot binding, lack of inheritance rights, the
patriarchal marriage system, and the paucity of education and employment
opportunities.

Study societies and patriotic associations often provided the cover for
women involved in organizing along feminist lines to overthrow the Qing
government. In China the major cities were the major sites of activity. But
the more radical anti-Qing groups prospered away from Qing government
influence—especially in Tokyo among the expanding body of Chinese students studying abroad.[34] Almost all of the leaders of the suffrage movement
in the first years of the Republic of China spent time in Tokyo as students
and activists.

For groups located in China, patriotism was a useful protection from
Qing government surveillance. For example, the Guizhou Women's Patriotic
Association (*Guizhou funü aiguo hui*) formed in 1910 described its commitment to promoting love of the country among women. It did not mention
explicitly that it was supportive of the overthrow of the Qing dynasty, but
most of the so-called patriotic associations of this period were at their core,
anti-Manchu. Its founders' concern to present the association as a morally
upright organization, despite inciting women to engage in public political activities, is evident from its membership codes. The Guizhou Women's
Patriotic Association explained that it was open to all women regardless of
their financial status, but prostitutes were explicitly excluded.[35] To maintain
the moral status of the association, the point had to be made that not all
women "in public" were prostitutes. However, sometimes the divide between "chaste" and "unchaste" women was blurred in the course of the anti-
Qing movement. Both prostitutes and elite women were active members
of intelligence-gathering groups, such as the China Women's Spy Society
(*Zhonghua nüzi zhentan tuan*).[36]

In contrast to the underground or "patriotic" groups formed within China, the women organizing in Japan espoused explicitly anti-Qing policies, and their feminist politics even included anarchism. Most commonly, however, the women worked as sisterhoods that provided practical support for fellow female students. The first feminist group specifically for women studying in Japan was called the Mutual Love Society (*Gong ai hui*), established on 8 April 1903. Only about ten women were present at its inaugural meeting. Hu Binxia (circa 1887–1920s), the daughter of a wealthy scholar-gentry family from Suzhou, led the small group.[37] She would later return to China to serve as editor for the most important women's magazine of the republican period, *The Ladies' Journal* (*Funü zazhi*) from 1916–1919. In the 1920s she led the women's suffrage movement in Shanghai.[38]

In an article publicizing the formation of the Mutual Love Society, Hu wrote of the importance of equal rights between men and women and of the urgent need to eradicate the mentality of "venerating men and subordinating women" (*nanzun nübi*). She explained that the society aimed to win women their rights and freedoms based on the principle of women's fundamental equality with men. Their belief in the transformative powers of education led the society to provide practical support and advice for women studying in Japan in order that this new overseas education venture run as smoothly as possible for the women concerned.[39] Allusions to women's sexualized virtue also penetrated this society's constitution. The society declared that it aimed to "tap the strength of resolve of those women citizens who have committed suicide."[40] The women referred to were those who had committed suicide during the Boxer Rebellion in 1900, after suffering rape by foreign soldiers. As we will see below, appeals to women's sexualized virtue would diminish over the course of the next two decades as women gained increasing access to public virtue through education alone.

In November 1904 the group changed its name to the Society for Achieving Mutual Love (*Shixing gong ai hui*) under the influence of two new prominent feminists—Qiu Jin (1875 or 1877–1907; discussed in detail later in this chapter) and Chen Xiefen (1883–1923). The Hunanese Chen became a cause célèbre among Chinese women in Japan when her otherwise progressive father tried to persuade her to become a concubine to a Chinese merchant. With support from her feminist friends Chen was able to resist her father's pressure. Later, she married a man of her own choosing.[41] Her prominence in the feminist movement had been developed well before her arrival in Japan. At the age of sixteen in 1899 she founded *Women's News* (*Nü bao*). Her father, Chen Fan, was editor of the radical paper *Subao* and he aided her in the radical project of promoting women's rights. His own paper published highly inflammatory anti-Qing essays from the relative safety of the foreign concessions in Shanghai.[42] The Qing government banned the *Women's News* within a year, citing the publication as treasonous. In 1902 Chen revived her publishing career with a journal by a slightly different name—*Women's Studies News* (*Nüxue bao*).[43] This monthly journal was distributed through *Subao*'s networks but it too was short lived. In 1903, under intense pressure from the Qing government, Chen Xiefen and her father left Shanghai for Japan where she became involved with the Mutual Love Societies.[44]

The Mutual Love Societies were small and transient, lasting only as long as key members were still in Japan. Nonetheless they drew together key figures in the struggle for women's equal rights like Hu, Chen, and Qiu and set a pattern of women's organizing under the rubric of education that would continue in subsequent groups of women students. In drawing together women from around China, independent of their clan or locality affiliations, these groups heralded the arrival of a new political constituency—women in the public sphere—although they would not realize their collective power for a few more years.

Other student organizations followed the Mutual Love Societies' lead. The largest women's group to emerge in Tokyo, the Society for Chinese Women Students in Japan (*Zhongguo liu Ri nüxuesheng hui*), was formed in September 1906. The society briefly published a quarterly magazine, the *Journal of the Society for Chinese Women Students in Japan* (*Liu Ri nüxuesheng hui zazhi*).[45] At its foundation it had around seventy people. The greater membership reflects an expansion in numbers of women studying in Japan between 1903 and 1906 as a result of the introduction of Chinese government scholarships for women. Until 1905, when the scholarships were introduced, all the Chinese women studying in Japan were self-funded.[46] Ironically, the government-funded scholarships for women students had the effect of furthering anti-Qing activism among a crucial sector of China's female population. The society also promoted women's rights and on a pragmatic level provided financial support for Chinese women students in Japan. Among the leadership of this new group were the Sichuanese student of English, Li Yuan (circa 1886–?), the redoubtable Hunanese suffragist, Tang Qunying (1871–1937; discussed in detail in the following chapter), and Henanese medical student and journalist, Luo Yanbin (1869–?). The latter was also known as Yan Bin, and her extensive publishing activities on women's rights to political participation are discussed below.[47]

One Chinese feminist association in Tokyo adopted the radical politics of anarchism. He Zhen's Society for the Reinstatement of Women's Rights (*Nüzi fuquan hui*) argued that regaining women's rights would require two methods of attack—first, to force men to relinquish control by use of violence and second, to intervene directly on behalf of women who are suffering oppression by men. The society published feminist writings in the anarchists' bimonthly journal, *Heaven's Justice* (*Tianyi*).[48] The anarchist principles of this group ensured that feminism, rather than nation building, was of prime importance. Peter Zarrow notes that He Zhen "severed feminism from nationalism, proclaiming 'women's liberation' not 'for the sake of the nation' but out of moral necessity."[49]

The anarchist principles of this group also ensured their opposition to the cause of women's suffrage. They regarded parliamentarianism as an insidious force since it reflected the concerns of upper and middle classes at the expense of the poor. On this view, granting women suffrage would merely ensure that the men and women of the oppressor classes would unite against the poorer classes. He Zhen described parliaments as "the source of myriad evils."[50] To the anarchists, reform of the government system was insufficient—the total destruction of the government was required. Similarly, the total destruction of the family was necessary. She continued with an explicit attack on the futility of the suffrage campaign. After describing the success of the Finnish women's movement in winning suffrage rights she explains: "The source of the world's myriad evils is precisely these government policies, and if women want true happiness and prosperity then they need to seek fundamental reforms and fundamental reforms are not found in the struggle to win electoral rights."[51]

Because men devised the government system, her argument ran, it necessarily defended male interests, and therefore women who participate in it would necessarily become supporters of a corrupt system: "Even if a few women get power it will not be enough to save the large bulk of the female population . . . if a few upper-class women participate in politics this will be of no benefit at all to the ordinary people . . . and in fact these women . . . will simply help upper-class men in perpetrating their evil."[52] He Zhen conceived of political rights for women as being best manifest outside of the parliamentary system. She wrote that women's rights needed recovering on three grounds: the right to participate in the military, in nonparliamentary politics, and in education.[53]

The anarchists' advocacy of the complete destruction of government as a path to recovering women's rights was not a common position among those who sought change in China. Most politically active Chinese women in Japan at this time were advocates of a democratic republic provided women were included as formal participants on an equal footing with men. The impact of the anarchist's writing on the other women activists of the time is unclear—but one would anticipate that they read each other's publications, thus the anarchist suspicion about parliamentary democracies would probably have been considered at some point by the mainstream reformists.

Apart from He Zhen, almost all women activists were members of the main anti-Qing Republican political party, Sun Yat-sen's Revolutionary Alliance, as well as being members of their respective women's societies. For example, Chen Xiefen, Qiu Jin, Li Yuan, and Tang Qunying were members of the Revolutionary Alliance as well as leaders in their various women's associations. He Zhen's position appears to be that of a radical outlier.

FEMINISTS IN THE REVOLUTIONARY ALLIANCE: PERFORMING WOMEN'S CITIZENSHIP

The Revolutionary Alliance was formed on 20 August 1905 with the merger of the Awaken China Society (*Xing Zhong hui*) and the Restore China Society (*Hua xing hui*). George Yu argues that the Alliance represents the "beginnings of popular participation by China's intelligentsia in the revolutionary movement." It expanded the existing anti-Qing movement's membership beyond the triads and overseas Chinese by including students.[54] Prior to the Alliance's establishment the movement to reform China had been divided on class grounds. The educated scorned association with the uneducated. The organization's manifesto included four points: expel the barbarians; restore China to the Chinese; create a republic; and equalize land rights. This last point was hotly contested since many wealthy students were uninterested in social reforms that would threaten their landholdings and therefore wanted to concentrate solely on the overthrow of the Manchu. The Revolutionary Alliance was riven with factional disputes. Racial hatred against the Manchu was a major unifying feature of the Alliance in these early years.

Shen Zhi notes that between one hundred and two hundred women signed for membership of the Revolutionary Alliance over a number of years, although many more participated in the activities of the group through its extensive, albeit loose, networks.[55] Li Yu-ning suggests that the party was attractive to women largely because it was "the first major political party in China to recognize the principle of equality between men and women."[56] In fact, although women were welcomed as members, the manifesto of the Alliance promulgated in 1905 made no specific mention of sex equality. It merely stated, "Now our revolution is based on equality, in order to establish a republican government. All our people are equal and all enjoy political rights."[57]

The Cantonese He Xiangning (1879–1972) was among the more prominent of the women active in the Revolutionary Alliance. He Xiangning was married to Alliance leader Liao Zhongkai, and most of the Tokyo meetings of this secret society were held in their house. He and Liao's home served as an important communication base during the Alliance's Japan years. From 1903 to 1910 she studied at various universities and colleges in Tokyo, and on its formation in 1905 she joined the Revolutionary Alliance. A son and daughter were born to her while there. With the collapse of the Qing dynasty He returned to Guangzhou and continued her work for both the Alliance and the women's suffrage groups that formed during the first few months after 1911. She later went on to hold prominent positions as women's adviser in the Nationalist Party and, after 1949, the CCP.[58]

Her first published writing on the question of women's participation in the revolution was "A Respectful Note to My Compatriot Sisters" published in 1903 in the magazine *Jiangsu*. She calls women to be awake to the danger that China faces. She wrote in the vein of the equality rhetoric favored by women activists at the time: "Every person (*ren*) has a share of responsibility for the rise and fall of the country. This clearly is the duty of men but are not women also people—able to see and hear just like men and made of flesh and bones capable of feeling just like men?"[59]

But she also echoed the "equal but different" perspective promoted by the 1898 reformers. He Xiangning's "respectful note" includes an explanation of women's roles as the "producers of civilization" and as "mothers to society" and emphasizes women's national duties.[60] She describes women as having distinct—but still valuable—roles in society, and while these aspects are different from those played by men, women should together with men shoulder the burden for saving the nation. In He Xiangning's political vision women's equality with men was infused with an assertion of their fundamental sex differences. In this respect she was unusual among the women activists in Japan. The majority espoused sex equality with undifferentiated social roles for men and women and sought to demonstrate this in every aspect of their struggle for a democratic republic.

For the most part the women in the Revolutionary Alliance did shoulder the same burdens as men and undertake the same roles as the men. As well as publishing in the Alliance's journals and newspapers, women were active in carrying out communication and underground liaison tasks. Many of the women based in Hong Kong were occupied with the manufacture of bombs for use in the many doomed rebellion attempts. Women formed assassination squads to eliminate prominent Qing officials. For example, the Fujianese radical Fang Junying (1884–1923) organized many such raids, including an unsuccessful attempt on the life of Qing military leader Yuan Shikai.[61] Fang Junying had family support for her radical political activities. Her father and uncle had long been sympathetic to the cause of political and economic reform for China and in 1901 arranged for the unmarried Fang and her widowed sister-in-law to travel to Japan for study. Once in Japan she soon became involved in revolutionary politics, and by 1907 had taken charge of the assassination section of the Alliance.[62] Other women committed to the republican cause became involved in more formal violent action through their participation in the several women's armies that emerged in the dying years of the Qing dynasty.

WOMEN IN MILITARY ACTION:
CITIZENS ARE SOLDIERS

Activist women were well aware that the rights of citizenship came with responsibilities, and so they embraced the duty of citizens to fight to defend their nation. If women wanted to vote, they would have to demonstrate willingness to fight. Participation in all aspects of military struggle was embedded within the early Chinese feminist movement. Claiming equal rights to access political power went alongside the claim for equal access to military power. Thus, China's early feminists formed women's armies and engaged in formal battles alongside men during the last stages of the Qing dynasty.[63] These women were at pains to win the appellation "citizens" or "nation-people" (*guomin*) and to avoid being labeled as "family-people" (*jiamin*)—as the *Hubei Students' World* magazine had described women who lacked the vital spirit of patriotism.[64]

Each of these armies invoked the famous women warriors of China's history—Hua Mulan and Liang Hongyu—and called on the women of China to discard their cosmetics and seek the courage modeled by these figures.[65] A nineteen-year-old woman, Wu Shuqing (1892–?), led one of the first women's armies, the Women's Revolutionary Army (*Nüzi geming jun*), and they took part in the battles for Nanjing and Hankou. It enlisted around one hundred women, and after a brief ten days' training they engaged in combat. Wu's philosophy was that there was no difference between men and women, and she wrote that all of the nation's people have the responsibility for defending their nation with military service. She was of the opinion that because both men and women were equal citizens of the nation, women should also take part in liberating their nation from Qing domination. The Great Han nation belongs to *all* the people, she asserted.[66]

Another young woman to take the initiative with military action in the last months of the Qing dynasty was the seventeen-year-old Yin Weijun who led a "dare to die" brigade of thirty people. At the ages of nine and fourteen Yin Weijun (1894–1919 or 1920) and her elder sister Yin Ruizhi (1890–1948) had joined the Shaoxing school of the revolutionary Qiu Jin. Here, the sisters came under the influence of radical revolutionary ideas and quickly became loyal followers of Qiu Jin. In 1909, at the ages of thirteen and eighteen, they joined a successful assassination squad charged with bombing two Qing officials in Beijing. Their expertise in bomb manufacture and explosives was to win them much respect in the battles against the Qing in the autumn of 1911. To provide a front for their anti-Qing military activities, the sisters opened the Guangfu Study Society (*Guangfu hui*) and the Female Citizens' Association (*Nüzi guomin hui*) in 1911 (see Figure 2.1 for a picture of the Yin sisters in military attire). Their first women's army was named the Women's Guangfu Army (*Nüzi guangfu jun*) and it became famous for its daring bombing raids around Zhejiang. After Hangzhou came under revolutionary control, Yin Ruizhi was badly injured while making a bomb in Shanghai's French Concession. She spent the rest of the next twelve months recovering. However, her younger sister regrouped the troops and organized a new group, the Zhejiang Women's Army, which took part in the famous battle on Nanjing's Yuhua tai.[67] Her partner in the establishment of this army was Lin Zongxue (see Figure 2.2). She was sister to Lin Zongsu, author of the preface to *A Tocsin for Women* and key leader in the

Figure 2.1. The Yin sisters in military attire (circa 1911). *Le Miroir* (undated clipping), Collection Laruelle, tome 89, ne 63, fo 1, Bibliothèque National, Paris. After Valerie Steele and John S. Major, eds., *China Chic: East Meets West* (New Haven, CT: Yale University Press, 1999), 129.

Figure 2.2. Lin Zongxue, women's army leader. *Minli bao* (People's Independence News), 11 January 1912.

women's suffrage campaigns of 1912. Where Zongxue demonstrated equality with men on the military sphere her sister Zongsu sought the same in the political arena.

As the rebellion increased in successes, more women's armies were formed in preparation for the final push into northern China. Various women formed military associations under the title of the Women's Northern Attack Brigade (*Nüzi beifa dui*) around the major cities of the South.[68] For example, Zhang Mojun (aka Zhang Shaohan; 1883–1965) organized a women's army that was known as the Shanghai Women's Northern Attack "Dare to Die Brigade" (*Gan si dui*). It had over seventy students enlisted as soldiers.[69] In Shanghai, Lin Zongxue organized the Women's Citizens' Army (*Nüzi guomin jun*), and after the establishment of the republic this group took the lead in lobbying the new republican government for women's right to participate in military affairs. In January of 1912, *The People's Independence News* (*Minli bao*) published a picture of Lin's soldiers and a cameo shot of Lin herself (see Figures 2.2 and 2.3).[70] The paper's favorable coverage of their actions included a headline, "The President salutes women warriors."[71]

The leaders of China's post-1911 republic had reason to be grateful to the women who were prepared to enter the battlefields. The famous medical feminist Zhang Zhujun (1879–?) achieved a position of authority in the Red Cross (*Chi shizi hui*), and through this status aided the rebels—rescuing the Revolutionary Alliance leaders Huang Xing and Song Jiaoren from the Qing troops during one battle.[72] The medical efforts of Zhang's team drew them into dangerous areas close to battlefields and, during the fight-

Figure 2.3. China's Women's Army. *Minli bao* (People's Independence News), 10 January 1912.

ing around Hankou, they are credited with saving over 1,300 lives within a two-month period. Of the Red Cross's one hundred and twenty members, fifty-four were women (fourteen doctors and forty nurses).[73]

The unique feature of these women, compared to those warriors in China's past such as Hua Mulan and Liang Hongyu, was that their campaign was to disrupt rather than buttress the existing gender order. China's Amazons prior to this time have been hailed in extensive histories and fictional accounts for their dedication to protecting China's idealized social and political structures against foreign invasion or internal disarray—but in every instance the social order that is restored is patriarchal. The women warriors of the first decade of the twentieth century were most likely perceived as a continuation of this patriarchy-reinforcing tradition—hence the glowing media reports of their actions. On this view the women armies were symbols of the dire straits into which China had fallen, and it was assumed they would return to their feminine roles when order resumed.[74] Women soldiers of the twentieth century were not of the same mold. They sought, through their military action, to confirm that sex equality would exist in their longed-for republic. The women's military activities were intimately linked with their political aspirations. For example, the army commander Zhang Mojun would leave her military interests aside and form one of the most important women's suffrage groups of 1912 after the formation of the Republic of China, as we will see in Chapter Three.

Many links existed between the women's schools and the women's armies. Both scholarship and warfare were male domains that women were keen to demonstrate they could enter. In so doing, they demonstrated their legitimate right to full citizenship. Women students comprised the bulk of the troops in the women's armies and the majority of the activists in the suffrage movement. Appealing to scholarship was important in asserting their virtue and equality with men. For example, the Guangdong Women's Northern Attack Brigade (*Guangdong nüzi beifa dui*) drew its troops from the many students and workers in the Revolutionary Alliance's main educational institution in Hong Kong, the Hong Kong Girls' Practical College.[75] The brigade's leader, Xu Zonghan (1876–1944), became a prominent suffragist once the republic was achieved—a role she continued into the 1920s.[76] Xu Zonghan also went under the name Xu Mulan during this time, invoking the martial glories of Hua Mulan.[77] But, in contrast to her namesake, Xu and other women warriors of the first decade of the twentieth century

engaged in military action to achieve a women's rights agenda, just as they used their newly gained access to education for the same ends.[78]

At the end of the Qing, the women activists' claim to equality in citizenship rights was demonstrated by their participation in all aspects of the struggle to create the democracy in which their citizenship could be realized. Military action was regarded as an integral part of the duties of citizenship, and with that logic the women radicals were enthusiastic in their participation. Some of the women harbored dreams of a career in the military, but their hopes to maintain a female army in the Republic of China were quashed with the 26 February 1912 ruling by the provisional government to disband all women armies.[79] Not everyone appreciated the radical nature of this military action by women. However, the women had other important platforms upon which to demonstrate their equal citizenship with men. Military prowess was an important but not the only avenue for demonstrating citizenship. Knowledge of national and international politics was also vital, and education was the key to developing those skills.

ERADICATING IGNORANCE: EDUCATING
THE WOMEN CITIZENS OF THE FUTURE

In China full and equal political citizenship demanded full and equal access to examinable education. The link between access to political power and formal, examination-based education had underpinned China's governance structure for centuries since bureaucrats were selected through a series of examinations. Women's education, unlike that of their brothers, was home based and did not include participation in the examinations—thus women were institutionally excluded from political power. Radical women activists of the first decades of the twentieth century perceived their explicit exclusion from attending schools that would give them formal academic qualifications to be a major block to their political aspirations. To overcome this problem, they sought equal access to education on the understanding that with equal opportunities, differences between the sexes' access to political power could be eradicated. In 1903 one feminist, Fang Junji, wrote of the link between education and rights:

> Several thousand years ago, Chinese women lost their rights and were reduced to piercing their ears and binding their feet. They did not leave the

house and did not read poems or books. Their experience was narrow and shallow . . . they were totally reliant on other people . . . Chinese women do not have access to their rights because they do not have access to education and because they do not have an education they do not have access to their rights. Thus, if we want to promote women's rights we must first promote women's education.[80]

The women at the forefront of the movement at this time began their campaign for the expansion of women's education outside the home from a strong position. They were highly literate women, having been educated within their family homes. But, importantly they were increasingly able to access nonfamily schooling as both private and government institutions expanded during the first two decades of the century.[81] In 1907, the Qing government encouraged education for girls with its ordinances announcing the opening of girls' primary schools and women's teachers colleges across China—these were the Regulation on Girls' Primary Schools (*Nüzi xiaoxuetang zhangcheng*) and the Regulation on Women's Teachers Colleges (*Nüzi shifan xuetang zhangcheng*).[82] That same year, Shen Zhi notes, twenty-two provinces had 428 different women's schools and 15,496 students, with 1,501 teachers.[83]

Significantly, formal education also permitted women to depart from their segregated lives in the domestic realm and step into the public realm with their virtue partly protected by the prestige of learning. Elite women's virtue was built around isolating them from public view, and attendance at school threatened this control mechanism. Cheng Weikun noted that schooling for girls bridged the gap between the inner and outer, the private and the public and "sent women into the public world."[84] Achieving a public presence was crucial to strengthening women's status, but maintaining woman's virtue was important to building credibility for the "public-ness" of the movement as well. Confucian philosophy had long advocated the acquiring of virtue through education, but this kind of virtue had primarily been a male moral economy. So women activists had to emphasize that this equation could equally apply to women. In 1907 one feminist, Zhao Zhi, challenged the old maxim "a woman without talent is virtuous" to just such an end. She wrote, "talent (*cai*) accompanies virtue (*de*)—they are connected—if you have talent then virtue will follow. If you don't have talent then what sort of virtue can you have."[85] On this logic, developing women's talent through education could only enhance their virtue.

However, where some supporters of women's public schooling regarded it as a radical shift in fundamental gender norms, others saw it simply as the modernization of the education of virtuous mothers. Wang Zheng has written of this tension as follows: "For many women, an education was a step into the men's world and a qualification for citizenship, rather than merely a means to become a virtuous mother of good citizens."[86] The 1898 reformers, Kang Youwei and Liang Qichao, had recommended the expansion of public schooling for girls in order that they become superior mothers to China's sons. Ye Weili has noted that Liang Qichao "did not feel it necessary for women to be educated for their own benefit" even though he was "the most forceful advocate of female education at the turn of the century."[87] Similarly, Jing Yuanshan (1841–1903), founder of China's first Chinese-operated school for girls, "featured the teaching of mothers as a major argument for women's education" in his memorials to the Qing government.[88] In Beijing in the first decade of the twentieth century, Manchu reformers and local merchants started a range of private girls' schools based on the philosophy that an educated woman would become a proficient teacher for her children and would thereby strengthen the nation.[89] Similarly, the North Ocean Girls' Normal School aimed to reinforce the value of traditional Chinese virtues. At a meeting of the school held in February of 1908 the girls were exhorted to protect the old Chinese female qualities—women's virtue, women's speech, women's deportment—and not to be influenced by the strange talk about women that was circulating in society.[90]

Sally Borthwick describes the situation in many schools as follows: "Girls' schools attempted to stress conservative values in the social realm: regulations forbade visits from non-family members and correspondence from unauthorized persons, and students were warned that 'equal rights' meant simply 'an educated woman, able to manage her own household and tasks, and thus the same as a man,' while freedom was the self-regulation which ensured that every act accorded with what was right."[91]

However, despite these best efforts many schools created the space within which women conceived of themselves as independent individuals with responsibility for their own fates.[92] Qian Nanxiu convincingly demonstrates that rather than being passive recipients of the male reformist agenda, women involved with the schools soon developed their own "agenda, agency, organizations, and specific strategies for forming a new Chinese womanhood and for national strengthening."[93] Typical of the feminist politics informing many who attended these schools was the sentiment that without women's schools "women's rights will not be revived and millions of Chinese women will live a paint and powder life bitterly imprisoned as playthings for men."[94]

They were assisted in this political program by some of the private institutions that were considerably more radical than the government-regulated schools. Some, like the Datong school, employed radicals such as Qiu Jin and included knowledge of military matters in their curriculum. Of these private schools the most significant was Cai Yuanpei's Shanghai-based Patriotic Girls' School (*Aiguo nüxiao*) that opened in 1902. It was radically anti-Qing in its political leanings and was able to function with this philosophy largely because it had the protection of the foreign concessions where it was located. Sister schools in other major cities soon followed, and together they served to spread not only the important cause of a broad education for women, but also the importance of establishing a democratic government controlled by Han Chinese.

Radicalism was also promoted through the increasing scope for women to study abroad. The prime destination was Japan, and Xing Long notes that in 1907 there were over one hundred women from China studying in Japan.[95] Most of the women there enrolled in teaching courses and probably intended to return to China to fill positions in the expanding girls' school sector. Japan was the preferred location for a number of pragmatic reasons. In 1903 an article promoting the value of overseas study for women argued that they should come to Japan to advance their learning in a country that is relatively close to China—in terms of cultural background and script. The author, Chen Yan'an, stressed that the current education system in China was discriminatory since it regarded women as useless and kept them in conditions of poverty and dependency—this combined to deny women their humanity. She concluded by asserting that only with education could women assume their responsibilities as citizens.[96] Similarly, in another article urging women to come to Tokyo, the Mutual Love Society reiterated the importance of education to strengthening the nation by embedding a notion of egalitarian mutuality between men and women's roles into the discussion: "The essence of the nation rests in its educated people. Therefore to recover the nation both men and women must be educated . . . if this is so then women will not be dependent upon men and men would not be dependent upon women. The nation would certainly be strong. Unless we undertake this, the nation will continue to be weak."[97] Discussion around the Japan-based schools routinely and explicitly promoted such radical equal rights agendas.

Progress on women's overseas education varied between localities. The first province to embark on this radical path for women's education was Hunan. As a result of a succession of enlightened governors, the Hunan provincial government had been progressive in outlook since before the 1898 Reform Movement. In keeping with this tradition in July of 1905 they sent twenty women on scholarships to study at a women's college in Japan. These women formed the core of the women's suffrage movement on their return to China and include such eminent figures as Wang Changguo (1880–1949) and Zhang Hanying (1872–1915). Wang was among the province's first elected women parliamentarians in 1921, and Zhang was part of the group that stormed the Nanjing parliament in 1912 to demand that the constitution guarantee women's rights to participate in politics.[98] Another prominent Hunanese suffrage activist to benefit from the Qing government's education policies for women was Tang Qunying. Tang began her studies in Japan as a self-funded student but later received a scholarship from the Hunan provincial government.[99] As we shall see in the following chapter, Tang was destined to become China's most famous woman suffragist. Instead of educating women to become better mothers so that they would produce better sons, many of the women who entered schools at this time emerged as enthusiastic women's rights campaigners.

Despite the rapid growth in the education sector, schooling for girls was still an elite preoccupation, as were all the social reforms of this period, and Sally Borthwick notes that by 1909 less than 0.1 percent of the school-age population of girls was attending school.[100] Although the Chinese women studying in Japan would be important figures, the numbers actually graduating from formal colleges, rather than from less official schools, remained very small. For the ten-year period leading up to 1911 the total of Japan graduates came to a paltry thirty-five.[101] Many women there focused on revolutionary rather than scholarly pursuits. These small numbers reflect the broader situation in the Chinese women's movement at this time. For the first two decades of the twentieth century the women's movement was largely composed of privileged women. But the entrance of these "good" women into the public realm through access to schooling outside the home presaged an important shift in elite attitudes. It challenged the notion that women should aim to remain out of the public domain in order to present themselves as virtuous individuals. Education provided a mechanism to access a moral schema that could at least partially replace that of female segregation. The schema simply had to be

extended from men to include women. Once women were included in the
"public education = public virtue" matrix, then it was more possible for
them to claim "right to rule." By performing equally as well as men in the
education realm women could legitimately claim the right to equal access
to political power since they "had virtue too."

The rapid expansion in women's newspapers and journals at the turn of
the century presented women with ample opportunity to publicly demonstrate that they were sufficiently well educated to participate in ruling
the nation.[102] They routinely displayed an exceptional level of erudition
through their writings. Moreover, by publishing their ideas these women
broke centuries of resistance to the public circulation of women's writing,
a practice considered improper for women of literati families.[103] The new
woman citizen was an individual with an independent, public voice.

The women contributing to these journals often used their new public
voice to criticize their sisters around the nation. They repeatedly bemoaned
the widespread lack of knowledge about citizenship rights and responsibilities. As the 1907 publication announcement for one of the more successful
journal of these years, *China's New Women's World*, declared, "Although there
are many, many women citizens (*nü guomin*) in China, there is not much
spirit of women's citizenship amongst them."[104] China's women's rights
activists set themselves the task of creating just that spirit of citizenship
through their publications.

One of their key lines of argument was to attack the scourge of dependency that they regarded as hampering women's political consciousness—
only once women had achieved independence could truly effective women
citizens emerge.[105] Dependency and slavishness, it was understood, prevented women from taking responsibility for their own and their nation's
fate.[106] In a dramatic illustration of the extent of the perceived task ahead,
an article in *China's New Women's World* described a fantasy tale where the
protagonist undertakes a journey to seek the meaning of the term "woman
citizen" (*nü guomin*) in an ancient dictionary. The journey to find the word
"female" (*nüzi*) involves a trek to a dark, threatening place: "There was a
deep hole leading under the ground. Looking down you were presented

with a series of levels connected by small ladders and . . . on the first level were the characters for 'slave'. . . . Underneath 'slaves' was the level for the characters 'female' (*nüzi*)."[107]

On the "female" level a great ocean of blood and tears stretched to eternity, filled by the centuries of women's misery. Slavery and imprisonment rhetoric abounded at this time among China's feminists. For example, in *Women's World* (*Nüzi shijie*), the longest-running and most influential women's magazine prior to 1911, Ding Chuwo wrote: "If we have no rights, then we are slaves; if we have no freedom, then we are imprisoned."[108] This dismal picture of China's women being imprisoned, lower than slaves, and burdened with limitless misery simultaneously amplifies the injustices faced by women in China and acknowledges the difficulties inherent in the task of creating the desired spirit of citizenship.

Independence, both financial and emotional, was advocated as the key to escaping from slavery and achieving freedom. The 1907 "Song for Women Citizens" draws this connection in its evocative lines: "The spirit of independence is rising like the red morning sun, and the tide of freedom is gushing forth, and a world of women's rights and equality stands strong."[109] Luo Yanbin wrote of the importance of promoting women's independence in her *China's New Women's World* magazine and outlined two main causes of dependency: "the first is the lack of education and the second is the absence of organizational support. If you don't have an education then you lack knowledge and if you don't have an organization then you lack public spirit. It is no wonder that for thousands of years women have been like slaves."[110]

In the *Women's Studies News*, Chen Xiefen wrote a piece titled "On Independence" in which she stated: "Those who are independent have escaped from oppression, fought obstructions. . . . They are no longer maintained by men nor do they suffer from meddling by men."[111] An article by Jiu Si titled "Self Respect" presented a psychological solution to the dependency problem. She argued that dependency and self-denigration were endemic in the women of China and that the promotion of self-respect among this same group was crucial to winning their freedom.[112]

Education was presented as a key method for eradicating women's dependency. For example, in 1903 Yi Qin wrote an article serialized over two issues of the radical magazine, *Jiangsu*, explaining the intricacies of women's dependence on men in relation to education. She argued that as a result of the centuries of dependency, women needed men's help to break the cycle.

Education was regarded as the key to achieving this independence, and ironically women depended on men to provide them with access to this education.[113] This was a common position. In 1902 Chen Xiefen's *Women's News* had earlier included an article that connected independence to education, national strength, and women's rights. "If we want the nation to be strong then we must recover women's rights; if we want to recover women's rights then we must popularize women's education; only once women's education is popularized can women be independent and no longer be appendages to a man's world."[114]

Family reform was also seen as a vital focus for social change if women wanted to achieve the missing spirit of citizenship. The first issue of the *Journal of the Society for Chinese Women Students in Japan* exposed the commoditized, dehumanized position of women in families: "In current marriage customs fathers demand bride-price (*pinqian*) [from the groom's parents]. Parents treat daughters as commodities to be bought and sold like the household pigs, sheep and cattle."[115] This situation would have to change if women were to fully understand their status as equal citizens to men. One 1907 commentator, Pei Gong, challenged China's women to learn from their sisters in Europe and America arguing that these women had worked hard to carve for themselves free and independent lives where they were able to choose their own husbands, develop careers, and maintain their own property and finances. Their victories had not come without hardship, and so China's women needed to find the courage to strive for these benefits as well.[116] Similar international comparisons were made in the *Journal of the Society for Chinese Women Students in Japan*. It declared that women's independence from men was an imperative but it would require persistence and resolve to achieve this goal. The editors wrote that despite the fact that women in England had repeatedly lost their bids for suffrage rights they were undeterred by failure and with each defeat revived their campaigning.[117] China's early feminists were well aware that their task would require enormous effort, persistent struggle, and unflinching courage. Women's progress in Europe and America stood as markers of hope for Chinese women in an age where international communication and exchange occurred.[118]

The national struggle for survival also provided women with an opportunity to purge themselves of their dependent behaviors. Ding Chuwo described a "direct link between women's rights (*nüquan*) and people's rights (*minquan*)." She continued, "if you want to create a nation, you must first create a family; if you want to build citizens, you must first build women. The political revolution emerges when striving for the freedom of the entire body of citizens."[119] Similarly, women activists in Japan were determined to demonstrate that women's action in politics was normal by appealing to patriotism. In an open letter to the women of China, the Japan-based students wrote that because the nation was in desperate straits they felt it appropriate to widely publicize their responsibility for saving it as women compatriots.[120] By embracing their duties as citizens of China the women assumed that they would be afforded the rights of the citizens of China.

One of the many songs *Women's World* published shows the strength of the radicalism among women at this time. Titled "Women Citizens" (*Nü guomin*), the lyrics of the first two verses proceed:

> Rage, rage, rage! Choking on shame and interminable misery. There is none in the world as good as a man, yet in the North they are in court managing for the enemy scum. In the midst of chaos they talk of reform, their heads shaved like criminals, yet so conceited. Only we women, uphold the light, free from the spirit of dependency.
>
> Speed, speed, speed! The energy of civilization is moving through East Asia. The spirit of independence is red in the sunrise, and the currents of freedom are flooding forth. The world of women's rights is weighty, and the principle of equality is mighty. Then turning back we see the gold, powder, paints, and rouge of the ordinary pitiful insects.[121]

These journals were as radical as they were short lived but their feminist credentials were never in doubt. Their vision of a "woman citizen" was one that had the identical attributes of (male) citizens. They provided translations of material on natural rights and the women's movement from Japan, USA, and Europe, spreading knowledge about the principles behind the editors' enthusiasm for social and political change. Their audience would have been extremely small, limited to the urban upper and middle classes with education. They conceived of their task as that of a vanguard that would lead the masses on the correct path to national strength and cultural revival by proclaiming women's natural equality with men. Yet within a few years, as we will see in the following chapter, it would become apparent that their campaign to be recognized as equal to men even by their elite male peers was a failure.

QIU JIN: SOLDIER, TEACHER, JOURNALIST,
AND WOMEN'S RIGHTS CAMPAIGNER

The most famous of all the remarkable women who participated in the
struggle to prove women's equal status with men in China is Qiu Jin (1875
or 1877–1907).[122] Martyred for her anti-Qing activities, Qiu Jin's work en-
capsulates the diversity of the tasks activist women undertook during these
years to demonstrate this equality. They simultaneously embraced political
and military action, education, and publishing on the understanding that
through these actions their claim as women to an equal role with men in
any future political order would be furthered. From Zhejiang Province,
Qiu Jin was married by her parents to a Hunanese merchant whose behavior she later described as "worse than an animal's. This man is devoid
of virtue."[123] Married life became increasingly unbearable, but it had the
effect both of sharpening her awareness of the urgency to revolutionize relations between men and women in China and of raising her consciousness
of the importance of political activism for women. She was in Beijing at
the time of the occupation of the city during the Boxer Rebellion of 1900,
and the humiliation of this debacle kindled her patriotic sentiments. During this time she corresponded regularly with like-minded women—the
widowed Tang Qunying and the disaffected wife Ge Jianhao (1865–1943).[124]
In a move that combined their twin political goals, Qiu Jin and Tang Qunying resolved to travel to Japan to study. Qiu Jin left her husband and
their two young children, literally and figuratively unbinding her feet, and
traveled to Japan aiming to restore China to its former strength and work
to unshackle China's women from the binds of slavery.[125] In Japan she lived
for nearly two years in relative poverty since her savings had remained in
the possession of her husband. In her lucid description of Qiu Jin, Mary
Backus Rankin points out that her mother and brothers also supported
her through this time.[126] From her earliest days as a foreign student, she
was active in the anti-Qing associations and, as mentioned earlier, she also
joined the Mutual Love Society for Chinese women studying in Japan.[127]
In August of 1905, Sun Yat-sen's Revolutionary Alliance was formed, and
Qiu Jin joined and was appointed representative for Zhejiang. She was active in publishing in the various anti-Qing journals that emerged, and the
poems and prose from these and her remaining years stand as evidence of
her considerable literary skill.

Frustrated variously by the slow pace of reform in China, a sense of isolation from China, and harassment by the Japanese authorities, Qiu Jin returned to her homeland at the start of 1906.[128] Back in China she aimed to put her feminist and nationalist aspirations into direct action. During this year she taught in a middle school in Shaoxing. In January 1907 she went to Shanghai and started a newspaper designed to spread the notion of gender equality as a natural right among the population of literate women. Titled *China Women's News* (*Zhongguo nübao*), it published only two issues before it was closed. In this short-lived publication, Qiu Jin called her fellow countrywomen to wake themselves and prepare for the dangerous times ahead. Women, she declared needed to unite in action to fight against the darkness into which the country had sunk.[129] She called on women to shoulder their responsibilities as women citizens in repeated poems and articles. In one of her most famous poems, "Striving for Women's Rights," she forcefully and eloquently wrote: "Ours is a generation that loves freedom, we strive for freedom on one single cup of wine. Equal rights for men and women is endowed by nature, how then is it that you willingly live in subordination? . . . Outstanding women citizens must not fail to shoulder national responsibilities."[130] In her essay "A respectful announcement to my sisters," Qiu Jin bemoans the current state of Chinese women, declaring:

> While the men of China are entering a civilized new world, China's women still remain in the dark and gloom, mired in the lowest of all the levels of hell's prisons, not even contemplating raising ourselves one level. Feet bound so tiny, hair combed so shiny; tied, edged, and decorated with flowers and bouquets; trimmed and coiled in silks and satins; smeared with white powders and bright rouges. We spend our lives only knowing how to rely on men—for everything we wear and eat we rely on men.

Qiu Jin stressed that the misery of women's lives is not necessarily visible but the pain of daily subordination to one's husband remains. "Husbands always stand as the masters and women everywhere take the position of slaves. By relying on other people, you strip yourselves of any shred of an independent character." From here she urges her younger sisters to join the girls' schools and develop their careers. By these means women can win freedom and happiness and by "scrubbing off the name of 'useless woman' earn the respect of men."[131] Throughout her writings she promoted the importance of financial and political independence for women and she too based her arguments on the notion that men and women were born with the same inalienable rights to liberty and equality.

From this brief excerpt it is clear that Qiu Jin's audience were women in the same privileged class as herself—literate and sufficiently wealthy to be living a life of dependency. The vast majority of China's women would only dream of being able to be trimmed with silks and satins or smeared with powders and rouges. There is little evidence in the feminist writings of this time to suggest interest in the converting the female masses into political action on their own accord. Rather, like their brothers, they conceived of themselves as an enlightened elite who should persuade other members of an educated political class into leading China's masses forward.

With the closure of her newspaper, Qiu Jin returned to Shaoxing later in 1907 where she was employed as a teacher in the Datong Girls' School. This school was a thinly disguised front for anti-Qing activities, and the students were trained in military affairs as well as more regular academic subjects. The school's revolutionary activities soon made students targets for the attention of the Qing police. During the failed Anhui-Zhejiang uprising Qiu Jin's activities and those of the women in her school clearly implicated them in treasonous activities. Despite warnings that she was scheduled for imminent arrest, Qiu Jin remained at the school and with around thirty students put up heroic, albeit brief, resistance to the Qing officers as they arrived. Once captured, the treasonous woman citizen, Qiu Jin, was executed.[132]

TOWARD THE REPUBLIC

Qiu Jin's life, with its revolutionary interest in women's rights, education, and publishing coupled with daring military action, exemplifies the spirit of the women involved in the early women's rights movement of China. High-minded but elitist, these women regarded themselves as a vanguard, leading the Chinese population into new cultural and political terrain. The first decade of the twentieth century saw a dramatic transformation of women's attitudes regarding their right to participate in politics and public life. Women citizens were conceived and promoted as equal to men in both rights and duties for the first time. The embracing of ethical principles of natural rights provided a discursive foundation upon which equality with men would be fought, complementary to but also independent of the campaign for national salvation.

Women's rights activists regarded their participation in every aspect of the republican movement as being crucial to the assertion that women were equal to men. Women were demonstrating their preparedness to take all the responsibilities of citizenship and this, they anticipated, would lead to full and equal rights with men in the new Han China. Women activists of this period saw that women needed to assert their abilities and strive for equality themselves and not wait for men to bestow equality on them. As Qiu Jin stated: "Women must get educated and strive for their own independence; they can't just go on asking the men for everything. The young intellectuals are all chanting, 'Revolution, Revolution,' but I say the revolution will have to start in our homes, by achieving equal rights for women."[133]

The hopes and aspirations of the women who worked alongside Qiu Jin in this 1911 revolution period to create a woman citizen with full and equal rights to men citizens were to be dashed with the establishment of the republic. Perseverance would become a significant virtue in the struggle for women's suffrage rights.

Women's Search for Political Equality in the New Republic, 1912–1914

In October 1911, after two and half centuries, the once glorious Qing dynasty was crumbling. Control of the country was slipping from the Qing government's hands, and by 12 February 1912 the emperor had abdicated. A provisional government of the Republic of China emerged with a mixture of governors, assemblymen, anti-Qing rebels, and literati as its core and with Sun Yat-sen at its head. The women activists were soon to discover that the Han patriarchy that had assumed control of China was no more interested in giving political rights to women than the Manchu patriarchy had been. They had to contend with the many influential men who had participated in the Qing self-government movements and not just the men in the Revolutionary Alliance. And, the more conservative men from the old assemblies were far from convinced of the benefits of women's suffrage. As anticipated by Qiu Jin, the main political groups would betray the women's suffrage campaigners, despite the latter's participation in the overthrow of the Qing.[1] The women activists came to realize that they could not rely on their nationalist, Han-patriot credentials to deliver feminist goals. Despite their efforts to prove women's independence and equality with men during the struggle to create the republic, they found that the age-old perceptions of sex differences were reinforced under the new government—women's difference from men equated to women's subordination.[2]

In the course of attempting to overturn this new opposition, during the two years between 1911 and 1913 the women developed a political consciousness and public profile that was singularly feminist in perspective—their activism was premised solely on feminist politics, rather than in concert with nationalist or anti-Qing agendas. The Chinese women's movement began to enunciate a platform that took men, specifically their elite, educated male peers, as the opposition. To undermine patriarchal notions of sex difference they continued to promote the view that women, given equal opportunities, would be equal to men in performance and to advocate that women were essentially and inherently entitled to be considered men's equals. In their high-profile activism on the issue of suffrage, the aspiring women politicians and voters presented to a Chinese audience a vision of a public woman in a democratic political context rather than one of warfare. Women's public participation in the latter was simply dismissed as a temporary aberration within the rubric of the long-standing conceptions of women warriors in China's past—extraordinary women achieving extraordinary goals during times of national crisis who return to the domestic sphere when order is restored. The suffragists appearance in the public realm demanding long-term political rights presented a different woman altogether. Thus, while the activists of this period were unsuccessful in winning changes to constitutional documents, the campaign did raise awareness about women's aspirations for public political roles and also established a new mode of thinking about representation and governance. In so doing, these earlier activists laid the foundation for the more successful campaigns of the 1920s and 1930s by creating the space in which a sense of a legitimate women's political collective identity could develop.

In addition, during these two years the suffragists established a pattern of drawing on their connections with the global women's suffrage movement. In hosting well-publicized and well-attended visits by IWSA activists, such as Carrie Chapman Catt, China's activists demonstrated that theirs was a cause of global significance. They pressed the case that this was a far-reaching, modernizing force of international import. Simultaneously, newspapers during these years regularly reported on the dramatic actions of women in Britain and the USA with their campaigns of vandalism, public nuisance, and civil disobedience. The "extremism" of China's activists in these years was thus contextualized within this narrative of persistent, widespread activism within strong nations with established democracies. Suffragist campaigning was presented to a Chinese reading audience as being part of the package that came with democracy and not an aberration by small numbers of radical Chinese women.

THE EARLY YEARS OF ASIA'S FIRST REPUBLIC

The much-anticipated Chinese republic commenced with considerable optimism among the political elite. This hope for a better-governed nation was to prove to be largely misplaced. On 1 January 1912, Sun Yat-sen formed a provisional government in the southern city of Nanjing but he did so only through a compromise with a key military and political strongman, Yuan Shikai. Yuan had been influential in the Qing military modernization and held considerable influence with its military forces throughout the first decade of the century. Through clever manipulation of competing interests he had also secured the position of premier in the Qing government in Beijing. From this position Yuan appeared to the rebels to be indispensable to securing the republic. Thus Sun's provisional government was formed on the understanding that Yuan would eventually assume the presidential role—a duty he undertook after formal inauguration on 10 March 1912. Then, in blatant disregard of an agreement that the republic's government would be based in Nanjing, Yuan moved the capital to Beijing since he was reluctant to leave his power base in the north of the country. He quickly revealed himself to be a traitor to the republic just as he had betrayed the Qing. Yuan Shikai was ruthless in his suppression of dissenting voices, and many politically active citizens lived in fear of his ruthless henchmen. With relentless ambition Yuan Shikai moved in 1915 to reestablish the monarchy with his own dynasty. The democracy that the suffragists had sought to build was in grave peril.

How was the women's suffrage movement placed throughout these dramatic political changes? At the start of the republic in 1912 the women had been imbued with great hope for full political recognition of their equality with men. But within six months of the establishment of the republic their hopes were dashed. In March of 1912 the Provisional Constitution was approved, and it implicitly excluded women. This defeat was compounded by the promulgation of the electoral laws in August of the same year that reiterated the disenfranchised state of China's women. Nonetheless, throughout

1912 and 1913 women's suffrage activists maintained lively, vocal and disruptive campaigns to win support for equality between men and women in political rights. Yet even these actions were to come to a grinding halt with President Yuan Shikai's banning of women's involvement in political activity in a series of regulations from November of 1913 to March 1914.

WOMEN'S SUFFRAGE AND THE
EARLY REPUBLICAN CONSTITUTIONS

Women's status in the republic's first constitutions was problematic from the outset. In October 1911 only days after the successful Wuchang uprising that precipitated the demise of the Qing dynasty, Song Jiaoren seized the initiative and wrote the first version of a republican constitution to replace the Qing documents. This has become known as the Ezhou Constitution, and the precepts Song devised formed the basis of the more formal and nationally recognized Provisional Constitution promulgated in March of 1912.[3] The statement that all people were equal was included among the Ezhou Constitution's sixty items, but it remained unclear whether the concept of "people" included women. The women's rights activists of the time were astute enough to realize that this ambiguity could support or hinder their cause and knew that, while Sun Yat-sen's Revolutionary Alliance advocated equal rights for women (though not universal adult suffrage),[4] the general feeling among political leaders was one of opposition. The campaign to ensure that both men and women were explicitly included in the constitution's provisions for national multiparty elections then began in earnest and, in the six months after October 1911 the issue was hotly debated. The crucial decisions that denied women the right to vote were made in the context of the factions competing for interest in the formation of the new political bodies that were to govern China.

The Nanjing-based provisional parliament comprised forty-three elected and nominated representatives from seventeen provinces around the nation. Of these, twenty-three were members of Sun's Revolutionary Alliance and eighteen were Constitutional Faction (*Lixian pai*) members.[5] No women were included. The first and most important of their tasks was the finalizing of a draft constitution that would govern the nation and provide for national parliamentary elections. Accordingly, during February of 1912 the provisional parliament deliberated on the nature of China's first republican constitution. This revised constitution was promulgated on 11 March 1912 and overruled the Ezhou document in which the general reference had been made to equality of all people. The revised version was more specific and explicitly stated that all people were equal regardless of race, religion, and class—sex was omitted and "people" was understood to refer only to men.[6] The Alliance's commitment to sex equality had been traded away in the negotiations. But significantly, the documents also consolidated the notion that educated and moneyed men were the republic's authorized political leaders and participants. Suffrage was not to be universal for men.

The first elections of the new republic were held in the winter of 1912–13. John Fairbank described these as based on a "very restricted and indirect franchise. . . . Voting was still an elitist activity."[7] It was nonetheless a vastly more expanded electoral list than the 1909 equivalent. John Fincher notes that forty million voters were on the electoral lists in 1912, compared to eight million in 1909. He comments that this was around "20 and 25 per cent of the adult male population and 10 per cent of the total population. This increase was accompanied by a lowering of the education requirement from secondary to only elementary schooling or its equivalent." Property requirements were similarly loosened from "ownership of a business or real property worth $5,000 ($10,000 for non-natives) to ownership of immovable property worth only $500 or annual payment of at least $2 indirect tax. Any male over 21 years of age with either of these qualifications and who had resided in his district for at least two years and was not disqualified by certain crimes could vote."[8] Those prohibited from voting were "illiterates, opium smokers, bankrupts, and those of unsound mind."[9] Importantly, the women's suffrage activists were not struggling for universal suffrage, merely equality with men in suffrage rights. In many of the women activist's minds, illiterate and propertyless women should also be excluded.[10]

Women greeted the announcement of the new constitution and electoral laws with outrage. Indeed, the period between October 1911 and November 1913 was one of intense activity for the women's suffrage campaigners. Among the several different groups that formed to fight for women's rights to vote during this time, three are most important—the Women's Suffrage Comrades' Society (*Nüzi canzheng tongzhi hui*) and the Shenzhou Women's Assistance Society (*Shenzhou nüjie gonghe xiejishe*). The former merged with a number of other women's groups in February of 1912 to form the Women's Suffrage Alliance (WSA; *Nüzi canzheng tongmeng hui*). This amalgamated group and the Shenzhou Women's Assistance Society participated in joint actions in the struggle for women's suffrage until late 1913. The Shenzhou Women's Assistance Society group adopted a more moderate approach than the WSA. Importantly, the women leading these groups had all been members of the Revolutionary Alliance. As the fortunes of Sun's Revolutionary Alliance weakened over the course of 1912, the support the women garnered from this source diminished considerably.

FIRST FORAYS: LIN ZONGSU AND THE
WOMEN'S SUFFRAGE COMRADES' SOCIETY

As Qing rule came closer to collapse, the first major organization established to advocate specifically for the right of women to participate in politics was Lin Zongsu's Women's Suffrage Comrades' Society. This society formed in Shanghai on 12 November 1911 and was a subbranch of the newly formed Chinese Socialist Party, of which Lin was a member.[11] The goals of Lin Zongsu (1878–1944) and her group were to enhance women's knowledge of politics, nurture women's political strength, and to win women the right to political participation.[12] The Women's Suffrage Comrades' Society was prominent in educating women about politics through study sessions, public speeches, and the publication of articles in magazines and newspapers. They aimed to ensure that women would be well informed when it came time for them to exercise their political rights and also to counteract the repeated accusation that women were too ignorant to participate responsibly in national political debates. Reflecting the primacy it placed on women's engagement in politics, the society was divided into two sections: full members, comprising women above the age of sixteen, and honorary members, including "supportive" men, such as the head of the Socialist Party, Jiang Kanghu. With this structure the Women's Suffrage Comrades' Society was able to maintain vital support from sympathetic men while keeping control of the movement firmly with its women members.

The founder of the Women's Suffrage Comrades' Society, Lin Zongsu, was typical of the women active in this first stage of republican suffrage activism.[13] Originally from Fujian, Lin Zongsu attended Shanghai's Patriotic Girls' School in 1902. She soon moved to Japan for further study in what was to become a pattern for revolutionary-spirited men and women during the first few years of the century. She enrolled at the Tokyo Women's Normal

College in 1903 and participated in the numerous anti-Qing activities organized by Chinese students in Japan. While there she established vital contacts with other revolutionary women, like Qiu Jin, and some would later form part of her suffrage networks. She was among the three women who wrote prefaces for one of China's earliest feminist manifestos, Jin Songcen's 1903 *A Tocsin for Women* discussed in the previous chapter. In this brief text Lin repeatedly stresses the importance of parity between citizens' rights and women's rights in the republic that she and Jin were encouraging women to build.[14] In 1904 she returned to Shanghai where she immersed herself in the publishing industry as both a journalist and editor. During the next year, despite her return to China, she maintained her links with the revolutionary groups based in Japan and joined the Revolutionary Alliance when it formed in August of 1905.

Lin holds the esteemed position as China's first woman journalist.[15] Her brother, Lin Baiyong, was prominent in the newspaper business, so she initially worked with him on the *China Vernacular News* (*Zhongguo baihua bao*). Lin Zongsu became associate editor for the revolutionary *Warning Bell Daily* (*Jing zhong ribao*) and in 1911 established the *Women's Times* (*Funü shibao*).[16] The *Women's Times* published numerous items of importance relating to the Women's Suffrage Comrades' Society that reflected Lin's political aspirations, but items on women's education also featured regularly. Its lengthy articles relating to women's suffrage in China represent the beginnings of the long campaign for consciousness-raising among women. As the national political scene became more conservative, Lin's political activities drew government displeasure—she was forced into hiding during 1913, moving around the Jiangsu region to avoid arrest and to escape persecution by Yuan Shikai's enforcers. When political pressure eased she settled in Nanjing where she engaged in teaching and embarked on numerous business ventures in conjunction with her brother's newspapers.[17]

An important feature of Lin's journal was its introduction of comparisons with the contemporaneous international suffrage movements. Many issues of the journal included translations of women's suffrage propaganda from overseas or reports on the international suffrage movement.[18] Locating the Chinese women's movement within the global women's movement became an increasingly important strategy for China's suffragists over the next two decades. This sort of international unity helped develop their struggle as a feminist movement, rather than a part of an anti-Qing campaign or an elitist political reform project. Their allies were women's suffrage activists the world over. In the new political space afforded them by the republic, with its democratic aspirations and desires for international recognition and respectability, the women's suffrage advocates publicized their new global allies with increasingly broader enthusiasm. Prior to the establishment of the republic, advertising such allegiances would have been less useful, and potentially even counterproductive, since the women's first steps into public political activism had been smoothed by anti-Qing rhetoric and widespread acceptance of women acting outside of the domestic realm in times of national crisis. Once the republic had been won, women like Lin moved to promote their campaign in a more direct fashion.

Her actions on behalf of the women's suffrage campaign set a trend for the style of lobbying to be employed by other activists in the first few months of the republic. Their position was one of "seeking rightfully earned entitlements to equality," and they expected that their male comrades-in-arms would respect these entitlements. This assumption and invocation of a unified purpose with like-minded brothers in politics would soon dissipate as the schism between men and women activists developed.

Lin made the journey from Shanghai to Nanjing as soon as there was a parliament to lobby. Representing the Women's Suffrage Comrades' Society, she met the provisional president Sun Yat-sen on 5 January 1912. The Shanghai-based *People's Independence News* (*Minli bao*)[19] reported that "Socialist Party member Lin Zongsu, representing the Women's Suffrage Comrades' Society, saw the president and requested that once the national legislature is established, women be given full rights to participate in politics."[20] Lin told Sun Yat-sen that her association represented all the women of China in their request for suffrage rights. The activists regarded themselves as a vanguard representing a political constituency composed of women and spoke publicly and repeatedly of themselves in these terms.[21]

For the women's suffrage activists, rapid action was deemed crucial—the first and most important task charged to the provisional parliament was the drafting of the constitution under which the republic would be governed. This document, they believed, would decide the status of China's women for years to come. The principle of equality between men and women would be enshrined or ignored depending on the parliamentarians' response. By approaching Sun Yat-sen, Lin hoped to add the prestige and authority of the republic's most respected leader to her cause. In their amicable meeting she presented the women's demands to Sun, and he reportedly declared affirmatively: "In the future, women will certainly have complete political rights. But, women must immediately seek knowledge of law and politics to understand the truth of freedom and equality."

Lin replied that her group was holding study sessions on law and politics in preparation for their political engagement. Sun then stated that although these actions were most praiseworthy, "it is unavoidable that opponents of women's suffrage will abound. I will certainly take up the responsibility of mediating in defense." Lin then asked, "if the women from my party submit a petition requesting women's suffrage how effective will this be?" To which Sun replied, "I recognize your esteemed party as the representatives of the women compatriots of the whole country and respect it." Lin then told him that she would spread news of their conversation in order that it serve as evidence in the future. Sun supposedly agreed with this tactic.[22] Lin promptly printed her version of their conversation in the national papers to publicize her cause and emphasize the high level of support women's suffrage enjoyed.[23]

She stressed that Sun Yat-sen regarded equality between men and women as crucial to the success of the republic. However, Sun was also convinced of the special ignorance of women in relation to politics and remained certain of the pressing need for the education of women in political studies.[24] Perhaps in reaction to the doubts cast on women's educational attainments, Lin Zongsu's contributions to *Women's Times* are written in highly scholarly style and are unpunctuated, dense texts. The sophistication of her prose possibly stood as evidence of her erudition and women's scholarly talents more generally. Unfortunately for the women's suffrage activists, the men whose duty it was to devise the constitution were to prove harder to persuade than Sun.

Lin's publication of the conversation with Sun drew him into criticism from more conservative members of his party. One such man, the conservative Revolutionary Alliance member Zhang Binglin, made the following formal written complaint to Sun:

> I do not know whether women's political participation would be a good social custom or not, and, not daring myself to presume to have such knowledge, I think that the judgment of the appropriateness of such a measure should await public discussion. Yet, I have heard that Your Excellency gave approval in a few words to a certain woman's verbal request, even though the constitution has not yet been precisely enunciated. When unconsidered talk gets out of hand, once such statements are endorsed, things will become even more unruly.[25]

Sun's reply revealed the embattled nature of his provisional presidency and of his prestige in the Revolutionary Alliance. He was not to be the legitimizing force Lin and her colleagues had hoped, as his letter attests:

> Of course the matter of women's participation should be decided by public discussion. The other day when a certain woman came to see me, I only had a personal chat with her. However, she immediately published the contents of our conversation in a newspaper and claimed that I had approved her request. This sort of incident is difficult to correct each and every time one occurs. As to your advice about being careful about what I say, I certainly accept it with respect.[26]

Lin's media campaign for women's suffrage continued through January. In a manifesto published in *Heavenly Bell News* (*Tianduo bao*), Lin declared: "As we enter a new century women will leave behind thousands of years of darkness." She explained that the happiness and prosperity of all women depended upon women's suffrage and highlighted the injustice in the electoral system that planned to exclude women even when they had the same education qualifications as men.[27] Lin's campaign was soon to be reinforced by the formation of a new umbrella women's suffrage organization.

EXPANDING INFLUENCE: TANG QUNYING AND THE UMBRELLA WOMEN'S SUFFRAGE ALLIANCE

Lin's enthusiasm for suffrage continued when she merged her association with several other women's military and political associations. Formed on 20 February the umbrella Women's Suffrage Alliance (WSA) was established in Nanjing as a reaction to the dismal deliberations of the provisional parliament on the national constitution. It had over two hundred members and unified a disparate range of women's groups.[28] The leaders of these associations were also simultaneously members of Sun Yat-sen's Revolutionary Alliance, and they agreed that the time had come to unite under a larger banner to lobby more forcefully for the suffrage cause on a gender-specific platform while invoking the now-respectable base of the Revolutionary Alliance. The regulations of the WSA state that its aim was to "realize equality between men and women and achieve participation in politics."[29] The organization established the Nanyang Women's Political and Legal University (*Nanyang nüzi fazheng daxue*) to serve as the basis for the achievement of their long-term goals.[30] The formation of this umbrella alliance of women's groups signals the broadening of the realization among women that their interests within the new republic were likely to be distinct from the men that they had supported so vehemently and forcefully in the overthrow of the Qing.

One of China's foremost women's suffrage activists, Tang Qunying, assumed leadership of this new Women's Suffrage Alliance. Her biography is typical of women in the militant wing of the suffrage movement.[31] Tang Qunying (1871–1937) had a long and distinguished career as a feminist radical participating in military and political actions. She was born in Hunan and, like Lin Zongsu, went to study in Japan, where she became the first woman to sign herself a member of the Revolutionary Alliance in 1905. She was active in publishing articles in the Alliance's organ, *The People's News* (*Minbao*), and in 1906 formed the aforementioned Society for Chinese Women Students in Japan. In the summer of 1911 she returned to China and helped form the military organization the Women's Northern Attack Brigade—later known as the Women's Reinforcement Association (*Nüzi houyuan hui*). Her military background ensured that the WSA had a militant and forceful approach in its 1912 activities, as will become evident below. But in the long term she focused her energies on building educational and publishing opportunities for women in order that they were able to assume positions of political authority when the time arrived. For example, she started newspapers in Beijing and her home province of Hunan, the *Women's Rights Daily* (*Nüquan ribao*) and *Women's Vernacular News* (*Nüzi baihuabao*). Tang also suffered during Yuan Shikai's crackdown on democratic forces. In March of 1913 she was briefly arrested and both her newspapers were forcibly closed. Nonetheless, Tang remained active in fighting for women's rights and continued to participate in politics throughout her life.[32]

Tang's umbrella WSA incorporated Lin Zongsu's original group as well as her own and three others: the Women Citizens' Association (*Nüguomin hui*); the Women's Society for the Respect of Military Affairs (*Nüzi shangwu hui*); and the Women's Alliance (*Nüzi tongmeng hui*). Tang's group, the Women's Reinforcement Association, was established in December of 1911 and saw its role as facilitating the speedy military suppression of the Qing government. This group organized financial, medical, and other auxiliary support for the revolutionary military forces.[33] The Cantonese Shen Peizhen led the Women's Society for the Respect of Military Affairs, and it advocated the overthrow of the Qing and called on women to shoulder their responsibilities for reviving China. Shen declared that women had been reduced to powdered and decorated playthings for men. They had to fight for their freedom alongside men so that they would have the skills to work with men in all aspects of life.[34] The Women Citizen's Association was formed by Wang Changguo (1880–1949) and was based in Changsha, Hunan Province.[35] As we shall see later in this chapter, Wang was not averse to violent action in the pursuit of women's suffrage. The Women's Alliance was yet another Shanghai-based group and was formed by Wu Mulan. Its manifesto advocated promoting women's rights and women's participation in political affairs, and to this end they established in January of 1912 the Women's Training Troop (*Nüzi jingwu lianxi dui*) so that they could prepare for military action and promote ethnic (Han) "nationalism" (*minzu zhuyi*) among women.[36] Wu, another activist with experience studying in Japan, had worked with explosives as a member of the Revolutionary Alliance.[37] She contrasted men and women, arguing that unlike "stinky men" women are noble and pure, flexible and agile, and are the most strong and steadfast in heart.[38]

The WSA held a major conference in Nanjing on 8 April 1912, and its manifesto was released to the press.[39] The key tenets included the attainment of equality with men and women's suffrage rights. Apart from the key principle of fighting for women's suffrage, the WSA declared its policy interests as follows: (1) the realization of equality between men and women, (2) the implementation of universal women's education, (3) the reform of the family customs, (4) the prohibition of the buying and selling of slaves and servant girls, (5) the implementation of monogamy in marriage, (6) prohibitions on divorce without reason (but on the understanding that later freedom in choice in marriages will be realized), (7) the encouragement of women's vocations, (8) to build philanthropic industries, (9) to strengthen the enforcement of unbinding feet, (10) to reform the customs relating to women's clothing, and (11) to enforce the prohibitions on prostitution.[40]

These tenets provide a succinct overview of the breadth of the women activists' political concerns. Apart from their core preoccupation with achieving equality in opportunity for women and recognition of women's inherent equality with men, the suffragists outlined their concern for women's physical and moral health in their discussion of sartorial regimes, foot binding, and prostitution. While demanding full participation for women in the public sphere, they were at pains to distance themselves from those "other" public women, prostitutes.[41] The suffragists would maintain lengthy campaigns against prostitution for decades to come, in part to declare their high moral worth within a cultural system that had long regarded women's appearance in public as a less than respectable act. Through their repeated self-differentiation from prostitutes, the suffragists reinscribed a long-held patriarchal code, wherein responsiblility for proof of sexual morality rested with women. At this stage in their struggle they felt no compunction about engaging in very public military battles, or acts of public nuisance such as window smashing, yet they repeatedly asserted their moral worth in echoes of old codes of female chastity.

LET'S LEARN ABOUT POLITICS FIRST: ZHANG MOJUN'S SHENZHOU WOMEN'S ASSISTANCE SOCIETY

Not all the women activists of this time were as enthused about violent action as Tang's group. The third group dedicated to winning equal rights for women in the new republic was the moderate Shenzhou Women's Assistance Society.[42] Zhang Mojun (aka Zhang Shaohan; 1883–1965), another active Revolutionary Alliance member, formed the society.[43] The Shenzhou Society's stated aims were to promote women's education, industry, and political knowledge, and they adopted a reformist, gradualist approach. Fundamental to their platform was equality between men and women in all legal, social, and political aspects of life in the new republic, but they accepted the view that achievement of these goals would be incremental. They requested that if women were unable to have full suffrage then, at the very least they should be granted observer status in the parliament so that women's political knowledge and skills would be developed. The society's major organ was the *Shenzhou Women's News* (*Shenzhou nübao*), which published an issue every ten days between November 1912 and February of 1913.[44] The journal explains its purpose as "to promote the cause of women's suffrage." Women's suffrage, they argued, was an inevitable development for the twentieth century and that women in China were undertaking the necessary preparations for suffrage by improving their knowledge of politics.[45]

Zhang Mojun's Shenzhou Society referred to Tang's group as "radicals" whose actions were "unlikely to yield results."[46] The difference in the composition of the leadership accounts for their different approaches on the best method for realizing women's suffrage. Where Tang's group comprised leaders of key women's military units, Zhang's society comprised wives of prominent government and party men such as He Miaoling, Wu Tingfang's wife.[47] The explicitly moderate and gradual approach of the Shenzhou Society accorded more with Sun Yat-sen's own position than with Tang's.[48]

The Shenzhou Society was typified by both its commitment to sex equality and its commitment to the men of the Revolutionary Alliance and, later, the Nationalist Party. To this end, the society was involved in many activities that were devised to strengthen the democratic institutions the men were establishing. Nonetheless, they were committed to the eventual realization of equality between men and women in China. On the first two days of March, just prior to a key parliamentary debate, Zhang had sought an audience with President Sun during which she had expressed their concerns that women's equality with men be a core principle of the new republic.[49]

In the letter to Sun Yat-sen, Zhang and her supporters wrote of the importance of equality between men and women for the strength of the nation. They stressed that women had been active in the revolution that led to the formation of the republic and through these actions had demonstrated women's patriotic feelings for the "fatherland." The letter then introduced to Sun the Shenzhou Society's goals stressing their interest in "spreading education, researching law and politics, promoting industry, and promoting the emergence of pure spirited female citizens." Zhang requested financial support for the establishment of the Women's School for Law and Politics. Its emphasis on the preparation of women for political activism "in the future" reflects relative to Tang Qunying's group.[50]

The reply from Sun was supportive—just as had been his reply to Lin Zongsu. However, it also came with a donation of 5,000 yuan for Zhang's Shenzhou Society. Sun's letter reaffirmed his support for egalitarianism but also warned against hasty appeals for sex equality in suffrage rights.

> The natural rights of human beings are identical for both men and women. Equality is for everyone. . . . With the establishment of the republic it is hoped that the whole country can progress forward together. There is much ability amongst women. Some joined the Revolutionary Alliance and busied themselves with national affairs, remaining undaunted by repeated setbacks. They are just as admirable as the revolutionary men from every province. . . . In the future women must most certainly have the supreme right to vote. Members of your organization are talented and knowledgeable. You are in no hurry to acquire suffrage rights but endeavor to unite women, popularize education, study law and politics, promote commerce and industry, and in these ways assist in the nation's progress.[51]

Zhang thus opened her school in the name of the society, the Shenzhou School for Girls (*Shenzhou nüxue*) with Sun's financial support and assumed the position of principal. Enhancing China's education system, and particularly educational opportunities for girls, was to become a major focus for Zhang throughout her life. She assumed many high-level posts in the Nationalist government related to education and is still recognized as one of China's foremost women educationists.[52]

That formal education was a prerequisite to suffrage rights was still unproblematic. Just as dynastic China had recognized the scholar literati's legitimate right to political power, so too did the early republic. For women this was a serious problem since formal schooling for girls and women was still in its infancy at this point. Consequently, moderate activist women like Zhang concentrated their efforts on providing the educational opportunity girls had long been denied. Women like Zhang regarded an expansion in girls' formal educational experience as an important step toward proving women's legitimate right to exercise power. However, their more radical sisters did not see that a staged approach was necessary. While supporting an expansion in women's education they sought equality in suffrage rights immediately so that those few women privileged with formal schooling would be able to enter parliament alongside their equally privileged brothers. Tang Qunying was of the latter opinion, as the actions she led in March of 1912 reveal.

TAKING THE PARLIAMENT BY STORM IN NANJING

The provisional parliament was to discuss the constitution during March 1912, and to Tang and her more radical supporters this was the appropriate time for action. The events of this time have placed Tang Qunying as preeminent among the suffrage activists. She became the effective leader of the entire movement—moderates and radicals alike—for her efforts to influence constitutional deliberations. At the end of February 1912, the Tang contingent and around twenty people submitted a petition to the parliament declaring:

> The political revolution has already taken place and the social revolution will follow in the future. To ensure that the social revolution is not a miserable failure we must first strive for social equality. To strive for social equality we must first seek equality between men and women. To strive for equality between men and women first we must have women's right to participate in

politics. . . . We request that the constitution clearly specify equality regardless of sex, and also declare explicitly equality between men and women in
the right to vote and stand for election. . . . Moreover, the statement describing the "people (*renmin*) of the nation" should specify that this include
both men and women.[53]

Their suggestions were ignored despite reports that they had threatened
to blow up the parliamentarians if it was not granted.[54] The humiliation of
this defeat became apparent on 11 March 1912 when the new constitution
was promulgated and publicized. As noted above, the provisional parliamentarians had taken the trouble to clarify the statement in Song Jiaoren's
constitution that "all people are equal" in article 5 with the phrase "regardless of race, class or religion." "Sex" had been deliberately and consciously
excluded. Disgusted by this result, the more radical women activists decided
that desperate measures were required if women were to be able to reap the
rewards of a republican government in China.

In a bid to maintain momentum among women activists, *Women's Times*
published a rousing article by Lin Zongsu. Lin alerted readers to the fact
that women suffragists throughout Europe and the USA had maintained
their struggle despite repeated setbacks over decades. She reminded her audience that the final decision had not yet been made; that although she
was disgusted with the current situation "the president had promised it, the
parliament had promised it, the people had promised it"; and that "sisters
around the country are encouraging her" to keep on with the struggle until
women's suffrage is realized.[55]

They responded to the proclamation with a further letter to Sun and the
parliament with the request that the words "regardless of sex" be included
in article 5.[56] This petition was scheduled for debate in the chambers on
19 March. Tang and about a dozen other women requested permission to
enter the parliament to speak on behalf of their proposal. They received a
flat denial in response. Not so easily deterred, Tang's delegation entered the
chambers via the public gallery and simply sat among the parliamentarians.[57] At the point when the women's proposal was introduced, conservative male assemblymen stymied discussion by scoffing and guffawing. In
these conditions, it was impossible for the issue to be debated sensibly and
so parliament adjourned for lunch. On their return to the afternoon session
Lin Sen, head of the parliament, informed them that any changes to the
constitution should be addressed to the first National Assembly upon its
election. The women would not be fobbed off and engaged Lin in a lengthy

and vigorous argument. A newspaper report described the women as "raging wantonly" and "using harsh language."[58] Eventually, with no further progress being made, the women reluctantly left the chambers.

The following day, 20 March, Tang and her supporters returned to the parliament and requested an interview with Lin Sen. Refused entry, their path was blocked by troops stationed for this purpose. In retaliation the women smashed the windowpanes of the chambers and staged a noisy demonstration outside the building that lasted for more than five hours. The women kicked to the ground a policeman attempting to stop their vandalism (see Figure 3.1 for a cartoon on this event).[59] *The Eastern Times* (*Shibao*) reported that the women had bleeding hands as a result of their window smashing.[60] One commentator, Meng Huan (a supporter of women's suffrage) from Tianjin, wrote that the violent actions by women in Nanjing were not surprising given that these women shed their blood in battles in the revolution to win equality. However, Meng went on to say that their violence was not indicative of their level of culture and that it was hoped they would use their scholarly talent (*cai*) to further their cause.[61] The violence in Nanjing was in direct imitation of recent British suffragists' activities—over

Figure 3.1. Women's suffrage activist with natural feet kicking a policeman during a protest in Nanjing, by Dun Gen. *Shenbao*, 30 March 1912.

two hundred women smashed windows around the commercial and political center of London simultaneously, resulting in thousands of pounds of damage.[62] China's suffragists had moved to a stage where their connections with other women around the globe also fighting against male privilege were useful and significant. Their pragmatic liaisons with the republican, anti-Qing cause were failing to deliver their desired results, so China's feminists sought inspiration and stamina by conceptualizing their campaign as part of a global women's movement.

The Nanjing campaign continued the next day with Tang and an even larger group, of over sixty women, marching on the parliament. *Shenbao* reported that the women were carrying weapons but that the two hundred–odd soldiers stationed around the parliamentary building prevented their entry to the chambers.[63] Again, their path was blocked by the military. In an effort to sway Lin Sen and his parliament, the women then requested an interview with the "father" of the republic, Sun Yat-sen. Sun granted this interview and in the course of the discussion agreed to act as mediator. He and two of the women, Jin Yan and Jin Wan then entered the parliament accompanied by a news reporter from a Beijing daily. Confronted with this delegation and under pressure from Sun, the parliament agreed to add women's suffrage to their agenda again but gave no indication of the date for the discussion.[64]

In order to maintain the momentum provided by Sun Yat-sen's support, Tang's Alliance wrote a lengthy letter addressed to Sun. This was published in *The People's Independence News* on 23 March, accompanied by a condemnatory report on the actions of the women over the previous several days.

> The inequality of men and women is an impediment to human progress. The common people have long denounced it. The present republic was established for the prosperity of the people . . . although the Provisional Constitution of the Republic of China is only a temporary document, it does have the same effect as a constitution and will form the basis for the future constitution. It outlines the rights and responsibilities of the government and of the citizens. . . . In Chapter 2 Article 5 it speaks of the people and states that the citizens of the Republic of China are equal and then specifies that this is so regardless of race, class or religious belief . . . these differences are clearly stated . . . we women demand the right to participate in politics . . . and the equal rights of men and women should be expressly specified in the Provisional Constitution. . . . This could be achieved with the insertion of the two characters "male or female" into the text between "class" and "religious belief."[65]

Relentless in their campaign the women decided to attempt to expand their support base by speaking to the internal affairs minister, Tang Shaoyi. This request of 25 and 26 March was refused. Some women sent telegrams to newspapers in an attempt to encourage Sun, Tang, and Yuan Shikai to discuss women's suffrage together.[66] Their patience was wearing thin, and on 30 March, Tang and her group stormed the parliament shouting their demands for equality. Apparently, blows were exchanged, and threats of violence against members of the parliament were made when security guards were called to forcibly remove the women. Media reports described the women as being "armed." The troops were called in, and Tang's activists were forced to retreat. As they retreated someone shouted, "If you don't allow it [suffrage for women] then be prepared to face military force."[67] From here the parliamentarians' attitudes toward the activists hardened, and the two parties became irreconcilably polarized.

CIVILIZED SPEECH AND BARBAROUS DEEDS:
FIREBRANDS LOBBY THE BEIJING GOVERNMENT

The Nanjing focus for this stage of suffrage activism drew to a close in April when, on the first of the month, Sun formally relinquished his duties as provisional president in favor of Yuan Shikai and on 5 April, when the parliament voted to make Beijing the capital. The women suffrage activists reorganized and moved to Beijing to continue their campaign. The Beijing media announced the arrival of the women's suffrage activists from Nanjing reporting that the Nanjing women aimed to inspire local women to join the cause.[68] The women continued to lobby Sun for his support with the *Shengjing Times* (*Shengjing shibao*), publishing a letter from the Women's Suffrage Alliance to him as "former" president reiterating their claim to have "regardless of sex" inserted into the relevant constitutional clauses.[69] As the center of power shifted to the north, the more conservative forces behind Yuan Shikai increased in influence. *L'Impartial* (*Dagong bao*) reported on 6 April that Yuan Shikai had sent a secret telegram to the Nanjing parliament saying that under no circumstances should they legislate to give women suffrage rights.[70] In this new circumstance the women's suffrage struggle, along with that of other democratic forces in China, grew increasingly perilous.

Although the Provisional Constitution did not explicitly specify that all citizens were equal regardless of sex, it had not specifically excluded women either. The legislators' intent was to suggest that women were not "citizens," but this sentiment had not been explicitly written into the document. This ambiguity in the text provided the women's suffrage activists with an opportunity for further action. The electoral laws by which the "citizens," whomever they may be, elect their legislators had yet to be determined. And so, once in Beijing, Tang Qunying led the suffragists in a campaign to ensure that women were included in the electoral laws as eligible voters.

In July they became aware that the draft legislation did clearly state that "men" had the right to vote and stand for election. Newspapers published calls for women to send telegrams of protest to Beijing.[71] On 10 August the women's fears were confirmed when the electoral laws were announced excluding women from participation as voters and candidates. Mongolia and Qinghai were guaranteed minimum quotas under the laws, but the women's claims for representation were ignored.[72] Tang and her group then entered the chambers and requested that a "law on women's suffrage" be immediately promulgated. The reply they received was, "The Assembly has already debated this matter and there would be no purpose in repeating the process." *Shenbao* reported that Yuan Shikai refused the women's demands and instead requested that the Education Department examine the level of women's education.[73] This latter move served to indicate that he was not opposed to women's suffrage per se but rather felt that women's educational levels were insufficient at that point in time. This prompted Tang's Alliance to submit a petition to the legislature. The petition proceeded: "The host of public and private rights are based on the principle of the natural rights of human beings. Regardless of whether one is male or female, these rights are inherent to every single person and cannot be granted or removed by other people." It continued with the accusation that the passage of these electoral laws demonstrated that the current legislature did not consider "women to be people."[74]

The persistent campaign by the women to have the law on women's suffrage reconsidered eventually forced the parliament to discuss the issue during a November sitting. However, the parliamentarians only reiterated their opposition, stating: "Only the national president has the authority to overturn [rulings], and if we overturn the ruling then we are handing the president's authority to the female world." Another parliamentarian pointed out that "the petition repeatedly insulted members of the Assembly, and on these grounds it should most certainly not be considered."[75] The petition was granted only cursory attention and was finally rejected.[76]

Women commentators raged against the injustice. Some invoked natural rights philosophy and slave imagery from the anti-Qing struggle. Jiang Jilan wrote that "natural rights don't discriminate over whether one was born a man or a woman" and the current parliamentary decisions rendered women to the status of "Africa's black slaves."[77] In the conclusion to her article she declared that "equal political rights for men and women was proof of sex equality. How could men be citizens and women be citizens and yet they do not have the same political rights?"[78] Others attempted to counter arguments that women were incapable of ruling by arguing that women's comparatively poor educational attainment was a result of traditions that had favored men and had nothing to do with innate ability or intelligence. This same commentator argued that China was a laughing stock among the strong nations of the world for her backward traditions on the roles and status of the sexes.[79]

The electoral laws were publicized in the first week of December and made no provisions for women to participate as voters or candidates.[80] In disgust, on 9 December 1912, Tang Qunying, Shen Peizhen, and several supporters marched on the parliament and vehemently put their case to the Chair, Wu Jinglian.[81] Tang declared: "During the armed uprisings, women assumed responsibilities as secret agents, organized bomb squads and undertook a whole host of dangerous tasks—risking both their lives and their properties—just like men. How is it that now that the revolution has been achieved women's interests are not taken into account!"[82] They went on to argue, "If President Yuan does not recognize women's right to participate in politics, we will not recognize him as president. . . . If in the future, civil laws of the Republic of China [fail to grant equality] women and others will have no choice but to use military force to resolve this problem."[83]

During the last two months of 1912 Tang and her supporters continued to rage indignantly about the injustice they saw transpiring. Shen Peizhen was reported as raiding the East Asia News Office cursing and shouting about the injustice of the electoral system. A report in *Shenbao* described her as being "civilized in her speech but barbarous in her deeds."[84] Shen Peizhen's reputation as a firebrand was further enhanced by reports that she recommended to the women's suffrage activists that unless women were granted suffrage rights, then unmarried women should refuse to marry for ten years and married women should refuse to speak to men for the same period.[85] In her journal, *Women's Vernacular News*, Tang published a moving article commemorating the anniversary of the founding of the

Women's Suffrage Alliance. The anonymous author, reporting on a meeting where Tang Qunying gave a speech, declared (rather optimistically as it has emerged), "In the future, when women's suffrage has succeeded, [the date of the founding of the association] will be commemorated forever by women."[86] In a dramatic statement emphasizing the extent to which women are subject to decisions made in parliament it continued, "Aren't the bullets that split women asunder those discussed by men [in parliament]? . . . Women have careers and assets and make direct contributions to the republic's taxation, therefore women also should have the republic's public rights."[87]

The next issue of the same journal published a challenge to the parliamentarians:

> They opposed women's suffrage, boldly declaring that we were not hardy. Now I would like to ask that group of parliamentarians, if there are among their members those who would qualify on this criterion. A year after the founding of the republic, what is the value to our people's future of their discussions or their political views? Each month they squander two hundred silver dollars and create chaos from their debauched lives. They have completely forgotten about the matters of significance to the nation. Is not each and every one of these parliamentarians detestable?[88]

The diatribe continued with Kai Yun declaring that the parliamentarians all have mothers, wives, and sisters and yet they are prepared to act like criminals toward these very same women. Their behavior warranted a violent reaction from the suffragists, and as Kai Yun reminded readers, in the first months of the republic women activists had armed themselves with guns and explosives to counter opposition just as the British activists had used violence in their struggle. Kai Yun then went on to describe the parliamentarians as mice who were terrified of death. "They treat us as if we were the enemy and send the police to raid us."[89] The increasing venom in their tone indicates the women's increasing identification of their opposition—male parliamentarians.

These efforts proved to be the last concerted push by the suffrage activists of these years to influence the formulation of national documents relating to equality in political rights. At the beginning of 1913 Tang Qunying and fellow Hunanese, Zhang Hanying, returned to Hunan to build support for women's rights in their home province. Tang started her newspaper, *Women's Rights Daily*, and opened girls' schools for the arts and industry as well as forming the Hunan branch of the Women's Suffrage Alliance, on 2 February. It is reported to have had eight hundred members at its formation.[90] Tang's threats at violent action were far from idle. Back in Hunan her supporters caused a stir when they ransacked the offices of the *Changsha Daily News* (*Changsha ribao*) after it published slanderous material about Tang Qunying. The paper had published reports that a certain Zheng Shidao had been romantically attached to Tang. Tang declared the man to be mad and accused him of deliberately slandering her good name simply because she had rebuffed his unwanted attentions. In retaliation at this slander, Tang and her supporters forcibly entered the offices of the newspaper and wrecked crucial printing equipment. This rendered the newspaper useless—as well as incurring the costs of the damage, they also lost sales during the days they were unable to print.[91]

The incident again points to the considerable extent to which the women suffrage activists were concerned to defend their moral status in matters of sexuality but were completely unconcerned about their reputations in regards to violence and the destruction of property. Women's morality at this time almost entirely revolved around questions of female chastity. Women's virtue was sexualized, and since virtue had long been a prerequisite for political participation, women suffragists would publicly defend themselves against claims of immorality in order to further their goals for equal access to political rights.[92]

BRIEF DABBLES WITH POWER: WOMEN POLITICIANS IN THE GUANGDONG PARLIAMENT

There were difficulties for women's suffrage activists at the provincial level as well. During 1912, as women suffrage activists watched the likelihood of winning equal political rights with men at a national level diminish, the women in Guangdong Province saw the removal of their existing equal rights. With the collapse of the Qing dynasty, Guangdong had established a military government under the control of Revolutionary Alliance member Hu Hanmin in November of 1911. Hu has a strong reputation as a supporter of women's rights and this was evident in the political system he established for his province.[93] The province established guidelines for the provincial assembly that made no restrictions on the sex of candidates or their property and education qualifications. The seats in the assembly were to be divided among different interest groups to ensure that representation was broad. The widow Zhuang Hanqiao, former bomb commander for the Revolutionary Alliance and currently a teacher in the Hong Kong Girls' Practical College, led the women activists. She argued that women should be guaranteed half of the seats since women were half the population of the nation. This was overwhelmingly rejected.[94]

Nonetheless, the Revolutionary Alliance was allocated twenty seats (out of a total of one hundred and twenty); and with Hu's support of principles of equality between men and women, women Alliance members were allocated a quota of ten of these twenty places. The various women groups that had emerged in the previous years around the expanding girls' schools elected the women to fill the women's seats. These ten Revolutionary Alliance women were the first women political representatives in China's republic and were the very women that Carrie Chapman Catt had sought out in her visit to China.[95] Among the successful women were Zhuang Hanqiao, Li Peilan (an overseas Chinese), Zhang Yuan (a principal of a girls' normal school), Liao Bingyun (from Guishan), and Deng Huifang (aka Deng Aiming, 1891–1976).[96] Like Zhuang, Deng Huifang was in the Explosives Section of the Alliance, and she had joined the rebels in 1908. Her commitment to women's suffrage was to continue throughout the republican period. As we will see in the following chapter Deng was to storm the Guangdong parliament in 1921.[97]

At the start of 1912, the equal rights of women with men were confirmed in the Guangdong Provincial Constitution, wherein article 2, section 3 stipulated that all people were equal and in article 8, section 47 that "the people refers to both men and women." These successes were to be stripped away when on 4 September 1912 the provincial assembly election laws were standardized by the national parliament and explicitly excluded women from participation.[98] Only men over the age of twenty-one that met certain property, education, or tax criteria could vote, and only men over the age of twenty-five could stand for election.[99] The conservative interests at the center of political power constrained the progressive elements influencing Guangdong Province. Li Peilan's objection to this imposition was publicized when her petition to Yuan Shikai was discussed across the national press. She pointed out that the Guangdong provincial parliament had set a successful precedent on women's suffrage and that this should not only be maintained at the provincial level but it should also be extended to the national level.[100]

The women delegates began a campaign to prevent these national laws being implemented in Guangdong, and a proposal to this effect was put to the assembly only to be rejected by a margin of sixty-five votes to thirty-eight.[101] Once Hu Hanmin was no longer the dominant voice in the parliament, women's rights were subject to the majority male opinion that was far more conservative. Thus, by the close of 1912 women in Guangdong Province had lost their right to vote and stand for election.

Nonetheless, their success in winning access to power for even this limited period provided moral support for many suffrage movements around the world. Suffragists in both the USA and Britain invoked the Guangdong example in their attempts to shame their own governments into action. For example, in 1913 Mrs. Pankhurst defended herself at her trial on the window-breaking incidents in London: "Even in China—and I think it somewhat of a disgrace to Englishmen—even in China women have won the vote, as an outcome of a successful revolution."[102] Similarly, in 1917 Mrs. Richard Wainwright spoke to the U.S. Congress about the importance of her nation's international standing: "We resent the fact that our great nation stands behind so many countries of the world, even China, in giving the share of its government to its women."[103] The "even in China" argument smacked of racist and imperialist sentiment but it demonstrated the extent to which women's suffrage had been successfully presented as a marker of civilization and advancement internationally. In fact, even Guangdong had stripped its women of their briefly held right to vote by 1913 and 1917.

As the connections between the Chinese suffragists and their sister suffragists around the world increased—problematic as these links were—their ties with the men in the Revolutionary Alliance ruptured. Compounding their struggles at the national and provincial level, the women's suffrage activists also had to face direct betrayal by their male party comrades.

SLAPPING, RAGING, CURSING:
THE FORMATION OF THE NATIONALIST PARTY

As was evident in the discussion above, almost all of the prominent women's rights activists were active members of the Revolutionary Alliance, and women members presumed equality with their male comrades from its inception. This situation was to change once the Revolutionary Alliance made the transition from rebel party to ruling party. In the political reorganization that occurred in the first year of the republic, the Revolutionary Alliance struck deals with several other major political parties and formed the Nationalist Party. In the process of achieving this merger the Revolutionary Alliance's practice of sex equality was removed to satisfy the demands of the conservative parties. Thus in March 1912 the Revolutionary Alliance had a political program that included equal rights for men and women, but by August of the same year the new Nationalist Party reaffirmed patriarchal rule and denied women equality with men.

The Alliance itself had been riven with factional disputes, and as it moved to reinvent itself for the new "democratic" era, the women's suffrage movement was exacerbating these internal divisions. Many men in the Alliance were more than happy to rid themselves of these troublesome women. The women in the party knew they faced increasing opposition. At a July meeting of the Revolutionary Alliance, Tang Qunying questioned Song Jiaoren, Alliance leader and fellow Hunanese, about the likely consequences of the proposed merger on the principle of equality between men and women. When the women learned that it was indeed a point of negotiation they were furious. Wang Changguo cursed and wept: "The Revolutionary Alliance was built on the blood, sweat, and tears of untold women members. I am driven insane with despair [over this decision]." Song Jiaoren was left speechless by the vehemence of their reaction.[104] Less than a year earlier, as we saw in the preceding chapter, women Alliance member Zhang Zhujun had risked her position in the Red Cross by rescuing Song from Qing troops. Knowledge of such sacrifices made Song's betrayal intensely personal for the women in the Revolutionary Alliance.

That evening the women called an emergency meeting of the female members of the Alliance where it was resolved to telegram their sisters in the various provincial branches of the party. They wrote, "The Revolutionary Alliance is amending its constitution for its own profit, thereby betraying our revolutionary martyrs. Today, they have again removed equal rights for men and women summarily dismissing the financial contributions made by women, thus trapping women in a despotic system forever. These [actions] are extremely, and utterly hateful."[105]

The Beijing branch of the Alliance held a meeting on 13 August, deliberately excluding the women members, and here the plans for the merger were ratified. The women twice stormed the meeting to demand that equality between the sexes be upheld. On their second entrance Wang Changguo physically assaulted Song Jiaoren, shouting and cursing that sex equality should remain in the party platform. To calm the tense situation the chair of the meeting, Zhang Ji, recommended that they wait for Sun's arrival in Beijing.[106] Sun was due to address the new party later that month.

Wang Changguo (1880–1949) was a radical feminist from Hunan, whose activism would see her elected to the Hunan provincial legislature in 1921. She was one of the first women students to go to study in Tokyo on a government scholarship. While there she joined the Revolutionary Alliance in 1905 and other radical groups, such as those led by fellow Hunanese, Tang Qunying.[107] Wang's daring physical assault on such a prominent party leader demonstrated her frustration at the betrayal of the principle of sex equality by her own party simply for political expediency.

Despite the women's objections, on 25 August in Beijing the merger was concluded and the Nationalist Party was formed. During this conference only around fifty women were among the total of three to four thousand participants. When the issue of equality between men and women was raised and put to the vote, the tremendous size of the opposition became clear. Only forty-odd people supported the women (whether this number includes the women themselves is unclear), and thousands stood in opposition.[108] The debate on this issue was, to say the least, heated. Tang Qunying was reported to have walked over and slapped Song Jiaoren and Lin Sen on their faces in disgust at their betrayal of the women who had long been their comrades in arms.[109] News of the party's elimination of the equality provisions spread around the country by telegram and was subsequently reported in the media.[110]

Arriving in Beijing, Sun Yat-sen addressed the new membership and concluded his speech to the new party members with a comment on the issue of equality between men and women:

> The principle of sex equality was originally part of the Revolutionary Alliance manifesto. Currently, in the hope of constructing a strong political party, based on the political views of these five large parties, this plan has been postponed. . . . Based on the decision of the majority we have no choice but to postpone it. However, if we can thoroughly consolidate the republic then we will certainly see the day when sex equality is realized. Otherwise, even the men will be slaves, and then what would be the condition of women?[111]

Immediately following Sun's speech, Zhang Ji began his report as chairman. At this point Tang, Wang, and Shen moved onto the stage and interrupted him. Shen Peizhen, continuing the suffragists' use of physical demonstrations of anger, "struck out at the men on the platform with her fan," and another woman "gave an impromptu speech about how the new party constitution betrayed women."[112] Zhang was unable to regain control of the meeting and so he called an adjournment until the afternoon. David Strand notes that fisticuffs competed with oratory at many political meetings in these years of early republicanism. The women were clearly not going to miss the chance to use this new political tool.[113]

The meeting did not proceed well for the women despite the ferocity of their actions and vehement arguments. When the meeting considered the issue of equality between men and women it was decided that the country was in such dire straits that the party could not risk giving women "freedom."[114] The most important thing was to ensure the security of the country. In contrast to the sentiment common among reformist intellectuals in the pre-1911 period (that women's emancipation was a vital prerequisite for national strengthening), the Nationalist Party resolved in 1912 that national interest demanded a delay on women's emancipation.

Tang and Shen visited Sun after the meeting to press the case for equal rights. *Shenbao* described Shen Peizhen as "crying loud enough to shake the room." During the revolution women had undertaken dangerous work on behalf of the nation in order that they win freedom. It came as a major blow that their own political party denied them equality.[115] The women left the interview resolved to press the case for equal rights at the parliament—a course of action that as we saw above was doomed to failure. The sentiment reflected in the Nationalist Party was clearly in accord with that of the national legislators.

In private correspondence with the women activists, replying to a letter from the Nanjing branch of Tang's Alliance, Sun wrote on September 2:

> I am fully in support of sex equality and have vigorously publicized the cause and moreover have taken the lead in putting this into practice. . . . The decision to delete the clause providing for equal rights for women from the party program was made by a majority of the men and cannot be overturned by the minority. It would do you no good to continue to trouble one or two leaders. In my opinion, at the present time women should promote education and women's organizations to spread knowledge among women more widely. Later, when your strength has increased you can struggle for rights with men, and then you will be assured of victory. . . . Don't rely on men to exert themselves on your behalf, since it is not at all to men's benefit.[116]

Sun perceived the struggle for women's rights to be threatening the overall stability of the republican cause. To him, and many other men in the party, women's rights and sex equality were optional extras to democratic constitutional government. To the women in the party, women's rights and sex equality were integral and indivisible parts of the democratic government they had struggled to establish. They now had learned the bitter lesson that for women's rights to be advanced they had to be extricated from men's vested political interests.[117]

UNNATURAL DEMANDS, UNNATURAL WOMEN:
PUBLIC DEBATE ON WOMEN'S SUFFRAGE

During the two years of this vigorous parliamentary campaign, heated debate on the issue of women's suffrage raged in newspapers. Supportive articles on women's suffrage were printed in the journals linked with the various women's associations, but articles in the mainstream media provide evidence of the deep distrust with which many educated Chinese regarded women's suffrage. One long-running debate took place in *The People's Independence News* from late February to early March 1912. The debate was prompted by a 28 February letter titled "My Doubts about Women's Suffrage" submitted by someone writing under the Buddhist pen name Kong Hai (Empty Sea). The anti–women's suffrage arguments used in China had striking parallels with those invoked in Europe, the USA, and Australasia in regards to their appeals to "the natural order" and "essential sex differences," but there were also particularly Chinese expressions of these anxieties in regards to the connections between family stability and national stability. The arguments presented by the opponents to women's suffrage at this period center almost entirely around women's difference (inferiority) to men. The late Qing and early Republican activists' repeated assertions of women's inherent equality with men were thus strategically targeting the opponents' reliance on these "sex difference" arguments.

   Kong Hai raised three main objections to the case for equality between men and women in political rights: "First, we must examine the abilities of men and women. Second, we must research the special natures of men and women. Third, we must consider its effects on social order." Of the first point s/he stated that those who have the right to participate in politics must have knowledge about politics and the ability to participate in politics. Since not even all the men of China had these abilities, how could women have these skills? Women have been preoccupied solely with household (inner) matters and thereby have no understanding of affairs external to the household. On the second point, regarding the special natures of men and women, Kong Hai argued that the special characteristics of men were to concentrate on financial matters beyond the confines of the house and to ensure that these external affairs are well managed. A woman's special nature is to manage the household and to bear and raise sons—all her activities should be centered on the inner domestic realm. "These distinctions evolved through nature and one cannot force the [sexes] into similarity." S/he continued by saying, if women undertake tasks that are against their nature then there is no possibility of a successful outcome, just as it would be impossible for men to bear sons. Indeed, it would be as futile as trying to "teach a hen to crow at dawn." This famous maxim continues with the phrase "there will be disorder in the household by nightfall." Women's inherent difference from men was deemed to produce a balance of skills in society, a rational division of labor, and natural harmony. On the third point, regarding the consequences of women's suffrage on social stability, Kong Hai reproduced a classic Confucian maxim—s/he stressed that the family was the foundation of society and that harmony in society grew from harmony in the family. If women engage in politics, they will argue with men and vie for power with men. This would cause chaos in society because it would cause chaos in the family. Women would be assuming roles that were not in their nature, the family would no longer be a foundation for society, and consequently society would descend into chaos.

The preoccupation with women's and men's spheres, with the former dwelling in the inner domestic realm and the latter in the outer public realm, had been realized in elite families around the nation for centuries. Women lived segregated lives and ideally were rarely seen in public. This practice was the cornerstone of women's virtue, conceived as it was in terms of chastity. The suffragists advocated the dismantling of this structure by simply deploying the logic of women's equality to men as opposed to women's difference from men. The media debates sparked by Kong Hai reveal the depth of anxiety felt about the blurring of the divisions between inner and outer work, women's and men's work. Kong Hai reasserted the case for sex difference in the face of the suffragists' logic of sex equality. According to Kong Hai, women had neither the education nor the natural talents for participation in politics and if China were to allow women's suffrage then Chinese culture and society would be certain to decline as a result.[118]

This single article generated a flurry of responses. On 5 March, Shenzhou Society member Yang Jiwei replied to Kong Hai. The paper published Kong

Hai's response immediately below Yang Jiwei's. The debate on women's suffrage had well and truly begun. Yang declared, "We women have long borne
unequal treatment as human beings. Today unexpectedly we share freedom." She argued that women's contribution to the winning of this freedom
was considerable and that to ensure the future peace and stability of the
nation it was vital that women have the right to participate in politics. Yang
pointed out that if knowledge of politics were to be a prerequisite for suffrage, as Kong Hai had asserted, then many men would be eliminated from
participation as well. Without sex equality women alone were being explicitly excluded from demonstrating their competencies in political affairs. On
the matter of the special characteristics of the two sexes, Yang argued that
there is very little that cannot be taught and learned by human beings and,
indeed, turned into talent. With regards to the third point about the social
chaos that would ensue, Yang stressed that women were already performing
a far greater range of roles than Kong Hai had acknowledged. The manner
in which they organize their families is their own concern and need not be
legislated. She concluded by pointing out that the improvement in the status of women would raise the standard of the nation as a whole.[119]

Kong Hai countered with the comment that if women's nature had included the skill in politics then how is it that for thousands of years they
have not demonstrated this skill. S/he argued that it was not just the Confucian East that "revered men and denigrated women" and spoke of women
being inner and men being outer. Kong Hai claimed that the West never
had an egalitarian ideology either and dismissed the examples of Queen
Victoria and Empress Wu Zetian as extremely special circumstances.[120]

Four days later a reaction came from Madame Zhang Renlan who had recently returned from studying in America. Zhang wrote that even the USA,
the country that is most devoted to freedom and equality of all the nations
in the world, does not have sex equality in voting rights. So why should
China? The "even in China" argument used in the USA had its counterar-
gument in China—"not even in the USA." She declared that women's rights
activists were misinterpreting the system of separate spheres for men and
women, where women govern the household while men govern the outside,
as being unequal when in fact it was merely a natural difference. "Men have
men's natural abilities and women have women's natural abilities." The existence of separate spheres does not mean there is no equality, she argued,
rather that there is mutual cooperation in roles. Zhang described the wom-
en's suffrage activists and their supporters as being so uncivilized that they

are "neither Western nor Eastern, neither male nor female, and neither monk nor nun."[121] Moreover, she argued if the "no husband-ism" views of the women's rights activists were propagated then within a few years there would be a sadly diminished Chinese race. The view that women's suffrage activists were lacking proper male guidance and control was clearly a major opposition charge. The forerunner of the women's suffrage campaigns, Lin Zongsu, describes how opponents to her views sometimes described her as being a "woman without a husband in the boudoir."[122]

By 14 March the editors of *The People's Independence News* declared that reaction to the letters on suffrage had been so voluminous that they had devoted space in the next several issues of the paper to debate "The Question of Women's Right to Participate in Politics."[123] Madame Zhu Lun's letter published on 16 March explained how it was no longer accurate to say that China's women were uneducated and ignorant. Zhu pointed out that in the previous decade women had made dramatic improvements in education and many had studied overseas. She countered Kong Hai's argument that men and women have distinct characteristics by saying that the differences were largely learned and taught in society and were not "natural." Unless women have the right to vote and stand for election they will remain the "playthings" of men and nothing more. Women's suffrage, Zhu concluded, is one of the most pressing issues for the progress of the nation since it reflects the application of principles of equality.[124]

Two days later, Madame Zhang Xiaofen's letter argued that women's suffrage activists were opposed to marriage and the family. Her evidence was that the suffrage movements in the USA and Europe were also promoting the use of contraception and "no husband-ism." Separate spheres for men and women, she argued, does not imply inequality—merely difference. Of a far more pressing concern is the winning of equality in education opportunities.[125] In reply to the accusations that women's suffrage advocates were opposed to marriage and children, the prominent Hunanese activist and member of Tang Qunying's WSA, Zhang Hanying (1872–1916), wrote that the calls for women's suffrage derived from patriotism. She claimed that "no husband-ism" and women's suffrage are two separate issues. Nonetheless, women's rights activists were most certainly devoted to eradicating the system of marriage that reduced women to mere horses and cattle for trade.[126]

The arguments presented by Kong Hai were widely held. In an anonymous article published in two parts in *L'Impartial* in March of 1912, the same themes appeared. The author argued that men and women had separate spheres of labor and this should not be interpreted as meaning women are not equal to men. Rather, there is equality based on differences that draw from the special characteristics granted men and women by heaven. Women's special strength lies in their domestic and child-rearing skills, and for women to enter in an area of weakness—politics—would result in poor politics. Women had neither the education, the experience, nor the natural ability to engage in political work. Moreover, if they enter political life they will be unable to perform their vital functions in the family. People cannot live alone, and if the family is in chaos then the country will be in chaos. Men cannot possibly manage the household, because it runs counter to their natural abilities. In sum, the author argued that women should not feel that they are not valued as equal citizens to men simply because they cannot vote or stand for election—men and women simply have separate spheres of labor.[127] An article reporting the women smashing the windows of parliament pointed out that since the "civilized nations" of America and Europe had not granted women suffrage, there was no need for China to grant this right.[128]

The response to this article from a supporter of women's suffrage, Meng Huan, argued that the absence of equality between men and women in China was the most unjust aspect of Chinese society. In particular, because women's learning, women's knowledge, and women's thinking have all progressed rapidly over recent years there is no longer any need to allow China to be retarded by clinging to an old superstition.[129]

The Kong Hai debate ended in early April, but for the remainder of the year leading Chinese dailies continued to publish articles on the women's suffrage movement and public debate on sex equality.[130] One commentator wrote in a witty poetic series, "It's a pity that pure and refined women want to enter the dirty, polluted world of politics. It's frightening that the women's suffrage activists attacked the parliament and then were dispersed with troops."[131] Many others indicate that the women's public political activism was regarded in some quarters as being an amusing aspect to political life. For example, *Shenbao*'s regular columns "Amusing Articles" and "Straight Heart, Fast Mouth" regularly featured sarcastic or humorous commentary on the women's suffrage movement and its leaders. In November of 1912 one commentator writing under the self-satirizing pen name Dull Root (Dun Gen) challenged prominent suffrage activist Shen Peizhen to change her name so that it was more in keeping with the spirit of her political goals. *Pei* means "to pay respect to" and *Zhen* means "chastity." Dull Root regarded her current behavior as being out of step with this ancient sentiment and humorously recommended a name change.[132] Earlier this same author had written an ironic article describing how in the suffragists' world "men would be imprisoned in the inner chambers, wearing women's clothing, using women's speech and acting like women."[133] In October s/he published a series of "ideal telegrams" that included a congratulatory message from the governments of Europe and America for the election of a woman to the Chinese presidency and celebrating China as a forerunner of women's rights.[134]

In the same month Dull Root wrote a satire of the new government's continued attempts to force men to cut their queues—seen as symbol of backwardness and even pro-Qing sentiments—by preventing men with queues from voting.[135] The article was presented in the form of actual legislation, adding to its comic effect. Any men with braids (queues) or braid-like beards would be barred from voting or standing for election. Any men with daughters sporting braids, or wearing braid-like apparel on their clothing would lose their suffrage powers as well. The only people eligible to vote were monks, since they had shaved heads.[136]

Yet another contributor to *Shenbao* had created an imaginary exchange between the women's suffrage activists and local prostitutes. Making light of their democratic ideals, the author has the "suffrage activist" explain that she would address them as "sisters" because that was egalitarian.[137] The joke relied on the disconcerting ranking of elite women's suffrage activists and prostitutes as social equals. It established a parallel between suffragists and prostitutes as women who dared to act publicly and mingle with men—directly casting doubt on the suffragists' virtue. Madeline Yue Dong discusses a satirical piece in *The Patriotic Vernacular News* (*Aiguo baihua bao*) that took a similar approach. A "Constitution for Equality between Men and Women" is outlined for readers' amusement. It includes the provision that male prostitutes and concubines should be available for women's pleasure.[138]

Women suffragists faced constant attacks on their moral standing and had repeated aspersions cast on their virtue. A satirical work of "unofficial history" described by Madeleine Yue Dong created a composite caricature of the three radical suffragists, Shen Peizhen, Tang Qunying, and Wang Changguo, called Shen Beizhen. Shen Beizhen is depicted as being barbaric (relieving herself noisily on a chamber pot while smoking and discussing women's equality with men with two male senators) and unfeminine (having a loud voice, big feet, short hair, and an excessive degree of self-assurance).[139] Such satirical pieces were clearly designed to ridicule these public women for their "outrageous" demands. Exaggerating the consequences of sex equality by caricaturing suffragists' bizarre physical attributes and immoral behaviors sought to produce in readers a sense of comfort with the status quo—a world where men and women were presented as differentiated and the moral order of the respective codes of virtue remained upheld.

Those opposed to women's suffrage were fearful that such dramatic political shifts would change the existing family structure and this in turn would lead to the destruction of national stability. At a personal level they correctly perceived that women's suffrage would undermine the supreme power of men over their wives and daughters. Almost all the suffrage groups included in their manifesto the call for the abolition of the marriage system that allowed men to take concubines and a raft of other provisions that would reduce the totality of men's legal power. Men had reason to fear that their considerable personal powers in the family order would be eroded if the activists were able to participate in national policy making.[140] As we saw above, this anxiety would sometimes manifest itself in ribald imaginings about women suffragists imitating men's sexual habits. Aiming to discredit the suffragists for their lack of feminine virtue, these comments also reveal men's anxiety about being subordinate to women's independent economic power—which, if they so chose, could be used to buy sexual favors, thus reducing men to the status of chattels.

Yet the challenges to male privilege posed by the women's suffrage activists reached even deeper than household power relations or economic power in the sex market. Women's suffrage challenged the fundamental, centuries-old premise of political virtue in China—that it was a male preserve. Whether it is household politics, village politics, provincial politics, or national politics, masculine virtue revolved around the exercise of political power just as feminine virtue revolved around sexual morality.[141] The women's suffrage campaign threatened the borders of both gendered notions of virtue. Masculine attributes of virtue, as Chinese to that point conceived of it, were threatened by women's demands to perform politics. With equal education opportunities for women and men, formal learning would no longer serve as the signal of the legitimacy of male political rule. While public debates focused frequently on the loss of feminine virtue that was feared to emerge from women's suffrage, an undeclared anxiety was the disruption this equal political order would produce in the matrix of masculine virtue. How could men perform virtue if their sequestered right to formal education and thus, political power, was open to women?

DEMOCRACY CRUSHED

Despite all the media debate, comic or vitriolic, political events were to overtake the women's suffrage cause and eventually silence it for half a decade. Yuan Shikai's dismantling of democratic structures across the nation over the course of 1913, 1914, and 1915 led to the crushing of the women's suffrage movement. Outspoken Nationalist Party member Song Jiaoren was to receive a far worse reaction to his political views than the slaps delivered to him by Tang Qunying and Wang Changguo. On 20 March 1913, Yuan Shikai's henchmen assassinated Song at the Shanghai train station. Song's death signaled grave times ahead for the forces of China's nascent democracy—patriarchal or otherwise. Yuan Shikai meant business, and that business was to install himself as emperor.

An attempt to resurrect the democratic ideals of the 1911 revolution against Yuan Shikai was defeated. The parliament tried to curb some of Yuan's excesses by hastily writing a new constitution in October of 1913, known as the Temple of Heaven Draft. It ignored women's claims to political rights and granted a limited elitist suffrage based on property and education.[142] This draft did, however, plan to increase the cabinet's powers as a balance to those of the president. Yuan Shikai was not deterred by these efforts and continued to extend his monarchist campaign into 1914, when on 4 January the National Assembly was suspended, the provincial assemblies and local councils were abolished, and the Nationalist Party was no longer recognized as a public body. The constitution of 1912 was annulled.

By the middle of May the following year, Yuan promulgated his own constitution that extended the presidential term to ten years, renewable without limit. This "Constitutional Compact" not only ensured him lifelong tenure, but it also gave him the right to appoint a successor. Yuan made a mockery of the democracy he was rapidly dismantling, reportedly calling for a referendum on the question of whether China should return to a monarchy. A Washington-based journal published by the Congressional Union for Woman Suffrage titled *The Suffragist* reported on Yuan's referendum: "Should it happen that China really returns to the monarchical form of government through this election, one-half of the citizens of the country will have voted away the freedom of the remainder, since women have no voice in the decision."[143] Indeed, the women's suffrage movement was in no position to influence the content of Yuan's constitution since, as democratic activists, they rightly feared for their lives.

Yuan's direct campaign against women's political activism commenced on 13 November 1913 with an Internal Affairs edict that banned Tang Qunying's Alliance.[144] Until this point the women had continued to hold public meetings promoting the value of women's education as preparation for participation in politics and to resist being mere "playthings."[145] They had continued despite repeated police harassment. For example, in May the Tianjin women's suffrage offices were raided and their propaganda material seized.[146] The harassment campaigns were accompanied by the "Police Ordinances on Public Order" of 2 March 1914 that prohibited women's participation in political associations and public meetings. This law was in direct imitation of one imposed in Japan in 1900.[147] The Women's Political and Legal University was ordered to close since educating women in such matters was no longer acceptable. Not only had the women's suffrage activists lost the optimum position advocated by radicals (sex equality in the constitution), but even the position of the moderates (the right to "prepare" women for future political participation through the training of women in politics and law) had been removed.

Yuan's complete mockery of constitutional rule was exposed in December of 1915 when he announced that the following year would begin a new imperial reign titled "Glorious Constitution." Reaction to this betrayal of his mandate was swift. Province after province declared independence, and antimonarchist armies sprang up under the command of former military leaders. Calls for his resignation increased daily, and with his grand plan beginning to unravel, Yuan Shikai died in June 1916 at the age of fifty-six. China's politics at a national level then descended into a period of political chaos as semirepresentative governments formed and reformed in Beijing. Beijing held elections to national and provincial legislatures—each marked by greater or lesser degrees of chaos and corruption—over the latter half of 1917 and 1918. Women did not formally participate in any of these events as voters or candidates.[148] Sun Yat-sen returned to political leadership, formally setting up a Constitution Protection government in Guangzhou in opposition to that based in Beijing. Jonathan Spence notes that "some one hundred former members of parliament who followed him south gave a kind of overt legitimacy when they elected him grand marshal.[149] Further political energy in the nation concentrated around the provincial governments that had reformed; and in a dogged adherence to the position that a constitution would create stability in governance, the provincial parliaments all devoted time to inaugurating a constitution.

As will become evident in the following chapters, the 1920s would prove to be a period of considerable intellectual ferment where radical new ideas about the importance of creating new social and political relations facilitated the emergence of the next wave of suffrage activism by women. This campaign would also focus on constitutional reform, but it would do so from the new perspective women had developed during their period of earlier defeats. It was a perspective that had no need to subsume feminist issues into other political projects in order to claim legitimate public voice. Within their new, albeit complex, republican political space the women were able to build their constituency with greater independence. Moreover, they were able to more effectively mobilize their knowledge that the international women's movement was an increasingly influential ally. During the next stage of activism this perspective strengthened to create a politically powerful notion of the unity of disadvantage common to all women.

FOUR

Suffrage and Provincial Constitutions

Building a New Culture, 1919–1923

The women's suffrage movement's recovery from the demoralizing defeats of 1912–1913 occurred as part of the major social reforms of the epochal New Culture Movement (1915–1925). This period is often called "China's Enlightenment," and indeed it was a time of significant shifts in China's intellectual and political leaders' conceptualization of the relationship between individuals and the state—China's social and political structures both faced major overhaul.[1] In this milieu the women's suffrage activists reinvigorated their movement with renewed optimism. The radical challenges to both the Republican and the Qing political orders generated during the New Culture Movement ultimately challenged cultural practices that had made female subordination appear natural.[2] The increasing structural stability of provincial governments that occurred over the New Culture period, when combined with the rethinking of the fundamental premises of Chinese culture, provided the legislative mechanisms and ideological space for the women to press their case for equal political rights with men.

The suffragists of the New Culture Movement years mobilized with increasing efficacy the concept of women citizens as a political category deserving of representation. They created a sophisticated political conception of "women" by establishing a collective notion of women's unity of disadvantage; that is, women's common political interests derived from their collective disadvantage relative to men. Prior to 1911 their predecessors had argued that women were people and citizens, and in the immediate years after 1911 they had promoted women as equal political actors to men with independent political agendas. During the New Culture Movement, activists built upon these foundations to publicize a broader sense of political unity among women. A significant aspect of this new gendered notion of collective political interests was that by discussing women's collective political concerns, divisions along class lines that had kept the suffrage movement narrow were reduced. Increasing numbers of women joined the feminist movement as they came to appreciate their similar political interests to other women, regardless of such differences as class, race, religion, or creed.

By producing a broad consciousness of women's unity of disadvantage, the activists argued for women's collective right to representation by women. Their case for women's equal political rights with men was thus imbued with the understanding that women, as a collectivity, were *different* from men. Within this logic, women's difference from men was not accepted at an individual level; rather it was at a collective level (women as a group were disadvantaged and therefore different from men as a group). In presenting their campaign in this light, China's women's suffrage activists ensured that the benefits of arguing for women's *special* political needs and interests within the logic of a politics of difference did not revert to old "different but equal" logic embedded in customs of essentialized separate spheres—in which women were deemed to be adequately represented as individuals by their fathers and husbands. Not relinquishing their claim to women's natural rights within the egalitarian rubric, the suffragists deftly won recognition for women's collective difference from men. Their increasing awareness of the politics of class differences contributed to an appreciation of women's collective political interests. Rather than splintering the women's movement along class lines, as had occurred in Britain, an increasing understanding of class differences in China helped create broader acceptance of the notion that disadvantaged groups deserved political representation. China's women's rights activists of the New Culture Movement established women as just such a distinct group based on their collective disadvantage relative to men.

Some of the women active in the earlier campaigns served as leaders for the revived campaign, but most important of all, young women who had not experienced the many indignities and hardships known to their mothers and aunts swelled the ranks of the women's suffrage movement. By the end of the first two decades of the twentieth century, urban intellectual families no longer routinely bound their daughters' feet, nor did they keep their daughters closeted in the family home. Industrialization in the coastal cities gave greater numbers of working women independence from their parents and husbands' families.[3] Many more of the women who reached their late teens and early twenties in the May Fourth era had confidence in the justice of their claim to equal rights. These women not only had knowledge of changes in the status of women around the world, but they also had models of radical Chinese feminism from the actions of women like Qiu Jin, Tang Qunying, and Lin Zongsu. Similarly, the men who grew up alongside the new-style woman of the New Culture period had different expectations about women's roles in society than those held by their fathers. Thus, a new generation of men and women were aspiring to claim their place in the political life in China.

Building from their predecessor's experience, the New Culture period's women's suffrage activists realized from the start that Chinese culture needed to change if their campaign was to be successful. Tang Qunying's February 1912 declaration to parliament that China required a "social revolution" emerged as words of prophecy. In the wake of the collapse of Yuan Shikai's failed monarchy, the subsequent decade of political instability produced conditions that were ripe for the required brutal reexamination of the fundaments of Chinese culture. During this aptly named New Culture Movement, a broader spectrum of China's intellectual and political elite than ever before questioned the validity of female subordination and came to appreciate women as a collectivity with similar political interests.

POLITICAL AND MILITARY CHAOS

The New Culture Movement is also known as the "May Fourth Movement," taking this latter name from a political demonstration of 4 May 1919 that protested the apparent willingness of sections of the Beijing government to sign the Versailles Treaty. The treaty transferred German territories in China to the Japanese rather than returning them to Chinese control. To China's patriots such acquiescence to foreign interests was emblematic of the dismal state of Chinese cultural and political life. China's intellectual class began to question naturalized assumptions about China's place in the world, and about ideologies behind core relationships in China itself—between the individual and the family, the individual and the state, the rich and the poor, the educated and the uneducated, and importantly, between men and women.

However, the instability of the government made a mockery of the intellectuals' ideals for a revived nation. The first task was to restore some form of legitimate representative government to the republic, and accordingly many invoked the power of that symbol of order, the Constitution of the Republic of China. But which constitution should be revived? The government in the South, led by Sun Yat-sen, argued that the 1912 Provisional Constitution should be the basis for government. The government in the North had directly inherited control from Yuan Shikai and, led by Premier Duan Qirui, argued that the 1912 document had long been abrogated. Nonetheless, by 1917 both groups agreed that China be ruled temporarily under the 1912 provisional document while work continued on the refinement of the 1913 Temple of Heaven Draft.

This period of agreement was to be short lived. Disputes about China's role in World War I led China's president, Li Yuanhong, to dismiss the premier and dissolve parliament in June of 1917. Chaos ensued in Beijing, and for the month of July power passed between President Li, the warlord Zhang Xun, ex-premier Duan, and another warlord Feng Guozhang. This unstable situation in the North led Sun and his supporters to reestablish their government in the South. Sun Yat-sen established and headed a series of military governments from Guangdong that purported to represent the nation in the name of the Constitution Protection Movement. However, his control of the city was tenuous because it depended on the whims of the southern warlord, Chen Jiongming. Yet more versions of the "national" constitution were created in the North over the next few years.[4] The split between North and South was to continue until 1928, when China was reunited from the South after a military campaign led by a reformulated Nationalist Party in concert with the CCP. The connections between the two parties and their influence on the women's movement are discussed in the following chapter.

During the unsettled years prior to the unification of the nation in 1928, many provinces declared their "independence" and established their own forms of republican democracy within subsections of China. These governments legitimized their rule with constitutions, and the women's suffrage activists were quick to press their claims for sex equality at these provincial levels. This chapter focuses on the key women's groups that formed during this provincial constitution movement. Indeed, China's first victories on women's suffrage were to appear in the constitutions of the "independent" southern provinces. As one feminist commentator noted at the time, the debates about constitutionalism and provincial independence that emerged during these tumultuous years provided the opening for a discussion on the questions of equality between men and women and "women's rights as people" once again.[5]

RETHINKING "WOMEN" IN THE NEW CULTURE MOVEMENT

The transformation in understandings about China's gender order occurred amidst these chaotic political realignments and military uncertainties. Influences from foreign philosophy, politics, and literature were driving many of the reassessments. Journals such as *New Youth* (*Xin qingnian*), *Renaissance* (*Xin chao*), and *Short Story Monthly* (*Xiaoshuo yuebao*) promoted democracy, pragmatism and science, and the destruction of Confucianism. They called for the youth of the nation to smash the traditions that had led China to stagnate and fall under foreign domination. The intellectual youth of China were called to develop a new and modern Chinese culture that would awaken the masses from their slumber.[6] This was truly a New Culture Movement—iconoclastic, nationalist, and cosmopolitan. Overseas-educated students were returning to China with plans for reforming the nation that were more international in focus and pragmatic in vision than those of the 1898 reformers. Public debate in mainstream newspapers discussed women's status in relation to freedom in love and marriage, equality in inheritance rights, as well as the right to participate in all political matters of national and international significance. They saw the intimate link between political rights and all other social and educational rights. Debates raged about the double standards of sexual morality and the strict codes on female chastity.[7]

Coeducation was expanded, enabling many women—who previously had access only to the few women's schools and colleges—the possibility of joining their brothers at universities and colleges and further dismantling the fundamental nexus between advanced learning and male access to political power. (See Figure 4.1 for a cartoon on education.) Chow Tse-tsung notes that before the May Fourth Movement "there had been very few girls' schools of higher learning. In 1922, however, twenty-eight universities and colleges had girl students."[8] The single-sex girls' schools, as Gilmartin has argued, created a sense of community among girls that was crucial to their formation of a political identity.[9] And, the coeducational universities and colleges created the forum within which this political identity could be exercised. The division was collapsing between masculine education-based virtue and women's sexualized virtue as coeducation meant that women increasingly joined men in the very sites of training for modern political virtue. For centuries, sex segregation had been a key marker of the feminine virtue of sexual chastity, but in the New Culture Period coeducation provided the mechanism by which women could undermine the link between sex segregation and female virtue by invoking the masculine-coded virtue of education.

Opponents to women's suffrage found that the main tenets of their argument, the conservative appeal to the stability of the old order, were undermined in the growing popular enthusiasm for modernizing Chinese culture. In particular, the New Culture Movement attacked Confucian ethics and claimed to strike at the fundament of the Chinese traditions that had for centuries supposedly denigrated women and elevated men. The demoniza-

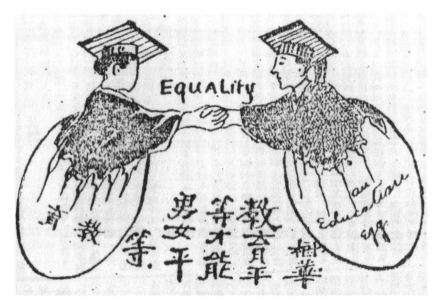

Figure 4.1. "Equality between men and women can only emerge from equality in education." *Shenbao,* 7 April 1921.

tion of Confucian traditions, whether accurate or exaggerated, was central to the imagining of a new Chinese culture. Thus, arguments against women's suffrage that invoked the importance of tradition or Confucian custom were thoroughly discredited during the early and mid-twenties. Opposition to women's suffrage appeared more desperate and venal as it was linked more clearly with the traditional moral codes that were perceived to have led China into its current desperate straits.[10]

In this atmosphere, the discursive space for broad intellectual acceptance of the necessity for "recovering" women's rights was opened. Radical journals regularly canvassed issues of women's rights. Feminist arguments about women's natural rights and status as people derived from the first decade of the century were among these pieces. An article in *Renaissance* declared that women's liberation was needed because: "pitiful women all over the world have suffered under myriad fetters, both historical and social, and these have made women as appendages to men—slaves. Now we must break free of those fetters and enable women to shift from being 'appendages' to having the status of 'people'; allowing them to be people, to be their own people."[11] Liang Qichao, one of the 1898 reformers, reiterated this sentiment and pronounced at a speech to the Nanjing Women's Normal College in November of 1922 that "women are people, and when we speak of people's rights we are naturally including women's rights within that."[12]

Feminist editor Zhang Peifen used the apparent disjunction between the terms *woman, citizen,* and *people* to expose the ambiguities in the existing rulings on suffrage. She declared:

> The constitution states that citizens have the right to vote and to be elected. Both men and women make up the body of citizens, so naturally they should have equal rights to vote and be elected. However, the articles on the electoral process do not uphold this view. So, this indicates that women are not citizens and women are not the same as citizens. In respect to every other law, if what was indicated as "person" only meant men, then women wouldn't be included, so I would like to ask if the law is supposed to be interpreted as only referring to men? If the law is interpreted as meaning "men" when it states "person" then clearly women have been forgotten and women are not recognized as people. Is it the case then that the law does not recognize the existence of women . . . ? It does not mean this at all—when it comes to issues of duties and punishments, women are clearly recognized as being in existence. It seems that women can only face the punishments of the law and can gain none of the rights conferred by the law. There is nothing more unequal than this in China today![13]

Likewise, these journals published news of victories for women's suffrage from around the world, and these provided hope for the women activists and also increased pressure on male politicians keen not to be seen as lagging behind international political trends.[14] In particular, news about the recent successes of the women's suffrage movement in the legislatures of the major international powers of England, USA, and Germany gave increased credibility to the revived campaign in China.[15] An article published in *The Ladies Journal* in 1919 described the "women's suffrage campaign as one of the most important issues in the world today."[16] To increasing numbers of people it was inevitable that China, with its democratic and modern pretensions, should proceed down this path. Wu Yuxiu describes women's suffrage as an inevitable international trend for the twentieth century and states that with nations like Britain already recognizing women's right to vote and stand for election there was no doubt that China would follow suit.[17]

In this milieu, with its enthusiasm for radical social change, the women's suffrage movement and the women's rights movement in general were able to make significant advances. They focused on whatever government in China was available to be lobbied, refusing to wait for national unification. They took their cause to both the "national" governments in Beijing and Guangzhou as well as to independent provincial governments. Over these years, the women's suffrage cause had gained a new legitimacy once their collective interests and collective right to political representation, as distinct from those of men, were more broadly promoted. They undertook their task with a consciousness of universal suffrage rights in a major advance on their immediate predecessors—but, as we will see below, even then education remained a key signifier of the right to exercise political power. The main groups that waged these campaigns for constitutional change in the provinces were the United Women's Associations that formed in the capital cities.

UNITED WOMEN'S ASSOCIATIONS AND THE PROVINCIAL CONSTITUTIONS CAMPAIGN

In 1919, at the height of New Culture activism, a number of women's organizations were formed under the general title of United Women's Associations (UWA; *Nüjie lianhe hui*). These groups formed when it became evident that the discussions about provincial independence emerging from amidst the fractured political landscape had created an opportunity for winning women's suffrage at a provincial level. The establishment of Sun's military government in Guangzhou, with its pretensions at national jurisdiction, gave the Guangdong women's movement a quasi-national legislative body on which to focus. The first UWAs were established in Shanghai and Guangzhou in the summer and autumn of 1919, respectively. Other regions soon followed suit—including Zhejiang in 1920, Hunan in 1921, and later Sichuan and Jiangxi.[18] Specifically, the UWAs aimed to ensure that any legislation written by provincial governments include the notion of sex equality in political rights. Equality in all other rights, it was assumed, would flow directly from this premier right of women to vote and stand for election. The UWAs were remarkably effective in changing provincial constitutions. By December of 1921 Guangdong's constitution included sex equality, and on 1 January 1922 Hunan's achieved the same. In the Double Ninth Constitution of Zhejiang Province, promulgated on 9 September 1921, sex equality was guaranteed. Equality provisions were later enshrined in the 1923 Sichuan constitution as well.[19]

While these constitutions also included provisions for the equality of all social classes, they stipulated literacy as a prerequisite to voting.[20] So, although they removed the property requirements that had ensured the very limited suffrage of the earlier constitutions, these new documents reinforced the political power of those privileged with access to education by specifying literacy as a prerequisite characteristic of a voting citizen. For example, the Hunan constitution granted voting rights to all citizens who were over twenty-one years in age but prohibited illiterates (*bu shi wenzi zhe*), bankrupts, opium addicts, those deemed to have improper employment, and people with mental illness from voting.[21] The Zhejiang constitution allowed all people over twenty to vote but excluded illiterates, the unemployed, and people with mental illness.[22] The Sichuan document made similar exclusions on the basis of mental illness and illiteracy.[23] In the case of Zhejiang and Hunan, the criteria for determining illiteracy were not specified. In Sichuan the constitution identified the ability to read the constitutional document itself as the benchmark literacy standard.[24] These restrictions on voting rights demonstrated the close link between literacy and "right to rule" that remained from the dynastic epoch of Confucian literati bureaucrats. This position effectively disenfranchised the bulk of China's population and, given that women's literacy rates were likely to be well below those of men, empowered only a small section of the female population. Up to this point, China's women's suffrage activists had argued that sex was an inappropriate category for exclusion. They had not argued that education, a privilege of the middle and upper classes, was an inappropriate category for discrimination. However, to their credit the women did win specific rulings on sex equality in educational opportunities within these constitutions. They did not challenge the notion that the educated, or at least the literate, had the right to rule China, but they did aim to enhance educational opportunities for a broader cross-section of China's women.

The fundamental premise of the UWAs was basically the "sex equality" argument that women were people and therefore women's rights were an integral part of a generic category of people's rights. The manifesto of the Zhejiang group declared:

> What we refer to as "women's rights" are not over and above those of men, nor do they stand separately from people's rights. Clearly, humanity comprises both men and women. People's rights are common to all and there are no so-called special rights for women. However, by custom, what are called "people's rights" has been monopolized by men. We must rectify this error in the meaning of the term "people's rights." We must recognize their true value and furthermore demand that they be equally shared with women. The women's rights campaign then, is a campaign for the equal allocation of people's rights. People's rights should not differentiate between men and women, but when we make our claim for their equal sharing between men and women, we also feel that the term "women's rights" is a useful tool for making our position and meaning clear.[25]

This last sentence points to the major new point of departure for the suffragists of the New Culture period. While not resiling from their "equality" premise, they simultaneously assert the importance of "women" as a legitimate political category and one that is different from "men." The collective political interests of women are declared within these lines and a constituency demanding political representation is created.

The UWAs were directly linked to the Nationalist Party, but the Shanghai group would develop close ties with the newly formed CCP (est. 1921). The CCP's main women activists were based in Shanghai at this time and, following directives from their Central Committee to work for the Nationalists in a united front, many became active in the Shanghai UWA despite their distaste for "bourgeois" women's movements. The Guangdong UWA commenced with close ties to the Nationalist Party through its adherence to Sun's visions of the principles required for modernizing China with its constitution, stating that it aimed to "encourage women to exert themselves for the national revolution, to promote the realization of [Sun Yat-sen's] Three Principles of the People, to encourage a women's movement and to safeguard women's rights."[26] In contrast to the Guangdong group's early invocation of Sun's ideology, the Shanghai UWA manifesto of 1921 exhorted members to focus on the "international," "imperialist," and "class" nature of oppression.[27] In the dynamic and rapidly changing intellectual milieu of this period, a difference of two years had a dramatic impact on rhetoric and consciousness. The extent of left-wing influence on the UWAs increased as Marxism strengthened its influence on intellectual life in China.

Prior to the expansion in awareness of Marxism, Chinese feminism had been more elitist in outlook and adopted a philanthropic attitude toward "less fortunate" women, reflecting the paternalism of an "enlightened elite." In the new atmosphere, some UWA branches ruled that peasant or worker members needing financial support during childbirth would be eligible for Association funds. A sliding scale of membership fees reduced costs for worker and peasant members.[28] Soon the UWAs would move to a relationship with working women premised on active mobilization for labor and anti-imperialist causes.

A similar broadening of perspective occurred on the issue of sexual morality. Few suffragists in 1919 doubted the value of including working or peasant women, but some resisted tainting their movement with women whose feminine virtue had been compromised by employment as prostitutes or status as concubines. Such scruples were increasingly disregarded with broader acceptance of the notion that women as a collective formed a political category because of their unity of disadvantage relative to men. As women gained access to the arena of training for masculine political virtue through expanded educational opportunities, and waged campaigns against the backwardness of codes of female chastity, the latter were no longer the sole barometer of female virtue. Moreover, women were increasingly able to access public space without having aspersions cast on their moral state.

The evolution of the UWAs reveals how women political activists developed a heightened awareness of the breadth of the "female experience" in China and constructed it as a coherent and unified collective political experience. They also increasingly discussed class as a political rather than moral category. While the leadership of the women's movement remained largely urban, educated elites, they did represent a broader constituency of women than ever before.

ARE CONCUBINES PEOPLE TOO?
THE GUANGDONG UWA

Typical of the transformation in the suffrage movement's conceptualization of women as a political category with unified political interests is the evolution of the first UWA formed, the Guangdong branch. In 1919, the Guangdong branch was largely a club for "good" women that excluded those of dubious morals, yet by 1921 its members were engaged in highly public violent actions within their provincial parliament.

The Guangdong UWA was formed on 23 December 1919, when a group of Guangdong women activists organized a meeting boldly titled the "Women's National Assembly." Held at the Tianmagang Women's Physical Education College, more than one thousand women attended. At the assembly Dr. Wu Zhimei (1897–?) proposed the formation of the Guangdong UWA.[29] The first committee chosen to lead the branch included Wu Zhimei, Tang Yungong, Cheng Yili, Li Lian, and Zhuang Hanqiao. Zhuang was one of the original women parliamentarians of the short-lived provincial assembly of Guangzhou in 1912. Wu Zhimei was a medical educator "who graduated from a medical college in America and received training at Chicago University Hospital."[30] She became an active member of the Nationalist Party when it reformed in Guangdong in 1923.[31]

The group saw as its broad tasks the promotion of a women's movement that would safeguard women's rights within the framework of Sun's southern military government. The suffrage cause was not mentioned in this establishment stage and took a few months to become its key focus. Instead, the Guangdong UWA initially specified the following areas of concern: (1) instituting universal education for women, (2) improving women's work and access to careers, (3) providing relief to unemployed women, (4) striving to eliminate the suffering of oppressed women, (5) promoting women's physical culture, and (6) developing women's morality. The absence of an explicit call for women's suffrage in these points was a matter of some dispute. Zhuang Hanqiao argued that this cause was a matter of great urgency, but there was insufficient support among the founding members to include

it. The majority decision was that the UWA needed to become a more organized body before taking on this "difficult" issue.[32] The group took great
pains to emphasize the good morals of its members. Its mechanisms for
achieving this mission read as follows:

> (1) liaise with women to open their consciousness to inculcate them with
> new ways of thinking; (2) ensure that women are regarded as being inde-
> pendent economically in all mercantile and industry reforms; (3) establish
> more tertiary, secondary, and primary schools, and pay particular attention
> to the industrial education of poor women, to enable women to have the
> knowledge to facilitate their liberation; and (4) pay attention to morality to
> prevent being misled; any decline in moral character would generate more
> trouble at a later date.[33]

Gradually the more politically active members, like Zhuang Hanqiao,
managed to inject advocacy for direct political reform into the Association.
At the conclusion of the meeting of 27 December 1919, the Guangdong
UWA had drafted a petition on women's suffrage directed to Sun's "National
Assembly." Titled "Submission Demanding Women's Suffrage Presented to
the National Assembly," it commenced with the assertion that women had
natural rights equal to men simply by being born human. Echoing the rhetoric of the 1911 campaigners, they declared that denying women the right
to participate in politics was a breach of their natural rights. Women's suffrage was deemed central to the construction of a strong foundation for the
nation's future progress.[34] This petition was circulated to the newly formed
Shanghai UWA in solidarity. From this meeting on, all further meetings
of the Guangdong UWA highlighted women's suffrage.[35] The UWA meeting hall was hung with a banner listing recent international successes for
women's suffrage reminding members that sex equality was being recognized with increasing rapidity throughout the world.

Nonetheless, while the radicals managed to bring women's suffrage explicitly into the group's agenda, the conservatives remained a contentious
force. Indeed, sexual morality threatened to divide the suffrage cause in
Guangdong. At the end of January 1920, debate raged within the UWA over
whether concubines should be permitted to become members. Despite their
recognition of the special needs of unemployed and poor women, many
members of the Guangdong UWA clearly did not feel great empathy with
concubines. Concubines were perceived to be of low moral worth, and some
members felt that the Association's mission to "develop women's morality"

would be compromised by the participation of concubines. Concubines were clearly more problematic and threatening to the UWA membership than poor women or factory women. After all, it would be men of their husbands' class who would have the wealth to procure concubines.

On 20 January 1920 the importance of "maintaining the high personal character of the membership" was discussed at formal meeting. Wu Zhimei proposed that the Association exclude concubines on the grounds that such women were necessarily of dubious character. Cheng Liqing spoke in opposition to Wu, arguing women's liberation was for all women regardless of social standing. She asked if the Association was truly a women's association or was it in reality a "madams and young ladies' association." Were Wu and her supporters suggesting that concubines were not women, Cheng asked? Furthermore, she declared it was the system of taking concubines that required condemnation and not those who had been oppressed by the system. In the final vote twenty women, led by Li Lian, opposed restrictions on concubines while ten, led by Wu Zhimei, voted to prohibit their membership. The vitriolic meeting disbanded with no change to the original constitution that permitted all women over the age of sixteen (who had been nominated by two existing members) to join.[36] The debate provides an excellent example of the transformations taking place in activist women's consciousness at this time. The victorious group enunciated the case for a collective women's political consciousness based on the common unity of disadvantage experienced by all women, regardless of social status or position in the hierarchies of sexual morality.

The internal dispute over the membership of concubines attracted media attention, but the UWA's actions over the issue of sex equality in the provincial constitution also gave the Association considerable public profile. The direct involvement of the Guangdong UWA in the reformulation of a provincial constitution began in 1921. The UWA organized a petition requesting that women's suffrage be guaranteed in the provincial constitution. To this end, on 19 February 1921 around seven hundred women marched on the parliament led by a group of seven that included Deng Huifang (one of the original parliamentarians of the 1912 provincial legislature), Dr. Wu Zhimei, and a student, Zeng Suxian. Arriving at the parliament at 1 o'clock PM, they presented their petition and waited while it was appraised.[37] Their petition requested that the provincial constitution concur with the national constitution (the South was working from the 1912 document), which vested sovereignty in "all of the people." Article 5 of this national document had also declared: "All people are equal."[38] The women of the UWA reasoned that in 1921, unlike in 1912, there should be no argument that women were people too. Thus, the exclusion of "those who are not men" was now inappropriate. The petition then provocatively asked what difference there would be between the lawless warlords of the North and the provincial government if the law were not passed?[39] Ironically, the suffrage activists of the 1920s were attempting to insert into their provincial constitution the very statement about "equality of all people" that the 1912 suffrage activists had attempted to clarify. The intellectual transformation that was occurring during the New Culture Movement ensured that the suffrage activists were no longer particularly worried about being considered "nonpeople" or "less than equal" people. Moreover, they were making the case that women were people with "special" political interests that required "special" political representation—representation that acknowledged women's difference from men.

According to house procedures, petitions required vetting before being included on the agenda for later discussion. During this initial debate it became clear that conservative members of the house, Feng Heqing and Lin Chaonan, were speaking persuasively against the proposal. It appeared that the petition would not even be considered eligible for full debate. The women leading the rally then entered the chambers with their supporters gathering outside the door. Deng Huifang asked if the women could take the stand and speak to the main points of their petition. A summary of the events in the left-wing paper *Labor and Women* (*Laodong yu funü*) described how the response from the conservatives, Lin and Feng, was both noisy and rude as they banged their fists on the table and cursed the women as troublemakers.[40] These actions failed to frighten the women, so Lin and Feng began throwing ink boxes and, in an instant, a ruckus ensued. In the attack Deng was cut on the chin and left hand, Cheng Yili received an injury to her left foot. Most seriously of all, Zeng Suxian was knocked unconscious by a chair that had been thrown at her head. In reaction to the chaos inside, the women waiting at the door flooded into the chamber, and after a further hour of arguing and fighting, the congressmen vacated, bringing parliament to a close for the day.[41]

Undeterred by the violence and strength of opposition to their cause, the women then marched to the headquarters of the southern Constitution Protection government, where Sun Yat-sen had his offices. Even Zeng Suxian, recovering from her recent concussion, made the journey. Sun spoke to the rally declaring that women's suffrage was an integral part of the original, provisional constitution that he had helped create, which had not explicitly precluded women from participation. Moreover, it explicitly stated that all citizens are equal. At this point the provincial head and southern warlord, Chen Jiongming, on whose goodwill Sun maintained his position in Guangzhou, addressed the rally. He too expressed his support for including women's suffrage in any revisions of the constitution. Chen told the women not to become overly anxious on the issue and said that he would counter any obstructions placed by the provincial parliamentarians. Chen pointed out that "the regulations on self government do not state that women do not have suffrage rights and if the parliament moves to decide against women's suffrage, I will of course counter their arguments."[42] With this high level of support for the cause, the women gave shouts of victory and immediately organized a meeting for the following day. However, they were to face an even graver setback before victory was finally achieved.

The violence meted out to the women suffragists inspired a measured and controlled response from the women. One of the most severely beaten women, Huang Bihun, explained her feelings on the issue in an article in the local left-wing newspaper *The Social* (*Guangdong qunbao*) on 7 April. She wrote that although she could have sued Li Chaonan for assault by invoking the judiciary, she chose not to take this path. Her reasons were twofold. First, she noted that the main goal of the movement was to win suffrage rights for women and any legal case against Li Chaonan would distract from this effort. Second, she noted that the episode revealed that although the perpetrators were men charged with writing laws, their flagrant abuse of these laws indicated that legal action would have no impact on them at all. She said that justice was partly served by the publication of reports about the behavior of the men because this would serve to discredit their case. Taking the opportunity to further the public's understanding of the debates about suffrage, Huang elaborated on the differences between men and women. She noted that usually opposition to women's suffrage was framed within arguments about women's reproductive role and their failure to participate in military action to defend the nation. It was assumed, she noted, that because women did not risk their lives in military action they should not have voting rights. She then asked how many of the current legislators had ever seen military action and noted that most would not have served the nation in this way. Huang continued her attack delineating the implications of the different roles that women and men play in building China from within the sex-differentiated functions of childbirth and military defense. She noted that military action involved "(1) killing people, (2) being cruel and brutal, and yet (3) it did not include all men as participants, (4) it was not necessarily dangerous, (5) it did not always involve suffering, and (6) it sucked the nation's vitality." She contrasted this list with one about childbirth, which she claimed "(1) creates human life, (2) is loving and compassionate, (3) is experienced by almost all women, (4) always involves danger, (5) always involves suffering, and moreover (6) expands the vitality of the nation." She concluded by arguing that there was not one man in China who had not been born from a woman's womb whereas there were many women who had fought in the military.[43]

Such media coverage supported more direct action. On 29 March the Guangdong UWA held a general meeting on the third floor of the Guangxi meeting hall. There were about one thousand people in attendance, some bearing placards with "Long live Sun and Chen," "Equal rights for men and women," and "Assemblyman Feng Heqing beat and injured women delegates." At the meeting there was unanimous support by a show of hands for the motion that women should have the right to participate in politics. At two o'clock these one thousand women commenced their march on parliament.[44] A photograph taken before they departed on their rally was later published in the premier Shanghai women's journal, *The Ladies Journal* (see Figure 4.2).[45] The rally presented two requests to the chair of the provincial assembly. First, that the assailants be expelled from parliament and second, that a law confirming women's suffrage be adopted. The chair acknowledged the UWA petition and expressed his sincere wish to "come to an understanding" on the issue. Furthermore he assured the petitioners that he would endeavor to ensure the successful passage of a women's suffrage bill through parliament. On the matter of disciplining the "assailants" he was less forthright. There were, he declared, aggressors on both sides. Such a complex issue required lengthy consideration and as such would be most effectively dealt with at a later date. The women greeted this supportive statement with enthusiasm. It was regarded as a major victory by the women rallied outside his office, and with shouts of "Great Victory" they dispersed.[46]

Under such sustained pressure from the UWA, on the first day of April the parliament held a heated debate about the issue of the wording of the provincial constitution in relation to sex equality. The conservatives dominated the parliament and were adamant that women be excluded from political participation. To this end they removed the current ambiguity about the sex of the citizens who had the right to be treated equally with regards to voting rights. The new bill specified that "*men* over the age of twenty" had suffrage rights whereas the previous draft had merely stated "*citizens* over the age of twenty."[47] This amendment was passed by fifty votes to thirty-two. The women of Guangdong had again failed to regain their 1912 rights to political participation despite the support they had won from Sun and Chen.[48] The reasons opponents to women's suffrage presented in support of their case focused on the low level of women's education—most women were illiterate—and the fact that women do not participate in military service—they cannot defend the nation. The women countered the latter argument by reminding the parliamentarians that women had been very active in bomb squads and formal armies during the 1911 revolution to establish the republic. Indeed, women had been expressly prohibited from engaging in military activities after the formation of the republic, against their own desires.

Nonetheless, the passage of this amendment demonstrated that it was becoming increasingly difficult to argue that women were not inherently part of that group called "people." If the old notions of "people" meaning "men" still had credence there would have been no reason to specify men in the document. The perversity of the conservatives in deliberately specifying "men" must have been particularly enraging. The events of March 1912 were

Figure 4.2. Cantonese suffrage movement gathering before its 1921 rally. *Funü zazhi* (The Ladies' Journal) 7, no. 7 (1921).

being replayed—the only difference was that they were located in Guang-zhou rather than Nanjing. Sun's guarantees proved to be as ineffectual as they had in 1912.

Before the words "regardless of sex" could be inserted, the word "men" had to be removed. Weeks of intense lobbying on the part of the women ac-tivists ensued. *The Social* provided regular reports on the campaign.[49] These included repeated petitions by the UWA and individual women to Gover-nor Chen for his intervention. Liu Shaobi argued in her petition to Chen that rights are embodied in the people regardless of whether they are men or women and that the province's constitution would do well to reflect this fact.[50] Their sustained pressure ultimately produced the desired results at the end of May.

L'Impartial (*Dagong bao*) reported on 20 May 1921, "The Cantonese women's suffrage movement has success." The article outlined the events of March and April and noted that by the end of May the chair of the as-sembly had announced that women could participate in elections and that the word "men" had been removed.[51] The provincial constitution of Guang-dong presented on 2 December 1921 finally officially acknowledged women's equal political rights with men. The violence of Feng and Lin in March had been the last burst of conservative opposition to women's suffrage in Guangdong. The Guangdong women's suffrage activists were not alone in their struggle. In another part of southern China, Hunan, women had been simultaneously active.

EXPOSING THE INCOMPETENT
CHINESE MAN: HUNAN UWA

The Hunan UWA formed in January 1921, and within only six months it achieved victory—without the violence that caused such a sensation in Guangzhou. As a direct result of the Hunan Association's lobbying, on 1 June 1921 the revised Hunan provincial constitution indicated that, once formally promulgated, women would have equal political rights with men. The constitution did not come into effect until 1 January 1922, but the June announcement ensured that Hunan, along with Guangdong, was among the first provinces to officially grant women suffrage rights. Just as it had led the way in 1905 when it sent the first batch of women students to Japan, Hunan had demonstrated its progressive and daring political leadership.

The comparatively late formation of the Hunan UWA, two years after the Guangdong group, resulted from the later realization of political stability in Hunan. In the last few months of 1920 democratic forces finally overcame the warlord who had dominated the region, and in January of 1921 Hunan self-government was declared. Thus, the formation of the province's UWA came only weeks after the return of a semblance of democracy to the region. Two students at the Hunan Teachers College, Chen Chu and Wu Jian, established the group in Changsha (it also went by the name "Changsha UWA"). It drew together a range of staff and students from the various women's schools and colleges around Changsha, indicating the continued dominance of educated women within the suffrage movement.

At the end of January, the *Republic Daily* (*Minguo ribao*) published the Association's foundation manifesto.[52] The declaration summarized the historical nature of women's oppression and the vital importance of "recovering for women their rights as people." It then outlined a four-point rationale for the recovery of these rights:

> First, we firmly believe that people's rights are derived from the natural order and since women are part of this natural order we also ought to have people's rights. Second, we firmly believe that people's rights are the "life of humanity" and since women have life they therefore should have people's rights. Third, we firmly believe that "people's rights are equal" and since in China men and women do not have equal rights and powers we must recover for women their people's rights. Fourth, we firmly believe that people's rights are "mutually reinforcing" and now we strive for social assistance, and so demand a campaign for recovering women's rights as people.

From these fundamental principles the manifesto explained that the two immediate and tangible goals of the Association were to realize within the provincial constitution the legal right to inherit property and the right to participate in politics.[53]

In March of 1921 deliberations on the detail of the constitution were begun, and the UWA began its campaign to ensure that "women's rights as people" were recovered. UWA founder Chen Chu was one of the examiners appointed to devise the document. The women faced stiff opposition from conservative members of the legislature, as encapsulated by the statement that "it is the natural order that men should have three wives and four concubines just as it is natural that women concern themselves with the provision of food and drink. The current discussion about wanting to participate in politics is extremely bizarre and totally ridiculous."[54]

Nonetheless, the women maintained their lobbying campaign to win constitutional change. To this end, they submitted a six-point petition to the newly formed Constitutional Drafting Committee. The main points were:

(1) women should have the right to vote and be elected, (2) women's education should be equal to that of men, (3) women's employment should be regarded as being the same as men's and should invite no discrimination, (4) women should have the right to freedom in choice of marriage, (5) women's right to inherit parents' property should be guaranteed, and (6) men ought to adopt the practice of monogamy in marriage.[55]

As part of the remarkable increase in feeling over this issue, the UWA organized a rally for 16 May 1921 to exhibit the volume of its support. Over two thousand women demonstrated, marching around the chambers and eventually sending a delegation in to present their demands to the constitutional committee.[56] During the same month, *L'Impartial* published a running series of articles and opinion pieces on the potential effects of women's suffrage. One letter serialized over 6–7 May stated explicitly how their requests could be met in the constitution: "Insert into article 1, item 3: 'The people referred to in this constitution includes all men and women.' . . . for many thousands of years it has been the Chinese custom to regard women as property and therefore often the common people have not considered women to be people . . . therefore we would like this statement included to prevent any confusion." The author further requested that the phrase "regardless of sex, religion, or class differences" be added to article 2, item 5, where it currently stated, "all people are equal before the law."[57] The following day, the UWA's advice on amending the constitution's ruling on inheritance and property rights argued that the document should be amended to read "all people, regardless of sex, have the right to own and inherit property." Similar amendments were stipulated for the items referring to the "people's" rights to vote and stand for election. The explanatory statement accompanying these rather dry legal statements stressed the importance of individuality and people's rights.[58]

A lengthy article by a male supporter of the suffrage activists, Li Liuru, was serialized over four days. Li argued that men have the responsibility to liberate women since women have had limited opportunities in the past and therefore require men's help and support. Men have for centuries regarded women as chattels or slaves for their use, he argued, and this has had the effect of reducing women's concerns to household drudgery or frivolous and inconsequential matters (see Figures 4.3 and 4.4). This practice de-skilled women who, Li asserted, do not differ at all from men in abilities. With equal access to education women would be able to achieve the same level of independence as men. Only once women have equal opportunity and economic independence can they be liberated from their position as slaves, dependent on men for their existence. To those critics who argue that women are currently lacking the ability to undertake a full range of careers, Li asked, "Do all men have these abilities?" Such skills he argued are based on individual differences and are not monopolized by one sex in particular.[59]

In opposition to Li's article was a lengthy reply by a male member of the Constitutional Drafting Committee, Cheng Xiluo. Cheng was deeply concerned about social change, and this exposed the extent to which he was out of step with the rising intellectual mood of the New Culture period. The young intellectuals driving media debate embraced change partly on the grounds that nothing could be worse than the chaotic pres-

Figure 4.3. A book titled *New Culture* is snatched from a girl student who is restrained by the hand of the "evil family." *Shenbao,* 31 March 1921.

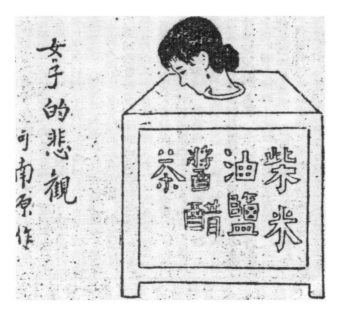

Figure 4.4. Women trapped in household duties and domestic trivia. *Shenbao*, 22 March 1921.

ent. Cheng asserted that in the nations of Europe and America that had granted women full suffrage rights, social problems had emerged. He did not specify the exact nature of these problems, and his vague references to "problems" were to draw ridicule from readers of *L'Impartial*. He then took the dangerous step of insulting the abilities of all women in his province. He declared that while it was true that in Europe and America women had assumed positions of responsibility in a range of careers, few women in Hunan would be capable of performing well alongside men—only one or two in a hundred. He continued his provocative argument with the assertion that political chaos would result from such unenlightened government. Women in Europe and America had the vote because these are advanced nations, whereas China was a mere "beginner" and could not risk granting women the vote. Moreover, throwing women into the hurly-burly of political life would jeopardize the safety of women. "Would such a move be respectful of women or is it sacrificing them?" he asks. Finally, he doubts the wisdom of women's participation on the grounds that they are physically incapable of maintaining political activities simply because of limitations imposed by their physiology.[60] (See Figure 4.5 for a cartoon critiquing separate spheres for men and women.)

Figure 4.5. "Path to free public interactions between men and women blocked," by Huang Younong. *Shenbao*, 19 March 1921.

An impassioned response to Cheng's article came from Jiang Zhaoxiang the following day. Jiang called for Cheng to provide evidence of the "problems" caused by women's suffrage in the West and then asserted that Cheng's claim to this effect was complete fabrication. Uncertainty of outcomes is an integral part of politics, Jiang continued. "So Mr. Cheng, how many hundred years would it take for you to feel comfortable before allowing women to vote with a democratic constitution?" The barrage continued, with Jiang asking if Cheng also felt that the men of Hunan province compared unfavorably with foreign men. After all, the chaos of China over the past decade hardly indicates competence in the ruling men. Moreover, Jiang countered that Cheng's argument about protecting women from the rough and tumble of political life is complete nonsense:

Have women not suffered untold hardship during the [current] tumultuous period? And yet, what of the suffering of politicians during this same period? . . . Looking at politicians during this same period we can see that they are not to be pitied at all. The ones that should be pitied are the millions of women who have been trapped in the inner chambers. They have not exercised political power, and yet with every change of political circumstance they are subject to hardship; now we want to ease or even erase this suffering.[61]

A joint letter of opposition came from students at the Number 1 Girls' Normal School. They too queried Cheng's assertion that the effects of women's suffrage in Europe and America had been problematic. They wrote that extensive research on the topic has shown that women's suffrage has overwhelmingly positive results. Regarding the issue of Hunan women's inability to rule, the students argued that illiteracy was a problem across the entire rural sector and that a sufficient number of women were adequately educated to participate productively in political life. Cheng's fears that women's physiology was unsuited to politics, they argued, should be allayed by the experience of women in Europe and America. Their reaction to his purported concern for women's welfare contained the most venom:

> Your concerns about the safety of women are repulsive given the fact that for so many years women have been trampled on by men. Is being subjected to this sort of hardship your idea of "protection?" . . . Your suggestion that we should wait until after the national revolution is successfully completed is abhorrent and such promises have been made in the past and have come to naught. We women have waited long enough and we will not wait any longer. We want to participate in the building of this new system.[62]

Only days later, Class no. 8 followed their fellow students with another response to Cheng, declaring that his arguments against women's suffrage were so insubstantial as to be simply a waste of ink.[63] Later on in the debate Yi Chuheng asked Mr. Cheng whether or not he regarded women to be citizens. Yi argued that if women were citizens then the constitution should rule equally over all citizens and not merely reinforce the power of those who drafted the document. Yi queried the ability of anyone to decide when China would be sufficiently advanced to permit women to vote.[64]

Education rights were a fundamental part of the campaign for equality between men and women in political participation at this stage in the feminist movement, in Hunan as elsewhere. In most people's minds, women who want to participate in ruling the nation needed to gain education so as to prove their moral capacity to rule. In almost all the letters to *L'Impartial* an expansion of educational opportunities is asserted as a prime goal of the political and constitutional campaign. In an article published on 5 May,

L'Impartial reported the opinion that while including sex equality in the constitution would not immediately solve all problems related to women, it would provide the method for solving these in the long term. Women's equal participation in education and politics would facilitate great progress toward improving the overall status of women.[65] In a later report a jubilant note was adopted since it was clearly assumed that women would be granted full suffrage rights with men and that Hunan would be the province to break new ground for China. The paper expressed the hope that the women of Hunan would wake the rest of China's women to the importance of winning these rights and would stride along the path of learning and knowledge and set examples for the rest of the nation to follow.[66]

The success of the Hunan UWA campaign was made public on 1 June 1921 when the provincial constitution was announced. It included the crucial statement that all citizens were equal "regardless of sex." It even went so far as to include Chen Chu's statement on equal rights for sons and daughters to own and inherit property.[67] Clearly the arguments for sex equality had fallen on more sympathetic ears than they had during the 1912 Kong Hai debates in *The People's Independence News*, discussed in the previous chapter.

In the winter of 1921 three women activists, Wang Changguo (1880–1949), Wu Jiaying, and Zhou Tianpu, were elected as legislators in the provincial assembly. The impact of the sex equality provisions was also evident at the lower levels of government. In the accompanying county elections seven more women won seats.[68] Both Wang Changguo and Zhou Tianpu were prominent women educators in local women's colleges, and Wang had strong ties to the suffrage movement from its inception.

With its own considerable victory on the provincial constitution to its credit, the UWA continued to work for equal rights in education and other broad social matters related to Hunanese women. Appraisal of their contribution was not always positive. Yan Shi wrote in the influential magazine *The Ladies' Journal* that having women in the Guangdong and Hunan parliaments was not all that "terrific" because the results of their participation were hard to gauge. Yan Shi warned that it was important for suffrage activists to raise the political consciousness of all women in the nation and not simply win seats in parliament.[69]

For women in Hunan, their continued vigilance about their victory was required. In November of 1924 a bill was presented to the provincial parliament to strike women's suffrage rights from the constitution. Only after the women suffragists had mobilized their supporters and rallied at the parliament was the bill defeated.[70] Media reports mentioned that the person proposing the bill feared women suffragists would "beat him to death."[71] There was no evidence that physical violence was used, but clearly the matter was one that generated high emotion. For the women activists the episode was a reminder that their opponents could use a constitutional reform process for their own ends just as had the women themselves.

INTELLECTUAL LEADERSHIP ON CLASS STRUGGLE AND IMPERIALISM: SHANGHAI UWA

Formed in mid-1919 the Shanghai group was the earliest of the UWAs, but given the political domination of Shanghai by foreign powers it focused instead on providing important intellectual leadership on women's rights and social progress in general. Where the Guangdong and Hunan branches directed their attention to the provincial governments, the Shanghai group directed their energies toward mobilizing women, activists and nonactivists alike. The Shanghai Association was to become crucial to the connection between the CCP and the Nationalist Party on women's issues. In December 1921 it was renamed the Shanghai China UWA (*Shanghai Zhonghua nüjie lianhe hui*) with the support of the newly formed CCP.[72] The CCP needed the UWA's access to politically active women in the city, and in return the Shanghai UWA benefited from the intellectual energies of the CCP—specifically in the production of a journal, *Women's Voice* (*Funü sheng*), and the establishment of a women's school, the Pingmin Girls' School, under the guidance of CCP activist Wang Huiwu (1898–?).[73] The Shanghai China UWA devoted much time to propagandizing among middle-class women to promote an awareness of class consciousness among these already politically active women. *Women's Voice* included a range of materials including essays, fiction, poetry, and political commentary, including works by Marx and Lenin, and became the main CCP organ to address women in Shanghai. It published numerous stinging critiques of the "middle-class" interests of the women's movement and the importance of uniting with the working masses.

Like the other branches, the Shanghai UWA included a core of older women who had been active in the 1911 revolution as well as younger women who had been politicized by the recent anti-imperialist May Fourth demonstrations they had either witnessed or participated in as students in

Chinese secondary and tertiary institutions. The central core of the Shanghai UWA included the 1911 suffragist Huang Zonghan (aka Xu Zonghan, 1876–1944) as chair and prominent Revolutionary Alliance member Cui Zhenhua (1886–1971).[74] Li Guo (?–1920), Huang Shaolan, Zhong Peiyu, and Zheng Bi were also members of this central organizing group. The premier radical journal *New Youth* published its manifesto on 1 September 1921. It declared that the oppression of women in China was similar to that of other women around the world—it resulted from the imposition of religious beliefs that denigrated women and economic structures that treated women as chattels. Class consciousness and anti-imperialist sentiment permeates the document.[75]

This group's impact on the women's suffrage movement after 1924 was considerable, as we will see in the following chapter. Beijing was its main rival for intellectual leadership of the women's movement, and yet practical success for women suffragists was to remain a feature of the "independent" provinces of the South for another few years to come.

DIVISION AND RADICALISM IN BEIJING

The situation in Beijing, the national capital, differed markedly from that elsewhere in the country. As the UWA groups established the notion of women's suffrage as an acceptable part of China's political life in the provinces, the women's groups in Beijing aimed to effect change to the "national" constitution. Political instability in the Beijing government hindered their campaign for suffrage rights. The suffragists' successes in Guangzhou and Hunan depended on the relative stability, albeit recently won, of the governments in these provinces. The women in Beijing were not so fortunate.

The remnants of Yuan Shikai's government lurched from crisis to crisis. In a period of twenty-eight months the presidency had changed three times. Not to be outdone by Sun Yat-sen's government in the South, the northern government decided to write a new constitution, and by 12 August 1919 China had yet another national constitution. Much to the disgust of the women's suffrage campaigners, article 4 of this document stated that "the people of the Chinese republic shall be equal before the law and there shall be no racial, class or religious distinctions."[76] "Sex" was deliberately omitted. Discussion between North and South about national reunification on the basis of this document ceased abruptly when the two major factions of the

Beijing government went to war against each other in July 1920. The ruling clique, led by Duan Qirui was ousted, and a new leadership under Xu Shichang assumed control with backing from the military strongman Zhang Zuolin. Xu instructed the provinces to reelect their representatives based on the 1912 regulations. The southern provinces were unimpressed, and only eleven provinces held elections. Military instability then drew Xu into strife. In June of 1922, Xu resigned from the presidency and Li Yuanhong was recycled, returning to the position he had lost in his spat with Duan Qirui in 1917. The political ambitions of another faction leader, Cao Kun, were to make Li's presidency equally as impotent as and even more short lived than Xu's. Cao Kun bankrupted Beijing politics completely by bribing his way to power. Despite widespread condemnation he succeeded Li on 10 October 1923, and in the twelve months of his presidency another new constitution was completed. It too denied women equal rights with men by declaring in article 5, "Citizens of the Republic of China shall be equal before the law without distinction of race, class or religion."[77] In this short-lived constitution manhood suffrage was limited to those who attained strict property and education requirements.[78] By 1924 the flawed Cao Kun constitution had been replaced by a number of regulations that led in 1926 to a string of regency cabinets.

With each of these changes in government and announcements of constitutional reform, the women's suffrage activists attempted to have sex equality provisions inserted. For example, in the brief period of Li Yuanhong's presidency from mid-1922 to mid-1923, a Constitutional Drafting Committee was established. The Beijing-based women activists lobbied this committee on the issue of sex equality, and on 27 August the committee agreed that the phrase "regardless of sex" would be included in the relevant section of the constitution. On the strength of this promise, jubilant women paraded in the streets making premature celebratory speeches.[79]

Cai Yuanpei, a former president of Beijing University, took up their cause in a very public debate with President Li. In October 1922 he published in the major daily paper *Chenbao* his objection to Li Yuanhong's statement that "at the present time, the level of women is still low and is far too insufficient to consider their participation in politics." Cai responded, saying:

On the question of women's suffrage it is inadvisable to ask whether their [educational] level is sufficient or not. Rather, we should ask whether this issue is correct or not. If women ought to be able to participate in politics, then we ought to immediately grant them suffrage rights, even if their level is insufficient, might it not be that education could remedy this. You absolutely cannot be so stingy as to refuse to grant them this right on the basis that the current level of women is insufficient.[80]

The debate between Cai and Li had been sparked by the activities of two major women's groups that had formed only two months earlier—the Women's Suffrage Association and the Women's Rights League. On 15 July 1922 several women called a meeting to create a single Beijing group to lobby the new constitutional committee for equality between men and women. During the meeting it became apparent that there were irreconcilable personal differences between participants, and in the final analysis two groups were formed. Christina Gilmartin noted that, although the differences were often spoken of as doctrinal there was also an element of personality conflict in the division. She writes, "according to the recollections of Zhou Min, a founding member of the Women's Rights League, the actual—though not stated—reason for the split into two groups was more personal than political: it ultimately boiled down to who was friends with whom."[81] The two groups vied for support in Beijing and across the nation as they attempted to establish sister organizations.

MODERATE RADICALS: WOMEN'S SUFFRAGE ASSOCIATION

The Women's Suffrage Association (*Nüzi canzheng xiejinhui*) was formed in Beijing by a group composed of students from three institutes of higher learning in the city. Wan Pu was from Beijing's China University (*Zhongguo daxue*), Shi Shuqing was enrolled at the National School of Law and Political Science (*Fazheng zhuanmen xuexiao*), and Wang Xiaoying (1901–?) studied at the Women's Normal College (*Beijing nü shida*). Wang was elected president of the group at its inaugural meeting. She would later go on to serve as principal of the Fujian Teachers College.[82]

The Women's Suffrage Association's basic platform centered on the struggle for women's suffrage, but their manifesto reveals how they regarded legal, economic, and education reform as integral to improving women's overall status. It outlined the following three goals: "overthrow the constitution that was written specifically for men and ensure that there are guarantees for women's rights; overthrow the property and inheritance laws that are designed for men and demand economic independence; and overthrow the education system of the power holders and demand equality in access to knowledge."[83] These three points demonstrate the extent to which women's difference from men—indeed women's relative disadvantage to men—was clear within the suffrage movement of the time. No longer speaking just of recovering equality with men, this Beijing group identified men as having more than their fair share of power. Women, within this rhetoric, were implicitly a political collectivity unified by disadvantage.

The Women's Suffrage Association published a journal in which Wan, Shi, and Wang published articles and poems on the importance of suffrage. In the introduction to the first issue the editors explain that winning the right to vote would enable women to fully rely on themselves for economic independence. This self-reliance would emerge from women legislators developing laws that facilitate women's full and equal participation in the economy.[84] Shi Shuqing included an article that reasserted the "right of all people to political participation . . . regardless of their class—and even more so, regardless of their sex. Thus, in the last few hundred years there has been a rising tide of women demanding suffrage and of workers demanding equality . . . this is an unstoppable tide."[85]

Recognizing the familiarity of readers with arguments against suffrage, Wan Pu's contribution to the edition outlined the major objections presented to women's suffrage:

(1) women are physically weak and would not be able to cope with political life, (2) politics is dirty and would pollute women's purity, (3) women are insufficiently educated and therefore should not be involved in politics, (4) women should start with a reform of women's society rather than demand suffrage now, (5) once women get into politics the political scene will be even more crowded with people and even more chaotic, (6) the women who demand suffrage rights are simply those few who want to become officials, and (7) once women enter politics the stability of the family will be destroyed.[86]

Wan refuted each point in turn. If physical strength were the measure of eligibility to vote, then there would be many current male politicians who would be ineligible! Besides, she retorted, although women are generally a little weaker than men this is primarily a result of differences in upbringing. On the matter of politics sullying women's purity, Wan argued that women had obligations as citizens to participate in the reform of the political system to ensure that it ceased to be in such poor shape. Acknowledging the poverty of women's education Wan asserted that not all women had been denied education and therefore assumptions about knowledge levels based on sex were inappropriate. She also queried, "Do all men that currently have the vote come up to this standard [of knowledge]?" In response to the criticism that the suffrage advocates simply wanted to win power, Wan expresses her "boredom." People, she says are "political animals" and women are people just like men. Moreover, she declared, women have been discriminated against for generations precisely because they have been excluded from political power. Thus, of course women want to win power! As to the damaging affects on the stability of the family, Wan declared, the ideal "big family" was already a figment of a distant past imagination. The traditional family was already changing because it had been proven unsuitable for contemporary economic and social changes—keeping women out of politics would not stop this inevitable historical trend.[87]

In a petition to the Beijing government the Women's Suffrage Association made two specific requests for constitutional change. The petition asked that the words "sex" be included in article 3, item 4 where the constitution guarantees equality regardless of class, race, or religion. Secondly, they request that the words "men" should be replaced with "people" in the electoral laws within items 4 and 5. They argued that the stipulation of men's participation in the electoral laws "violates the spirit of the constitution and requires urgent rectification" because the "sovereignty of the Republic of China is vested in the whole of its people." They addressed the common concerns of those opposed to women's suffrage that women were insufficiently qualified to participate in a meaningful fashion by arguing "human knowledge and ability are in direct proportion to the duties and responsibilities one bears. The heavier the burden of duty and responsibility, the faster will be the development of one's knowledge and ability. Therefore women's suffrage would bestow duty and responsibility and thereby cultivate knowledge and ability."[88]

The group was not immune to police harassment. At its first meeting in August 1922 at China University, the police forced the women to disband on the grounds that the Police Ordinances on Public Order—Yuan Shikai's 1914 ruling—prohibited women's political activity. The various Beijing governments' claims to have inherited the mantle of national rule directly from Yuan Shikai provided them with a raft of antidemocratic legislation. Undeterred, the women reconvened their association under the guise of a speech society for women.

Building on the impetus of the Beijing group, a Shanghai branch of the Women's Suffrage Association was established on 15 October 1922. Wan Pu from the Beijing group had gone to Shanghai to help mobilize potential members. WCTU member Wang Liming (aka Liu Wang Liming, 1897–1970), Zhu Jianxia, and Huang Ren'ai were the leaders of the Shanghai branch of the Women's Suffrage Association.[89] They wrote petitions to the Beijing government in relation to the constitution in December 1922. Tan Sheying notes that they started a short-lived monthly journal called *Women Citizens* (*Nü guomin*).[90]

IMMODERATE RADICALS: WOMEN'S RIGHTS LEAGUE

The alternative women's group in Beijing, the Women's Rights League (*Nüquan yundong tongmeng hui*), stood in direct opposition to the Women's Suffrage Association. These women centered on the Women's Normal College and declared themselves to be broader in approach to women's issues than the Women's Suffrage Association.[91] Leading this group were Zhou Min and Zhang Renrui. Their manifesto explored class consciousness and drew heavily on Marxist epistemology where the Women's Suffrage Association had not, and many of the members of the Women's Rights League eventually aligned themselves explicitly with the CCP. The first woman member of the CCP, Hunanese Miao Boying (1899–1929), was one of the league's founding members.[92]

In August 1922 *Shenbao* reported that the group had held a three-hour meeting on suffrage issues. The meeting commenced with participants hearing a history of the suffrage movement in China at the start of the republic indicating that these May Fourth activists knew they were carrying on from a preexisting struggle of a decade earlier. Beijing University professor Li Shouchang addressed the meeting and concluded with three key demands: first, that the Police Ordinances on Public Order be revoked since these restricted women's ability to mobilize for political action; second, that the government include women in the electoral laws; third, that women be included in the workers' protection law.[93] From the League's perspective, women's political rights and workers' rights were intertwined and should be simultaneously advocated. Following this meeting, a petition was organized, and on 8 September 1922 the parliament received the League's letter of demand that the constitution clearly state sex equality in all political rights.[94] League activists also engaged in public media debate. They explicitly defended their members' political competence in response to an article by Fei Juetian that declared: "The significance of the women's suffrage question in China today is not one of whether we ought to grant suffrage or not, but rather whether the competency [among women] exists or not."[95]

Once the central branch of the Women's Rights League had been established, sister associations formed around the nation. On October 29 a Shanghai branch was established with the veteran feminists Hu Binxia and Huang Zonghan at the helm. Huang was also a member of the Shanghai UWA, indicating the degree of convergence among left-leaning women's groups at the time.[96] On 20 December Shandong established a sister branch. It drew over one hundred people to its first meeting at the Women's Normal College. Participants heard that China's thousand-year history of keeping women in the "inner chambers" rendered women dependent upon men and slaves of men.[97] A Tianjin group was established on 28 October 1922 and included among its founders Deng Yingchao (1904–1992), who would become one of the top women leaders of the PRC. The Tianjin branch produced a journal, *Women's Star* (*Nü xing*), that commenced in March 1923. It published broadly on the importance of women's rights, but the rhetoric of its publication announcement is clearly influenced by socialist notions of oppression, class, and gender. The journal's editors point out that both women and the laboring classes suffer untold oppression but because women also suffer the effects of traditional patriarchal practices their oppression is greater than that of the laborers.[98] The study group that formed around the *Women's Star* also published a short-lived newspaper called *Women's Daily* (*Funü ribao*). In October of 1924, after less than a year of operation, the Cao Kun government closed the publication for its radical views.[99]

The general regulations of the Shanghai branch state that the aims of the league are to "extend women's rights and to gain constitutional and legal equality for men and women."[100] Women's particular needs are acknowledged as the concept of women's collective disadvantaged political identity gained acceptability. The manifesto provides a seven-point summary of their demands: (1) all educational institutions in the nation should be open to women; (2) equal rights for men and women should be reflected in the rights enjoyed by citizens in the constitution; (3) in regards to private law all relations between husband and wives, parents, and children in terms of inheritance, conduct, and right to own property should be based on the principle of sex equality, (4) legislate a marriage law that is based on sex equality, (5) include provisions on "age of consent" and legislate that "those who take concubines are in breach of the marriage law," (6) prohibit prostitution, the buying and selling of girls, and foot binding of women, and (7) legislate to protect women factory workers based on the principles of "equal pay for equal work" and the "protection of maternity."[101]

The league's manifesto reveals the tensions between class and sex differentials as understood at that time. It presents sex difference as a form of class difference that must be overcome but maintains that inequality between men and women is more deep-seated and fundamental, and therefore likely to be more difficult to eradicate. In the early 1920s China's left-wing feminists embraced class analysis within an appreciation of disadvantages and inequalities based primarily on sex difference. Indeed, for these women, class consciousness and revolutionary aspirations were integral to their feminist project.

Manifesto of the Women's Rights League

In this era of people's revolution we women should participate in such a revolutionary movement. This is not only our duty but also our right. At the same time we should also not lose sight of our specific responsibility, that is, the women's rights movement. All movements that resist power are revolutionary movements so our women's rights movement is also a kind of revolutionary movement. In terms of our personal interests it is even more important.

We do not believe that true democracy can exist unless we smash the two classes of sex that are men and women. We do not believe that it is possible to have the true happiness that comes from equality in a society where one half are oppressors and the other half oppressed. If a society only allows men opportunities for agency and excludes its female half from all of life other than family life, then how can that society not be a despotic society? How can it be a society that is imbued with the spirit of democracy? In politics the meaning of "people" naturally encompasses both sexes. Democratic politics that are limited to men are *definitely not* pure democratic politics. The term "people" is not a special term for "men," rather it is a general name for the whole of the people that includes both men and women. The only true democracy is one in which all the people have the right to participate in politics. In society, differences of class can be easily eliminated. It is only the natural differences between the two sexes that have any permanence. If we do not completely eradicate the class differences that have occurred along with these permanent natural differences, then class oppression will continue to exist on the basis of these differences. For this reason our demand for democracy between the sexes is imperative! The responsibility we shoulder with respect to the revolutionary campaign for democracy between the sexes is also of paramount importance.[102]

NEW CULTURE, NEW WOMEN, NEW POLITICS

The women's movement of the New Culture period was typified by its increasingly confident assertion of the necessity of women's equal political rights with men, but more important, this claim was made within the context of their simultaneous assertion that women's political interests were fundamentally different from men's and thereby deserving of representation. China's feminists engaged with the increasingly broad acceptance of cross-class alliances for political purposes promoted by the emerging left wing, but they adapted this awareness to their own cause. Women of all classes were a diverse but still distinctly definable group with collective political interests that drew from their similar disadvantage to men.

The constitutional successes of the early 1920s placed more women into the formal political roles than had ever been seen before in China's history. The impact of this public role would be felt in the next decade as women lobbied from within and without the CCP and Nationalist Party structures. Indeed, the maturing of the women activists' political knowledge and skills that occurred during these years happened in tandem with the consolidation of the broader political scene in China. The emergence of the CCP in 1921 and the reformulation of the Nationalist Party in 1922–1923 were major influences on the women's movement of this time. As we will see in the following chapter, both major parties had immensely complex attitudes toward the women's suffrage movement. The united front between the two parties presented an unusual set of alliances among the increasingly politically diverse women's movement: the suffrage movement originally conceived as being situated within a parliamentary democracy was evolving into a movement to participate in politics, whatever the shape of that politics.

FIVE

Nationalists, Communists, and the National Assembly Movement, 1924–1926

The women's suffrage activism in the New Culture period achieved important but partial successes. While key provinces had promulgated constitutions embedding sex equality in political rights and several women were serving in Hunan and Guangdong assemblies, victory at a national level remained elusive. The major stumbling blocks were competing claims to leadership by Sun Yat-sen in Guangzhou and Duan Qirui in Beijing, as well as the continued presence of powerful regional warlords. Nationwide women's suffrage would be impossible to lobby for without a unified government to persuade. Achieving constitutional uniformity remained an important legitimizing goal for those who claimed to rule the nation—including the women activists. Nonetheless, as we saw in the previous chapter, this period of dramatic intellectual shifts in thinking about Chinese culture had produced a consciousness of women's different political interests from men as a group—and importantly that this difference was based on women's common disadvantaged status relative to men. Moreover, nationalism and patriotism were important catch cries for all people active in politics during these years, but in contrast to the first fifteen years of the twentieth century, in the New Culture period these terms invoked "national unification and anti-imperialism" whereas in the earlier period they signified anti-Manchu or antiforeign sentiments.[1] The relationship of China's feminist movement to these nationalist or patriotic goals necessarily evolved as the scope of the latter agenda changed.

The situation for political parties in China was undergoing equally fundamental reorientations. In the early 1920s the ground was laid for the emergence of the key political tensions of the next several decades—the variously symbiotic and fiercely competitive relationship between the CCP and the Nationalist Party. This chapter explores the explosive impact of the changing relationships between these two parties and their ideological positions on the women's suffrage movement. In so doing it reveals the extent to which the women's movement was central to the evolution of both practical planning and philosophical conceptualizations about improving the quality and effectiveness of formal politics in China. In regards to the CCP's evolution, Gilmartin has pointed out that gender provides crucial insights into "the development of the party as an institution, the meaning of the party to its early members, and the process through which leaders gained power and legitimized their exercise of authority."[2] This excellent point is no less the case when one considers the evolution of the Nationalist Party. Now recognized as a legitimate political constituency deserving of representation, women activists were able to influence formal politics with greater efficacy than ever before. Indeed, women's engagement with formal politics in both the party and legislative arenas was to become a central feature of all subsequent political reforms in the republican period. During the New Culture period, suffrage activists demonstrated the strength of women's collective political identity in their influence on party politics. In contrast, Lucien Bianco noted that China's peasants, even as late as 1937, did not have a class or patriotic consciousness that enabled their ready participation in politics.[3] Women activists created women's collective political identity over the course of the decades from the start of the century, and by the New Culture period they had won recognition for the legitimacy of this identity among their male peers—the intellectual and political reformist, urban elites. Thus recognized, the women activists' influence on formal politics emerged.

China's women's suffrage activists, and women's rights activists more generally, joined forces with the two parties just as they had with the Revolutionary Alliance in the years prior to 1912. The challenge for the women of the 1920s remained, as it had in 1912, to ensure that each party's political machinery did not use women's rights as an optional extra or a bargaining chip to win other political goals. Indeed, as this chapter will argue, both major parties were more firmly committed to the basic principle of women's equal rights with men than China's political leaders of a decade earlier, but they were also very concerned to make sure that feminism did not jeopardize their "primary" political campaigns. Moreover, as a wider variety of women joined the movement, a broader and more complex array of political views and party agendas needed to be considered. Women's suffrage, conceived as it primarily was along parliamentary-democratic lines, was more problematic for the CCP than it was for the Nationalist Party. The latter espoused an ultimate vision of parliamentary-like democracy for China whereas the former linked this government system with bourgeois political interests and was at best a staging post on the way to rule by the proletariat. Yet the women's suffrage call had mobilized many urban women and neither party could ignore them, as we will see below in the discussion on the 1924–1925 National Assembly movement.

For the Nationalist Party, at the time the largest and most organized of the two parties, the major political agenda was reunification of the North and the South and the suppression of the warlord-led military domination of some sections of the country. For the newly formed CCP, while national unification was no doubt important, fomenting class consciousness and mobilizing China's workers into a political movement remained an important dual agenda. The boundaries between the two parties blurred during the period known as the First United Front (1924–1927). The cooperation between the two parties had emerged as part of Sun's campaign to revitalize the Nationalist Party when in the first few years of the 1920s the Comintern had provided finances and organizational strategy advice to the Nationalists. Sun was keen to improve party discipline in order to confirm premier status for the Nationalist Party as the body that could reunite and lead China. Following advice from his Comintern mentors, Sun welcomed members of the newly formed CCP to join the Nationalist Party. The Comintern deemed cooperation between the two as necessary for a successful "socialist" revolution. Sun welcomed the Communists for he hoped that their networks in the labor and agrarian movements would draw wider support for national unification from among the working classes and peasantry and prevent fragmentation based on class divisions. Similarly, the Communists made ready use of the larger Nationalist Party—especially its

Comintern-funded military wing and its well-established links with various urban women's groups. The immediate goal of the United Front was national reunification, but both political parties also saw in it the chance to strengthen their position relative to the other.

The campaign to unify the country began in Canton in 1926 when Sun Yat-sen embarked upon his long-awaited Northern Expedition with forces that combined members from both the CCP and the Nationalist Party. Led by the military commander Chiang Kai-shek, it was completed by the end of 1928 and China entered a period of Nationalist government in which the population was to be "prepared" for democracy again. Sun's death in 1925 prevented him from witnessing this moment of national unity. It also spared him the brutality of Chiang's attempt at eradicating the CCP and other left-wing members of the Nationalist Party in 1927.[4] The imprisonment, persecution, and execution of the left wing ruptured the cooperation between the two parties. As we shall see later, the schism between the CCP and the Nationalists had dramatic effects on the women's suffrage movement. China's feminist movement drew supporters from the left, the right, and the middle ground between the two parties, and the split in the United Front made such cooperation highly problematic, but not impossible. Nonetheless, in the dark days of Chiang's crackdown politically active women like the suffrage activists were in grave physical danger, and some paid with their lives.

EQUALITY BETWEEN COMRADES: EVOLVING PARTY CONSTITUTIONS

Women's suffrage activists had good historical reasons to be suspicious of the male-dominated Nationalist Party system. In 1912 women within the Revolutionary Alliance had been betrayed by their male comrades when sex equality was removed from the party platform of the newly formed party. Yet by the early 1920s almost all the major women's suffrage groups had rallied behind the Nationalist Party. The crucial difference between 1912 and 1922 was that the dramatic intellectual changes that had occurred as a result of the New Culture Movement ensured that women's equal rights with men was no longer perceived as problematic, and in Sun's revamping of the party this became evident. By the end of 1922 Sun's committee to revise the new party constitution had completed its task, and on 1 January 1923 Hu Hanmin announced a manifesto of the reorganized Nationalist Party.[5]

The one hundred and sixty-five delegates that attended the first party congress passed the new party constitution. This document confirmed women's equal status with men in the party organization and, without any of the vitriolic debate that had occurred in 1912, overturned the ruling on male membership. Point 12 of the manifesto stated, "Legal, economic, educational, and social equality between the sexes should be recognized, and the development of women's rights should be encouraged." It also committed the revitalized party to universal suffrage through the eradication of "class suffrage based on property qualification." But in a statement that reaffirmed the importance of education to political power, the following provision declared, "Competitive examinations should be established to supply the deficiency of the electoral systems."[6] This caveat provides evidence that the literacy provisions in the provincial constitutions discussed in the previous chapter reflected a widely held position among China's political class—the belief that only educated citizens should be directly represented and serve as representatives.

Significantly, the revised Nationalist Party also introduced a number of standing committees or bureaus to its department structure. These standing committees included peasants, workers, and women and had duplicate bodies at the provincial level around the nation. Each was charged with the duty of investigating the current experience of their constituents in China and overseas and then presenting recommendations to the party. The goals behind the establishment of the women's bureau were outlined as: "To acknowledge the principle of equality between the sexes, to help promote the development of women's rights."[7] The establishment of these women's bureaus is evidence of the broad acceptance of the notion that women had special political interests distinct from men's—women were by the early 1920s a legitimate political collectivity with legitimate political rights. The ideological space created by left-wing conceptions of the importance of representing disadvantaged groups was central to this breakthrough. Women, like peasants and workers, developed a collective identity based on their disadvantaged status. Women's right to equality with men was never questioned within this rubric—indeed, their distinct political needs as a group was premised on recognition of this point. Women's political needs were thus institutionalized in the party structure.

The CCP had formed in July 1921 in Shanghai from the merger of the Shanghai and Beijing left-wing groups headed by Chen Duxiu and Li Dazhao. Its constitution had from the outset provisions for sex equality of members, and its rhetoric of emancipation was appealing to many women. The early CCP leaders regarded participation in and integration with existing women's organizations as crucial to winning support from politically active women, and accordingly prominent male CCP members became active in publishing and making speeches to women through the existing channels forged by the UWAs and more directly through participation in the formation of the Women's Rights League.

The incorporation of the CCP into the Nationalist Party also resulted in a core of CCP women eventually dominating the Nationalist Party's Women's Bureau. CCP leader Xiang Jingyu (1895–1928) was named head of the Shanghai Women's Movement Bureau of the Nationalist Party in April of 1924 (see Figure 5.1). She performed vital functions in establishing the bureau's structures and was responsible for disseminating information about national affairs to women and developing contact with the full range of women's groups.[8] It was hoped that the Nationalist Party's women's committee would be able to act in a coordinating role for existing groups as well as encourage participation from women who were yet to be involved. Andrea McElderry summarized the paradox of the CCP women charged with

中國國民黨上海執行部婦女運動委員會全體會員

Figure 5.1. Nationalist Party, Shanghai, Women's Bureau. *Funü zazhi* (The Ladies' Journal) 10, no. 8 (1924).

mobilizing women for the United Front as follows. "Communist women were to seek to establish themselves at the centre of the national women's movement but were to avoid being absorbed by it."[9]

The Bureau included many women who would become prominent in the communist movement in China. Yang Zhihua (1900–1973) and Wang Yizhi (1901–1991) assisted Xiang Jingyu in Shanghai. He Xiangning (an early Revolutionary Alliance member discussed in Chapter Two) headed the Guangzhou office. Deng Yingchao and Cai Chang (1900–1990) assisted her in the South. Christina Gilmartin describes in detail the difficulties these women faced in mobilizing women for the CCP cause in Guangzhou.[10] Cai Chang's family had strong connections with radical politics in China. Her mother, Ge Jianhao, had been a close friend of the revolutionary martyr Qiu Jin and had continued her support of radical change by traveling to France in 1919 where she grew increasingly supportive of the communist cause. Cai Chang's brother, Cai Hesen, was Xiang Jingyu's common-law husband in the early 1920s and was one of the most active Marxist theorists of the CCP throughout the 1920s. Cai Chang herself was to become one of China's most resilient women activists. She traveled in Europe, visiting France and the Soviet Union in the 1920s, returning to China to assume her positions in the CCP and United Front hierarchy.[11]

Yang Zhihua's life is a microcosm of the travails of the United Front over the 1920s. She married the son of a Nationalist Party member on her parents' advice and was drawn further into politics under the influence of her father-in-law. However, with the establishment of the CCP her interests gradually shifted farther to the left. By 1922 she had joined the Communist Youth League and by 1924 had become a full member of the CCP. She met prominent CCP intellectual Qu Qiubai while studying at university in Shanghai, and amid much scandal she divorced her husband and married Qu.[12] It was during this turbulent emotional situation that she undertook political work for the Women's Bureau.

These CCP women were no doubt committed to the feminist cause, yet they were subject to their political party's ambiguous perspective on so-called "bourgeois feminism." Women were a recognized disadvantaged group, and thereby deserving of special political consideration, yet among their members were women who sought power in a noncommunist system. Gender politics thus constructed were complex and ambiguous in ideological significance. Internationally the suffrage cause was aligned with a broad cross-section of political forces—only one of which was the communist

movement, and for the most part Communists remained skeptical of suffragists. The CCP came to view women's suffrage as a deviation and a tan-
gent to the real cause of class revolution. There were clear tensions within
the CCP about the connection between the internationalism of "bourgeois
feminism" and the internationalism of communist philosophy's principle of
class struggle. How did the CCP understand the links between these twin
global movements?

The first few years of the 1920s saw considerable CCP involvement in the
mainstream women's movement, including the women's suffrage campaign,
ostensibly on behalf of the United Front and the national revolution. In
this regard the Communists gained an important introduction into the active and enthusiastic women's movement. Ultimately, however, the CCP
was more interested in incorporating women in the labor union movement
than it was with facilitating the cause of women's suffrage. CCP founder
and Marxist theoretician, Li Dazhao, had been sympathetic to the women's
suffrage cause. In 1919, prior to the formal establishment of the CCP, Li
had hailed the virtues of the women's suffrage movement as a natural consequence of the burgeoning spirit of democracy wherein people have equal
opportunities to develop themselves in all spheres regardless of race, gender,
class, or background. He asked, "Why should women allow themselves to
be trampled under men's feet? Even before the Great War the movement
for women's suffrage had its own history of struggle. The movement was
already in progress in many American states." However, he closed his speech
by stating that, internationally, the women's suffrage movement has been
relevant to middle-class women and not to the working classes. Ultimately,
he argued, class issues must be addressed for the following reasons:

> The interests of middle-class women do not represent the interests of all
> women; the expansion of middle-class women's rights cannot be called lib-
> eration of all women. I think that the way to resolve women's problems
> completely is, on the one hand, to consolidate the power of all women to
> smash the patriarchal system; on the other hand, we must also consolidate
> the power of the proletarian women of the world, to smash that arbitrary
> social system of the capitalist class (including men and women).[13]

In fact, both CCP elders, Li Dazhao and Chen Duxiu, had already become well-known figures in the UWAs around the nation as speakers and contributors to various women's journals. One of Chen's speeches, titled "Women and Socialism," was presented to the Guangdong UWA on 30 January 1921—six months prior to the formation of the CCP. It argued that "the women question will be fundamentally resolved only when socialism arrives." This, Chen stated, is because socialism will ensure that everybody, including women, is given economic independence, and once women have economic independence they will have the dignity that is currently denied them restored.[14] Access to middle-class women was clearly imperative for the propagation of theories of class struggle because, as the left-wing writer Shen Yanbing (aka Mao Dun) had noted in 1920, "since upper- and lower-class women cannot take on the important tasks of the women's movement, middle-class women—the wives and young ladies of middle-class families—are our only hope. . . . Have no fear; you have your little sisters of the lower-class, and you can raise them up and fight together with you."[15]

Indeed, even into the early 1920s any CCP opposition to women's suffrage by both men and women members remained muted. The CCP was careful not to alienate the existing women's suffrage groups in their political messages. For example, the CCP's National Congress Resolution on the Women's Movement of 23 July 1922 noted that there were three immediate struggles for the women's movement. These were imperfect in and of themselves but were nonetheless necessary stages in the progress toward true liberation for women. True liberation would occur after the establishment of a proletarian dictatorship, but in the meantime CCP activists should assist women to win ordinary suffrage rights and all other political rights and freedoms; protect the interests of women and child workers; and smash the fetters of the values of the old society.[16] While performing these tasks in concert with existing women's groups, CCP members were instructed to teach women that any successes on these three fronts would merely be "staging posts" on the path to full liberation under a Communist revolution. On this view, Communist support for the women's movement was a political convenience—not an unpleasant or completely calculating convenience, but a complex alliance nonetheless.

The 1923 congress expressed a similar sentiment with the comment that the "regular women's movement such as the women's rights movement, the suffrage movement and the movement to abolish prostitution are extremely important." Moreover they warned, "First, we must not look down upon these young ladies and madams or the women politicians' movement and second, the color of the doctrine of class should not be too sudden or too concentrated, this could cause them to be frightened."[17]

In 1926, only months prior to the collapse of the United Front, a meeting of the CCP Executive Committee reiterated the importance of maintaining good relations with all women's groups in order to strengthen the CCP's reach among politically active women: "We must (1) pay attention to women's own interests, (2) give appropriate respect to the objectives of the various other women's organizations when movements occur, and (3) avoid situations where we monopolize or cause other types of unnecessary conflicts."[18]

The amount of space devoted to explaining the CCP's connection to the existing women's movement in these very brief documents reveals the extent to which early Communist efforts at garnering support among women depended on these groups. Indeed, these early years of the CCP are marked by its public tolerance of women's suffrage as a legitimate and immediately achievable goal. In private, many CCP members had strong reservations about the suffrage cause.

Through this same period CCP documents show the party's concern to maintain class as the key focus. At the Fourth Communist Party Congress held in January of 1925, party workers were advised not to allow the "general women's movement" (*yi ban de funü yundong*) to hamper broader political goals: "We must clearly demonstrate the pointlessness of disputes that divide men from women for they hamper the closer integration of the women's movement into the nationalist and workers' movement."[19] At the third meeting of the party's Central Executive Committee in September 1926, party workers were exhorted to be careful about integrating too closely with the general women's movement in case it led them to ignore the needs of the masses. The party's main focus should be workers, peasants, and students.[20] The Women's Bureau reported in February of 1927 to the Central Executive Committee that the ordinary women's movement "certainly will not be much use in the real revolutionary battle front."[21]

Clearly, negotiating the tension between the struggle for sex equality and the primacy of the class revolution was central to the CCP's engagement with the United Front women's campaigns. Notions of women's collective unity of disadvantage were constantly negotiated against their conceptions of class divisions. The women's movement was able to maintain its identity and credibility as a legitimate political interest group in part because of the expanding left-wing rhetoric about the importance of giving voice to the disadvantaged. While women promoted themselves as unjustly disadvantaged they could maintain a dynamic and complex relationship with groups like the CCP that focused on class differences. Nowhere is this negotiation more evident than in the writings of a key woman CCP activist, Xiang Jingyu.

BATTLING FOR THE BOURGEOIS MIND: XIANG JINGYU ON WOMEN'S SUFFRAGE

Xiang Jingyu is second to none in the communist hagiography of the party's women's activists. As a martyred revolutionary she has been readily hailed for her great sacrifice to the cause. She was born in Hunan and took advantage of the growth in girls' schooling opportunities in China by attending local institutions before leaving to study in France for two years with leading Communist, Cai Hesen. Cai became her common-law husband during this time. On her return to China in late 1921, she joined the CCP and in the following three years assumed the task of mobilizing the women of China. In 1925 she was relieved of her post as a result of a romantic affair that exacerbated internal conflict within the central committee. She requested to be sent to the Soviet Union to study. When she returned in 1927, Chiang Kai-shek's purge of the CCP was at its peak, and in 1928 police in Hankou's French Concession handed her to Nationalist authorities. She was executed by firing squad on 1 May 1928.

Her opinions on women's suffrage were clearly influenced by European Communist opposition to "bourgeois" movements. What good would it really do for women to vote in a bourgeois parliamentary democracy when working-class "miseries will only be prolonged in this system?"[22] Yet the objective conditions of the United Front in China dictated unity with the bourgeois classes. In Xiang Jingyu's writing we see the fraught nature of the CCP's early connections with the women's suffrage movement. She acknowledged, in her 1923 summary article "The Chinese Women's Movement at the Present Moment" for the communist magazine *The Vanguard* (*Qianfeng*), that the women's suffrage movement was a major force for mobilizing women in China. However, she tempered this comparatively supportive comment with a statement that the suffrage cause reflected only privileged women's concerns. It was merely a diversion for those women

who relied on their fathers, husbands, and sons for a livelihood by dab-
bling in "freedom."[23] As would be expected from an orthodox Communist,
Xiang Jingyu's great passion was manifest in her energetic organizing of the
women workers in Shanghai, and her writing directed at the middle-class
feminists aimed to draw them into this movement. Catherine Gipoulon
has argued that during the two years prior to her departure for the Soviet
Union in 1925, Xiang "persistently tried to integrate them [the 'bourgeois
feminists'] into the workers' movement. . . . This interest in bringing these
'class enemies' over to the right cause testifies to a certain open-mindedness
and shows an absence of scorn for educated bourgeois women."[24] This political perspective did not mean that Xiang was a Communist in feminist
disguise. Gilmartin has demonstrated clearly that "she poured an extraordinary amount of energy into creating a voice for herself in the world of
independent women's groups in Shanghai, establishing a foundation for a
broad-based women's movement, and utilizing the resources of the Nationalist Party to consolidate her program."[25]

Xiang also attempted to increase the women's awareness of the global
struggle against capitalist oppression by invoking the internationalism
of their own movement. In the December issue of *The Vanguard* she ex-
pounded on the importance of internationalization of all anti-imperialist
forces in a report on the International League for Women's Rights congress
held in Rome in May of 1923. Xiang stresses that the women's suffrage movement—with its twin agenda of gender equality and world peace—required
unity with all oppressed groups.[26] In the same issue she published a short
article on the Chinese women's movement describing their efforts in 1923
as miserable and noted that the media routinely ignored their campaign
initiatives. Their voices are "like footsteps in an empty valley."[27] That same
year she wrote that the women's suffrage activism of the provinces in recent
years was simply "wasting the energy of nine oxen and two tigers, and even
though there may be the occasional victory, in the end it is bound to be
only a rather short-lived and pitiful movement."[28]

In a 1923 article responding to one by Wang Bihua, president of the
Zhejiang UWA, Xiang provides a comprehensive critique of the women's
suffrage movement—scathingly referred to as the "movement to become
officials." Wang had advocated the importance of women's participation in
the political process as a key method of ensuring that women's legal rights
with men were attained. In response, Xiang first highlighted the class-
specific nature of Wang's concerns. So what if women get equal inheritance

and property rights with men? This is only a cause for celebration among the women whose family has property to distribute. Second, she argued that women's involvement in the present corrupt political process would simply corrupt those who enter parliament, since their lives as officials would cause their commitment to principles of women's rights to wither. These women will "enter white and exit black," she wrote. Xiang summarized her arguments about the sullying effects of political participation by saying, "In reality, the movement to become an official is like immersing a mud Buddha in water." Third, she raised the point that the current political situation in China was so chaotic and prone to rapid change that it was very doubtful that any legislative gains would ever be implemented. Would they not merely be reduced to nominal reforms of "black words on white paper?" She then went on to draw the reader's attention to the effects of women's rights activists in parliament by raising doubts about the effectiveness of the presence of Wang Changguo in the Hunan provincial assembly.[29] Thus, to Xiang, women's participation in the parliamentary system is destined to be ineffectual and, worse still, would have a negative effect on the personal lives of those women who participate.

She elaborates further, arguing that "the true significance of the women's movement is not in the battle of the sexes. When women's rights are suppressed, society is paralyzed. So who would object when women themselves take action? But if women are only concerned with 'women's rights' (*nüquan*) and show no concern for 'national rights' (*guoquan*) . . . then they will themselves strip away their human dignity (*ren'ge*) and people's dignity (*min'ge*)." She continued to argue that women should be active in politics in order to prevent enslavement of China by imperialist aggression. If China were enslaved, it would not matter whether women had their rights or not. "Thus, truly awakened women of China will be active in both the movement for political reform and the women's liberation movement."[30]

The CCP's attempts at integration with the existing women's movement posed particular challenges for Xiang Jingyu—she played a key role in enunciating the importance of links between the workers' movement and the women's movement. In 1923 she wrote a lengthy article on the state of the women in the national revolution for the bourgeois women's magazine, *The Ladies' Journal*, in which she concentrated primarily on exploring issues of Marxist theories of imperialism and capitalism and the importance of workers to the overthrow of that structure. Her link to women's liberation appears more than a little strained when she finally

comes to the issue in the last three paragraphs. There was a natural partnership between women's liberation and workers' liberation, she asserted.
Women and workers both occupy positions as slaves because of the economic circumstances that she had earlier elaborated at length. However,
relying on the women's movement alone would not solve women's problems—for that to occur a total revolutionary transformation in the economic system was required.[31] "If the suffrage movement is successful then
it simply means that a whole bunch of women will enter the pigsties of
Beijing and the provinces where together with the male pigs, they can pre-
side over the nation's calamities and the people's misfortunes."[32]

Despite Xiang's disdain for the strivings of women's movement activists to "become officials," under her leadership the Shanghai Women's Bureau produced a manifesto that demonstrated the extent to which in 1924
women's suffrage rights, national political unity, and constitutional reform
were bound to the United Front. In this manifesto we again see clearly the
deep suspicion with which CCP women like Xiang regarded the notion of
constitutional parliamentary democracy. Instead, unity with the masses and
not the male parliamentarians was proposed:

Manifesto of the Shanghai Women's Movement Committee

For several thousand years, we, the women of China, have been nothing but appendages of men, baby-producing machines and domestic slaves
but gradually we have become aware of our individual status and consequently, we are demanding our rights. Thus, the women's rights and suffrage
campaigns that have already been played out in various Western nations are
being reenacted for the Eastern stage. . . .

What then exactly is our ideal benchmark for the women's rights and suffrage campaigns that we are so ardently and bravely about to undertake?

Regarding our demand for women's rights—is it enough to merely attain
equal status with that of the average man in current-day China?

Regarding our demand for women's suffrage—do we want to wallow in
the mire and with the likes of the present stinking warlord-kept swine of the
parliamentarians and be the equals of that bunch of pigs? . . . Can we bear to
throw our open and honest suffrage movement into this pigsty?

Fundamentally speaking, China's movement for women's rights and suffrage is a progressive movement, an innovative movement, a movement that
carries the style of twentieth-century human liberation. Then its ideal objective does not just consist of achieving equal status with ordinary Chinese
men. Rather, on the one hand, it demands legal, economic, educational, and
social equality between men and women. On the other, it demands enthusiastic participation in the mass revolutionary movement to overthrow the

various big power holders and northern warlords, in order to prevent domestic and foreign oppression of the Chinese. An innovative path, in the sense of cooperation, is the only path for the suffrage movement because only through this method can we build the foundations of our women's rights and suffrage movements. Only by this method can we, from our principles of the mutuality of rights and responsibilities, make the leap from a position as stragglers to one at the vanguard.

The Chinese Nationalist Party, all in all, has more than thirty years of revolutionary history. After this year's reorganization it has even further determined its historical mission. . . . Sisters, if you have completely woken to the necessity of the participation of the women's rights movement and the women's suffrage movement in the national revolution then you had best unite under the Nationalist Party's banner with the awakened masses in your locality and wage persistent and widespread struggle!

The Nationalist Party is the representative of the interests of the masses. The representatives of the masses' interests absolutely cannot neglect women who constitute half their number. Moreover, women have their own special interests. The Nationalist Party faithfully and sincerely vows to represent the special interests of women. Consequently, after reorganizing its Central Executive Committee it has worked together with the Beijing, Shanghai, and Hankou executives to establish a Women's Bureau to specifically handle the task of fighting for women's interests. We hope that politically awakened elements . . . will bring to fruition the following article of the Nationalist Party's political platform:

> "To legally, economically, educationally, and socially affirm the principle of equality between men and women and to help advance the development of women's rights."[33]

This manifesto reflects the ambiguities of building United Front political constituencies based on common disadvantage. Women were disadvantaged and therefore different from men, yet they did not uniformly have the same markers of disadvantage relative to other identifiable disadvantaged groups—like workers. Yet, the strength and diversity of the women's movement ensured that they could not be subsumed into another group or ignored. Activist women were a force to be contended with in China, and through women like Xiang Jingyu, their collective political identity within party politics was sustained. Xiang Jingyu's disdain for the long-term benefits of the suffrage movement, and her impatience with the urban middle-class women's movement in general, influenced the movement's rhetoric on women's suffrage—stripping it of some of its optimism about parliamentarianism. To Xiang, revolutionary political change, not constitutional reform, was required for the liberation of women. Indeed, in her writing we see the

beginning of the transformation in the connotation of the term *canzheng*.
To Xiang "suffrage" was already best conceived as "participation in politics"—parliamentary-style democracies were not central to her notion of
political engagement. Regardless of her discomfort with parliamentary suffragism, in November of 1924 she was instrumental in the success of a new
women's group that formed to press the case for the inclusion of women in
a National Assembly that Sun Yat-sen announced he would convene.[34]

ASSERTING WOMEN'S COLLECTIVE IDENTITY: THE NATIONAL ASSEMBLY MOVEMENT

Looking back on the history of the Chinese women's movement from a
1927 perspective, Yang Xianjiang described the Women's National Assembly
Conference campaign of 1924–1925 as the important third stage of the overall
Chinese women's movement. Yang identifies the first stage as women's participation in the 1911 revolution and the second as their involvement in the
May Fourth activities.[35] The 1924–25 National Assembly Conference campaign was prompted by Sun Yat-sen's call for a national summit designed to
reunite the country under one government by drawing the political interests
of the North and the South to the negotiating table. It was among the first
major political initiatives Sun undertook after revamping the Nationalist
Party in 1923. Accordingly, in communication with the newly restored head
of government in the North, Duan Qirui, Sun sought to end the divisive
schism between North and South with this National Assembly conference.
Seeing the opportunity to ensure that women's rights were embedded in
any foundational agreements, the women in the United Front formed an
umbrella organization called the Women's National Assembly Promotion
Association (WNAPA; *Nüjie guomin huiyi cucheng hui*).[36] The WNAPA was
a women's version of the National Assembly Promotion Association. The
latter simply aimed to promote Sun's meeting whereas the former had the
additional agenda of ensuring that women were included in all aspects of
the meeting and the assembly that would emerge from the meeting. Xiang
Jingyu and WNAPA drew all major women's groups into the campaign for
a National Assembly. The major suffrage groups were naturally enthusiastic
about the notion of a National Assembly, and they regarded women's participation in the campaign to form this new body as central to ensuring sex
equality in a future national constitution and ancillary laws.

Ultimately, like most of the political strategies employed in China during these years, the National Assembly Promotion movement was to be a short-lived campaign. Duan Qirui announced that he would convene an "Aftermath Conference" (*shanhou huiyi*) in a matter of weeks and the National Assembly within three months. However, the division between the two men proved too great. Duan and Sun failed to reach agreement on the participant list—Duan wanted to include more military interests and Sun favored a greater civilian involvement (dominated of course by Nationalist Party members and sympathizers). Duan and Sun continued their struggle over the participant list for the Aftermath Conference through the winter of December and January 1924–25. Eventually, the Nationalist Party pulled out of talks with Duan. The Aftermath Conference was held on 1 February 1925 without Nationalist Party imprimatur and specifically excluded women's organizations.[37] In response, Sun decided to hold a "people's" National Assembly conference and excluded Duan and his supporters from the meeting. This assembly was convened during the whole of the month of March 1925 and, as we will see below, resulted in a number of statements about sex equality. The optimism of the "people's" assembly meeting was overshadowed by Sun's declining health, and midway through the conference he died of liver cancer. With both North and South at an impasse, a military solution to national unity appeared to be the only available option. Following the demise of the movement's leader, WNAPAs also gradually ceased their activities.

Although a short-lived campaign, in the five months of their existence the WNAPAs demonstrated the high level of political and organizational skills present within the United Front women's movement at this time. As they had demonstrated with speedy action during the provincial government movements, the WNAPA women moved quickly as soon as they saw an opportunity to promote their cause. As soon as they heard about Sun's plan to convene an assembly, the women acted to advocate for women's participation. As November drew to a close and publicity about the formation of a participant list circulated, the Shanghai WNAPA lobbied Sun Yat-sen directly, arguing that women's special interests deserved specific representation in the assembly. They pressed their case invoking the importance of mobilizing all the people, not just men for the antiwarlord, anti-imperialist push. Finally they reminded Sun that the Nationalist Party's constitution explicitly espoused sex equality and the importance of promoting women's rights.[38]

In subsequent weeks WNAPA members were active in their publishing and media activities. One article in *Shenbao* stressed the necessity for the proposed assembly to include representatives from women's organizations. The women did not simply want women members participating in the assembly; they also wanted specific representation from women's groups so as to ensure that the feminist agenda would be addressed in any deliberations.[39] Zhang Xichen wrote that a common logic circulating was that "the National Assembly is the citizens' assembly. Women are also citizens. Therefore women ought to participate in the National Assembly."[40] The Women's Suffrage Association supported the campaign by releasing press statements about the National Assembly of their own accord. One article traced the genealogy of the women's suffrage movement from 1911 and presented the National Assembly movement and WNAPA as the contemporary culmination of this struggle for women's political rights. They exhorted women to join this noble struggle.[41] This group later released a three-point plan of action for its members. First to send messages to all the women's groups around China about the movement, second to send messages of complaint to Sun Yat-sen and Duan Qirui, third to encourage the holding of the National Assembly as quickly as possible.[42]

As a key leader in this movement, Xiang Jingyu promoted awareness of the women's campaign in a discussion paper in the *Women's Weekly News* (*Funü zhoubao*). The article argued that specific women's representation in the National Assembly was vital because, as a result of historical and institutionalized prejudices against women, it was unlikely that women would be nominated as representatives in any other sectors. Moreover, she pointed out that the existing women's groups had the mandate to represent women's concerns and to ensure that they are addressed within the assembly's deliberations. The matters of particular concern to women included protection of mothers, equality in political rights, marriage laws, inheritance rights, employment opportunity, and access to education. In an echo of the strategies used by women in the 1911 revolution, Xiang concluded by arguing that women's rights would benefit the entire nation of China. "This would not only benefit women but would also benefit men and the nation."[43] A woman writing in Xiang's paper by the name of Chen Wenqing saw China's reform as embedded within women's rights. She wrote that the reform and repair of China's currently chaotic political system would commence once women participated in formal politics.[44]

In early December the women began coordinating the diverse women's groups in joint action. *Shenbao* reports on 9 December 1924 that a meeting of over ten women's groups was convened to develop strategies for enhancing women's involvement in the assembly. In addition to the Women's Suffrage Association representatives from student groups such as the Jing Ping Women's Students' Association, the Chinese Women's Physical Education School Association, the Shanghai University's Pingmin Women's School, and the Shanghai University Women Students' Association attended. Workers associations' representatives, such as the Hua Shang Tobacco Workers' Association, also joined the meeting.[45] As was common to every women's association of the previous two decades, the inaugural WNAPA meeting produced a constitution.[46] In order to promote the cause more broadly among women, they sent a telegraph alerting women to the problem and calling on them to mobilize quickly; "time is running out for this matter of life or death."[47] WNAPA resolved to convene a general meeting as a show of strength later in the month.[48]

Held in Shanghai on 21 December 1924, this larger gathering drew over six hundred women. Prominent suffragist Liu Wang Liming (1897–1970) chaired the meeting. The women linked their campaign for women's rights to that of the national crisis in government, with one speaker explaining that women wanted to participate in the National Assembly in order to help solve the nation's problems and also liberate women. Women, the speaker argued, had no freedom in marriage choice, nor did they enjoy equality in inheritance rights, and moreover, the education of women had not flourished. Those attending the meeting heard that to achieve these feminist goals in conjunction with the agenda of national unification, it was crucial that women participate in that assembly.[49]

Following quickly on the establishment of the Shanghai branch, affiliate WNAPAs formed around the country, including Beijing, Nanjing, Hangzhou, and Guangzhou. Prominent CCP member Deng Yingchao formed the branch in Tianjin. In its first major announcement, the Tianjin group identified several non–gender-related issues that they recommended the assembly address. These included matters such as overturning the unequal treaties, the provision of support for China's refugees, the suppression of corruption, tax reform, and an improvement to the living conditions of soldiers.[50] Like the Shanghai branch they included the usual log of claims for women's rights such as winning equality in politics, economics, inheritance and marriage laws, and educational, employment, and career opportunities. However, they also sought government support for specific education opportunities for women workers, a prohibition on prostitution and the commercial trade in women and girls, and initiatives eradicating hypocritical double standards relating to female chastity.

There was a flurry of activity by WNAPA after the provocative actions of Duan Qirui in his exclusion of the women's groups from his Aftermath Conference. Women's groups around the nation protested by sending telegrams to Duan Qirui and Sun Yat-sen, and many were also published in newspapers. The Shanghai group's telegram declared that Duan's decision had "totally deprived women of their rights as citizens to vote and stand for election. Moreover, it insults the dignity of women citizens and trifles with the will of women citizens."[51] The Henan group declared in an open letter accompanying the press release of its telegram, "If we women of China are to liberate ourselves from layer upon layer of oppression, to hold the status of 'people' and 'citizens,' then participating in the National Assembly movement is one joint struggle that magnifies our influence."[52]

An article by Zhang Yangchen had argued that the participation of women in a national convention was vital since the words *Guomin huiyi* imply that it is a citizens' convention and since women make up half the citizens of China so too should they be able to express their views. She also notes, however, that at this stage most women do not conceive of themselves as citizens so there is a need for some education of women in political affairs. Her final line is a challenge: "Bring about a real citizens' convention! Bring about real women citizens!"[53]

Sun's rival "real" meeting, the "people's" National Assembly conference, commenced a month later on 1 March 1925 with women's participation. The women's press celebrated the event, with one commentator in *Women's Weekly News* writing evocatively of Sun Yat-sen's National Assembly, "We women ought to liberate ourselves from our prison of darkness now. This [event] truly is a remarkably rare opportunity."[54] The Shanghai branch sent two representatives to Beijing to join the local women's group there. The report of the meeting to nominate the representatives was filled with enthusiasm and hope.[55] During the month-long proceedings WNAPAs from around the nation held meetings reporting on the Beijing conference.[56] They sent messages to the conference reminding the delegates of the centrality of equality between men and women and that this should be embedded in the formal National Assembly regulations.[57] In Shanghai the women held a parallel Women's National Assembly meeting where their key demands were reiterated. Xiang Jingyu's speech to the meeting stressed that "women not only ought to have equal rights with men to vote and stand for election, but ought to have women's association representatives explicitly included in the National Assembly."[58] Only with this method could women's broader interests be guaranteed. As Xiang warned, China had previously had high-flying women leaders, such as Wu Zetian, but such women did little to alleviate the conditions of the larger mass of women. Representatives from women's associations would ensure that women's interests would be protected and advanced.[59]

Ultimately, the convention lasted over a month and with its thirteen women delegates produced a specific statement on women.[60] Section 8 of the assembly's report discussed women's issues. The program it outlined largely reiterated the UWA concerns of the early 1920s:

> (1) Women should have equal rights with men in political, economic, legal, educational, vocational spheres; (2) women and men should have equal inheritance rights; (3) protection for women and girls; (4) complete deregulation of education such that principles of coeducation are implemented at each level; (5) women should have absolutely total freedom of vocation; (6) both male and female workers should have eight-hour workdays and receive equal pay; (7) strictly punish the evil customs of female infanticide, maltreatment of wives and daughters-in-law, and trafficking in women as well as foot binding and ear piercing; (8) eradicate entirely the "buying and selling" marriage custom; women should have absolute freedom in marriage and divorce, and moreover promote the right of women to initiate/object to marriage on their own accord. Furthermore, there should be equal treatment both of women who are virgins and of those who marry more than once; eradicate the encouragement of the hypocritical and inhumane rites and laws of chastity.[61]

This explicit attack on the double standards of chastity—wherein women were solely responsible for sexual virtue—reflects an important shift in the public political presence of women. The full impact of this shift would become apparent in the 1930s during the revision of the family and marriage laws. However, there was another key difference between the earlier UWA documents and this current "people's" National Assembly statement—the latter emphasized economic rights as being the key to overcoming the historically rooted oppression of women and enunciated the importance of class unity. The second paragraph commences, "Naturally, behind women's problems are economic problems. The institution of property is the principle of these economic problems." The third paragraph explains that the women's movement should "broadly encourage immersion with the women masses." Women activists are advised that the current political scene demanded unity, and "this type of unity can include working women, middle-class women, and even upper-class women."[62] Asserting women's disadvantage relative to men in terms of economic standing provided an important avenue for promoting women's collective political interests.

This document's promotion of the women's rights agenda was a success, but a highly qualified one. Yet again, the overarching political situation prevented legislation-focused women's activism from achieving success. Despite Sun's best efforts to achieve a political settlement over the winter of 1924 and 1925, the situation in the North continued to be unstable. Duan Qirui was but a nominal leader, and warlords continued to wreak havoc. The failure of the National Assembly movement to produce a legitimate national government meant that this segment of the women's program of action ceased with the dismantling of the National Assembly movement as a whole. The special column dedicated to the National Assembly movement in the *Republic Daily* received smaller and smaller space. One-time editor of *The Ladies' Journal*, Zhang Xichen, advised women to move away from a legislative rights campaign toward one that promoted changes in the way people conceived of women's place in society. He contrasted the rights-based approach of "suffragism" (*sai fo la ji shi mu*) to that of "feminism" (*fo mi nie shi mu*), where the former focused on eliminating inequalities between men and women and the latter aimed to change the fundamental ways men and women regarded each other. To Zhang, suffragism was a component of the larger feminist "mental revolution" and was of the opinion that even without suffrage rights women activists could still seek such a revolution.[63] Zhang strategically saw the limitations for women of tying their campaigns too intimately with the national political situation. In another article Zhang argued that the National Assembly of 1925 was a sham, and one of the indicators that it lacked credibility was that there was any discussion at all about whether women should participate. "There will without doubt come a day when a real National Assembly will convene. In that real National Assembly women certainly will not demand to participate because there would be no thought that women could be excluded."[64]

Other commentators expressed the view that suffrage was still an important goal, particularly as women in Britain and America had won this right in recent times. Reports on women politicians in Britain continued to interest publishers.[65] Se Lu wrote in 1924 that the success of the suffrage movement internationally sadly had a limited impact on China. Nonetheless, in the years since the 1911 suffrage movement Se Lu declared that the women's movement had broadened and had won many notable successes in terms of women's education and employment even without the formal recognition of equality in political rights.[66] However, an unexpected event propelled politically active women further along the anti-imperialist path. The suffrage struggle would remain on the back burner for a few more years.

MAY THIRTIETH MOVEMENT: ANTI-IMPERIALISM SIDELINES SUFFRAGE

By the middle of 1925, with the National Assembly campaign waning, China's women activists rallied around an incident that was to draw them further to the left. On 15 May 1925 a striking worker at a Japanese-owned cotton mill was killed in Shanghai. By 30 May there were mass demonstrations protesting the Japanese imperialists' treatment of Chinese workers. During these protests, British police shot and killed eleven students and workers. Political activists and patriots around the country rallied in protest in a wave of anti-imperialist anger that came to be known as the May Thirtieth Movement.[67]

The women's movement turned its energies to support this campaign, and the networks active during the National Assembly campaign expanded as women students and workers joined the cause. Gilmartin writes that the May Thirtieth incident saw a large growth in the numbers of female student activists and a tenfold increase in the number of female CCP members.[68] Women were active at all levels of this movement—participating in strikes, holding rallies, and distributing materials. The suffrage movement was sidelined by the anti-imperialist agenda of the Nationalist Party and the workers' rights agenda of the CCP. The WNAPA networks transformed into May Thirtieth networks. Gilmartin notes, "The timing of the May Thirtieth incident proved to be quite fortuitous in expediting the transformation of a women's rights organization [the WNAPA], into a mass women's movement organization."[69] To complete the transformation, Xiang Jingyu established a new umbrella body—the Shanghai All-Women's Association (SAWA; *Shanghai gejie funü lianhe hui*) on 5 June 1925. In Shanghai SAWA drew on exactly the same base women's organizations as had WNAPA, yet its manifesto ignored the question of sex equality or women's rights. Under Xiang's leadership, SAWA demanded that foreigners cease bullying and exploiting Chinese workers and that workers be granted the freedom to organize without outside interference. They also demanded that the unequal treaties be overturned.[70] The Shanghai branch of this body achieved the CCP's goals—it harnessed the women's movement for the communist cause.

Indicative of the influence of Marxist notions of historical materialism that flourished at this time is an article by Yang Xianjiang. Yang described the progression of the Chinese women's movement as starting first with the aristocratic and capitalist class women and their claims for sex equality and women's suffrage. It then moved through a stage where women reflected the influence of imperialist economics and desired simply individual happiness within the family setting. Yang's third stage was a petty bourgeois demand for economic and family reform that still revolved around sex equality and women's suffrage. The fourth stage is the proletarian women's movement that grew among the women factory workers.[71] The May Thirtieth Movement and the activities of SAWA were perceived as a step along the path to the fourth stage.

Not all women involved in the May Thirtieth Movement felt that the women's rights agenda was insufficient. The Guangdong group that paralleled Shanghai's SAWA preferred to call itself the Guangdong Women's Emancipation Association (*Guangdong funü jiefang xiehui*). From its formation in May 1925 it adhered to an explicit commitment to women's rights. Its May manifesto placed the Association's calls for sex equality in schooling, wages and vocation, politics, and marriage within the context of the workers movement and the anti-imperialist movement.[72] The agenda to maintain the momentum of the National Assembly movement for women continued. Alongside promoting the "national products" campaign (that encouraged householders to buy Chinese goods rather than foreign ones), one meeting also asks women around the country to send telegrams in support of the women representatives to the National Assembly.[73]

Yet the movement was unable to bridge the increasing gap between the CCP and the Nationalist members. Reflecting on the ultimate break that was to come between the two parties, Tan Sheying wrote, "the CCP and the Nationalist factions could not cooperate."[74] The impact of CCP leadership of the national women's movement and the mobilization of women for all major political campaigns saw the dilution of the sex equality agenda and the emphasis on economic and class-based oppression. The suffrage campaigners' dependency on the emergence of nationwide stable, political structures reduced their ability to maintain consistent pressure for their cause. Yet, at the same time, the broadening enthusiasm for giving voice to identifiable political constituencies of disadvantaged peoples ensured that the women's movement continued to have influence on political debate in China.

EXECUTING REVOLUTION:
THE COLLAPSE OF THE UNITED FRONT

As the Northern Expedition gained success so did Chiang Kai-shek's distaste for the communist influence in his party. In late 1926 the link between the left wing of the United Front and the big-business section of the Nationalists became increasingly strained. When the Northern Expedition troops reached the Yangtze River, Chiang resolved to turn east to take Shanghai before resuming the journey north. In anticipation of the liberation of the city from the warlord Sun Chuanfang, the labor movement organized a general strike in February of 1927. Betraying the trust of the union movement, Chiang's troops waited outside Shanghai while Sun rounded up and executed the main activists. The job of clearing the city of left-wing "troublemakers," who had until this point believed that they too were part of the Nationalist Party, was completed once Chiang gained control of Shanghai. In the months that followed many prominent CCP activists were killed, like Xiang Jingyu, or fled into hiding. Executions of "radical" women were conducted throughout the country—Leslie Collins notes that "over 1,000 women leaders were killed in China in 1927 by KMT [Nationalist Party] rightists; many of them were not Communists but simply active participants in the women's movement." Collins notes that incidents in which women's breasts were cut off before being beheaded were reported.[75] The sexualized mutilation of the women political activists' bodies reveals that for some people at this time such women had lost their feminine virtue.

The life and death of Zhang Yilan (1893–1927) is a case in point. The Nationalist Party's 1923 reorganization involved the revival of party cells around the nation, and among the women who joined the Beijing branch was Zhang Yilan. Another of the many politicized Hunanese women, her scholar father married her into the Long family in 1910, but on the death of her child in 1915, Zhang left her husband. In 1919 she went to Beijing to pursue her studies at Beijing Women's Normal College and in 1922 passed the entrance exams for Beijing University. It was during this time that she formally divorced her husband. Her commitment to Sun Yat-sen's cause of national unification under the Three Principles and the Nationalist Party began in earnest in 1925 when she joined the Society for the Realization of Sun Yat-sen-ism. She took responsibility for editing the radical journal *Women's Friend (Funü zhiyou)* and in 1927 became head of the Nationalist Party's Women's Bureau in Beijing. This connection with the women's wing of the Nationalist Party was sufficient to link her to radical left-wing politics, and this made her a target for attack. At the close of the Northern Expedition, the warlord Zhang Zuolin arrested Zhang Yilan as part of his support of Chiang Kai-shek's campaign to eradicate radicals. She was executed on 28 April 1927 along with twenty other "revolutionaries," including CCP founder Li Dazhao.[76]

The women's movement in Nationalist Party–controlled areas was not completely silenced in 1927, despite the brutal excision of CCP members from within its ranks. But, as Christina Gilmartin has pointed out, "after 1927, feminist programs lost their political backing as neither party was willing to repeat the full-scale assault on patriarchal social controls over women that had occurred in the 1920s."[77] Yet, in the face of wavering support from the top party leadership, the women's movement continued to mobilize. After Chiang's troops entered Shanghai, twenty-two women were involved in discussions with the Nationalist Party's Second Route Army in Shanghai about the importance of mobilizing women in the new political order almost as soon as the Nationalists had control of the city. With official support, they established the Women's Movement Committee (*Funü yundong weiyuan hui*) on 28 May 1927. Invoking the Three Principles of the People, the Nationalist Party's constitutional commitment to sex equality, and women's responsibilities to engage in patriotic action, the Women's Movement Committee was silent on issues of defending workers' rights. Instead they advocated improving women's education and knowledge, encouraging economic independence among women, and eradicating the scourge of concubinage and prostitution.[78] Their middle-class perspective was clear within their manifesto. Headed by Chen Yiyun, this group would produce the prominent women politicians of Nationalist China for the next two decades, as we will see in the following chapter. The committee existed only very briefly since its sponsoring organization, the Second Route Military Command, was disbanded, but the alacrity with which it was established is typical of women's activism in China. As soon as any form of government had been formed women engaged it in direct lobbying to press the women's cause. It is unlikely that Chen's colleagues would have been unaware of the brutal purges of their one-time allies like Zhang Yilan or Xiang Jingyu. However, such events were commonplace in 1927 as comrades turned on comrades in the Chiang Kai-shek–led scramble for total power as the end of the Northern Expedition appeared in sight.

By June of 1927 the Nationalist Party developed a more coherent approach to the integration of the women's movement into its party structure. Over the course of the next few months, cities like Nanjing, Beijing, and Shanghai established Special City Women's Associations (*Tebie shi funü xiehui*), and provinces like Henan and Anhui also linked equivalent committees into their own Nationalist Party structures. Their allegiance to the Nationalists was explicitly declared in their manifestos. The Shanghai committee wrote, "This committee is entirely under the direction of the [Nationalist] Party."[79] Women in these new associations distanced themselves from the Communists and maintained middle-class agendas within the overall Nationalist Party platform. Although by the autumn of 1928 when the Beijing committee was established, women workers and peasants were included in their plan for action. Improving the life and education of women workers and peasants was included as a matter for concern, alongside the unspecified "hygiene" and "clothing" problems of female students—revealing the members' more detailed knowledge of the problems faced by women students as a result of their common social status. Women's suffrage was given explicit recognition as well. The Association aimed to ensure that women politicians were nurtured and that equality with men in political rights was achieved.[80] The Fuzhou city committee manifesto concluded with the rallying cries of "Destroy the enemies who look down on women! Freedom in marriage and divorce! Long life to the Nationalist Party! Long life to the Nationalist government! Long life to the success of the women's movement!"[81] Clearly, the women in the Nationalist-controlled areas connected their cause directly and loudly to the fortunes of the Nationalist Party and its Nationalist government.

FROM NEW CULTURE TO WHITE TERROR

In the years between 1925 and 1928 there was limited discussion of women's suffrage issues. The occasional piece in the women's press kept the issue alive, but there were no major campaigns around which suffragists mobilized until the end of the Northern Expedition. A 1927 article by Chen Jiangtao traced the legislation on political rights in regards to women, pointing out that women were currently regarded as being in the same political category as the insane by being barred from voting. Chen also summarized the main arguments presented to oppose women's suffrage. The anti's arguments had not progressed over the years, despite dramatic changes in attitudes about women among large sections of the urban educated class as a result of the New Culture Movement. Chen lists the anti's positions as being: women are too weak physically to compete with men in this arena; women will neglect the family, and children will suffer; and women are subject to emotional instability. In contrast, the conclusion of the article outlines a concise and mature summary of the full scope of political rights women demanded—indicating the increasing sophistication among activists of the intricacies of democratic systems. Chen writes that China's women required not only the right to vote and stand for election, but also the right to criticize government policy, to participate in recall and referendum, to hold official positions in the government administration, and to serve on juries. Moreover, women should have legal rights to freedom of speech and thought, to hold the status of an independent individual before the law, to be able to inherit property and the rights to divorce and marriage within a monogamous system.[82] A small reader titled *Women and Society* published in 1929 by Qian Di likewise represents feminist thought of this time:

> From now on our women's battle lines ought to have these two objectives: (1) Overturn the male-centered society and establish one that is publicly owned by both sexes. (2) Women become people of society and don't be the wives or lovers of men, nor the daughters of parents, or the mothers of children. . . . In the period of hard work in building this society of the two sexes we propose the three slogans below: Women are not men's property! Women are not society's decorations! Women are the owners of society![83]

The progress made in the New Culture Movement toward a more liberal and openly individualistic society came to a grinding halt with the unification of the country under Nationalist Party rule. To win sex equality at a national level the cowed and numerically reduced women activists had to deal with a government that espoused notions of Confucian harmony and family values and was suspicious of outspoken and radical women. As we will see in the next chapter, a fine line had to be walked to survive as a feminist activist in the newly unified Republic of China. The "White Terror" of 1927 forced women activists to choose their political allegiances with great care. For those that remained in the urban areas, the Nationalist government remained the focus of their attentions. Others relocated their activities and moved to the countryside with the CCP and worked among rural women implementing and propagandizing for broad CCP policies. Only very rarely did the urban-based women's magazines raise the question of the women's movement among rural women.[84] Some opted to avoid the CCP and the Nationalist Party altogether by occupying the equally dangerous middle ground as advocates of human rights, national salvation, and democratic principles. This group became effective advocates for women's suffrage and sex equality in cooperation with women in the CCP and the Nationalist Party throughout the 1930s and 1940s.

As we will see in the following chapter, by the end of 1928, the Nationalists were poised to reformulate all the documents that governed the newly united China. The suffragists, still overwhelmingly focused on effecting legal and constitutional gains for women, turned their attention to participation in these Nationalist-authorized document-revision processes. Keeping their political leaders honest on their publicly espoused support for women's rights became the main task. History had taught them that vigilance was necessary and attention to detail was crucial.

SIX

Feminists in the Nanjing Decade, 1927–1936

In October 1928, at the end of the Northern Expedition, the Nationalist Revolutionary Army reunited the country by suppressing and coopting the warlords and their various puppet politicians all the way through to Beijing, and the Nationalist Party established a single national government. China was reunited under one government, and the women's rights activists, despite the expulsion of left-wing women from the urban base of the movement, saw in this new structure the hope for fundamental, long-lasting legal and constitutional reforms. However, the Nationalist Party did not immediately establish a fully democratic electoral system, despite the provincial experience of such processes in the early 1920s. Instead, they announced a period of tutelage government. Sun Yat-sen had devised the notion of tutelage government in his 1924 *Fundamentals of National Reconstruction for the Nationalist Government.*[1] The document was premised on the understanding that the Nationalist Party would guide the population in its political and civic consciousness so that constitutional democracy could be achieved at a national level. One of the reasons why the 1911 revolution had failed, Sun thought, was because the population was not ready for democracy. Where some had argued that women's suffrage could not be granted because women were not adequately prepared, the Nationalist Party leaders of China declared both men and women ill equipped for democratic responsibilities. The tutelage period would supposedly facilitate the development of the requisite skills in the mass of the population. Calls to convene a conference to revise the national constitution appeared almost immediately once the country was united since the democrats hoped this would be the first step in ensuring the transition from a military/party rule to a fully democratic China.

However, the tutelage period became one of Nationalist Party control dominated by Chiang Kai-shek, during which his campaign to eliminate the CCP continued unabated. Chiang was wary of dissent and extremely concerned not to allow the CCP to threaten his control.[2] Edmund Fung has noted that the increasingly authoritarian nature of the Nationalist government during this period alienated many sympathizers and led to the formation of several smaller democratic political groupings despite an official ban on the formation of political parties outside of the Nationalist Party.[3] At the same time, the CCP, badly hit with Nationalist Party attacks on its ranks, was licking its wounds first in the Jiangxi-Fujian border area and then in the remote Shaanxi-Gansu border regions. Ultimately, the increasing Japanese aggression rescued the CCP from continued attacks by the Nationalist armies. Indeed, the Nationalist Party's hard-won control of the nation was destroyed by the Japanese invasion of 1937.

Nonetheless, during the 1930s the Nationalist government achieved success in building its state apparatus. Institutional structures to deal with taxation, education, health, and foreign relations, as well as military development, were formed at this time despite the "hostile environment" within which the new government of China operated.[4] Moreover, an important shift in Chinese political culture can be detected in this period—such as the absence of literacy requirements in constitutional documents and also in actual voting practice, in the case of village elections for local heads in Nationalist Party–controlled areas.[5] Women in the CCP similarly saw significant social reforms that challenged established divisions of power in both village and family structures, and elections in their occupied areas did not require literacy from voters either. Between the mid-1920s and the start of the 1930s there had clearly been a transformation of attitudes regarding political representation. This shift is probably attributable to a combination of an increasing awareness of the nature of universal suffrage practiced elsewhere in the world and left-wing political philosophies. However, the comparatively successful expansion in democratic political engagement resulting from the provincial electoral systems and structures in the early and mid-1920s, discussed in the previous chapter, would also have contributed to this remarkable transformation in attitudes about political representation.[6] China's political elite gained more confidence in electoral democracy as a result of these previous successes.

The political structures of the 1930s also delivered benefits to the women's movement. The Nationalist Party government's construction of a formal state institutional apparatus provided the women's rights activists in Nationalist areas with broad scope for intervention at a policy level. In rural areas the County Organization Act of 1929 had already delivered universal suffrage in elections for village heads for all adults over the age of twenty—although the extent of women's participation in elections was limited.[7] Women's voices in urban areas were also increasingly heard from within "third force" groups that were patriotic but not aligned with either major party.[8] Thus, this chapter argues that the 1930s was a period of substantial feminist activism and mobilization around China. Although official promotion of traditional Chinese values by the New Life Movement prevailed midway through the decade, women activists in the Nationalist government–controlled areas ensured that women's rights causes continued to be represented. Urban-based women's groups held fast to their belief in the importance of winning constitutional and legal equality for women in political rights at a national level. They ultimately achieved success in winning formal recognition for women's equal political rights with men in a constitution that claimed national jurisdiction in 1936. But their path to this victory involved working through complex, newly established legal and institutional structures designed specifically for the period of tutelage rather than for the long-awaited democratic China. They campaigned on the basis of the notion that once the tutelage period was complete, such theoretical gains would stand ordinary women in good stead at any future democratic elections. They also saw quite clearly that the scope for achieving their second-tier goals—such as effecting changes to marriage and inheritance laws and employment structures—could be readily furthered with the tutelage government.

TUTELAGE GOVERNMENT STRUCTURES

The political and social system that women's groups sought to influence was compromised. The tutelage period was initially designed to last for a period of six years, and democratic constitutional rule was supposed to be implemented by 1935. Chiang Kai-shek's reluctance to relinquish power, his preoccupation with the annihilation of the CCP, and Japan's increasing aggression combined to ensure that the six-year political tutelage period passed without Sun's schedule being fulfilled. Pressure on Chiang to end the tutelage period was brought to bear by the numerous democratic and constitution support groups that formed around the nation, including sections from within the Nationalist Party itself. The invasion of Japan in 1937 provided Chiang with the pretext of a "crisis" that could ensure his continued delay of democratic election.

Sun Yat-sen had noted in his plan for the country's political evolution that China should pass through three stages: military unification, political tutelage, and constitutional government; thus, "whatever the realities of Chinese politics may be at any particular moment, the history of the Kuomintang [Nationalist Party] is closely linked with the objective of constitutional rule."[9] The women's suffrage activists and their sisters advocating the broad women's rights platform trusted in this deterministic vision—constitutional rule was inevitable and therefore constitutional change was a worthwhile goal.

Sun had devised a five-power government structure for the tutelage period, and Chiang's party/government duly implemented this in 1928. At the top was the Central Executive Committee of the Nationalist Party and a state council. The head of the latter was also president of the republic. Five controlling organs, named Yuan, divided the business of government among them. The Executive Yuan supervised the various ministries (such as Foreign Affairs, Internal Affairs, Agriculture, and Forestry) and was theoretically the highest executive organ of the government. The Legislative Yuan served as a parliament through which all national legislation would be passed. The Judicial Yuan managed the administration of justice. The Examination Yuan selected suitable people for official postings, and the Control Yuan audited the government's accounts and served to oversee administrative functions of the government as a whole in much the same way that the censorate had in China's imperial past. The plan for the tutelage period was that national democratic institutions would build from the provincial level and, once constitutional rule had been achieved, then the national constitution would be implemented. The movements toward self-government in provinces like Hunan and Guangdong that had occurred throughout the 1920s indicated that this process was in progress by the time the Tutelage government was established in 1928.[10]

China's feminists and democrats alike anticipated that the tutelage period would provide the space for broad reformulation of all national laws. For the women suffrage activists this was clearly a significant opportunity, and they ensured that their voice was heard in all aspects of legal and political reform. With the advent of the Nationalist government's tutelage period, the serious work on drafting national laws—codes and regulations that would remove the vestiges of customs designed for a rapidly disappearing world order—had begun in earnest.[11] Such laws could ensure that political equality and also social and economic equality could be assured.[12] Women activists continued to focus on suffrage rights since these were fundamental to ensuring access to the right to control and amend any laws drafted. Having inheritance rights, equality in marriage, and other protective measures simply bestowed upon women by men was not the sort of guaranteed long-term independence the women activists sought. It was rightly felt that such provisions could easily be removed by less enlightened governments unless activist women were themselves participating in legislative affairs. Women's fundamental guarantee of power, self-determination, and independence, according to the suffrage activists, depended upon women's right to vote and stand for election.

REORIENTING THE WOMEN'S MOVEMENT IN NATIONALIST-GOVERNMENT CHINA

Knowledge of women's sustained pressure on the Nationalist government on the issue of increasing women's formal political rights during the Nanjing Decade is not widely recognized. In her seminal work, *Women and Socialism in China*, Elisabeth Croll wrote of the absence of feminist activism on political rights during the Nationalist government period: "Political work smacked of Communist influence and was strongly suppressed." She continued by arguing that, in writings of the women activists of the period, politics was "carefully avoided" since it was deemed an "inappropriate interest for women."[13] Croll also maintained that in the mid- and late 1930s many previously active women declared their goal of equality between men and women to be achieved and their work on political matters completed. "On the basis of the new constitutional gains [which enshrined the principle of equality], the leading feminists proclaimed the emancipation of women." These "leading feminists" then purportedly queried the need for "further organization of women in pursuit of these same ideals."[14] More recently, Wang Zheng has argued that in the 1930s the Nationalist Party regarded "feminism as a subversive ideology . . . of little use to a ruling class trying to maintain social stability by promoting Confucian norms" and that "radical agitation for a feminist revolution disappeared."[15] However, as this chapter will show, rather than a silencing of the feminist movement's political aspirations in Nationalist-controlled areas, instead there was an astute reorientation of the movement. Moreover, the political structures established in the Nationalist government areas enabled this feminist activism to continue.

For women in Nationalist Party–controlled areas, activism on women's rights had to be carefully distinguished from that of their one-time colleagues—the left-wing women activists. Sometimes this was achieved by explicit and vociferous expressions of anti-CCP sentiment. Edith Pye, representative of the Women's International League for Peace and Freedom (WILPF), toured China soon after the end of the United Front and noted that International Women's Day rallies in 1928 included "Execute the CCP" among the banners calling for "Equal Pay," "Equal Education," and "Women Participate in the People's Revolution."[16] The WILPF had been formed in 1915 from a core of left-leaning activists from the International Women's Suffrage Association protesting against World War I. While the WILPF would have found the banners problematic, for China's feminists explicit anti-CCP rhetoric was an important prerequisite for publicizing their goals in Nationalist government areas.

To achieve progress in their women's rights agenda without attracting suspicions that they held communist sympathies, women activists also aligned their campaign closely with the rhetoric of "building and strengthening the Nationalist government." Thus, in the decade from 1927, a further evolution of feminism's connections with nationalism occurred that reveals the long-term dexterity and flexibility of China's feminist movement. No longer was "national unification or anti-imperialism" the implicit meaning of "nationalism" as it had been only a few years earlier. With the advent of

Nationalist Party governance, achieved in tandem with the brutal expulsion of the Communists, women's appeals to patriotic nation strengthening deftly assumed new significances—unswerving publicly declared support for the Nationalist government's processes and structures. Many activists asserted their support for the government and deflected official criticism by starting their articles with phrases like "Under the leadership of the Nationalist Party, women have already achieved complete equality in political rights" and then proceed to argue how these gains could be improved upon for the remainder of the article.[17] One commentator writing in *New Femininity* (*Xin nüxing*) celebrated the Nationalist Party's assertion of equality between men and women in its own documentation and then called on the government to ensure that these same provisions were implemented across all the nation's laws.[18] Yet others argued that women's suffrage would help eradicate unspecified weaknesses in government.[19]

As this chapter reveals, advocacy for improvements in women's rights and status did not in and of itself draw negative attention from the Nationalist government authorities. Women's legitimate political identity as a group was accepted by the Nationalist Party and was institutionalized in its government structures during this period. The left wing did not have a monopoly on the gender reform agenda. International Women's Day was still celebrated, and extensive press coverage for feminist ideals was received throughout these years.[20] In part the women's continued leverage emerged from the strength of their collective political identity built during the New Culture Movement. Women's equality with men was by 1927 broadly accepted by China's leading political actors—how this principle would change interpersonal relations and family politics was about to be tested within a newly unified China. However, the new government's own desire for international recognition and respectability was also a factor in ensuring that the women's rights agenda was not completely expunged with the expulsion of the Communists. The Nationalist government sought international credibility as a progressive and modern regime in order to consolidate its control, and a moderate women's rights agenda was helpful rather than harmful to this cause. Women activists' awareness of the government's desire to be accepted on the international stage thus provided scope for increased lobbying on suffrage. (See Figure 6.1 on unity of women from India and China in national liberation campaigns.)

Publications reporting on the international women's suffrage successes continued to press the case that such a policy change was inevitable in

Figure 6.1. Women of India and China cooperate on watering the garden of national liberation. *Funü shenghuo* (Women's Life) 1, no. 1 (circa 1936).

China.[21] One commentator argued that women's suffrage was vital because it would improve the efficacy of government and sweep away weaknesses in government as well as extend women's rights.[22] Others presented the case that China was simply lagging behind on an inevitable international trend. One article published in 1929 declared, "Truly, the high tide of the women's suffrage movement has passed! Most countries around the world have already won suffrage rights! However, in contrast the state of the women's suffrage movement here in China makes us feel quite ashamed."[23] Liu Wang Liming wrote that Chinese women warmly welcomed the tide of women's suffrage that was sweeping in from overseas.[24] Chinese women maintained a presence in the international suffrage movement during these years as well. Luo Xiuying attended the Twenty-fifth Congress of the International Women's Suffrage Association held in Berlin in 1929 as China's representative.[25] Reports in the women's press that more women than men vote in the British elections reminded readers of the suffragists ultimate democratic goals.[26]

PROVING THEIR WORTH:
WOMEN IN THE CITIZENS' CONVENTION

In accordance with the notion that the tutelage period was preparing the nation for constitutional, democratic rule, in November 1930 the Central Executive Committee of the Nationalist Party announced that a citizens' convention (*guomin huiyi*) would be held in May of 1931. Its task was to approve and debate a constitution for the period of tutelage government. The constitution was to be drafted by a committee of eleven.[27] News of this forthcoming Convention provided the women with the focus for their enthusiasm, and much energy was expended in ensuring that sympathetic women representatives were included as participants. The Convention's recommendations would set the ideological groundwork for this newly re-united nation, and in this regard the women activists were keen to ensure that equality between men and women be implicit from the beginning.

The Tutelage Constitution of 1931 that resulted from the convention's deliberations did indeed grant women national equality in political rights. Article 6 of the "people's rights" states, "All citizens of the Republic of China shall be equal before the law, irrespective of sex, race, religion, or caste."[28] However, this did not give women the right to vote since the Tutelage Constitution, by its very nature, was establishing the rules for the period of Nationalist government dictatorship during which time the nation would be prepared for democracy.

Nonetheless, women activists wanted to be involved in the formulation of this Tutelage Constitution from the outset. Women's groups regarded this convention as a crucial juncture in which to ensure that equality between men and women was guaranteed at the national level as it had been in various provincial documents. The convention was conceived as a people's convention with five hundred and twenty elected delegates chosen by qualified voters in the provinces and municipalities. The five categories of delegates included farmers unions; workers unions; merchant guilds and industrialist associations; educational organizations, universities, and professional associations; and the Nationalist Party. The citizens' convention's electoral laws made no provision to include representatives from the women's groups, but women could be appointed within any of the above categories.[29] While women's collective political identity had been affirmed during the New Culture Movement within party political structures (through the Women's Bureaus), under the Nationalist's tutelage government, this identity was not recognized in equivalent institutional structures. As one article in the *Republic Daily* stated, one prevalent view was that because women's equality had been established in the Nationalist Party structure there was no need to have a special category for women in the citizens' convention. This view was commonly countered by the perspective that women were a special class of humans united by their lesser ranking compared to men. On the basis of this difference, the argument ran, women deserved a special category of women's representation that would speak specifically on women's issues. Having women within the party, enterprise, or educational groupings was inadequate since these representatives would lack the mandate to lobby on issues of concern to the women's movement.[30]

The women's campaign thus began to establish a separate sixth category for women's associations within the convention. In an article in the influential journal *The Ladies' Journal*, Xu Yasheng posed the rhetorical question of why the tutelage government cannot ignore women. Her answers reflect the conservative tenor of the time but also reveal that vociferous, feminist argument had not been silenced. On the one hand she invoked women's prime family responsibilities and on the other their right to revolutionary change in gender politics led by the new government's policies. For example, she pointed out that families were the bulwarks of Chinese society and that women were the bulwarks of families. Therefore, if the government wished to ensure that society progressed politically then it needed to ensure that there was no disjunction between family and state—and to guard against any potential disjunction, women needed to be included in political discussions. She also invoked the ancient segregationist principle about women being in the inner realm and men being in the outer realm (*nü zhu nei* and *nan zhu wai*) to press her point home about integrating family values with state values. Moreover in an appeal to traditional maternal virtues of early childhood education, she declared, how can women adequately educate children if they are inadequately prepared in political knowledge themselves? Yet, in contrast to these appeals to conservative values, she simultaneously asserted that women were a separate class of people and that they were collectively identified by their oppression by men. On this basis, she argued, the tutelage government's responsibility to educate all the people in revolutionary practice demands that one person's happiness does not depend on another's misery. Therefore the government has a duty to women as a special group to eradicate inequalities based on sex.[31] In this single article China's feminists have deployed arguments of sex difference rather than sex equality to appease the conservatives while still pressing for radical political change in a key political convention.

As the convention drew closer the women increased the intensity of their campaign for women's representation. In the spring of 1931 women's groups around the nation petitioned the government to allocate a quota for women.[32] As a result of the enthusiasm for this issue a new society was established in major cities around the nation. Named the Association for the Promotion of Women's Participation in the Citizens' Convention (*Funü canjia guomin huiyi xiejinhui*), it was formed in major cities around the nation with the largest groups being in Nanjing and Guangzhou. The Guangzhou group was formed on 24 February 1931. One of its initial actions was to organize a rally where more than three thousand women participated in a march to the provincial party headquarters to demonstrate the breadth of support for the inclusion of a quota for women in the national convention. The leaders of the group were Deng Huifang and Wu Zhimei—both long-term suffrage activists. The provincial party leaders took the demonstrations seriously and sent a telegram to the central party headquarters in the capital to communicate the women's demands.[33]

The women in the capital, Nanjing, were in the happy position of being able to lobby both the national Nationalist Party headquarters as well as the municipal party organs. Like their sisters from Guangzhou, the Nanjing women commenced their campaign by petitioning both Nationalist Party authorities to establish a special category for women in the convention. They followed this with the election of fifteen women representatives during a meeting held on International Women's Day to demonstrate their preparedness for political involvement. After several days the central government replied that the laws had already been determined and could not be changed.

The women activists were incensed, but rather than retire they intensified their campaign. Women's groups all across the city and the nation were mobilized to form a united front on the issue.[34] For example, the women's magazines promoted women's participation in the national convention by featuring articles on the issue. One example is Jin Zhonghua's article, "From the Family Realm to Political Realms," in which she argues that most women prior to the May Fourth era lacked the awareness of how society functions to adequately participate in political life. However, the extensive education women have received over the last decade has ensured that they are ready and capable of a broader level of participation. Her main argument is that from the stage of being primarily within the family confines, women have passed through the stage of interacting within society as a whole and are now ready to enter the third stage where women participate in national politics.[35]

The Nanjing women organized a meeting on the issue and identified a core of women who were to press the case for a "women's quota" with the Nationalist government. Eventually their lobbying achieved results, with permission being granted for ten women to attend the convention, although with nonvoting, observer status only. This was a partial victory since women would at least be able to speak at the convention, and it appeared by this stage that full participation rights by a special women's quota was unlikely to be achieved. Accordingly, the Nanjing women sent a telegram to their provincial support groups requesting delegates to elect representatives. On 25 April twenty women from major women's organizations of the urban areas attended a meeting in Nanjing. These included the Kaifeng Women's Progress Association (*Funü xiejin hui*), the Tianjin city Association for the Promotion of Women's Culture (*Funü wenhua cujin hui*), and the Shanghai Women's Association (*Funü xiehui*). The strength of the southern provinces with regards to women's rights is clear from the strength of the Cantonese contingent. Guangzhou and Shanghai each sent representatives from two groups—the Guangzhou's Women's Relief Association (*Funü jiuji hui*), the Guangzhou Women's Rights Movement Alliance (*Nüquan yundong da tongmeng*), the Shanghai Women's Association, and the Shanghai-based Chinese Women's Suffrage Association (*Zhonghua nüzi canzheng hui*)—and the Women's Youth Encouragement Society (*Nüqing nian lizhi she*) also sent delegates.[36]

At the April meeting ten women observers were duly elected—Chen Yiyun, Tang Guozhen, Tan Sheying, Mo Xiangzhi, Yu Weihua, Tan Hanxia, Ma Zhiying, Li Zhishan, Xie Weipeng, and Qian Yanshu. Another five were nominated as secondary representatives since the increasingly unstable political situation determined the need for backup delegates in the event of the first being unable to attend. These five include Cao Mengjun, Li Yingying (Sichuan), Yang Meizhen, Mao Yunqin, and Chen Yingmei. This selection represented a cross-section of the various provinces.

These "observers" from the nation's various women's associations were not the only women involved in the convention. Six others were nominated as delegates under the other regular categories open to men and women. These included Cantonese suffrage activists Deng Huifang and Wu Zhimei, mentioned earlier. The other four were Liu Chunyi (Shaanxi), Li Zhishan

(Hebei), Shi Zhiying (Zhejiang), and Yang Daoyi (Guangzhou). The three Cantonese delegates, Deng, Wu, and Yang, were eventually unable to attend, but two other woman attended as reserves: Tang Yungong, who attended as substitute representative for Guangzhou, and Ding Hansan who was a delegate for Henan. Women around the nation applauded their representatives with telegrams wishing them strength and success in their tasks.[37]

Although this was a Nationalist government initiative, not all the women delegates were blind party loyalists as the brief biographies of some of the women reveal below. The continued political diversity of the women actively working with feminist goals had diminished after 1927 but it was nonetheless more diverse than is commonly understood. By 1931 Tan Sheying (1891–1978) had many years' experience as a political activist, publisher, and commentator on women's political concerns. She joined the Nationalist Party in 1912 and joined the left-leaning Women's Rights League in the 1920s. During the traumatic years of 1927–1928 Tan aligned herself clearly with the Nationalist Party and remained a strong supporter throughout the remainder of her life, joining the New Life Committee in 1934 and being elected to the National Assembly in 1944.[38] Liu Chunyi was also a committed Nationalist Party member. In contrast, some women delegates had ties to the CCP. Li Zhishan was a Nationalist Party member but had worked closely in early days with the CCP leader Deng Yingchao on *Women's Star*. Others were members of neither party but would move to the left in later years. For example, the youthful Cao Mengjun (b. 1917) would join the CCP in 1937. Prior to aligning herself with the CCP Cao was active in the broad women's movement in the Nationalist government–controlled areas.[39] The division between Nationalists and Communists or sympathizers of the right or the left among the feminist movement in China was clearly not completely impermeable. Nonetheless, the convention was a Nationalist government agenda and the women delegates conformed to the rules established therein.

The appointment of female delegates within a special category was not without its critics. One commentator wrote, "In the future we must look at actual ability regardless of whether someone is male or female . . . if we only demand that the government exercises sex equality by appointing women functionaries regardless of the quality of their abilities, then the future dangers for women's liberation are too grave to contemplate."[40]

During the course of the months of April and May 1931 the first constitution with pretensions for national application to give women equal rights with men was promulgated. The citizens' convention thus passed the Tutelage Constitution. It gave women, for the first time, equal political rights with men—limited of course by the fact that the country was in a preparatory stage before democratic elections would confer a democratic government and that this constitution was only effective during the period of tutelage. Primarily, this was a victory on paper—there were no electoral structures in place to deliver voting rights.

Despite this limitation women activists garnered as much benefit as possible in pressing the case for women's rights. As Liu Wang Liming wrote, even though the constitution recognized equality women had to be even more vigilant than ever about political participation.[41] Newspaper articles declared that women's participation in the convention proved the point that women's increasing and expanding involvement in government was vital. One article expressed concern that even though women were successful in winning seats at the convention, much work needed to be done to bring the bulk of China's women into political engagement.[42] A publication edited by the students of Jinling Women's University titled *Women Pioneers* (*Shijie funü de xiandao*) revealed the need to maintain a firm resolve. They wrote that even though there were men in China that opposed women's suffrage, "we should not be afraid because when overseas women demanded suffrage rights they experienced this phase." The article then narrated the struggles of American suffragist Annie Howard Shaw in the path to winning voting rights in her country.[43]

Nonetheless, with sex equality recognized in the Tutelage Constitution the women turned their attention to the legal position of women more broadly than they addressed equality in formal political rights. They regarded access to political influence as central to winning equality in all aspects of law. Jin Shiyin wrote, "If there is no equality in politics there can be no equality in law." She continued arguing that the most important function for law was to protect people's freedom, and the old Chinese laws had suppressed women's freedoms while protecting only those of men.[44] Another article claimed that winning equality between men and women in the civil code was "the only path for eradicating women's common suffering. If we can produce a civil code that has total sex equality then in one hit we would wipe out the suffering caused by several thousands of years of unequal laws. This is such a magnificent task."[45] For women such as these, winning suffrage rights had long been conceived as an important strategy in the overall battle for women's complete legal rights.

GETTING HOLD OF THE INHERITANCE
AND RETHINKING MARRIAGE

The importance for women of having constitutional equality in political rights was made evident when laws relating to marriage and inheritance were undergoing revision. Having won the tutelage government's acknowledgment for women's participation in politics, the women sought to win changes to national laws that directly impacted on women's standing within the family. The two key aspects for China's feminists were ensuring sex equality in inheritance rights and the abolition of concubinage. These were issues that China's women's suffrage advocates had sought to change from the start of their movement, and their engagement with a legitimate, national government with a clear agenda to reform and modernize China's legal code provided the opportunity for these radical social reforms to be legislated. Lisa Tran has argued that in the first few years of the 1930s women's magazines "played a critical role in that struggle [to champion women's rights] by providing a forum for the public to air its grievances and denounce the Legislative Yuan every time it tried to pass laws contrary to the principle of gender equality."[46]

In the legal code effective from May 1931 there were substantial gains for women's legal status relative to men within family law.[47] Equality of husbands and wives in divorce was expressed for the first time. Bernice Lee writes of the document's "Book of Family": "The principle of the equality of men and women pervades the whole book, and was probably its most outstanding feature at the time of its promulgation. . . . This book radically changes the status of the wife. Formerly the wife was completely dominated by her husband and had very few rights of her own, but the 'Book of Family' establishes the equal status of husband and wife."[48]

Freedom of choice in marriage partners was guaranteed, and the traditional legal codes' practice that parents had the right to force their children into marriage was annulled. All this augured well for the legal status of women within the family. Yet, on the issue of concubines—still prevalent in the 1930s—the law remained ambiguous.

The May 1931 document had failed to deliver satisfaction for China's feminists on this front because it denied that concubinage was a form of marriage and therefore could not technically be considered a form of bigamy. Had it been recognized as bigamous, existing laws against bigamy would have rendered concubinage illegal. Bernice Lee wrote that while the

"Book of Family" did not recognize the institution of concubinage, it "provides that either spouse may apply to the court for a divorce when the other spouse has committed bigamy or adultery" as long as the injured party has not previously condoned the relationship or known of it for over six months. "Therefore, in reality, concubinage can continue if the wife does not object."[49] For China's women's rights activists this was unacceptable, and they sought to make concubinage illegal—on the grounds that it was adultery and therefore in violation of the criminal code—and ensure that the men involved in taking concubines were liable for punishment. In so doing the women would also be able to tackle the long-standing inequalities in adultery laws.

Crucial attitudinal changes had occurred over the years since the start of the century. These had made it possible for the changes to marriage laws to be implemented and also presented scope for changing the attitudes toward concubinage. Lisa Tran has argued that the Republican period saw a change in perceptions of the meaning of conjugal fidelity. Throughout the Qing, women were charged with responsibility for maintaining chastity, and female virtue focused upon women's sexual monogamy. And, until the Republican era, men were relieved of any notion of fidelity—enjoying recreational sex with sex workers and freely taking concubines after marriage. Tran notes that over the course of the Republican period, conjugal fidelity came to be a "gender-neutral term."[50] Marital fidelity was deemed to be monogamous for both men and women in this new understanding of the term. Thus, men's virtue was also linked to sexual chastity in a fashion that it had not been in the Qing.

The adultery laws presented China's feminists with a complex political fight, as Lisa Tran has deftly demonstrated. In 1928 the criminal code punished a married woman with a maximum of two years jail if she committed adultery with a man. However, her husband was not liable for punishment if his paramour was unmarried. If she were married he would receive the same punishment as his female partner. Effectively the law was ensuring continued male freedom in sexual activity and continued access to concubines while simultaneously protecting the family's patriline by controlling women's sexual activity throughout their lives. China's feminists in the Nanjing Decade argued that this law was in flagrant disregard of the Nationalist Party's own principles of equality between men and women and lobbied for change on this basis. Tran's work discusses how the women mobilized through rallies, telegrams, petitions and direct lobbying of government as well as through publishing polemical pieces in magazines.[51] After many protests that the government was "oppressing Chinese feminism" and appeals to the equality provisions in the constitution, Wang Jingwei assured the women that the laws on adultery would be amended.[52] Indeed, at the end of 1935 equality for both men and women in regards to adultery was confirmed in the criminal code.[53] This meant that men could be charged with adultery for keeping concubines. For women's groups this was a major victory, but the impact on concubines does not appear to have been considered. Nonetheless, as Tran has convincingly shown, their victory was a direct result of the women activist's sustained pressure—invoking at every turn the principles of sex equality in the party's own constitution as well as the Tutelage Constitution.

The inheritance laws passed during the Nationalist government's tutelage were equally as revolutionary. Women had argued that economic equality was crucial to women's liberation and that equality in inheritance rights was central to ensuring economic equality with men.[54] As Rubie Watson has outlined, in Qing Law, daughters were not entitled to inherit property from parents except in rare circumstances, and wives had control only of the dowry that they brought into the marriage.[55] In the Nationalist government's "Book of Succession," sons and daughters were granted equal rights to inherit parents' property, and spouses were given more generous rights in regards to their marital partner's property. The laws were detailed and complex and enabled men to ensure that patrilineal inheritance patterns could be continued if agreed contractually, but the code did acknowledge the wife's major interests in her husband's property.[56] The radical nature of these legal reforms demonstrates the extent to which China's political class had moved toward an acceptance of equality between men and women at a philosophical and moral level—even if there remained reservations in practice.

The new laws significantly improved the *legal* position of women. Yet Kathryn Bernhardt has demonstrated in her comprehensive study of women and property rights that "code and custom in fact came into conflict, with the result that daughters did not attain the full equality promised in the code. For all the good intent of the GMD [Nationalist Party] lawmakers, this development was the inevitable outcome of the imposition of an individual property regime on a society that continued to operate by the logic of family property."[57] Women did take advantage of these new laws, and Bernhardt provides numerous examples of court cases wherein women sued other family members for family property.[58]

The public and vociferous struggles for legal reforms that enshrined sex equality in both marriage and inheritance laws stands as clear evidence that women's rights activists in Nationalist Party–controlled areas during these years were by no means silenced or subdued. They cleverly developed their reform arguments from their newly won status as full and equal citizens within the new regime. Women's equality with men was a powerful legal argument in the 1930s. A decade earlier it had won recognition as a powerful moral argument among China's reformist intellectuals, but by the Nanjing Decade this principle provided women's rights activists with serious and practical political clout.

THE NEW LIFE MOVEMENT: WOMEN CITIZENS AS VIRTUOUS WIVES AND COMPASSIONATE MOTHERS

Curiously, these radical legislative successes took place within a social and political order that was increasingly conservative in public rhetoric on issues of women's place in the nation. Chiang Kai-shek needed to mold the women's movement in the areas under his control to suit his regime—in part to break the strong links between the women's movement and the CCP that had formed during the United Front. Chiang needed a strategy for conceptualizing the revolution in social gender mores occurring in 1930s China and harnessing these changes for his Nationalist government. The tutelage period was one in which political, social, and moral stability was a rhetorical priority— the appeals to iconoclastic change typified in the New Culture Movement were put aside. But "new" and "revolutionary" were still important notions for marketing stability, thus Chiang called his foray into moral engineering the New Life Movement. Begun in February 1934, the New Life Movement was a curious mixture of Confucian and Christian values and discipline alongside revolutionary mobilization of the population for hygiene campaigns and the promotion of conjugal fidelity for both men and women.[59] It was directed at generating traditional national virtues among the populace while not appearing to jeopardize the "new" and the "modern." Ultimately, this conservative movement aimed to improve social morals and remind women of their value as mothers—selfless nurturers and educators of the nation—as it promoted the age-old maxim of "good wives and wise mothers."

A national New Life Committee was formed with Chiang Kai-shek's wife, Song Meiling, at its head. The moral health of the nation, conceived

as a Confucian-Christian family, was under the wings of a conjugal dictatorship with Chiang as father and Song as mother. She led a team of women
Nationalist Party members, including many who would assume positions
as parliamentarians in China's wartime parliament, as we shall see in the
following chapter. One of these, Zhang Weizhen (b. 1911), an educationalist
and commissioner for the Ministry of Education in Nanjing, would go on
to become a member of the National Assembly in 1947 as a representative
of the Liaobei Occupational Groups.[60] The New Life Committee promoted
women's knowledge of household health and hygiene, the care of the elderly
and the disabled, as well as hygienic care of infants. Its broad-ranging moral
campaign also included encouraging women to buy Chinese-made products, to rid themselves of superstitions, and to learn to read and write.[61] The
New Life Movement was not an entirely negative program for women activists since its support of fidelity dovetailed with feminist campaigns for equal
legal rights in marriage, divorce, and adultery, and its education and health
campaigns suited the women's struggle for improvements in women's lot
more generally. It also drew together activist women in the noncommunist
areas and facilitated their continued involvement as a gender-specific political group. Moreover, the politically and morally constrained role adopted
by women activists may well have made possible the crucial constitutional
changes that were to emerge after the convention and the New Life Movement—their position in the conservative establishment being confirmed by
their participation in the movement's activities.

However, in the name of the New Life Movement's promotion of morals
and virtue, some provincial heads inflicted both idiocies and atrocities on
the women unfortunate enough to dwell in regions under their control. The
leader of Shandong's provincial government, General Han Fu-chu took it
upon himself to arrest "modern girls" for the supposed violation of the New
Life Movement's regulations of appropriate dress. Bobbed hair, wearing face
powder, short sleeves, and short trousers were offenses punishable with jail
terms.[62] The Confucian modesty demanded of women in the New Life campaign continued through 1936, with reports of the punishment of women
who were deemed to reach beyond the "acceptable" in their apparel. The
China Weekly Review published the following report on 22 August 1936:

> Changsha . . . is in the throes of a controversy concerning women's fash-
> ions. Chow Han, a staunch "moralist," who is head of the Bureau of Public
> Safety and concurrently sectional chief in the New Life Movement Promo-
> tion Association, recently ordered the confiscation of all waving machines in

barber shops, in pursuance of his campaign against curled hair, high heels, short sleeves, etc. It is even rumored that the police in Changsha have been instructed to shave the head of any women found on the streets with waved hair. The Changsha Women's Association lodged a strong protest against the "reform" wave, arguing that improvement of the art of dressing is a natural outcome of the advancement of material civilization; therefore in all modern countries in the West, women's dresses are becoming more and more artistic and fanciful. The women's protest was flatly turned down.[63]

This conservative backlash affected urban women from the middle and upper classes who had been radicalized during the New Culture Movement.

Not surprisingly, accompanying the official advocacy of "appropriate feminine modesty" was the unabated relishing of women's aesthetic and sexual appeal by men in those regions buffered from the full force of the campaign, like the "international" city of Shanghai. The English press, only months after reporting the crackdown in Changsha, noted the fascination of Shanghai men for "girls" in an article on high-class escorts and companions tantalizingly titled "The Girl Guides": "Shanghai is going mad after girls. By instinct, men love pretty girls, but this love as expressed by Shanghai men is more sensual than aesthetic." Demand for attractive girls willing to dance, sing, act, have sex, or adorn events was supposedly endless. "Shanghai's love for girls has made it a free hunting ground for enterprising girls to seek fame and fortune." The article ends with a challenge: "Why should we look at morality through a magnifying glass and raise a hue and cry over moral bankruptcy, when chances of employment for girls are so few in this man-ruled world? It is both natural and justifiable that they should 'sell' their natural endowments—beauty and charms—to the girl-crazy public as a means of livelihood."[64] These contradictory responses to the New Life Movement placed women's rights activists in the invidious position of fighting to expand the scope of women's public movement while simultaneously arguing against the "immoral and exploitative" industry of prostitution.

Gail Hershatter's study of interventions in the sex industry reveals how many women's rights activists coopted the New Life Movement's momentum in an attempt to win gains in an area they had long considered a social scourge. One concern was the supposed effects of prostitution on the national political "health." Tang Guozhen, a Hunanese Nationalist Party member, New Life Movement committee member and long-term suffrage campaigner (who would later go on to represent women in China's wartime parliament) declared that prostitution caused more harm to society than robbery because it distracted men from serving society.[65] Hershatter explains how many commentators in the 1930s linked the incidence of prostitution to a nation in crisis—economic and political instability generated higher levels of prostitution.[66]

Within this new and restrained environment the women's groups in Nationalist-controlled areas reorganized between 1933 and 1934 and reduced their explicit campaigning for women's suffrage rights. Tan Sheying calls these years the "period of women's associations" (*Funü hui shiqi*) since most of the various suffrage and philanthropic groups joined together to form locality-based women's associations under the direct auspices of the Nationalist Party and purged of any communist influences from the preceding UWA period.[67] In June 1933, the Nanjing Women's Association was formed, followed by ones in Jiangsu, Hunan, and Shanghai. In 1934 a central government ruling called for the reorganization of all women's groups under the Women's Association banner and conducted an audit of membership. In total, across nineteen provinces and municipalities there were over eight thousand five hundred women registered as members. The largest numbers came from Zhejiang, Nanjing, and Guangdong.[68] The manifestos to these associations make no explicit mention of struggling for women's suffrage rights. They express concern to develop "independence," "industry," and "knowledge" among women within the context of the Nationalist Party leadership.

Typical of the tenor of the times in Nationalist-controlled China is Huang Jiade's handbook called *New Types of Women* (*Xin nü xing*). In this 1936 volume, Huang explains how women's freedom should be expressed within the domestic sphere, and he recommended that public activities, like schooling, should be sex segregated. Coeducational schooling led to seduction, premarital sex, pregnancy, and moral decline, according to Huang. Moreover, participation in public life had simply led women to be distracted into frivolities of theatergoing, dance-hall hopping, and shopping.[69] Clearly, women's rights activists in Nationalist government–controlled China faced a very complex set of problems in undertaking their lobbying. On the one hand they achieved remarkable legal reforms that confirmed the power of the notion that women were equal to men, and on the other, they faced ongoing accusations that modernity was corrupting the very heart of women's virtue—sexual chastity.

CONTESTED CATEGORIES OF ENFRANCHISEMENT:
SUFFRAGE IN THE COMMUNIST BASE AREAS

As the women activists in the Nationalist government areas contended with the New Life Movement, women in the CCP-controlled areas faced a different challenge. The CCP had been keen to harness the "bourgeois" women's energies and networks but only insofar as it would further achieve their ultimate goal of fomenting class struggle. However, their expulsion from the United Front and subsequent exile to the remote rural regions of Jiangxi and then Yan'an drew them further away from the urban-based women's movement with its prime preoccupation with effecting constitutional and legal changes for women. This did not mean that women's issues for enhanced representation were ignored in the areas under CCP control. The CCP introduced numerous electoral processes among the villages that it controlled which demonstrated a commitment to realizing democratic participation among a long-disenfranchised group.

As early as 1931 while encamped in the borderlands between Jiangxi and Fujian—in their base known as the Jiangxi Soviet—the CCP signaled its commitment to equity between men and women in politics. On 7 November 1931 Ruijin Township held a National Representatives Assembly of Worker Peasant Soldiers and established the precedents for electoral rights in Communist Party–held territory. The laws outlined in the "All-China Soviet Electoral Laws" (*Zhonghua Suwei'ai gongheguo xuanfa dagang*) declared, "In the areas under the control of the Soviet all workers, peasants, soldiers, and working people and their families are equal under the laws of the Soviet regardless of their sex, ethnicity, or religion and are considered to be citizens of the All China Soviet." It continued with an explicit expression of support for women's emancipation: "In order to totally guarantee to advance the goals of women's liberation the Soviet recognizes freedom in choice of marriage, and it will introduce various plans to protect women . . . and to enable women to fully participate in society's economic and political spheres."[70]

Electoral laws introduced in 1933 likewise granted women voting rights on an equal basis with men in CCP-controlled areas. This did not mean universal suffrage since certain groups were excluded from voting (landlords, rich peasants, capitalists, Buddhist and Daoist monks, police, and bureaucrats in the Nationalist government). Poor and middle peasants along with workers and self-employed persons were eligible to vote. Significantly, there were no literacy requirements for voters in these elections—the age-old link between learning and the right to access political power had been broken in this remote part of China as well. The Soviet's electoral practices echoed the important broader shift in attitudes about democratic representation that had occurred throughout that nation from the mid-1920s onward—the removal of literacy as a prerequisite for voting.

Another distinctive feature of the Soviet's electoral system was the lack of a secret ballot. Instead an electoral meeting was held where everyone voted simultaneously by a show of hands.[71] The system did not appear to damage women's political prospects; in fact these elections returned strong results for women. By January 1934 most districts returned impressive results with more than 25 percent of the delegates being female.[72] Kay Ann Johnson notes that in some congresses the percentage of women reached as high as 64 percent as a result of the large numbers of men drawn away into military service.[73]

The changes to the marriage laws instituted in the base areas made divorce equitable as well as the division of property after divorce. They went further than the Nationalist government's civil code in outlawing polygyny and polyandry—the latter referring to the rare practice of women having more than one husband that occurred for decades among the poor.[74] They also gave women rights to raise all children under sixteen in the event of a divorce and legislated that the husband would be liable to make payments for their upkeep. Exceptions to the free divorce law were made in the case of wives of soldiers. In these circumstances wives had to obtain agreement from the husbands before winning a divorce.[75] While Delia Davin suggests that it was "unlikely that the law was very thoroughly implemented in those early years,"[76] Kay Ann Johnson's extended discussion of the debates among CCP policymakers about the problems this policy caused suggests that its impact was considerable and caused much anxiety among men.[77] Land reform legislation was also steeped in the principles of equality between men and women in the Jiangxi Soviet. The November 1931 "All-China Soviet Land Laws" (*Zhonghua Suwei'ai gongheguo tudi fa*) stated that all citizens of the Soviet regardless of sex were eligible for land. In the subsequent, albeit briefly held, land redistribution, married women, daughters, and widows were given equal amounts of land as their husbands, brothers, and fathers.

The careful social planning of the CCP in the Jiangxi Soviet was to be short lived. In January 1934 Chiang Kai-shek launched a full-scale attack on the Communists. This eventually forced the CCP to quit Jiangxi and embark upon its epochal Long March in October.[78] After twelve months of hardship the CCP regrouped in the north. The Yan'an period was one of consolidation of CCP policy and command. As we will see in the following chapter, typically of periods of consolidation, women's fundamental and radical challenges to social hierarchies are tempered for the "greater good." Despite the radical moves in support of women's rights in Jiangxi, conservative trends were to emerge within the CCP in the Yan'an years. Christina Gilmartin has pointed to patriarchal tendencies in the movement from its inception. She noted that "despite their ardent espousal of the cause of women's emancipation . . . early male Communists assumed that they should be the power holders . . . it seemed only too natural to them that men should hold the reins of power and serve as theoreticians and policy-makers while women filled less important roles."[79]

Moreover, a trend that would constrain women's full participation in the CCP became entrenched during these Yan'an years. Women's political engagement was increasingly conflated with the notion of "women's work" (*funü gongzuo*). Women's work was construed as the function of women party members, and their task was primarily to mobilize and politicize the mass of women in China to participate in party activities and implement party policy. Women party members found themselves allocated only work with women and children's issues.[80] Indeed, women's participation in party activity outside of the "women's work" realm was severely constrained. A form of party sex segregation emerged, replacing the older concepts of "women dwell in the inner realm and men in the outer realm." Women active in the CCP movement often felt that they were relegated to women's work and denied opportunities to take part in other aspects of the party's program.

This problem continued to plague the CCP policy on women's political engagement for years to come. A letter to *Women of China* published in 1939 described comments by cadres around the CCP areas. One of the discussants said, "Let's smash the mentality that has only women doing women's work. Let's give women's work to men to do." Another complained, "Once involved in women's work, that's all you'll ever do, it's really annoying." Yet another said, "I can't even behave like a woman, so how can they make me do women's work?" The editorializing accompanying the comments informs readers that such sentiments show that the speakers actually look down upon women while hiding behind words that supposedly show respect for women.[81]

Meanwhile, in Nationalist government China, the competition for political legitimacy was being accelerated. Chiang's government presented a new version of the republic's constitution with a promise of imminent national elections.

NATIONAL VICTORY?
DOUBLE FIFTH CONSTITUTION

Under the terms of the Tutelage regulations, democratic rule was to be implemented by 1935, but the Nationalist government was far less enthusiastic about convening the elections for a proper National Assembly than it had been about convening the Tutelage national convention. The December 1932 meeting of the Fourth Nationalist Party Congress had resolved to convene the National Assembly in March 1935 for the purpose of adopting a permanent national constitution. This date was to pass without a National Assembly convening. However, in anticipation of democratic elections, work on devising a new national constitution was taking place. The resulting document was made public on 1 March 1934, revised on the basis of the public comments and criticism received, and on 16 October 1934 submitted to the national government for its transmission to the Nationalist Party.[82] Revisions were requested and finally, in December 1935, the Fifth Nationalist Party Congress decided upon 5 May 1936 as the date for the promulgation of the document. However, still reluctant to share power, the Nationalist government and not the promised popularly elected National Assembly approved the draft constitution. The document could not become law until national elections established a popularly elected body that was empowered to formally promulgate a constitution. It became known as the Double Fifth Constitution and would later form the basis of the formal Constitution of the ROC of 1946–47.[83]

The Double Fifth Constitution confirmed for women that the generalized equality of the Tutelage Constitution was to be transformed into concrete political rights. In this document, equality between men and women was guaranteed alongside race, class, and religion. Articles 28 and 29 of the 1936 document state:

28. Delegates to the People's Congress [National Assembly] shall be elected by universal, equal, and direct suffrage and by secret ballots.

29. Citizens of the Republic of China having attained the age of twenty years shall, in accordance with law, have the right to elect delegates. Citizens having attained the age of twenty-five years shall, in accordance with law, have the right to be elected delegates.[84]

Celebration by women's groups after the constitution's passage was considerable. After a twenty-five year struggle, women had won the right to equal participation with men in the national political process.

After another series of false starts, it was announced that the National Assembly would convene on 12 November 1937, and so elections for representatives were begun.[85] Democratic groups around the nation began their campaigns with this date as their goal. Women's suffrage activists were among the more enthusiastic participants, and in the autumn of 1936 had campaigned across the nation for women candidates. A report from 3 October noted that "China's feminist movement will receive a serious setback as the nationwide campaign . . . to elect women's candidates to the National People's Assembly scheduled to open on Nov. 12 is heading for failure." The women's movement had hoped to elect women to as many as one-third of the one thousand two hundred seats, but "competent observers are inclined to predict that not more than four woman delegates will receive enough votes for the Assembly in the final elections to be held soon. Thousands of handbills have been distributed . . . asking the local populace to vote for Miss M. K. Sophia Chang."[86] The grim predictions by "competent observers" were reasonably accurate. This partial round of elections placed five women in seats, amounting to 0.5 percent of the total.[87] These included Nationalist Party members Lü Yunzhang, Wang Xiaoying, and Zhao Maohua.[88]

However, these few women, the first to win seats in a national parliament, were not to enjoy their newfound legislative power in quite the form of government expected. The invasion by Japan in 1937 placed the democrats' campaign for full elections in a less than desirable situation. Domestic concerns for constitutional democracy were shelved as the very survival of the nation was threatened. In place of the National Assembly, for which the complete election of representatives was now regarded as impossible, the national government decided to convene the People's Political Council (PPC)—known informally as China's wartime parliament. As we will see in the following chapter and despite the evident reluctance of the Nationalist government to hold elections, the women activists remained enthusiastic about participation in politics, probably still buoyed by their recent success with the constitution.

The commencement of the brutal and protracted war against Japan (the Second Sino-Japanese War, 1937–1945) marked the beginning of the end of Nationalist Party dominance of China. Chiang's loathing of the CCP continued unabated, but the threat posed by an external enemy forced him to reconsider the formal relationship between the CCP and the Nationalist Party. Popular disgust in major urban areas at Chiang's policy of "first internal pacification (fighting the CCP), then external resistance (fighting the Japanese)" was a major imperative to change. Accordingly, the Second United Front between the Nationalists and the CCP was forged. It lasted until the end of World War II in 1945, after which the two bitter enemies recommenced their civil war. During this period China's women's movement mobilized under a patriotic banner, and old alliances between CCP and Nationalist women from the New Culture period were reinvigorated.

SEVEN

Realizing the Power of Difference

Quotas, War, and Elections, 1936–1948[1]

The Double Fifth Constitution of 5 May 1936 acknowledged women's equal rights with men, but this success was certainly not the end of women's activism on feminist politics in China. In the decade from 1936 Chinese women's rights activists waged a successful campaign to win a set minimum quota of seats for women in the national legislative bodies. This goal was achieved at a time of national crisis—the Japanese invasion of China—during a decade of constant warfare. The group that formed to promote the quotas campaign was called the Women's Electoral Lobby for the National Assembly (*Funü guomin dahui daibiao jingxuan hui*), and it convened branches in all major cities.[2] This campaign is a pivotal part of the history of women's participation in politics since it reveals the results of the activists' strategic mobilization of lobbying premised on differences between the sexes. Special quotas for women were achieved because the case had been developed in preceding years that women's difference from men required special political provisions. This chapter explores the campaign through which Chinese women lobbied for this special quota and further demonstrates that, contrary to common perceptions, an independent feminist movement did engage in distinct activism on women's political rights during the war against Japan. Their efforts were rewarded with the inclusion of a 10 percent minimum quota in the national constitutional documents of 1946–1947. As a direct extension of the Chinese women's suffrage movement of 1911–1936 the legislative changes effected are still largely upheld in current Taiwan, ROC, electoral laws.

China's women activists were of the opinion that the maintenance of women's rights required constant parliamentary vigilance; only if women actually sat in parliament with full voting rights would the constitutional republic be able to represent their interests. They believed that a set minimum quota for women was the key to ensuring that women were able to win these seats. Importantly, the Double Fifth Constitution set a precedent for guaranteed quotas in its rulings on the elections of delegates from three minority groups: overseas Chinese, Mongolians, and Tibetans.[3] Feminists then identified winning a special category for women in this list of minority groups as their goal. With equality between men and women guaranteed, and women's collective political identity broadly accepted, the practical impact of the argument that men and women had distinctly different political interests could be realized.

WHAT "QUOTA CAMPAIGN"?

The quota campaign, like the women's suffrage campaign more generally, has been largely overlooked in Chinese political histories. There are several distinct explanations for previous scholars' lack of interest. One key reason is that it falls between the histories of the women's programs of the two dominant parties—the Nationalist Party and the CCP—that have attracted more attention. Many of the women involved in the quota campaign were aligned with neither party. Instead they occupied the middle ground between the two and, in some cases but not all, joined smaller democratic groups such as the Federation of Chinese Democratic Parties (FCDP).[4] Feminists active in the two major parties did participate, some taking leading roles, and there is no doubt that support and leadership from Nationalist Party women contributed greatly to the eventual success of the campaign. Nonetheless, the two major parties did not directly sponsor the issue, and the vitality of the campaign during a difficult decade originated from the alliance of feminists with disparate political perspectives.

The general disinterest in the campaign for quotas can also be accounted for by the belief that there was no activism by women relating to political participation during the war years at all. Norma Diamond declared the spring of 1938 as the "final death knell to an independent women's movement in the KMT-run [Nationalist Party] area of the mainland" because this date signaled the cooption (and supposedly, the silencing) of women activists into a united war effort against Japan at a meeting convened by Chiang Kai-shek's wife, Song Meiling.[5] So prevalent was this perspective that Chou, Clark, and Clark have stated in their volume *Women in Taiwan Politics* that the inclusion of quotas for women "required persistent and at times serious struggle on the part of many women and their male supporters between 1912 and 1936."[6] In fact, the struggle for a guaranteed minimum level of representation for women occurred in the years after 1936. As was clear from the discussion in the previous chapters, prior to this, feminists had been campaigning specifically for sex equality in the constitution and its accompanying electoral legislation while developing the narrative of women's collective political interests.

The general view presented is that a combination of Nationalist Party suppression, the exigencies of war, and the women activists' own lack of interest resulted in the removal of politics from the feminist agenda of the war years. This chapter will show that not all of China's leading feminists regarded their work as being completed in 1936, nor were they completely silenced by the Nationalist Party in 1938; rather, they directed their political campaigning along new paths, building upon the foundation of the newly won equality. These women regarded constitutional equality not as the end of their work but rather as the point for fresh departures. Moreover, they took advantage of the limited space for freedom of expression provided by the Nationalist Party's need to present a face of democratic intent for the international community during the war against Japan, to pursue a distinctly feminist agenda in regards to political participation.

The existence of a vibrant feminist campaigning "postequality victory" is comparatively unique in histories of women's suffrage movements around the globe where, as Richard Evans has noted, feminist movements tended to decline once the suffrage was won: "Of course, it is a fairly obvious point that feminist movements were almost bound to be weakened by winning the vote. . . . When it was won, many feminists felt there was little more to do."[7] For China's feminists the battle to ensure that women's suffrage was not merely an empty theoretical right began on the platform provided by their newly won equality. Unlike their Western counterparts who, Evans declares, slumped into destructive internal bickering after their suffrage wins, China's women's suffrage activists were galvanized to ensure that they personally, as the likely main benefactors of the newly won right to stand for election, would be able to actually win seats in parliament. The quotas campaign served to unify the feminist activists in China in a period when their organizations would easily have fragmented and disappeared.

"UNIQUELY CHINESE" POST-ENFRANCHISEMENT ACTIVISM

There are a number of possible reasons for China's unique unity after winning equality provisions in the campaign for quotas. First, over the preceding three decades, China's women's movement had successfully established a legitimate political interest group within the broader political scene in China. China's new political ideologies now recognized women as a group that deserved special political attention along with youth, peasants, and minorities. Moreover, the women activists themselves appear to have maintained an active sense of women's political collectivity. Such a political identity did not necessitate a uniformity of political opinion from all feminist activists except on one central principle—that crucial notion of women's unity of disadvantage relative to men. Communists, nationalists, democrats, and anarchists could all find some point at which they recognized the validity of this principle if they so chose. As a result of the strength of women's collective political identity within the broad Chinese political scene, the debilitating schisms that had occurred in Europe between middle-class feminists and working-class feminists did not develop fully in China in a manner that would hinder the progress of the campaign for suffrage or quotas.[8] (See Figure 7.1 for a picture of the CCP's international women's movement.)

Second, the continued activism of the Chinese women's movement post-enfranchisement is also due to the relative homogeneity of the women that composed the leadership of the group despite its broadening membership during the New Culture period. Almost all the leading feminists active during the war against Japan were middle-class women with considerably more education than the majority of the Chinese population, but importantly they were all committed to personal, active participation in formal politics. They realized that if minimum quotas for women in parliament were achieved,

Figure 7.1. "Women of the World Unite!" Cover page, *Funü zhoubao* (Women's Weekly News) 1, nos. 10–11 (1940).

it would impact all political parties' preselection procedures. Awareness of this fact no doubt encouraged cooperation from feminists across a disparate range of political persuasions. All the women activists stood to gain personally and directly since by default they were politically ambitious. This multiparty unity was important when it came to expounding the principle of special quotas for women in China's wartime parliament, the PPC, because the numbers of women in the council were tiny—between ten and fifteen out of a full complement of over two hundred.[9]

The existence of the PPC was an important third factor in encouraging feminist unity after the suffrage victory. Formed in 1938, the PPC was a Nationalist government body designed to advise the government during the war against Japan and to stem the growing demands for full and free democratic elections. It met thirteen times during the years 1938–1947, with the first council being held in Hankou on 6–15 July 1938 and the last in Nanjing on 20 May–2 June 1947. The PPC was to meet for ten days every three months, but meetings were postponed or cancelled several times.[10] It drew a broad cross-section of political interests into one structure and provided a platform from which women—regardless of their formal political affiliations—could lobby together on feminist issues. The existence of such a structure, under the framework of the Second United Front against the Japanese, provided the vital political space to facilitate this feminist cooperation. Importantly, this parliament was not a popularly elected body. In 1938, the formation of the PPC involved the appointment of one hundred eminent persons and one hundred representatives from the provinces and municipalities not under Japanese control. Through a complex process of nomination and approval, which assiduously avoided popular elections, the Nationalist Party had ultimate control over who was to join the PPC. This did not mean that CCP members were excluded; both Deng Yingchao and Zhou Enlai served on the PPC at various stages. The representatives from the provinces and municipalities "should be chosen from among those who had served for more than three years in public or private organizations" and, because there were no elections, these representatives were to be "nominated at joint conferences of the various provincial and municipal governments and Kuomintang [Nationalist Party] branches of corresponding location and level."[11] Over the course of the preceding decades women had established themselves and their activist groups as legitimate "organizations" so they were duly represented in the parliament.

This wartime body provided a valuable site for women councilors to demonstrate their political skill in a parliamentary arena, raise the issue of quotas to a broad spectrum of the politically active male population, and also to argue for an improvement of women's access to education and health facilities in the name of mobilizing the women for the war. These gains could be made without the pressure of imminent actual elections—since none were going to be held while Japan still posed a military threat. Most important, participation in the PPC enabled feminist activists to directly influence the revision of the Double Fifth Constitution, which resulted in the inclusion of minimum quotas in the 1946–1947 constitution.

While the PPC was a useful mechanism for enhancing the uniquely Chinese post-enfranchisement cooperation by suffrage activists, its record on more general politics is mixed. Ch'ien Tuan-sheng has declared, "altogether, from the First to the Fourth, the People's Political Council grew progressively impotent and disappointing."[12] Gerry Groot describes the PPC as "not a parliament but effectively an inclusive corporatist body."[13] Indeed, while the government ignored the PPC's repeated calls for a return to constitutional democratic rule it did set in motion a process by which recommendations on reforms to the Double Fifth document were possible. As Edmund Fung has noted "the war period was far from sterile in the democratic discourse."[14]

The war against Japan also created a patriotic cover for feminist unity among women activists. The Second United Front forged to battle the invading Japanese army, enabled women from all political persuasions to cooperate under a reinvigorated nationalism (now specifically defined in terms of anti-Japanese sentiment) to facilitate feminist constitutional reform and improved governance within the rubric of patriotic activism. This broad political consensus was cemented in the Lushan Conference of May 1938 where China's women leaders—including CCP, nonaligned, and Nationalist Party—agreed to coordinate women's activities in the struggle against Japan through the Women's Advisory Committee (WAC) of the New Life campaign.[15] While Norma Diamond regarded this conference as being the end of independent women's activism, the quotas campaign described below shows that this meeting was far from a totalizing silencing or cooption of all feminist forces. Indeed, the political party affiliations of the women involved in the quotas campaign were diverse, and this diversity gave the campaign its strength. When all other groups were disenchanted or silenced, the Nationalist Party feminist activists could maintain the struggle.

FEMINISTS IN AND OUT OF THE TWO-PARTY STRUCTURE

The political histories of women PPC members provide evidence of the diversity of voices in the PPC that enabled feminist voices to continue to be heard within China's only national political body at this time. While not all views were heard equally across the entire life of the PPC—left-wing voices were often silenced—all voices were heard at some point. The women PPC members range from nonaligned patriots to CCP and Nationalist Party members. All have a lengthy history of activism on feminist issues over several decades. Moreover, the non–Nationalist Party women often had checkered and fraught positions in the PPC.

For example, longtime suffragist Liu Wang Liming, national president of the WCTU, was expelled from the PPC in September of 1943 for her explicit sustained criticism of the Nationalist Party and her putative support of the CCP. By 1944 she had joined the FCDP and was elected to its central committee. Her "feminist left-democratic" status was confirmed in 1945 when she formed the Chinese Women's United Association (*Zhongguo funü lianyihui*); this association aimed to promote democracy among women in the face of the Nationalist's continued reluctance.[16] A close friend of Liu Wang Liming's and fellow FCDP member, Shi Liang (1900–1985), served as lawyer for the women campaigning for quotas in the PPC. She was committed to constitutional democracy and as a consequence was appointed to the PPC's Committee for the Promotion of Constitutionalism where she won crucial concessions for women, as will become evident below. Shi had been one of the leaders in the one thousand–strong membership of the Shanghai Women's National Salvation Society (*Shanghai funü jie jiuguo hui*) formed in December of 1935 that took the lead in promoting constitutionalism and affirmative action legislation for women in politics. Shi Liang trod the dangerous and narrow path of those critical of the Nationalist Party's continued emphasis on suppressing the CCP in the face of Japan's aggression. Her reputation as a daring patriot was furthered when, during the first anniversary commemorating the December Ninth Movement, she was injured in a demonstration and imprisoned by the Nationalist government. She and her fellow inmates became known as the "seven honorable persons" (*qi junzi*) for their patriotic stand.[17] Shi Liang's commitment to democratic constitutional government was evident when she organized a series of conferences on women and the constitution in 1939–1940. Her role as a leader of the FCDP was to continue in the PRC well after 1949.[18]

Another PPC member, China's first woman university president, Dr. Wu Yifang (1893–1985), was a prominent women's rights activist with apparent close ties to the Nationalist Party. In reality, her political affiliations were much more ambiguous. Wu Yifang's role in the quotas campaign was considerable since she was the only woman in the five-member presidium of the PPC (appointed in 1941 when Zhou Enlai withdrew) and was one of the few women members of the 1946 National Assembly that drew up the constitution. As chair of the National Christian Council and Chinese delegate to the Institute of Pacific Relations in 1929 and 1933 and the International Congress of Women in Chicago in 1933, Wu Yifang was internationally recognized. She was described in *Amerasia* as being "mildly liberal," and it was noted that she had never publicly criticized the Nationalist government.[19] Despite her unproblematic cooperation with the Nationalist Party, Wu remained in China after the 1949 revolution and assumed numerous prominent posts in the education sector, as well as being a delegate to the

National People's Congress and serving on the executive committee of the All-China Women's Federation (ACWF).

The Nationalist Party loyalists among those feminists campaigning for minimum quotas in the PPC included Dr. Wu Zhimei (1897–?), the Cantonese suffrage campaigner. She was a "member of the executive committee and of [the] supervisory committee of Canton Kuomintang headquarters" in 1932. Later in the decade, in 1938, she assumed a role as member of the Nationalist Party executive in Guangdong province.[20] Liu Hengjing was the Nationalist Party member who played the most active role in promoting the issue of special minimum quotas for women in parliament in the PPC. When tensions in the Second United Front made cooperation between the Nationalist Party and other political interests impossible, Liu Hengjing was able to continue raising the issue of quotas in the PPC. Fujianese suffragist and educator Wang Xiaoying (1901–?), although not a member of the PPC, was active in the Women's National Salvation Society, which served as a major sponsor of quotas through Shi Liang. She was elected to the National Assembly in 1946.

Two of the women active in the first stages of the quotas campaign that joined the CCP were Luo Qiong (1911–) and Wang Ruqi (1912–). From Jiangsu Province, Luo was a graduate from Suzhou Women's Normal College and began her activism on women's issues in 1935 in Shanghai where she helped organize the Family Women's Friendship Association (*Jiating funü lianyi hui*) and the Research Association for Women's Issues (*Funü wenti yanjiu hui*). She joined Shi Liang in leading the patriotic Women's National Salvation Society, calling for an end to hostilities between the Nationalist Party and the CCP. During the 1930s she published widely in women's journals and wrote persuasively on the issue of quotas for women in politics. By late 1938 Luo had aligned herself explicitly with the CCP by taking party membership. From this time on she undertook women's work around the country on behalf of the CCP, and after 1949 served on the executive committee of the ACWF as well as the National People's Congress.[21] Wang Ruqi was a law graduate from Fudan University in Shanghai. Like Luo she was spurred to political action by the tensions with Japan and the intractable schism between the CCP and the Nationalist Party. In 1935 she led the propaganda branch of the Women's National Salvation Society and was editor of their organ *Wartime Women's Weekly* (*Zhanshi funü zhoukan*). During the next two years she wrote extensively on constitutional matters relating to equality between men and women and the importance for women of participation in national politics. She joined the CCP in 1938 and left for

Yan'an in 1940 where she was a member of the Women's Bureau. In 1948 she became ACWF secretary in the areas under CCP control, and in 1949 headed the propaganda department of the ACWF from Beijing. Since then Wang has been active in politics holding numerous national government and party positions.[22]

Feminists active on the issue of quotas thus came from a broad cross-section of China's political interests. Their cooperation was crucial to the campaign's success and was predicated on mutual interests being met. Their commitment to the promotion of women in politics regardless of party affiliation attests to their feminist credentials and their sense that women were a distinct political grouping requiring special representation. However, the realization of any success in the quota campaign was dependent upon the return to democratic constitutional rule. The continued reluctance of the Nationalist government to relinquish control meant that the promised National Assembly was repeatedly postponed. Moreover, increasing Japanese aggression further destabilized China's domestic political situation.

THE IMPACT OF WAR ON THE CASE FOR FEMALE DIFFERENCE

Although the advent of the war against Japan in 1937 provided further excuses for delaying the national elections that would have returned China to constitutional rule, it did provide different opportunities for China's feminist activists than would have emerged in peacetime. These opportunities arose in the spaces provided by the contradictory effects of war on gender roles. On the one hand, the cult of masculinity generated by war effectively shifted the entire spectrum further toward the masculine pole, yet on the other hand, it amplified the traditional notion of a separation of spheres. That is to say, although women did adopt habits, dress, and employment usually associated with men during the war, their femininity was inscribed by their prime roles as noncombatants and "supporters" of the men's war effort. As Penny Summerfield has stated, war has often "polarized gender relations rather than reducing the gap between masculinity and femininity."[23] The campaign for minimum quotas for women in parliament in China was not only *not* hindered by this polarization, but it may well have been aided. The identification of "women's difference from man" was precisely the point that the feminist activists were keen to exploit during this campaign.

In the nations of Europe where women's suffrage had not been achieved by the outbreak of World War I, the effects of war on their campaigns has been difficult to gauge. Some scholars, like Arthur Marwick, argued that the overall position of women in society was improved by the expanded opportunities provided by the war.[24] Others, like Richard Evans, have pointed out that the war had either a detrimental or a neutral effect on the timing of the awarding of the franchise to women and that improvements in the status of women were only indirect results of the war's impact on the general political situation.[25] For the women of China, the war against Japan began fortuitously just after their suffrage victory and in the midst of their campaign for quotas, when possible negative effects of the war were reduced.

During the protracted war, China's feminists enhanced their credentials as patriots and thereby reduced the chance that they could be perceived as self-seeking, radical fringe elements. China's feminists became superpatriots, just as the militant wing of the British suffrage movement led by Christabel Pankhurst had been during World War I. The link between feminism and pacifism that delayed the suffrage cause by casting doubt on the patriotism of the feminist movements in Italy, Germany, and America was not a problem for the Chinese feminists.[26] All the prominent campaigners were staunch supporters of the war effort in China (even if it was in the name of restoring peace), just as they had been supporters of the National Revolution in the 1920s and the anti-Qing movements prior to 1911. The war against Japan presented another opportunity for China's politically active women to demonstrate this patriotic commitment.

The war against Japan was also important for the feminist struggle for quotas because it drew a group of new, younger women into the feminist movement. Spurred by patriotism and anti-Japanese sentiment, many of these women joined political activities for the first time. The main association that the new wave of women joined was the Women's National Salvation Society. These societies were formed to press the case for Nationalist Party and CCP unity in the fight against Japan. Branches of this group emerged in the major cities of Nanjing and Shanghai at the end of 1935 and the beginning of 1936. The Shanghai group had over a thousand members including students, housewives, lawyers, doctors, nurses, and educators.[27]

Under the rubric of patriotism, the National Salvation Societies included women from a wide range of political backgrounds and provided feminists, whatever their political coloring, with the opportunity to make progress cooperatively. For example, the Shanghai group established in December of 1935 included Nationalist Party member Wang Xiaoying and the non-aligned Shi Liang. The main organ of the Women's National Salvation Societies was a journal called *Women's Life* (*Funü shenghuo*), and it became one of the main journals that repeatedly raised the issue of quotas for women in parliament. (See Figure 7.2 for the banner of the magazine's table of contents.) For the most part *Women's Life* saw its mission as patriotic. It aimed to increase women's knowledge about international and national political events but also included sections on fiction, science, health, and hygiene. Commenced in 1936, this journal was published twice monthly in Shanghai until late 1937 when, with the arrival of Japanese troops, it shifted to Chongqing. Its enthusiasm for discussions of imperialism and class invited Nationalist government displeasure, and in 1941 the journal was banned. As will become evident below, the articles in *Women's Life* provide vital sources for understanding the rationale China's feminists had for their quota campaign.

The war also helped open space for women's public political action in Nationalist Party areas by countering the narrowing trends of the New Life Movement. The official vehicle for mobilizing women in the war effort was the WAC of the New Life campaign led by Song Meiling. The advent of war prevented the campaign from further curtailing the middle-class women's sphere of public movement, as its invocations of domesticity threatened. To mobilize women for the war, greater freedoms—not fewer—were required. As Song Meiling declared in 1937, in her bid to rally women behind the military cause:

> Today, every one of us Chinese must fight according to our ability, in order to preserve national unity and defend ourselves against aggression. We women are citizens just as much as are our men. Our positions, our capabilities and our line of usefulness may be different but each must do that which

Figure 7.2. Women at a rally. Banner for contents page, *Funü shenghuo* (Women's Life) 1, no. 1 (circa 1936).

best can be done to contribute our share to rescue our nation from defeat and slavery.[28]

Equality of citizenship, only a year old for China's women, was presented as being bound by duties. These duties were different from those of men, but nonetheless valuable and patriotic. It was this discursive space, provided by the war, that the women lobbying for quotas were able to speak from and thus advance their cause within a nationalistic rubric.

A report by Shi Liang to the WAC in October of 1940 outlines the nature of the activities that women were exhorted to undertake as part of the war effort:

> [One hundred and thirteen] Chinese women's organizations had been established at home and abroad during the past three years. . . . About 20,000 women have joined the guerrillas in the "occupied" areas and self-defence corps. Five women's service corps have been organized at the front, its members doing patrol and rescue work. Nearly 1,500 women are engaged in child refugees' work, caring for and educating 20,000 war waifs and orphans housed in 48 homes throughout Free China.[29]

Opportunities for philanthropic work in the name of the war effort expanded considerably during the period that the campaign for quotas was being waged. The roles that these leading feminists played in mothering the nation's orphans and nurturing the nation's refugees confirmed women's special skills as distinct from those of men. More important, these "natural" feminine skills were linked closely with patriotism. Prior to the war, women like Liu Wang Liming had been active in building refuges for homeless girls. During the war she was able to continue the same sort of activity with orphans and refugees, but this time with the additional prestige of performing a patriotic duty.

In sum, both the lead-up to the war and the advent of the war itself provided fertile ground for feminist activists to press their case for quotas precisely because the war emphasized women's separateness from men. The gender roles that emerged within the context of a patriotic war by both sexes against Japan amplified these differences and buttressed the quota campaign. Assertions of women's "equal difference" from men became a powerful practical strategy in the campaign for a set minimum quota of seats for women in national legislative bodies, where in earlier years it had been a discursive strategy for creating a collective political identity for women.

ARGUING THE CASE FOR QUOTAS

While the PPC was the crucial forum for winning set minimum quotas, China's women activists argued the case for quotas prior to both the Japanese invasion and the establishment of the PPC. This was a direct result of the fact that, as a comparative latecomer to the list of nations that had granted sex equality in suffrage rights, China's feminists were in the fortuitous position of witnessing the international impact of women's suffrage on women's participation in politics. Elections around the world based on equal suffrage rights demonstrated the likely effects of women's suffrage to the observant Chinese feminists. It became clear that minimum quotas for women would be necessary to ensure that equality on paper would become equality in reality, since the numbers of women being elected or even nominated by their parties around the world were minimal. Feminist activists began their campaign to persuade women of the need to lobby for minimum quotas; after all, as equal citizens women would be able to vote on such an issue. A survey of articles from *Women's Life* on the issue provides examples of the political thinking of feminists in China at the time. *Women's Life*'s concern for promoting quotas for women occurred during the first two years of the journal's existence, 1936–1937, after which time the campaign shifted to focus on the PPC. As one of the main nonaligned journals of the period it provides an overview of the rationale and the logic used by China's feminists campaigning for special quotas for women.

In the first instance, China's feminists saw the importance of encouraging women to reposition their movement, rather than let it decline, within the changed context of actually being equal political citizens to men. In an article by Qin Jin published in August 1936, the importance of reframing the feminist political struggle was asserted. Appearing under the regular "Women's University" column, the subheadings reflect its goal to educate readers about the prospects of their newly won rights, such as "What Is the National Assembly?" "Election Problems for Women," and "The Powers Granted Women in the New Constitution." The article argued that women should not become complacent about their victory in ensuring that sex equality be included in the constitution.

> [The constitution] clearly states that people's rights and responsibilities are equal before the law and that there are no distinctions between men and women. You may ask, "Isn't it a little tiresome, then, for women activists to lobby the capital about the issue of quotas?" I would argue that it is far

from tiresome! In fact, we must support women's demands to the central government regarding the inclusion of a special quota for women within the electoral laws. I'm sure that there is nobody within the women's movement who opposes this type of quota system. This is because everyone is aware that China is an equal society only on paper and not in actuality. Unless we have a quota for women guaranteed by law then I predict that there will be problems for the election of women . . . Without a guaranteed quota how many women will actually walk the halls of the assembly?[30]

Qin Jin proceeds, saying that unless the constitution guarantees a quota for women in the assembly then it is failing to protect the rights of women as equal citizens of China. Indeed, she argues that currently Chinese women only have the responsibilities of citizenship and few of its rights, and only by instituting a quota that guarantees the presence of women's representatives in the assembly would this problem be rectified.[31]

Elections for the National Assembly were announced in 1937, only to be postponed again, but this false alarm provided *Women's Life* with further impetus for articles on women and political participation. In June 1937, an article titled "We Want to Participate in the Promulgation of the Constitution in the National Assembly" appeared on the opening pages of *Women's Life*. Building upon concepts developed in Qin Jin's article of ten months earlier, its author, lawyer Wang Ruqi, argued that ensuring that the legal gains of the draft constitution of 5 May 1936 had concrete results was a foremost concern:

If there are no sincere and conscious plans to act upon the law that men and women have equal rights to vote and stand for election, then the women of the whole nation will be excluded from participation in the National Assembly's work of promulgating a constitution. If this is the case, the so-called National Assembly will be nothing more than an assembly for those few who are men and would cut off that half of China's population that are women as if they did not matter. Moreover, if only one or two women are included then it would be nothing more than tokenism. We women of China want genuine equality of rights and not just equality on paper. If we are not able to achieve actual equality of rights then our legal equality is false and empty. To be even more frank, it would amount to little more than a several-thousand-year-old trick designed to cheat women.[32]

Wang continues her article with an explanation of why she regards the current policies of equality between men and women as being inadequate guarantees for women. Women, she argues, are in a weaker position in society relative to men, and as a result some amount of protection must be afforded women, if their voice is to be heard in national-level politics: "In reality, the elections for the National Assembly would result in very few women being elected because women's level of education, social status, employment opportunities, etc., are all far lower than men's. If we say that the National Assembly is 'to permit every person to have the right to speak' then that half of China's population who are women should have a voice."[33]

The demands Wang expresses are clear, albeit modest. In the knowledge that the government was proposing to include a mixture of elected and appointed representatives, she asked that the government use its powers to ensure that women have a guaranteed proportion of those appointed seats:

> We acknowledge that the government cannot change the current electoral laws since the elections are already in progress; however, we would request that within that category of appointed representatives, which has just been increased to two hundred and forty members, a quota for women representatives be determined. Moreover, we request that this quota be made as large as possible so that women can be granted electoral equality in reality and not just on paper.[34]

Wang argued on behalf of the women she represented that such a quota would benefit the government by strengthening the nation. She suggests that the authorities will respond to their requests because they will want to foster women's votes and encourage women to participate more fully in the task of national revival. She also makes a strong call to women readers of *Women's Life* to make themselves heard to ensure that the government be made fully aware of the broad base of support for the request for quotas. The importance of this is noted in the emphasis of the points concerned: "*At the same time, we also sincerely believe that, in order to truly foster women's rights, they will respond to these, the reasonable and legal requests, of all the women from the whole of China.*"[35]

Similarly, in her conclusion she writes of the importance of galvanizing the energies of women to present a unified and powerful force: "We hope that the authorities will sincerely address our reasonable and legal claims, but *we hope even more that women comrades across the whole of the nation do not delay any further but immediately unite and rise up to demonstrate in solidarity our resolve and our strength. Only when we use all our strength and resolve to support our demands, will our goals be realized.*"[36]

A few weeks later *Women's Life* followed Wang's initial article with a special issue on "Women and the National Assembly." Wang contributed the lead article and was supported by contributions from five others—Luo Qiong, Ji Hong, Wen Yang, Mo Yan, and Zi Jiu. In these articles we see Wang's arguments elaborated further.[37] She stresses the importance of having strong and united women's organizations with clear plans for action. She also argues that women need to put aside their prejudices about women in order to fight more successfully on the single issue of winning quotas for women in the National Assembly. Wang calls on women activists to publicize their movement in every possible manner, including public speaking and contributing to newspapers and journals. She says that it is imperative that the men and women of China be made aware that this struggle is not about pitching men against women. Rather, it should be conceived as an inevitable citizens' rights movement and a national movement that includes the struggle for women's rightful access to political power. Wang concludes her article by reiterating the basic points—that the authorities allocate women a guaranteed quota, that the authorities select more women in those portions of the representatives that the government itself nominates, and that the women who are chosen reflect the demands and wishes of the women of China. In making this third claim, Wang was clearly aware that the authorities could nominate women whose politics could hinder the progress of the women's rights movement. Her final words are a call for concrete action:

> What should we do? Generally speaking, we should implement the following as quickly as possible: (1) undertake consciousness-raising and organizing of all women; (2) unite all women's organizations around the country to form a national action group for the Participation of Women in the Formulation of the Constitution and form subcommittees at every location; and (3) ensure that every regional group should lobby their own representatives and local councils to represent our demands.[38]

The sense of urgency in her calls for action are premised on the erroneous understanding that the National Assembly would be convened in November and that the elections would be completed by mid-August. The Japanese invasion when combined with the government's lack of resolve to establish a constitutional democracy rendered this impossible.

Luo Qiong's article, "The Place of the Movement to Participate in Politics in Women's Liberation," draws international comparisons and then argues that equality with men in suffrage is not sufficient for the realization of complete equality in social and economic aspects. She declares that while most countries in the world recognized that men and women should have equal voting rights after World War I, this in itself has not helped women achieve their goals. The result of this, Luo argues, is that women are still scarce in parliaments around the globe. The international experience shows that women cannot break through the barriers to equally participate in politics in sufficient numbers to represent women even in a very modest way, despite equality being guaranteed in electoral laws. It is to China's advantage to learn from these weaknesses. Luo then explains why it would be difficult for women to be elected in the Chinese electoral system. She declares that because the majority of women in the country are poor and living in the rural areas and often lacking the education or the ability to organize, they will not vote and so the natural constituency for aspiring women politicians is weakened. She continued pressing her case by pointing out that women's long-term disadvantage relative to men across all sectors of society would prevent them from being adequately represented in the special quotas planned for different sectors of the workforce or in the provincial or municipal parliamentary representatives. According to Luo, women's political opportunities and interests were collectively and uniquely different from men's.

Luo then points out that greater representation for women is not simply a goal in itself. Crucial legislative changes that guarantee women equality of education, employment opportunities, marriage rights, and freedoms are the ultimate goal for women activists. However, these matters will only be seriously considered when women are able to speak on these issues in a legislative assembly. She argues that women should only regard the movement to participate in politics as being a tool for use in the larger struggle to achieve equality. For women, access to the National Assembly is merely the provision of the platform from which women can raise issues related to women and ensure that women's interests are considered at every point in the legislative process. Moreover, once in these public positions, Luo states, such women would serve as models that would rouse other women to action.[39]

Ji Hong's contribution argues that women should be regarded as a group with special electoral needs and therefore should be afforded the same treatment as ethnic minorities and overseas Chinese with a guaranteed minimum quota. She also argues that the legislators should make more specific constitutional guarantees with regard to women's special place in society, specifically articles that show a commitment to equality of educational and occupational opportunity, expansion of childcare centers, maternity hospitals and preschools. She notes that the constitution (1936 draft) only includes one item that specifically recognizes women as having different social positions than men—section 6 on "National Economic Life" includes an article that notes "women and children shall be afforded special protection in accordance with their age and physical condition."[40]

The rationales for allocating a set minimum quota of seats for women in national government bodies were clearly and forcibly argued. The challenge remained to harness the enthusiasm for such rationales in a women's political body similar to that formed in the months preceding the national convention in the mid-1930s. On 1–3 July 1937, the National Association of Women Representatives Electoral Lobby (*Guoda funü daibiao jingxuan hui*) convened a national conference of women political candidates in Nanjing. This body was initially formed on the news that the National Assembly would be convened on 12 November of that year and elections for representatives were in progress. The National Assembly was postponed and elections were fragmented; however, this unified, national action in support of increased representation of women established many of the "women leaders" whose absence Luo Qiong had bemoaned.

Wang Ruqi wrote a brief diary of the events that took place for *Women's Life*. Between fifty and sixty women (including reporters and representatives of the government) attended the first session. The matter of immediate importance was the election of the central committee. The women elected in this lively but chaotic procedure included progressive Nationalist Party members Chen Yiyun and Tang Guozhen. The afternoon was spent visiting the Sun Yat-sen memorial where a photo of the delegation was taken (this was republished in *Women's Life* accompanying Wang's report). The morning of the second day involved the task of passing resolutions for referral to the central government. These were (1) petition the government to include women in the government-appointed delegates, (2) petition the government to send telegrams to all regional party and government organs indicating that women candidates in the primary elections be considered as full and formal members, and (3) petition the government to nominate more women in the special electoral category.[41]

The main proponents on these three points were Nationalist Party members Wu Zhimei from Guangdong, Lü Yunzhang from Beiping, and Qian Jianqiu from Shanghai.[42] As we saw in previous chapters both Wu and Lü had a lengthy history of activism on women's rights, by this time having been involved in the movement since the May Fourth events. The petition that Wu, Lü, and Qian organized was taken in person to the central government offices by a full complement of the conference participants.

Wang notes that the atmosphere among the women after their visit to the government offices was not unlike that of the rustic, illiterate Grannie Liu visiting the luxurious Prospect Garden in the Qing novel *Dream of the Red Chamber* (*Honglou meng*). The morning of the final day saw discussion on the issue of quotas for women in the National Assembly. It was resolved that the government be petitioned to guarantee a minimum ratio of two women per ten representatives in the election of municipal and provincial representatives in the forthcoming polls. The afternoon was similarly successful with resolutions regarding broader issues such as women's education, employment, and health as well as requesting that the government establish a national women's organization.[43]

As the country mobilized to defend itself against Japanese incursions, the political geography was irrevocably altered. Chiang Kai-shek recalled the events of the time in his "Address Before the Commission for the Inauguration of Constitutional Government" (1 March 1945): "You will recall that in 1936 the government decided to summon a People's Congress [National Assembly] on November 12, 1937, for the inauguration of constitutional government and the termination of the period of political tutelage under the Kuomintang. On July 7, 1937, Japan suddenly made war on us, and the plan had to be shelved."[44]

In place of the National Assembly, for which the complete election of representatives was now regarded as impossible, the Nationalist government decided to convene the PPC. Participation in the PPC then provided the women activists with their first opportunity for national level political action. The formation of the National Association of Women Representatives Electoral Lobby had the desired effect of providing a recognizable group of female political aspirants when the PPC was formed and appointments were being made. Some of the women in this political organization including Tang Guozhen, Chen Yiyun, and Liu Hengjing were either appointed or elected to the PPC during the following few years. The campaign for a set minimum quota of seats for women was then carried into the chambers of the PPC for the duration of the war against Japan.

WOMEN PRACTICING POLITICS

Women's success in winning electoral quotas in 1947 can partly be attributed to their successful participation in the PPC. Not only was the issue of special quotas for women repeatedly raised in the council, but also the general performance of the women in the PPC generated respect for their abilities. Despite the weaknesses of the PPC, it was in this forum that women gained valuable experience in the political process. There were ten women in the first session of the first council convened in July 1938, fifteen in the March 1941 council at the first session of the second council, fourteen in October 1942 at the first session of the third council, and at least thirteen in the first session of the fourth council of July 1945.[45]

Most significantly for women, the PPC's system of dual categories for the selection of councilors—one group nominated from eminent persons and the other elected by provincial and municipal bodies—ensured that women could be appointed as eminent persons and did not require the support at a provincial party or government level. It is here that the importance of the repeated calls for the government to establish a national women's organization coupled with establishment of such a body by women themselves becomes evident. Without the appointment of female leaders to nationally authorized women's organizations, few women would be able to make the category of "eminent persons." Moreover, the possibility of women being selected over men for the provincial and municipal categories was regarded as being even less likely.

Nonetheless, over the course of the four PPC councils, the number of women being selected at a provincial level increased, and many who entered the PPC initially as special, eminent persons became provincial representatives in later councils and vice versa. In the first council, of the ten women included only two were representatives of the provinces—Luo Heng represented Yunnan and Dr. Wu Zhimei represented Guangdong. In the second council all the women were nominated "eminent persons." In the third council, four of the fourteen were selected by their provincial party government bodies—Zhang Weizhen, a University of Michigan master's graduate and vice-president of the Pan Pacific Women's Association, was nominated from Jiangsu, Liu Wang Liming from Anhui, Zhang Bangzhen from Yunnan, and Nationalist Party member Hu Mulan from Guangdong. In the final council another four of fourteen were provincial representatives—Tang Guozhen from Hunan, Liu Xianying from Guangdong, Zhang Weizhen from Jiangsu, and Zhang Banzhen from Yunnan. Of the seven CCP representatives, Deng Yingchao was included. Communication between Yan'an and PPC members reveals the support women in the base areas gave the constitutional reform campaign.[46] Bing Xin, author and educator with close contacts to other Wellesley alumni, like Song Meiling, was nominated within the special eminent persons' category. The majority of these women, despite their diverse interests and political leanings, were committed to improving women's position in Chinese society.

In the first council the issue of a special quota for women was raised within the Committee for the Promotion of Constitutionalism, which made recommendations on changes to the draft of 5 May. The woman's representative on the committee, lawyer Shi Liang, argued two points on behalf of women. First, that the article guaranteeing the equality of all people before the law should be amended to include the statement: "With regards to absolutely all aspects of economic, national, cultural, political, and social affairs, women and men enjoy equal rights." Second, in the section relating to the composition of the National Assembly, that a percentage of guaranteed seats be allocated to women. The committee recommended that for the first thirty years after the promulgation of the constitution, a special quota for women's representatives be established.[47] In the explanatory note accompanying the document, the committee noted that it would be very difficult for women to be elected without this support, despite the general rulings on sex equality in all matters of popular elections. However, it was also felt that women should not receive special support for an indefinite period and so the limit of thirty years was chosen since it was predicted that genuine equality between men and women would have been attained by this time. This period of thirty years would see the formation of five separate assemblies (each with a term of six years).[48] Shi Liang was the only woman on the committee of twenty-eight persons, and her contribution to the debate clearly advanced the cause of establishing special provisions for women.

Shi Liang's success at the committee level was reinforced in later years by contributions by other women. Among these was the most senior of the PPC women, Dr. Wu Yifang, the only woman of the five-member presidium of the PPC. In 1941 she publicly expressed the concerns of the women PPC members about the evident difficulty women have in gaining political support from the party machines in the provinces and municipalities. On 19 March, in a broadcast to America, Wu explained the state of China's progress toward a democratic government and concluded by addressing the role of women in the PPC. Here she explained the difficulty for women of gaining seats as representatives of the provinces and municipalities, rather than as eminent persons:

> The women members are not satisfied with the present condition regarding the principle of equality between men and women. It seems as if we

are caught between the ideal principle and the actual practice. Theoretically and legally, women have the same privileges as men, and there is no need of asking for special consideration as women. Yet look at the status of the women members in this Council: there is not one woman among the ninety elected by the Provincial and Municipal People's Political Councils. Even after we make allowances that there are not many experienced women leaders, we cannot believe that in all these Councils there is not one woman who could not stand up well in competition with men candidates for election.[49]

Wu Yifang's commitment to increasing the numbers of women in the nation's representative bodies through a system of quotas, which granted special consideration to women, provided considerable weight to the campaign.

Another PPC councilor, this time from within Nationalist Party ranks, Liu Hengjing, raised the issue of a set minimum quota for women in several of the PPC councils. In April 1940, at the fifth session of the first council, during debate on "matters related to domestic government affairs," Liu put forward the motion that the government allocate a quota of places for women to overcome their low election rate in the district and municipal elections for the National Assembly. The motion was passed and referred to the central government for attention.[50] In 1944 Liu spoke again on the matter of constitutional rights for women when she put forward the motion that the Committee for the Establishment of Constitutional Government have the number of women members increased by two.[51] This was also passed and referred to the government. In 1945, as part of a broad log of claims to the government regarding the reform of the National Assembly, Liu again entered the motion that women be granted a set quota of places in the body.[52] Such constant reminders to the government and the PPC councilors generally that the issue of special quotas for women was still a top priority for women activists was vital to its eventual success.

The women in the PPC took their role as women's representatives seriously and raised in the forum a number of matters relating to the improvement of the status and well-being of women that reached beyond the matter of quotas. Foremost among these were concerns about women's employment and education and public health and welfare.[53] The women councilors' advocacy on broad national issues no doubt served as practical illustrations of the value of women's participation in the national political scene. Indeed, Luo Qiong's aforementioned 1937 challenge for women in politics—that once in the political arena women have the responsibility of developing sex equality in all spheres of life—was partly achieved in the PPC. An article published in 1941 praised the women PPC members saying that only the women members brought issues of maternal and child welfare into the debating chamber. On this basis alone, the article argued, the quota for women should be increased.[54]

In the first session of the first council, Wu Zhimei put forward a lengthy motion that the government support the formation of a national women's organization to coordinate the efforts of women during the war. It was noted that only a small minority of women could be mobilized through women's organizations because, as well as being small in number, such groups primarily focused upon educated women from urban areas. Her six-point recommendation covered a range of different issues and, being framed within the surge to "mobilize *all* people in the anti-Japanese war," was able to be more extensive in its requests on behalf of women than may have been possible in peacetime. She argued that women should be encouraged by the government to enter the productive workforce, not only because it would help their own economic situation, but also because it would strengthen the nation. In a similar vein, Wu stressed the importance of developing the educational level of women during the war period. It was only through expanding literacy that women would be able to play the vital roles of communication support for the soldiers in the field. Her final point was to challenge the government to use all its power to ensure that the general quality of life for women improved—foot binding, child marriages, selling of women, and concubinage should be more vigorously discouraged, and the conditions of women workers and peasants should be drastically improved.[55]

Terms and conditions of employment for women was a repeated focus for debate in the PPC, and one of the most widely publicized cases fought within the PPC was that of the women postal workers' struggle for equality in employment opportunity. In 1940, Shi Liang had put forward the motion that the government employ women in as many public service positions as possible, and this recommendation was duly passed to the central authorities.[56] Women campaigned against workplace discrimination on the grounds of marital status. Prior to 1941 women postal workers were prohibited from continuing employment after marriage. A successful action by the women in the PPC, including negotiations with the ministry of communications, ensured that equality for married women in postal work was achieved.[57] Public health was another issue that was repeatedly raised by the women councilors. For example, Wu Yifang spoke on the need for more and better public hospitals. Tang Guozhen spoke on the importance of providing relief for refugees fleeing the war, and Liu Hengjing spoke on the need to establish more childcare centers to better enable women to participate in the war effort.[58] The disparate nature of the political affiliations of the women in the PPC, including CCP, FCDP, and Nationalist Party members as well as nonaligned women, in concert with their preparedness to argue on a range of women's issues, may well have strengthened the campaign for a set minimum quota of seats for women in political assemblies.

Outside of the PPC, women also maintained a political presence and sustained pressure on the government about sex equality and constitutional reform. In 1940 Shi Liang had held a series of conferences on Women and Constitutionalism in Chongqing (which over two hundred women attended) and organized a rally on International Women's Day that attracted over five thousand women. (See Figure 7.3 for a line drawing of a woman orator.) At the meeting preceding the rally it was resolved "to send a petition to the national government asking that the new constitution include stipulations that women shall be given equal rights in civil, political and the economic field; that women should be given a representation of thirty percent in the National People's Congress [National Assembly] as well as in the

Figure 7.3. Woman orator. *Funü shenghuo* (Women's Life) 4, no. 1 (1937).

xian [county], municipal and provincial people's councils."[59] On 17 January 1940, women in the Yan'an base areas organized the Yan'an Women's Association for the Promotion of the Constitution (*Yan'an funüjie xianzheng cujinhui*) to increase knowledge of the opportunity for winning further gains and consolidating current victories in the new document among women in the CCP areas. In addition they sent messages of encouragement and support to prominent women like He Xiangning and Song Qingling. They also lobbied Chiang Kai-shek directly with a telegram.[60]

Recognizing the impossibility of eradicating the interest of China's feminists in constitutionalism, the Nationalist Party commenced a rival women's constitutional organization in March 1940. Headed by Nationalist Party stalwart Shen Huilian (1890–1974), this group called itself the National Assembly Women's Electoral Lobby (*Guomin dahui funü jingxuan hui*). Shen, a Cantonese medical doctor, had long-standing Nationalist credentials. She had joined Sun's Revolutionary Alliance in 1910 and maintained her commitment to its successor, the Nationalist Party, until her death. In 1937 she assumed a leadership role in the party's women's bureau and continued this role after 1949 when she left for Taiwan.[61] Progressive democrats like Shi Liang and Li Dequan (1896–1972) from the old Women's National Salvation Societies spurned Shen's Women's Electoral Lobby, regarding it as a stooge for Chiang's dictatorship.[62]

The emergence of these competing feminist groups was a likely product of the deterioration in the relations between the Nationalist Party and the CCP over the course of 1939 and 1940. The Second United Front was flawed from its inception, but the warming of relations between the Soviet Union and Japan fundamentally undermined the credibility of the Comintern's position on Chinese unity against Japanese fascism. Military clashes between the CCP and the Nationalists increased. These changing circumstances were soon to have negative impacts on the activities of China's women's movement. In November of 1940, with the promulgation of the National government's policy for the prevention of the activities of the illegal women's movement (*Feifa fu yundong huodong fangzhi banfa*), women's activism by non–Nationalist Party women was again more dangerous.[63] Progressive, left-leaning women's journals, such as *Women's Life* and *Women's Road* (*Funü zhi lu*), were disbanded, and the arrest and detainment of outspoken women prompted many others to go into hiding or reduce their activities.[64] The unity that had sustained the feminist movement in China was threatened. From 1941, Nationalist Party women in the PPC largely dominated the quota campaign. The increasing conservatism of the Nationalist Party authorities meant that the women who were regarded as belonging to legal organizations carried the weight of the entire national women's cause. The noncommunist women councilors in the PPC were among this reduced vanguard.

Nonetheless, the next national constitution of 1946–1947 did include provisions for quotas for women.[65] The campaign's success in a Nationalist Party–authorized constitution may thus in part be attributed to its perceived appropriate political links. The campaign was to end as a victory but unfortunately the democracy under which the constitution was formed was flawed. Before this constitution was promulgated the festering military dispute between the CCP and the Nationalist Party had to be resolved.

THE CIVIL WAR AND WOMEN PARLIAMENTARIANS

The war against Japan ended abruptly with the American bombing of Hiroshima and Nagasaki in August 1945. Neither the Nationalists nor the CCP were fully prepared for the absence of a common enemy. A scramble for control of the areas previously occupied by Japan began, and the country slid into the civil war that had been put on hold during the war against Japan. In an attempt to stabilize the situation and provide a constitutional rather than military solution to the dispute, a conference was called with the American General George Marshall serving as mediator. The so-called Political Consultative Conference was held on 10–31 January 1946 and included representatives from the two major parties as well as the FCDP and the Youth Party. Among the remarkable achievements of the conference, which included the merger of the CCP and Nationalist armies, were several rulings on the nature of the constitutional government that it was hoped would lead China into the last half of the century as a democratic nation. Among these was the resolution that "the equal status of women in the political, social, educational and economic fields shall be guaranteed."[66] By this stage the principle of equality between men and women was an unproblematic matter.

However, there were a number of rulings on which it proved more difficult to reach agreement. The conference decentralized power, giving weight to elected provincial governments and making the Executive Yuan responsible to the Legislative Yuan. Both provisions were abhorrent to Chiang

Kai-shek who preferred centralized power. Consequently, where the Political Consultative Conference stipulated the convening of the National Assembly only once a multiparty transitional government had been established, Chiang announced on 4 July that a National Assembly would be convened on 12 November 1946. The process drew on the 1936 electoral model for which elections had begun at various places sporadically over the course of the previous decade.

Meanwhile the military situation had also deteriorated. By April of the same year the civil war was back in full swing as both sides resumed the scramble for more territory. The Nationalist Party was confident of victory since it had an apparently stronger military and financial position, and after a series of victories Chiang was certain that he needed to make no compromises with the CCP.

Chiang had repeatedly stressed the importance of convening the National Assembly, but his unwillingness to form a coalition government with the Communists after January 1946 and his refusal to run entirely new elections generated the opinion that this was little more than a facade of democratization. Chiang's calls to reconvene the National Assembly were to some commentators his "chief weapon of deception."[67] The CCP issued a response declaring Chiang to be "playing up the trick of 'returning the reins of government to the people' and 'convening the National Congress' [Assembly] in order to preserve a fascist dictatorship."[68]

Deliberations on the amending of the Double Fifth Constitution took place during November and December of 1946 during the convocation of this compromised National Assembly.[69] Tan Sheying says that there were eighty-two women, led by Madame Chiang Kai-shek, at the meetings to amend the constitution. For the women activists involved, the 1946 deliberations saw victory in attaining their goal of set minimum quotas for women in *both* the representative bodies—not only the National Assembly but also the Legislative Yuan. Tan described the victory as "well surpassing the flourishing women's rights movements of those advanced nations of Europe and America."[70] Article 134 of the constitution notes that "in the various kinds of elections, the number of women to be elected shall be fixed, and measures pertaining thereto shall be prescribed by law." The March 1947 electoral laws guaranteed women 168 National Assembly seats that were to be filled by delegates from women's organizations in the ROC.[71] With regards to the Legislative Yuan, the electoral laws stated that the ratio of women to men should be at least one woman in every ten legislators from those legislators elected as municipality and provincial representatives.[72] Ch'ien Tuan-sheng describes this as follows: "in every group of constituencies one member must be a woman if the quota is below ten, and there must be one additional woman for every ten in excess of the first ten."[73] If this ratio is achieved through normal electoral processes then no further action is required. However, if less than one in ten legislators elected were female, then the women candidates' votes are tallied separately and the woman with the majority of votes is allocated one of the reserved seats. The ratio of women to men differed in each branch of government. In the Control Yuan, one in every five representatives should be a woman, and in the National Assembly one in every twenty-four representatives should be a woman.[74]

Chen Chih-mai notes that there were a "substantial proportion of women" among the representatives for the National Assembly.[75] As noted above, the initial round of elections a decade earlier had placed five women in seats, amounting to 0.5 percent of the total. The supplementary rulings on the election of National Assembly representatives then decreed that a further thirty-five women should be included, with twenty being nominated by various women's groups and fifteen from the various provinces and municipalities.[76]

Ten women's groups in Chongqing cooperated to elect the twenty women who were to be their delegates.[77] The ambiguous political allegiances of the women's groups active at the time reflected the instability of the relationship between the CCP and the Nationalist Party. Many of the women were sympathetic to the CCP but remained publicly aligned with smaller democratic third-force groups. Chiang ignored the elections, and not all the women identified by the women's groups were eventually to become delegates. One of the women's organizations was the China United Association. Established in Chongqing in July 1945, its goals were to promote the development of peaceful democracy and to provide famine relief and refugee aid. The group was opposed to the civil war and attempted to mobilize women in the Nationalist Party–controlled regions of China to facilitate a peaceful resolution. Li Dequan and Liu Qingyang (1894–1977) led the group—both women's activism drew from their base in the shifting middle ground between the two big parties. It also included other prominent women activists like Shi Liang and Tan Tiwu.

Liu Qingyang, of Hui ethnic origin, had been a member of both the Nationalist Party and the CCP through the 1920s and 1930s, but with Japan's invasion in 1937 devoted herself to women's patriotic activities and remained outside of the two major parties.[78] Li Dequan, a third-generation Christian, was secretary of the YWCA and one-time president of the Chinese WCTU. She maintained close ties with the Nationalist government despite her opposition to many of Chiang Kai-shek's actions and was one of forty members of Song Meiling's WAC.[79]

The coalition of ten women's groups elected eminent women activists such as He Xiangning, Tan Tiwu, Qin Dejun, Zhong Xiaguang, Zheng Ying, and Guo Yu.[80] The Shanghai women's groups underwent the same process, and eventually a list of three hundred and fifty candidates was compiled. Over 30,000 women participated in the vote for the thirty-five candidates. Xu Guangping (1898–1968), partner to the famous and revered writer Lu Xun, won the most votes. She had been active as a student in the New Culture Movement in Tianjin, although a native to Guangdong in the South. Along with Deng Yingchao and Zhou Enlai she had organized women's patriotic organizations and published women's magazines.[81] Tan Tiwu was born in Changsha, Hunan, and in her left-leaning but nonaligned political position reflected many of the women activists during the 1930s and 1940s. She joined the ranks of activist women as a student while studying law at Beijing University, and she helped found the FCDP in 1941. The FCDP boycotted the elections for the National Assembly, but as the candidature of Tan indicates, individual members were not barred from participation. She was a member of the Legislative Yuan in the Nationalist government period but remained in China after 1949 to assume numerous official positions although she never joined the CCP.[82]

In contrast, Qin Dejun was explicitly aligned with the CCP. Born in Sichuan she was active during the May Fourth activities while a student in Chengdu. Qin joined the party in 1923 and was involved in the First United Front's women's organizations. During Chiang Kai-shek's crackdown on the CCP in 1927 she went to Japan, where she remained for nearly three years. On her return to China her involvement with the CCP waned, and she joined the ranks of the women activists of left-wing sympathies. In 1937 she participated in the Women's United Friendship Alliance activities in Chongqing. At the close of the war against Japan, Qin Dejun resumed her connection with the CCP by becoming involved in underground liaison activities. She remained active in the government of the PRC for decades after 1949.[83]

Having won the right to access political power and even the right to specific quotas for parliamentarians, the women needed to mobilize their constituents—women voters. A book published in 1947 by Liu Hengjing stressed the importance of women's new national political responsibilities:

> Since the country recognizes that we are citizens and has placed all the responsibilities of citizenship on our shoulders, this means we have the right to get involved in politics and govern. But, if we don't understand politics, if we aren't concerned about politics, then chaos is unavoidable and this will cause chaos in society and bring the country into danger. Now that would not only harm us but it would also harm our children and grandchildren.[84]

Women, Liu argued, needed to get themselves prepared with an intimate knowledge of politics in order to ensure that their new citizenship rights and responsibilities not be squandered or poorly used. But the social and economic chaos that accompanied the military ruptures of the 1940s, and the rampant corruption among Nationalist Party officials that followed the defeat of the Japanese, would have dampened any optimism about the appearance of political progress.[85]

SUFFRAGE IN THE COMMUNIST-CONTROLLED AREAS

Competition for credibility between the CCP and the Nationalist Party during the war years extended to the sphere of electoral politics. Both sides were keen to demonstrate to both domestic and international audiences that they were committed to democracy. Both sides held elections, but complete authority was never vested in the elected bodies in either CCP or Nationalist government areas. The party, army, bureaucracy, and in the case of the CCP border regions, the mass organizations all had considerable influence on policy and planning.

The CCP undertook to hold elections in the remote Shaan-Gan-Ning regional base areas with universal franchise. The 12 May 1937 election law of the Shaan-Gan-Ning base area allowed everyone over the age of sixteen "regardless of sex, religion, race, financial situation, or culture" to vote and stand for election.[86] Voting was to be conducted by secret ballot and in order to cope with high levels of illiteracy variously relied on literate friends to cast votes or used a system of beans that were placed in bowls behind each of the sitting candidates—voters filed past and dropped beans in their preferred candidates' bowls. Significantly, the CCP ensured that the elections and the campaigns leading up to these ballots served to educate people about New Democracy, land reform, and even women's liberation.[87] During the Second United Front, Mark Selden noted that the CCP made efforts to reduce the distance between the Nationalist Party and itself in terms of the electoral processes. In its electoral legislation the CCP adopted "the precise language of model laws" in the style of liberal democracies as favored by the Nationalist Party bureaucrats—with no hint of "class struggle or other Marxist categories" that had limited the franchise in the Jiangxi Soviet back in 1931.[88] Moreover, the party deployed a system of Three Thirds—in which the CCP guaranteed to restrict themselves to a maximum of one-third of seats in the councils in base areas, leaving the other two-thirds to "advanced elements (of 'leftists and progressives') and 'neutrals.'"[89] This policy enabled them to win support from local elites and Nationalist Party members—the latter could join the councils but only as individuals rather than as representatives of the Nationalist Party.

In areas under CCP political management women had suffrage rights and were encouraged to participate fully as voters and candidates throughout both the war against Japan and the civil war periods. In 1939 the Yan'an journal *Women of China* (*Zhongguo funü*) would write that China's women had left their homes and entered the political stage with such success that women made up 5 percent of the PPC and 25 percent of the Shaan-Gan-Ning region's parliament.[90] The contrast between the percentage of women in Nationalist-controlled parliaments and Communist-controlled ones was clear in this statement. In the 1940 elections for the Shanxi-Chahar-Hebei border region, 85 percent of eligible women voted and 20 percent of all representatives elected were women. Similarly strong showings were made in north Shanxi where around two thousand women were elected as representatives and some even assumed positions as village heads.[91] In 1941 elections for the Shaan-Gan-Ning region women were elected to 8 percent of the seats in the township councils, including over 20 percent in two districts. Mark Selden goes on to note that an important part of this election campaign was its coordination with a women's rights agenda.[92] David Goodman has shown that in Shanxi "there was a requirement for each local government in the Taihang base area to ensure the election of at least one woman."[93] By the end of 1941 the results of this policy in Taihang were evident. Goodman's data reveals that 21 percent of elected village representatives and over 9 percent of village leaders were women.[94] In Long Bow during 1948, William Hinton reported that women featured strongly in village elections—in one case women had a segregated set of three possible seats, where men competed for seven. In other cases women and men appear to have competed for the same seats.[95] Deng Yingchao notes that by 1949, 30 percent of the elected village representatives were women, and within the party government, 20 percent of cadres at district level and 10 percent of cadres at county level were women.[96]

A major problem the CCP identified in its campaigns to mobilize peasant women into political action was sex segregation and the general community preference for women to remain in the domestic sphere. Illiteracy also proved to be a major stumbling block to broadening women's engagement with politics, so nighttime literacy classes were introduced. Songs and dramas were used to encourage women to participate actively. Yet there was much opposition to such shifts in gender roles, largely from men and older women. Sexual chastity was a major cause of anxiety since public political participation necessarily brought women into the public sphere. William Hinton reported that women faced beatings and accusations of sexual impropriety if they attended Women's Association meetings in Long Bow. If women took part in public activities outside the home it was regarded as "leading directly to adultery" or "flirtation and seduction."[97] Isobel and David Crook explain that in Taihang's Ten Mile Inn, middle peasant men "took pride in the chastity of their womenfolk" and were "zealous about their wives' reputations" to the extent that they prohibited them from attending "meetings of prostitutes" as the Women's Association gatherings were called.[98] The Crooks argue that this posed major problems for the local party's engagement of women because in the words on one cadre: "We felt that the militant women weren't virtuous and the virtuous women weren't militant. So though we knew we ought to recruit some women members into the branch, we couldn't find any who seemed suitable."[99] Where educated, urban women could make a transition to public political life aided by the respectability afforded those with formal and advanced education, peasant women had no such access. They faced accusations of immorality if they were involved in political activism, yet simultaneously if they upheld common notions of women's virtue—which required segregation from public activity—they were also deemed politically problematic.

There is little indication that the women elected to the National Assembly in the Nationalist Party areas had an in-depth appreciation of the particular difficulties faced by peasant women—who composed the bulk of the population these urban-based women claimed to represent. Moreover,

Hinton's study of Long Bow suggests that for rural women, real and immediate power emerged from their personal access to land tenure as part of the
radical land reform campaigns in the base areas. Access to formal or electoral politics was nowhere near as immediately empowering as economic independence from oppressive husbands and parents-in-law for these women.
Nonetheless, despite the divide between urban and rural women, the latter's
access to land reform under the CCP was attained in part by the decades-
long campaigns waged by urban women's movements to win recognition for
equal status with men in all spheres.

Meanwhile, at the level of party theory international Marxism's mistrust
of suffrage in a parliamentary system still circulated. A book by CCP member Du Junhui (1904–1981) published in 1936 reiterated the classic Marx-
ian suspicions of the women's suffrage movement. It notes that the suffrage
movement is premised on the equality of the sexes and then presents an
overview of key countries around the world in terms of women's suffrage
victories. Du presents that most countries changed their laws only after the
end of World War I but also proceeds to argue that only the Soviet Union
has ensured the broad spread and deep penetration of women's voting rights.
The reason for this is because in other countries, people without money
have no base for political action.[100] In keeping with Du's sentiment that
only the socialist system can establish conditions for broad-based exercise
of suffrage rights, in 1939 a CCP women's journal described the women's
movement as demanding "an expansion in the number of women who have
suffrage rights."[101] A 1935 article invoked the original suffragists' campaign
to have women recognized as "people" (*ren*) by pointing out that although
women had broken free of feudal strictures and had apparently become *ren*,
the reality belied these appearances. Women had become slaves of economic
institutions that were still controlled by men. Employment had trapped
women rather than liberating them because it was locked within the system
of private property. "Only once private property had been abolished and
class oppression had ceased, can women really become *ren*, and only then
can women really achieve the rights and powers that *ren* ought to have."[102]

Contradictions between class and sex oppression clearly continued
within the CCP culture well into the 1940s. Attempts to modify the patriarchal basis of party practice were quickly squashed. Writer and CCP member Ding Ling (1904–1986) expressed grave concerns about CCP progress
on women's emancipation in her 1942 article "Thoughts on March 8," and
she was quickly silenced.[103] David Goodman's work on women in CCP

base areas demonstrates that "at the start of 1942 the CCP abandoned any attempt to mobilize women behind appeals to emancipation and gender equality." Speaking to a meeting of senior cadres in the Taihang base area, Peng Dehuai "warned that raising women's political consciousness was generally permitted but that cadres should determinedly ensure it takes second place to economic mobilization, because of both war needs and concerns about potential resentment from male peasants."[104] Through the early 1940s family harmony campaigns softened the edge of the radical challenges of CCP divorce and land tenure policies while providing support to eliminate the commonplace beating of wives and daughters-in-law.[105]

In 1943 the CCP Central Committee attacked women communists who argued for more explicit equity programs. In February the Central Committee declared, "Women cadres must stop looking on economic work as unimportant" in keeping with the notion that women's liberation would emerge through participation in the work force. The CCP elite missed the fact that women throughout rural China, but especially in the South, had long been engaged in productive agricultural work within the confines of a patriarchal family structure without achieving liberation. Party women wanted access to power and not just access to work. That same month Deng Yingchao argued for greater women's involvement in political administration, saying, "Women's suffrage should not be separated from the war and it ought not be isolated with a small elite of educated women. Rather, women's suffrage ought to be expanded to the women masses and first we must lift the ban on vocational opportunities to give women the chance to engage in political administration."[106]

Yet the women's campaign in the CCP areas was largely submerged into broader party policy. Cai Chang, one-time urban activist, criticized her fellow women activists for their preoccupation with female emancipation, saying, "our slogans are no longer 'free choice marriage' and 'equality of the sexes' but 'save the children,' 'a flourishing family,' and 'nurture health and prosperity.'"[107]

A HOLLOW VICTORY

Over the course of 1947 in Nationalist Party areas, elections produced legislators for Chiang's National Assembly. Any citizen over the age of twenty regardless of sex could vote, and those over twenty-three could stand for election. However, the electoral process lacked credibility since many of the National Assembly's 3,045 members were selected in highly suspect processes. In a bid to ensure that the correct balance of prestige and pliability in membership was achieved, the Nationalist government appointed many delegates by decree and forced the resignation of others. Both regional and vocational interests were to be represented. The CCP and the FCDP insisted that the Political Consultative Conference's rulings be adhered to and declared the National Assembly a sham. Consequently they were excluded and, as Chiang Kai-shek had planned, the Nationalists dominated the National Assembly. The passage of the 1946–1947 constitution by this particular National Assembly was not cheerful news for many of those democratic activists who had long struggled to return China to rule by constitutional government.[108] Ultimately, the existence of the Assembly was a flagrant breach of the spirit and letter of the deal brokered in the Consultative Conference. This betrayal ensured that the civil war would continue with renewed ferocity, and constitutional government for China remained elusive.

For the women who had struggled for equality and protective quotas for women in parliament the passage of this constitution brought little satisfaction. It was clear that China's period of war-induced chaos was not over. Women may have won the right to vote and stand for election and even ensured that minimum quotas for women in parliament would be guaranteed, but Chinese democracy was still very fragile. Nonetheless an unprecedented number of women participated in politics at a national level. The National Assembly included two hundred and one women, the Legislative Yuan had sixty-five women members, and the Control Yuan had nineteen women.[109]

Conservative voices in the women's press gained ground. In 1947 on International Women's Day the first issue of the Nationalist Party organ *New Women* (*Xin funü*), sporting a picture of Madame Chiang on its cover, explained to its readers: "New Women should represent and speak for all women; they should seek to benefit women as a whole, but ought not to act as female politicos (*nü zhengke*). Service should not be limited to the women's sphere and should only come from what humankind requires . . . we ought to have an ambiance of cooperation with men."[110] Like their CCP counterparts, Nationalist Party women were exhorted to serve the "bigger" interests and not merely women's concerns.

Nationalist Party women's press was celebratory about their constitutional democracy. One report declared that theirs was "the world's most progressive constitution."[111] Yet another congratulated its readers saying,

"The constitution has already been implemented, the government elected by the people has been established . . . it's already the era of democratic constitutionalism." The author continues, explaining that this means open elections, the independence of the judiciary, and the protection of people's rights.[112] None of these features was guaranteed with any certainty in the "era of democratic constitutionalism" of the following few decades.

The constitution that guaranteed Chinese women the rights they had struggled to gain for the previous several decades, no matter how "progressive" on paper, was no panacea to China's woes. The document eventually came to rule the small island population of Taiwan, and even there Chiang's dictatorship curtailed its full implementation until the lifting of martial law in 1987. The constitutional gains the women won ensured that China's aspiring women politicians and patriotic political activists were equal to men in political rights. Yet, as the military chaos subsided after 1949 it became apparent that this equality and its protective quotas for women politicians were to be practiced in an impoverished democracy.

China's feminist activists had deftly advanced their cause during the years of war—first against the Japanese and second between the Nationalist Party and the CCP. They mobilized the rhetoric of women's collective status as a disadvantaged group, and from that basis they achieved concrete political gains by drawing on arguments that women's political rights were equal to but different from those of men. Yet this consciousness was only strong among middle-class urbanites. China's peasantry remained largely divorced from these ideas and activities. Sex segregation and regimes of sexual chastity for women dominated rural society. The CCP stepped into that vacuum, presenting the case for equality in rural areas, and with their victory over the Nationalists in 1949 would implement a 20 percent minimum quota for women in the various levels of PRC government. Moreover, the CCP established a social and political structure that legitimized women's public political action—reducing the moral risk for women active in politics. Women's difference from men, in terms of political needs and interests, was recognized and given formal representation within the PRC structure.

EIGHT

Conclusion

Over the course of the first half of the twentieth century China's women's suffrage movement evolved from an organization conceived by a small, radical group of women into a broadly based movement with networks into all key political parties in China. Where women had composed only a tiny proportion of the political elite in China in 1908, they were represented in all aspects of party and public life by 1948. Over the course of these years, women came to hold positions in formal politics and were influential and relentless advocates for women's rights in the public sphere. Women legislators and lobbyists had developed skills over the course of four decades that ensured the men leading the key political parties and heading government committees and councils could not ignore their concerns. Their movement for access to formal political power moved between arguments that "women were people equal to men" and those that boldly asserted women's difference from men. By the end of the civil war in 1949, China's women's movement was strong and diverse enough to survive partition and to continue in different forms in both Taiwan and China.

In the process of exploring their myriad campaigns, China's women's suffrage activists revealed the complex interactions between feminism, class, nationalism, and modernity that exercised the minds of China's critical thinkers and activists for decades. As this book has revealed, feminism was by no means a sideshow to the reformulation of the Chinese nation and the transformation of Chinese society. Rather, campaigns for women's equal political rights in China challenged fundamental conceptions about the nature of power, social order, and morality by revealing their gendered nature. They challenged deeply held beliefs about the embodiment of legitimate political power resting in a male form, and over the course of several decades presented a new model for political life in China. It was a model that not only claimed rule by the virtuous but also introduced gender to the emerging politics of representation.

GENDER, POWER, VIRTUE, AND EDUCATION

In 1911 China's political elite were comfortable with the idea that the moneyed and educated (and therefore virtuous) should legislate on behalf of the ignorant mass of the population. The absence of women from the category of legitimate power holders was naturalized since they neither owned property nor had formal education. Yet the ruling groups' veneration of education and its understood links to building and maintaining social order and "civilization" presented the very site for disrupting this naturalized exclusion of women from formal political power. Within this worldview, if the nation was in chaos, then it needed more education, not less. And China at the turn of the century certainly had reached its nadir. Thus, from the late nineteenth century reformers believed that women needed education so as to better contribute to the nation's revival. From this point on, with newly won access to formal education, women's exclusion from the "education = virtue = access to power" nexus was irrevocably undermined. The female body no longer connoted ignorance and weakness since it was being increasingly educated and exercised alongside the male body. The literati-intellectual class's privileging of the power of education thwarted claims that biological differences between the sexes justified differences in access to political power. Once women accessed schooling and performed well academically, rationales based on physiology were fatally weakened.

Gendered notions of virtue were also challenged by the women's suffrage activists' campaigns in the first half of the twentieth century. The centuries-old link between male virtue and political power contained within the Confucian concept of "legitimate rule" was undermined. China's political history within the imperial order revolved around the performance of virtue through education by examination. Education in the Confucian classics trained leaders for virtuous and wise rule until the end of the first decade of the twentieth century. Yet this type of virtue was solely the preserve of men. Women were unable to demonstrate their virtue through classical education and political prowess—instead, women's virtue was conceived as chastity and modesty. The construction of chaste widow arches and extensive elaboration on the lives of steadfast segregated and modest women in gazetteers created narratives of the virtue acceptable for women. Meddling in politics was anathema to these conceptions of women's virtue—constructed as they were around the ideal constrained and controlled sexual female body. Thus the suffragists' sustained and public claims to access formal political power challenged long-standing gendered norms of political virtue.

The New Culture Movement's challenges to prescriptions about female chastity, made famous by Lu Xun's article, "On Chastity," are well recognized.[1] Yet the obverse, the undermining of prescriptions about political virtue as a masculine attribute/responsibility, is less commonly perceived. China's suffragists' claims that women had the requisite skills to rule the nation wisely challenged the naturalized assumptions about masculinity and political virtue. They challenged men's ability to rule in repeated critical newspaper articles that linked China's current chaotic political scene with male incompetence. They emphasized that virtue and wisdom were not inherent in all men that reached political leadership positions in China. In so doing they participated in the ongoing democratization of China's political world: an individual's access to power, they had shown, did not always signify his proven ability to exercise virtuous and wise rule. Nor did it signify his continued unchallenged right to that power. In challenging long-standing norms about the sorts of people that "naturally" should have access to political influence, the suffragists opened new possibilities for political representation in China. Moreover, they promoted the notion that men had responsibilities to sexual virtue within new notions of monogamous conjugal fidelity. Political virtue was no more the sole preserve of men, just as sexual virtue was no longer the sole preserve of women.

Yet, within the suffrage movement itself, the challenge posed by the gendered nature of sexual and political virtue needed to be negotiated. Aspiring politicians needed virtue, and the women's suffrage activists were indeed aspiring politicians. For men, education provided signal markers of virtue, yet for women the signal markers had been sexualized. Do women politicians become superchaste as a bid to demonstrate their superior virtue? Would this superior feminized chastity then translate into political power? The answer was no on both counts for the majority of women activists. Indeed, in the arguments about the role of concubines in the suffrage movement we can see the transformation in public perceptions about gendered virtue. One group feared concubines would bring the whole movement into disrepute with their low-class, unchaste bodies. Other suffragists, the eventually victorious group, regarded concubines as part of that newfound collectivity called "women" and therefore deserving of representation and political voice. Thus, they disaggregated sexual virtue and politics.

In their critique of the national political health, the suffragists simultaneously disaggregated political virtue and maleness. Political arenas, from the early years of the republic, became recognized sites of polluting influences—pigsties of corruption—rather than gathering places of the wise and virtuous. The suffragists' consistent and highly public refusal to trust the judgment of the men in power with the representation of their interests stood as a constant reminder of the possibilities of political "alternatives." The new republic could not slip casually into a post-Qing patriarchal, elite-class leadership (be that in a republic, monarchy, or dictatorship) under the mantle of virtuous wisdom with the women activists' repeated and highly public declarations that they did not trust this group to adequately represent their interests. With each article that invoked the millions of women currently without a political voice, it was natural that other disenfranchised groups would begin to think along the same lines. It soon became *not* so natural to have power concentrated in such a small segment of society. Political power and male virtue eventually lost their previously unchallenged connection altogether.

CREATING A POLITICS OF REPRESENTATION AND CONSTITUTING A COLLECTIVE WOMEN'S IDENTITY

Simultaneously, the women suffrage activists invoked notions of representation and special interest by creating "women" as a specific category with discrete and identical political interests. These interests demanded particular representation by women themselves and not on behalf of women by men.

Significantly, this did not create a concomitant consciousness of "men's interests" because the sameness of "women's interests" hinged around a perceived unity of disadvantage. The excavation and reiteration of women's similar disadvantage was central to creating the political category for women that demanded representation. Women's journals and the constant stream of letters to newspapers were central to the creation of this new political category. It disclosed vast differences in interests across gaps in class and residency, and in education and opportunity privileges among the women of China. But this did not prevent China's aspiring women political leaders from building a new political category with legitimate claims to representation.

Without the public acknowledgment of women's unity of disadvantage, women's political representation was initially reliant upon appeals to the egalitarianism of natural rights. This proved problematic in its reception since it presented a far more real threat to individual men's experience of authority over individual women on a daily basis. Yet "women" as a collective category defined as having political interests whose sameness reiterated their unity of disadvantage was less personally threatening in its very abstractness. The collectivity of the new political category, publicly premised on women's disadvantage relative to men, simultaneously reified male dominance and undermined it. The reification of male privilege through the expanding narratives of women's relative disadvantage was vital to women's suffrage gains because it enabled a broader section of the population to accept the representation of women's special interests—there is after all less personal threat to male privilege from a group that is so abjectly disadvantaged.

However, by conceptualizing a political category of women, even if within the rubric of narratives of feminine weakness, women did indeed mobilize more effectively for their rights. Increasingly over the course of the first few decades of the century they saw these rights juxtaposed with male privilege—their targets drew more clearly into focus, and they promoted women's difference from men rather than simply women's right to equality with men. Arguments about Manchu incompetence, foreign imperialism, and the inclusion of concubines soon disappeared as the particularities of the feminist struggle, in and of itself, became more and more evident to more and more women. This did not render other struggles and causes less relevant in China or to the women themselves; rather, it meant the women increasingly identified more clearly which battle they were fighting at which point in time. If it was the feminist campaign for equal inheritance rights, then dismantling male privilege was the goal. If it was mobilizing women workers to strike, then challenging class privilege was the focus. Importantly, the newly imagined political collectivity also made it possible for women to work across political party divides for their feminist cause, even in times of great intraparty tension.

The global nature of the women's suffrage movement during the late nineteenth and early twentieth centuries also presented important reasons for Chinese men to share political power. Internationally women suffragists had astutely presented women's equal access to democratic political power as an emblem of modernity.[2] China's activists promoted this principle effectively in the domestic Chinese media. As more and more nations around the world acquiesced to their respective suffragists' claims over the course of the first thirty years of the century, China found itself in the company of fewer and fewer heavyweight nations. If China's male power holders wanted international respectability, they needed to adopt the trappings of modern, strong nations like the USA, Britain, and Germany. And Chinese nationalism in the twentieth century was nothing if not premised on the struggle for international recognition of China's rightful big-power status. China's great civilization risked being relegated to the category of the barbaric, the traditional, and the backward if it did not concede women's political equality with men.

Ramirez, Soysal, and Shanahan have argued that by the 1930s transnational influences eventually dictated a model of citizenship that included women's franchise on equal terms with men, and these influences overshadowed the effectiveness or otherwise of national women's suffrage organizations.[3] Yet, in order for a globally dominant notion of citizenship to include women's franchise, women's suffrage activists had spent decades working within that fraught place between the national and the international. The decades of national struggles, informed by and integrated with the international suffrage campaign, were central to the eventual naturalized acceptability of the transnational citizenship norm where women's political rights were recognized as equal to men's. Invoking the cross-national comparison, creating a conception of the inevitable modernizing trend of women's franchise, and mobilizing the language of "ladders of shame"—in which countries without women's suffrage were presented as having lower status—all contributed to ensure the post-1930s impact of transnational standards. The international women's suffrage movement established a global modernity competition—a women's suffrage ranking—where none had previously existed. In China it is clear that the national suffrage movement made effective use of the transnational comparison through repeated reminders of China's shamefully weakened state compared to other nations. Chinese women appealed to Chinese men's vanity and their aspirations for international recognition from foreign men as much as to their genuine willingness to find a modern solution to China's domestic and international woes.

Similarly, Lee Ann Banaszak's study of women's suffrage, *Why Movements Succeed or Fail*, highlights the importance of political opportunity structures wherein the political context that women suffragists' work within becomes a crucial factor in understanding their varying degrees of success relative to other national struggles.[4] The skills and resources mobilized by the women themselves become more or less effective depending on their political context. Indeed, the particular inflection of the women's suffrage movement in China reveals that Chinese women sought to strike at particular vulnerabilities in the national political psyche—resentment of China's low reputation on the global scene. The internationalism of the women's suffrage movement provided the leverage from which to achieve these attacks.

––––––––

China's women's suffrage activists challenged the foundation of Chinese conceptions of political power through their five decades of activism. They rendered the naturalized assumptions of sole male right to access political power questionable; they created a collective political identity for Chinese women and asserted the right of women to be represented. Over the course of the decades China's women politicians became increasingly savvy about the targets of their activities—they saw that politics enabled multiple targets and myriad goals simultaneously. With this knowledge, China's suffragists forged feminist bridges across deep political divides that affirmed the notion of women's rights regardless of political perspective. In waging their feminist battles, however, the impact was not simply one of reducing male privilege. Rather, they presented to Chinese politics a new vision and model of advocacy politics where changing and evolving groups and generations of activists maintain sustained lobbying for a single cause. In these respects China's women's suffrage activists revolutionized not only gender politics in China but also altered the entire Chinese political landscape.

Reference Matter

Commonly Cited Newspapers and Journals

Aiguo bao (Patriotic News)

Chenbao (Chenbao)

Chenbao fukan (Chenbao Supplement)

Dagong bao (L'Impartial)

Funü gongming (Women's Support)

Funü pinglun (Women's Critic)

Funü shenghuo (Women's Life)

Funü shibao (Women's Times)

Funü yuekan (Women's Monthly)

Funü zazhi (The Ladies' Journal)

Funü zhoubao (Women's Weekly News)

Funü zuzhi yu huodong (Women's Organizations and Activities)

Guangdong qunbao (The Social)

Jindai Zhongguo funü shi yanjiu (Research on Women in Modern Chinese History)

Laodong yu funü (Labor and Women)

Minguo ribao (Republic Daily)

Minli bao (The People's Independence News)

Minzhu bao (Democracy News)

Nüsheng (Women's Voice)

Nü xing (Women's Star)

Nüxue bao (Women's Studies News)

Nüzi baihua bao (Women's Vernacular News)

Nüzi canzheng xiejin hui hui kan (Women's Suffrage Association Journal)

Nüzi shijie (Women's World)

Nüzi yuekan (Women's Monthly)

Qianfeng (The Vanguard)

Renmin ribao (Peoples' Daily)

Shenbao (Shenbao)

Shenzhou nübao (Shenzhou Women's News)

Shengjing shibao (Shengjing Times)

Shibao (The Eastern Times)

Shishi xinbao (The Times)

Tianduo bao (Heavenly Bell News)

Tianyi (Heaven's Justice)

Xin chao (Renaissance)

Xin funü (New Women)

Xin nüxing (New Femininity)

Xin qingnian (New Youth)

Zhongguo funü (Women of China)

Zhongguo nübao (China Women's News)

Zhongguo ribao (China Daily)

Zhongguo xin nüjie zazhi (China's New Women's World Magazine)

Abbreviations

BDQP   Ho, Clara Wing-chung, ed. *Biographical Dictionary of Chinese Women: The Qing Period, 1644–1911*. Armonk, NY: M.E. Sharpe, 1998.

BDTC   Lee, Lily, ed. *Biographical Dictionary of Chinese Women: The Twentieth Century, 1912–2000*. Armonk, NY: M.E. Sharpe, 2003.

FNCD   Funü cidian bian xue zu, ed. *Funü cidian* (Dictionary of Women). Beijing: Qiushi chubanshe, 1990.

FNZZ   *Funü zazhi* (The Ladies' Journal)

MSD   Shang Hai et al., ed. *Minguo shi dacidian* (Big dictionary of the history of the republican period). Beijing: Zhongguo guangbo dianshi chubanshe, 1991.

ZFYLZ   Zhonghua quanguo funü lianhe hui, ed. *Zhongguo funü yundong lishi ziliao, 1921–1927* (Materials on the history of the Chinese women's movement 1921–1927). Beijing: Renmin chubanshe, 1986.

ZFYS   Zhonghua quanguo funü lianhe hui, ed. *Zhongguo funü yundong shi: Xin minzhuzhuyi shiqi* (The history of the Chinese women's movement: New democracy period). Beijing: Chunqiu chubanshe, 1989.

ZGNP   Gao Kuixiang and Shen Jianguo, ed. *Zhonghua gujin nüjie pu* (Annals of ancient and modern women in China). Beijing: Zhonghua shehui chubanshe, 1991.

Notes

Chapter One

1. See the debates in Gisela Bock and Susan James, eds., *Beyond Equality and Difference: Citizenship, Feminist Politics and Female Subjectivity* (London: Routledge, 1992).

2. On the emergence of "woman" as a category beyond kin relationships, see Tani Barlow, *The Question of Women in Chinese Feminism* (Durham, NC: Duke University Press, 2004), 44–54.

3. See Joan Judge's discussion of the simultaneous emergence of "the national question" and "the woman question" in "Talent, Virtue, and the Nation: Chinese Nationalisms and Female Subjectivities in the Early Twentieth Century," *American Historical Review* 106, no. 3 (2001): 765–803.

4. Peter Zarrow, "Citizenship in China and the West," in *Imagining the People: Chinese Intellectuals and the Concept of Citizenship, 1890–1920*, ed. Joshua A. Fogel and Peter G. Zarrow (Armonk, NY: M.E. Sharpe, 1997), 12. On third-world feminism and nationalism, see Kumari Jayawardena, *Feminism and Nationalism in the Third World* (London: Zed, 1985), 2.

5. Wang Zheng, *Women in the Chinese Enlightenment: Oral and Textual Histories* (Berkeley: University of California Press, 1999), 125.

6. On "national benefit" and suffrage, see Louise Edwards, "Moving from the Vote into Citizenship: Crafting Chinese Women's Political Citizenship," *Berliner China-Hefte* 29 (2005): 5–17.

7. Activist widows include Tang Qunying, Xu Zonghan, Song Minghuang, and Zhuang Hanqiao.

8. See Jing Tsu for an excellent study of the creation of a national identity centered on failure. Tsu Jing, *Failure, Nationalism and Literature: The Making of Modern Chinese Identity, 1895–1937* (Stanford, CA: Stanford University Press, 2005).

9. Frank Dikötter, *The Age of Openness: China Before Mao* (Hong Kong: Hong Kong University Press, forthcoming).

10. See Wu Shuzhen, "Zhongguo funü canzheng yundong de lishi kaocha," *Zhongshan daxue xuebao: She ke ban*, 2 (1990): 77–84.

11. Carole Pateman, "Three Questions about Womanhood Suffrage," in *Suffrage and Beyond: International Feminist Perspectives*, ed. Caroline Daley and Melanie Nolan (Auckland: Auckland University Press, 1994), 346.

12. Ian Fletcher, Nym Mayhall, and Philippa Levine, eds., *Women's Suffrage in the British Empire* (London: Routledge, 2000).

13. Ellen Carol DuBois and Robert Cherny, eds., "Woman Suffrage: The View from the Pacific," special issue, *Pacific Historical Review* 69, no. 4 (November 2000). See also J. E. Hahner. *Emancipating the Female Sex: The Struggle for Women's Rights in Brazil* (Durham, NC: Duke University Press, 1990); Ellen Carol DuBois, *Feminism and Suffrage: The Emergence of an Independent Women's Movement in America, 1848–1869* (1978; repr., Ithaca, NY: Cornell University Press, 1980).

14. Louise Edwards and Mina Roces, eds., *Women's Suffrage in Asia: Gender, Nationalism and Democracy* (London: RoutledgeCurzon, 2004).

15. Ellen Carol DuBois, "Woman Suffrage Around the World: Three Phases of Suffragist Internationalism," in *Suffrage and Beyond: International Feminist Perspectives*, ed. Caroline Daley and Melanie Nolan (Auckland: Auckland University Press, 1994), 252.

16. Sandra Stanley Holton, "The Making of Suffrage History," in *Votes for Women*, ed. June Purvis and Sandra Stanley Holton (London: Routledge, 2000), 14.

17. Roxanne Witke, "Woman as Politician in China of the 1920s," in *Women in China: Studies in Social Change and Feminism*, ed. Marilyn Young (Ann Arbor: Center for Chinese Studies, University of Michigan, 1973), 40.

18. Susan Kingsley Kent, *Sex and Suffrage in Britain, 1860–1914* (Princeton, NJ: Princeton University Press, 1987), 3.

19. Li Xiaojiang, "Economic Reform and the Awakening of Women's Consciousness," trans. S. Katherine Campbell, in *Engendering China: Women, Culture and the State*, ed. Christina K. Gilmartin, Gail Hershatter, Lisa Rofel, and Tyrene White (Cambridge, MA: Harvard University Press, 1994), 367.

20. The best of these overviews include Zhonghua quanguo funü lianhe hui, ed. *Zhongguo funü yundong shi—xin minzhu zhuyi shiqi* (Beijing: Chunqiu chubanshe, 1989); Liu Jucai, *Zhongguo jindai funü yundong shi* (Beijing: Zhongguo funü chubanshe, 1989); Lü Meiyi and Zheng Yongfu, *Zhongguo funü yundong, 1840–1921* (Zhengzhou: Henan renmin chubanshe, 1990); Ji Rong, ed., *Zhongguo funü yundong shi* (Changsha: Hunan chubanshe, 1992); Ma Gengcun, *Zhongguo jindai funü shi* (Qingdao: Qingdao chubanshe, 1995).

21. DuBois, "Woman Suffrage Around the World," 253.

22. Jane Rendall, "Citizenship, Culture and Civilisation: The Language of British Suffragists, 1866–1874," in *Suffrage and Beyond: International Feminist Perspectives*, ed. Caroline Daley and Melanie Nolan (Auckland: Auckland University Press, 1994), 141.

23. See Carrie Chapman Catt, "The New China: She Sits in the Gallery and Looks Down on China's Ten Women Legislators, Who Had Been Called a Myth," *Woman's Journal* (5 October 1912): 314–15. I am grateful to Mary Chapman for providing me with this article and excerpts from Catt's diary.

24. "In Heathen Lands," *Suffragist* 6, no. 47 (14 December 1918): 10.

25. "Womanhood Glorified," *Suffragist* 7, no. 30 (2 August 1919): 2.

26. For a full table of women's suffrage gains, see Daley and Nolan, *Suffrage and Beyond*, 349–52. Note that the date for China is incorrect: the chronology specifies 1949 as the year of victory for women's suffrage, but this is actually the year of the establishment of the PRC and the CCP's rule over China.

27. Louise Edwards, "Women's Suffrage in China: Challenging Scholarly Conventions," *Pacific Historical Review* 69, no. 4 (November 2000): 617–39.

28. See Sue Blackburn, "Winning the Vote for Women in Indonesia," *Australian Feminist Studies*, no. 14 (1999): 207–18.

29. Song Qingling, "Chinese Women's Fight for Freedom," in *Chinese Women through Chinese Eyes*, ed. Li Yu-ning (Armonk, NY: M.E. Sharpe, 1992), 91.

30. Witke, "Woman as Politician," 33.

31. Patricia Grimshaw, *Women's Suffrage in New Zealand* (1972; repr., Auckland: Auckland University Press, 1987).

32. Grimshaw, *Women's Suffrage in New Zealand*; Audrey Oldfield, *Woman Suffrage in Australia: A Gift or a Struggle?* (Cambridge and Melbourne: Cambridge University Press, 1992).

33. Li Ziyun, "Women's Consciousness and Women's Writing," in *Engendering China: Women, Culture and the State*, ed. Christina K. Gilmartin, Gail Hershatter, Lisa Rofel, and Tyrene White (Cambridge, MA: Harvard University Press, 1994), 304–5. For an analysis of this style of historiography, see Louise Edwards, "Co-opting the Chinese Women's Suffrage Movement for the Fifth Modernisation—Democracy," *Asian Studies Review* 26, no. 1 (September 2002): 285–307.

34. Ch'ien Tuan-sheng, *The Government and Politics of China, 1912–1949* (1950; repr., Stanford, CA: Stanford University Press, 1970), 325.

35. Louise Edwards, "Constraining Women's Political Work with 'Women's Work': The Chinese Communist Party and Women's Participation in Politics," in *Chinese Women: Living and Working*, ed. Anne E. McLaren (London: RoutledgeCurzon, 2004), 109–30.

36. On the ACWF, see Elisabeth Croll, *Changing Identities of Chinese Women: Rhetoric, Experience and Self-Perception in Twentieth Century China* (London: Zed Books, 1995).

37. See Louise Edwards, "Women in the People's Republic of China: New Challenges to the Grand Gender Narrative," in *Women in Asia: Tradition, Modernity and Globalisation*, ed. Louise Edwards and Mina Roces (Sydney and Ann Arbor: Allen & Unwin and University of Michigan Press, 2000), 59–82.

38. Susan Mann, *Precious Records: Women in China's Long Eighteenth Century* (Stanford, CA: Stanford University Press, 1997); Dorothy Ko, *Teachers of the Inner Chambers: Women and Culture in China, 1573–1722* (Stanford, CA: Stanford University Press, 1994).

39. Christina K. Gilmartin, *Engendering the Chinese Revolution: Radical Women, Communist Politics and Mass Movement in the 1920s* (Berkeley: University of California Press, 1995); Kathryn Bernhardt, *Women and Property in China, 960–1949* (Stanford, CA: Stanford University Press, 1999); Gail Hershatter, *The Workers of Tianjin, 1900–1949* (Stanford, CA: Stanford University Press, 1986) and *Dangerous Pleasures: Prostitution and Modernity in Twentieth-Century Shanghai* (Berkeley: University of California Press, 1997); Emily Honig, *Sisters and Stranger: Women in the Shanghai Cotton Mills, 1919–1949* (Stanford, CA: Stanford University Press, 1986); Wang Zheng, *Women in the Chinese Enlightenment*.

40. See Wang Xingjuan and Xu Xiuyu, eds., *Zhongguo funü canzheng de xingdong* (Beijing: Haitun chubanshe, 1995).

41. Ji Xin, *Nüren yu zhengzhi: 90 niandai funü canzheng yundong* (Taibei: Nüshu wenshu shi, 2000), 1–2. On women in current Chinese politics, see Jude Howell, "Women's Political Participation in China," *Parliamentary Affairs* 55 (2002): 43–56; Ellen R. Judd, *The Chinese Women's Movement: Between State and Market* (Stanford, CA: Stanford University Press, 2002); Stanley Rosen, "Women and Political Participation in China," *Pacific Affairs* 68, no. 3 (1995): 315–41; J. Tong, "The Gender Gap in Political Culture and Participation in China," *Communist and Post-Communist Studies* 36 (2003): 131–50.

42. Wu Shuzhen, "Zhongguo funü," 77.

43. An excellent example of this is found in Zhou Huan, "Nüzi canzheng tan," *Nüzi canzheng xiejinhui huikan*, no. 1 (10 December 1922): 6–14.

44. Andrew J. Nathan, *Peking Politics, 1918–1923* (Berkeley: University of California Press, 1976), 9. On constitutionalism in Nationalist China see Zhao Suisheng, *Power by Design: Constitution-making in Nationalist China* (Honolulu: University of Hawaii Press, 1996).

45. Edmund Fung, *In Search of Chinese Democracy: Civil Opposition in Nationalist China, 1929–1949* (Cambridge, UK: Cambridge University Press, 2000), 1.

46. Ch'ien, *Government and Politics of China*, 435.

47. "Manifesto of the First National Congress of the Kuomintang: January 30, 1924," repr. in Milton J. T. Shieh, *The Kuomintang: Historical Selected Documents, 1894–1969* (New York: St. John's University Press, 1970), 77.

48. See Zarrow, "Citizenship in China," 3–38.

49. Virginia Sapiro, "When Are Interests Interesting? The Problem of Political Representation of Women," *American Political Science Review* 75, no. 3 (1981): 701–16.

50. These international connections continued into the 1930s with Chinese participation in the Pan Pacific Conferences. Fiona Paisley, "Cultivating Modernity: Culture and Internationalism in Australian Feminism's Pacific Age," *Journal of Women's History* 14, no. 3 (Autumn 2002): 105–32.

51. "Wanguo nüzi canzheng tongmeng hui huizhang dao Hu," *Minli bao* (2 September 1912); "Nüquan da huodong," *Minli bao* (5 September 1912); "Nüzi canzheng hui," *Minli bao* (27 September 1912).

52. "Huanying nü canzheng huizhang," *Minli bao* (10 September 1912).

53. On the WCTU, see Ian Tyrell, *Woman's World Woman's Empire: The Women's Christian Temperance Union in International Perspective, 1880–1930* (Chapel Hill: University of North Carolina Press, 1991).

54. The fountain can still be visited today opposite Melbourne's Victoria markets.

55. Antonia Finnane has shown how important dress choices were in the first half of the century. See her article, "What Should Chinese Women Wear? A National Problem," *Modern China* 22, no. 2 (April 1996): 99–131. See also Louise Edwards, "Dressing for Power: Scholars' Robes, School Uniforms and Military Attire in China," in *The Politics of Dress in Asia and the Americas*, ed. Mina Roces and Louise Edwards (Eastbourne, UK: Sussex Academic, 2007).

56. June Purvis and Sandra Stanley Holton, "Introduction: The Campaigns for Votes for Women," in *Votes for Women*, ed. June Purvis and Sandra Stanley Holton (London: Routledge, 2000), 3.

57. For a discussion of the twin mechanisms for performing masculinity—literary and martial talent—and the dominance of the scholar, see Kam Louie, *Theorising Chinese Masculinity: Society and Gender in China* (Cambridge, UK: Cambridge University Press, 2002).

58. Key works on women's sexualized virtue in China include Janet M. Theiss, *Disgraceful Matters: The Politics of Chastity in Eighteenth-Century China* (Berkeley: University of California Press, 2004); Tien Ju-k'ang, *Male Anxiety and Female Chastity: A Comparative Study of Chinese Ethical Values in Ming-Ch'ing Times* (Leiden: E.J. Brill, 1988); Susan Mann, "Widows in the Kinship, Class and Community Structures of Qing Dynasty China," *Journal of Asian Studies* 46, no. 1 (1987): 37–55; Anne Waltner, "Widows and Remarriage in Ming and Early Qing China," *Historical Reflections* 8, no. 3 (1981): 129–46; Mark Elvin, "Female Virtue and the State," *Past and Present*, no. 104 (August 1984): 110–52. For discussion on elite Qing life, see Louise Edwards, *Men and Women in Qing China: Gender in the Red Chamber Dream* (Leiden: E.J. Brill, 1988; Honolulu: University of Hawaii Press, 2001).

59. See Louise Edwards, "Narratives of Race and Nation in China: Women's Suffrage in the Early Twentieth Century," *Women's Studies International Forum* 25, no. 6 (November–December 2002): 619–30; Patricia Grimshaw, "A White Woman's Suffrage," in *A Woman's Constitution? Gender and History in the Australian Commonwealth*, ed. Helen Irving (Sydney: Hale & Iremonger, 1998), 77–97, "Gender, Citizenship and Race in the Women's Christian Temperance Union of Australia, 1890 to the 1930s," *Australian Feminist Studies* 13, no. 28 (1998): 199–214, and "Settler Anxieties, Indigenous Peoples and Women's Suffrage in the Colonies of Australia, New Zealand and Hawai'i, 1888–1902," *Pacific Historical Review* 69, no. 4 (November 2000): 553–72.

60. On class in Germany and ethnicity in the USA, see Nancy F. Cott, "Early Twentieth-Century Feminism in Political Context: A Comparative Look at Germany and the United States," in *Suffrage and Beyond: International Feminist Perspectives*, ed. Caroline Daley and Melanie Nolan (Auckland: Auckland University Press, 1994), 234–51.

61. See John Fitzgerald, *Awakening China: Politics, Culture, and Class in the Nationalist Revolution* (Stanford, CA: Stanford University Press, 1996).

62. Fung, *In Search of Chinese Democracy*, 12.

63. Edmund Fung has argued that the 1930s liberal intellectual was "interested in a form of elite rule" and that "for them, the best form of democracy was that founded in elite consensus underpinned by a public philosophy." Ibid., 18. On education and suffrage, see Louise Edwards, "Chinese Women's Campaigns for Suffrage: Nationalism, Confucianism and Political Agency," in *Women's Suffrage in Asia: Gender, Nationalism, Democracy*, ed. Louise Edwards and Mina Roces (London: RoutledgeCurzon, 2004), 59–78.

64. Mann, *Precious Records*, 76–120.

65. Zarrow, "Citizenship in China," 23; Charlotte L. Beahan, "The Women's Movement and Nationalism in Late Ch'ing China" (PhD diss., Columbia University, 1976), 106–16. In 1904 one activist explained that equality between men and women was vital because it would create a sense of citizenship among mothers. Ya Chi, "Lun zhuzao guomin mu," *Nüzi shijie*, no. 7 (1904): 1–7.

66. Zarrow, "Citizenship in China," 12.

67. Ibid.

68. Kent, *Sex and Suffrage in Britain*, 7–11.

69. All chapters in Edwards and Roces, *Women's Suffrage in Asia*, as follows: Susan Blackburn, "Women's Suffrage and Democracy in Indonesia," 79–105; Gail Pearson, "Tradition, Law and the Female Suffrage Movement in India," 195–219; and Mina Roces, "Is the Suffragist an American Colonial Construct? Defining 'the Filipino Woman' in Colonial Philippines," 24–59.

70. Yukiko Matsukawa and Kaoru Tachi, "Women's Suffrage and Gender Politics in Japan," in *Suffrage and Beyond: International Feminist Perspectives*, ed. Caroline Daley and Melanie Nolan (Auckland: Auckland University Press, 1994), 180.

71. Barbara Molony, "Citizenship and Suffrage in Interwar Japan," in *Women's Suffrage in Asia: Gender, Nationalism and Democracy*, ed. Louise Edwards and Mina Roces (London: RoutledgeCurzon, 2004), 130.

72. On modern women in China, see Wendy Larson, *Women and Writing in Modern China* (Stanford, CA: Stanford University Press, 1998), 26; Tani Barlow, "Theorizing Woman: Funü, Guojia, Jiating," in *Feminism and History*, ed. Joan Wallach Scott (Oxford, UK: Oxford University Press, 1996), 58; Louise Edwards, "Policing the Modern Woman in Republican China," *Modern China* 26, no. 2 (April 2000): 115–47.

Chapter Two

1. For an excellent study of the gendered citizenship, see Joan Judge, "Citizens or Mothers of Citizens? Gender and the Meaning of Modern Chinese Citizenship," in *Changing Meanings of Citizenship in Modern China*, ed. Merle Goldman and Elizabeth J. Perry (Cambridge, MA: Harvard University Press, 2002), 23–43.

2. Roger Thompson has shown that this vibrancy extended to the levels below the provinces. *China's Local Councils in the Age of Constitutional Reform, 1898–1911* (Cambridge, MA: Harvard University Press, 1995).

3. Joseph W. Esherick, *Reform and Revolution in China: The 1911 Revolution in Hunan and Hubei* (Berkeley: University of California Press, 1976), 95.

4. John Fincher, *Chinese Democracy: The Self-Government Movement in Local, Provincial and National Politics, 1905–1914* (London: Croom Helm; Canberra: ANU Press, 1981), 111. Fincher also provides numbers of eligible voters by province, see p. 112.

5. Esherick, *Reform and Revolution in China*, 94.

6. For more detail see Chuzo Ichiko, "Political and Institutional Reform, 1901–1911," in *The Cambridge History of China*, vol. 11, ed. Denis Twitchett and John K. Fairbank (Cambridge, UK: Cambridge University Press, 1980), 398–99. See also the serialized articles on the electoral process in *Dagong bao* from 5 September 1910.

7. Fincher, *Chinese Democracy*, 16–17.

8. Sapiro, "When Are Interests Interesting?" 701.

9. For a succinct description of this reformist elite, see Esherick, *Reform and Revolution in China*, 105.

10. Zhou Yaping, "Zhongguo funü canzheng de lishi guiji," *Jishou daxue xuebao: She ke ban*, no. 2 (1992): 74.

11. Kang Youwei, cited in Min Jia-yin et al. eds., *The Chalice and the Blade in Chinese Culture: Gender Relations and Social Models* (Beijing: China Social Sciences Publishing House, 1995), 484–85. This equality sentiment became commonplace later. See the comment that "men and women are all the same" in Du Qingchi, "Nan nü dou shi yiyang," *Nüzi shijie*, no. 6 (1904): 13.

12. Wang Zheng, *Women in the Chinese Enlightenment*, 36. For a brief discussion of the contribution made by Tan, Liang, and Kang to women's rights in China, see Wang's discussion on pp. 36–38. See also Wang Shuhuai, "Kang Youwei dui nüxing ji hunyin de taidu," *Jindai Zhongguo funü shi yanjiu*, no. 2 (June 1994): 27–49; Zhang Pengyuan, "Liang Qichao de liangxing guan," *Jindai Zhongguo funü shi yanjiu*, no. 2 (June 1994): 51–64.

13. *Women's Studies News* commenced publication in July 1898 and is probably China's first women's publication. This paper was the organ of the China Society for Women's Study, a group established around the 1898 reformers. Their wives and daughters, Kang Tongwei (1879–1974), Kang Tongbi (1881–1969), Li Huixian (1868–1929), Huang Jinyu (1869–1936), and Li Run (1866–1925) were the main force behind this short-lived society.

14. *Nüxue bao*, cited in ZFYS, 26. *Nüxue bao*, nos. 4 and 7, cited in *The Chalice and the Blade in Chinese Culture*, ed. Min Jiayin et al., 488–89. Qian Nanxiu provides an excellent discussion of this journal and reproduces illustrations and cover shots in her article. Qian Nanxiu, "Revitalizing the Xianyuan (Worthy Ladies) Tradition: Women in the 1989 Reforms," *Modern China* 29, no. 4 (October 2003): 418–19. For further information on the Society and its journal, see Lü Meiyi and Zheng Yongfu, *Zhongguo funü yundong*, 92–100.

15. For a discussion of the impact of Mill and Spencer on China, see Beahan, "The Women's Movement and Nationalism," chap. 4.

16. Sandra Stanley Holton, "The Making of Suffrage History," in *Votes for Women*, ed. June Purvis and Sandra Stanley Holton (London: Routledge, 2000), 14.

17. Karl Gerth, *China Made: Consuming Culture and the Creation of a Nation* (Cambridge, MA: Harvard University Asia Center, 2003), 290.

18. Catherine Gipoulon, "The Emergence of Women in Politics in China, 1898–1927," *Chinese Studies in History* (Winter 1989–90): 47–48. See Zhao Zongpo, "Lun Xinhai geming shijian de funü aiguo huodong," *Shanghai shifan daxue xuebao: Zhe she ban*, no. 4 (1990): 60–65.

19. "Riben liuxue nüxuesheng Gongai hui zhangcheng," *Jiangsu*, no. 2 (1903): 155.

20. An article published in 1907 presented a slightly different logic to women's participation in national affairs. It noted that men dominated the political, military, financial, and educational aspects of national governance. Women played no part in any of these important functions, and as a consequence China was in dangerous straits. The failure to mobilize women to the national cause was a waste of national talent. "Nan nü bing zun lun," *Zhongguo xin nüjie zazhi*, no. 4 (1907): 3.

21. Hu Bin[xia], "Lun Zhongguo zhi shuairuo nüzi bu de ci qi zui," *Jiangsu*, no. 3 (1903): 156–57.

22. Chen Xiefen, "Nüjie kewei," *Zhongguo ribao* 26 (27 April 1904). Also available in English as "Crisis in the Women's World," trans. Jennifer Carpenter, in *Writing Women in Modern China: An Anthology of Women's Literature from the Early Twentieth Century*, ed. Amy Dooling and Kristina Torgeson (New York: Columbia University Press, 1998), 86.

23. Jin Songcen, *Nüjie zhong* (Shanghai: Datong shuju, 1903). This important text was presumed lost for decades until Professor Li Yu-ning located a copy in the early 1990s. For details on Jin's life and work, see Li Yu-ning, "Nüjie zhong yu Zhonghua nüxing de xiandai hua," in *Family Process and Political Process in Modern Chinese History: Part Two*, ed. Academia Sinica Modern History Institute (Taipei: Modern History Institute, 1992), 1055–82. Chen Yan of Fudan University has since edited another version. See *Nüjie zhong* (Shanghai: Shanghai guji chubanshe, 2003).

24. Zhang Yufa, "Women—A New Social Force," *Chinese Studies in History* (Winter 1977–78): 33.

25. Jin Songcen, *Nüjie zhong*, 46.

26. Jin Songcen wrote a preface to an important women's journal, *Nüzi shijie*, under his pen name Jin Yi, which read in part: "Women are the mothers of citizens. If we desire a new China then we must have new women; if we want a strong China, then we must have strong women, if we want a civilized China then first civilize our women; if we want to save China, we must first save our women, this is without a doubt." He advised China's men, "Don't look down upon women. Women are the mothers of civilization." Jin Yi, "*Nüzi shijie* fakan ci," *Nüzi shijie*, 1 (1904), repr. in Xia Xiaohong, ed., *"Nüzi shijie" wen xuan* (Guiyang: Guizhou jiaoyu chubanshe, 2003), 55–56.

27. Jin Songcen, *Nüjie zhong*, 56.

28. Ibid., 66–67. See also Louise Edwards, "Chin Sung-ts'en's *A Tocsin for Women*: The Dexterous Merger of Radicalism and Conservatism in Feminism of the Early Twentieth Century," *Jindai Zhongguo funü shi yanjiu* (June 1994): 117–40; Xiong Yuezhi, *Zhongguo jindai minzhu sixiang shi* (Shanghai: Renmin chubanshe, 1986), 419–33.

29. Jin Songcen, *Nüjie zhong*, 51–52.

30. Ibid., 58–59.

31. Ibid., 60–63.

32. Ibid., 83.

33. Lin Zongsu, "Lin nüshi xu," in ibid., 2. This translation is from Ono Kazuko, *Chinese Women in a Century of Revolution, 1850–1950*, ed. Joshua A. Fogel (Stanford, CA: Stanford University Press, 1989), 59.

34. The most comprehensive list of these organizations can be found in Lü Meiyi and Zheng Yongfu, *Zhongguo funü yundong*, 170–73. For an example of the reception these groups received, see "Dongjing liu xuesheng jie de zhentan," *Zhongguo ribao* (13 March 1907).

35. "Guizhou funü aiguo hui zhi daibiaotuan han," *Dagong bao* (2 September 1912).

36. See Tan Sheying, ed., *Zhongguo funü yundong tongshi* (Nanjing: Funü gongming she, 1936), 37–38.

37. Hu Binxia was one of eight women who went to Japan in June 1902. See Xie Zhangfa, "Qingmo de liu Ri nü xuesheng jiqi huodong yu yingxiang," *Jindai Zhongguo funü shi yanjiu*, no. 4 (August 1996): 66.

38. The group's leader Hu Binxia was to become an important figure in the women's movement for decades to follow. Hu's outstanding abilities won her a scholarship to study at Wellesley College in

1907, and after graduating in 1913 she explored the education system for women in the USA on behalf of the new Republican government in China. For more information on Hu's life, see Ye Weili, "'Nü Liuxuesheng': The Story of American-Educated Chinese Women, 1880s–1920s," *Modern China* 20, no. 3 (July 1994): 315–46.

39. Hu Binxia "Zhu 'Gongai hui' zhi qiantu," *Jiangsu*, no. 6 (1903): 162–63.

40. "Riben liuxue nüxuesheng Gongai hui zhangcheng," 155. It has become commonplace to describe the Mutual Love Society as highly patriotic, and some commentators have focused on the group's anti-imperialist sentiments. See ZFYS, 47. I can find no evidence of this as a central plank of the Society from its own documents.

41. Chow Kai Wing, "Chen Xiefen," in *BDQP*, 21–23.

42. *Subao* began publishing in June 1896 in Shanghai, and in 1902 it became the organ for the radical anti-Qing Patriotic Schools led by Cai Yuanpei. MSD, 44.

43. This was an identical title to a newspaper formed by the 1898 reformers.

44. For more information on Chen Xiefen, see Charlotte Beahan, "Feminism and Nationalism in the Chinese Women's Press, 1902–1911," *Modern China* 1, no. 4 (October 1975): 379–416.

45. "Zhongguo liu Ri nüxuesheng hui zhangcheng," *Zhongguo xin nüjie zazhi*, no. 2 (1907): 76–81.

46. Xie Zhangfa, "Qingmo de liu Ri nüxuesheng ji huodong yu yingxiang," 67.

47. Luo Yanbin's extensive writings were premised on the belief that women and men were equal in ancient times but gradually men used their superior strength to subdue women. The goal for women was to restore this ancient balance. She published in the main women's magazines of the time—*New Women of China Magazine* and *Chinese Women's Magazine*. Au Chi Kin, "Yan Bin," in *BDQP*, 258–61.

48. The journal lasted from June 1907 to 1910.

49. Peter Zarrow, "He Zhen and Anarcho-Feminism in China," *Journal of Asian Studies* 47, no. 4 (November 1988): 796.

50. Zhen Shu (He Zhen), "Furen jiefang wenti," *Tianyi* 8, 9, 10 (combined issue; 1907): 1. Zhen Shu was the pen name that He Zhen used for much of her writing at this time.

51. Ibid.

52. Ibid., 2.

53. Zhen Shu (He Zhen), "Nüzi fuchou lun," *Tianyi* 4 (1907): 1.

54. George T. Yu, *Party Politics in Republican China: The Kuomintang, 1912–1924* (Berkeley: University of California Press, 1966), 33.

55. Shen Zhi, "Xinhai geming shiqi de nü zhishi fenzi," *Shanghai shehui kexue yuan xueshu jikan*, no. 4 (1991): 58. Ma Gengcun provides a comprehensive table of the Revolutionary Alliance women in *Zhongguo jindai funü shi*, 219–25. See also Lin Weihong, "Tongmeng hui shidai nü geming zhishi de huodong," in *Zhongguo funü shilun wenji*, ed. Li Yu-ning and Zhang Yufa (Taipei: Shangwuyin shuguan, 1981), 129–78.

56. Li Yu-ning, "Sun Yat-sen and Women's Transformation," *Chinese Studies in History* (Summer 1988): 62.

57. For the full translated text, see Teng Ssu-yu and J. K. Fairbank, *China's Response to the West: A Documentary Survey, 1839–1923* (Cambridge, MA: Harvard University Press, 1961), 227–29. Quotation on p. 228.

58. Shang Mingxuan, *He Xiangning zhuan* (Beijing: Beijing chubanshe, 1994); Luan Xuefei, "He Xiangning yu Zhongguo gongchandang," *Dongbei shida xuebao: Zhe, she ban*, no. 4 (1992): 6–21.

59. He Xiangning, "Jing gao wo tongbao jiemei," *Jiangsu*, no. 4 (1903): 144.

60. Ibid.

61. Lü Meiyi and Zheng Yongfu, *Zhongguo funü yundong*, 231–32.

62. Lee Kam Keung, "Fang Junying," in *BDQP*, 34–37.

63. See Tan Sheying, *Zhongguo funü yundong tongshi*, 30–31 for names of the various military groups.

64. "Zhi na nüzi zhi aiguo xin," *Hubei xuesheng jie*, no. 3 (March 1903): 65–67.

65. Hua Mulan is China's most famous woman warrior. She replaced her ailing father in military service and returned home after years of outstanding battle performance. For an extended discussion on the various renditions of her story, see Louise Edwards, "Hua Mulan" in *Biographical Dictionary of Chinese Women: Antiquity to the Sui Dynasty*, ed. Lily Lee (Armonk, NY: M.E. Sharpe, forthcoming). Liang

Hongyu (circa 1130) was noted for her courage in the face of military attacks. She was wife of the Song general Han Shizhong and during a particularly difficult battle with the invading Jurched was credited with providing crucial battle plans that resulted in Han's victory. Yuan Shaoying and Yang Guizhen, eds., *Zhongguo funü mingren cidian* (Changchun: Beifang funü ertong chubanshe, 1989), 530.

66. Wu Shuqing, cited in Tan Sheying, *Zhongguo funü yundong tongshi*, 34–35.

67. Both sisters went on to marry fellow revolutionaries. Yin Weijun had a son and three daughters while Ruizhi remained childless. At the end of her life Ruizhi published an autobiography that was published in the 29 March 1948 issue of *Gongping bao*. See Zhejiang sheng xinhai geming shi yanjiu hui, ed., *Xinhai geming Zhejiang shiliao xuanji* (Hangzhou: Zhejiang renmin chubanshe, 1981), 483–91. See also Ma Gengcun, *Zhongguo jindai funü shi*, 216–18.

68. "Nüzi houyuan hui beifa jun qiujidui jianzhang," *Minli bao* (4 February 1912).

69. *Tianduo bao* reported that in Hong Kong a "Dare to Die Brigade" was formed that had over one hundred members. Their rules included cutting their hair short. "Nü gan si dui," *Tianduo bao* (14 December 1911). See reports of their actions in "Nü gan si dui ru jing," *Minli bao* (15 January 1912).

70. "Zhonghua nüzi guomin jun quandui," *Minli bao* (10 January 1912); "Zhonghua nüzi guomin jun faqi ren," *Minli bao* (11 January 1912).

71. "Da Zongtong jingli nüxia," *Minli bao* (19 January 1912). This enthusiastic praise for the women brigades contrasts with the provisional parliament's response. Fung describes the government's reaction as, "the appearance of a corps of 'Amazons . . . was a source of embarrassment to the military authorities." By the end of February the government had ordered the women's armies to disband. Edmund Fung, *The Military Dimension of the Chinese Revolution: The New Army and Its Role in the Revolution of 1911* (Canberra: Australian National University Press, 1980), 233.

72. A photo of Zhang Zhujun is printed on the inside cover of *Nüzi shijie*, no. 9 (1904). Born in Guangdong, Zhang trained as a doctor of western medicine in China under the tutelage of the American John Glasgow Kerr. She established hospitals for the poor and schools for girls in the province. Au Chi Kin, "Zhang Zhujun," in *BDQP*, 310–13.

73. Lü Meiyi and Zheng Yongfu, *Zhongguo funü yundong*, 236–37. See also ZFYS, 51. Tan Sheying has reprinted speeches of the Society in *Zhongguo funü yundong tongshi*, 38–41.

74. I describe this phenomenon as "crisis femininity," wherein women assume military roles in order to reinforce the patriarchy. See Louise Edwards, "Zhanzheng dui xiandai Zhongguo funü canzheng yundong de yinxiang: 'Weiji nüxing' de wenti," in *Bainian Zhongguo nüquan sichao yanjiu*, ed. Wang Zheng and Chen Yan (Shanghai: Fudan University 2005), 220–26. For discussion on how traditional women warriors buttressed the existing social order, see Louise Edwards, "Women Warriors and Amazons of the mid Qing Texts *Jinghua yuan* and *Honglou meng*," *Modern Asian Studies* 29, no. 2 (1995), 225–55.

75. The army numbered about one hundred. In February of 1912 the brigade joined the Guangdong Northern Attack Troops in the battle for Xuzhou. For a brief history of the brigade including a membership list, see Zhao Liancheng, "Tongmeng hui zai Gang Yue de huodong he Guangdong funü canjia geming de huiyi," in *Guangdong Xinhai geming shiliao*, ed. Zhongguo renmin zhenzhi xieshang huiyi Guangdong weiyuan huiweiyuan hui wenshi ziliao yanjiu weiyuan hui (Guangzhou: Guangdong renmin chubanshe, 1981), 101–6.

76. During the 1920s Zonghan led one of the most important suffrage organizations in Shanghai, the United Women's Association, and she provided financial support for the CCP magazine *Women's Voice*. Li Yu-ning, "Hsu Tsung-han: Tradition and Revolution," *Republican China* 10, no. 1a (November 1984): 20. Her name at birth was Xu Peixuan, see Christina Gilmartin, *Engendering the Chinese Revolution*, 243n30.

77. In 1908 Xu had a picture-mounting shop that served as a cover for smuggling arms and ammunition for the Alliance. Song Minghuang, another Revolutionary Alliance member, assisted Xu in forming the brigade. Song had been active in the Alliance's Hong Kong assassination squad. See the personal reminiscences of Zhao Liancheng in her "Tongmeng hui zai Gang Yue de huodong," 96.

78. Xu Zonghan's biography demonstrates the contradictions managed by activists at this time. In widowhood, Xu Zonghan became the second wife of a Revolutionary Alliance leader, Huang Xing, and from late 1911 onward changed her surname to Huang. Her friends in the women's movement had criticized this type of "polygamous" marriage in their various magazines. Zonghan's first marriage followed traditional

customs—her parents married her to the son of a high official at the age of eighteen *sui*. Her husband died only a few years after marriage, leaving Zonghan with two young children. Huang Xing's first marriage was also in the traditional style—his wife had bound feet and was illiterate. After 1912, Huang Xing established a household that included his first wife and Zonghan. The latter accepted the nominal position as "Huang's assistant" rather than concubine or wife. Huang had children by both women during these years. His first wife bore Huang five children and, during their brief five-year relationship, Zonghan also bore Huang Xing two sons. Zhao Liancheng, "Tongmeng hui zai Gang Yue de huodong," 96.

79. Ma Gengcun, *Zhongguo jindai funü shi*, 213.

80. Fang Junji, "Yu nüxue yi fu nüquan shuo," *Jiangsu*, no. 3 (1903): 157. This is likely to be a pseudonym for Fang Junying.

81. See discussion of the Japanese influence on Qing schooling during this time in Judge, "Talent, Virtue, and the Nation," 765–803. See also Paul J. Bailey, *Gender and Education in China: Gender discourses and women's schooling in the early twentieth* century (London: Routledge, 2007).

82. See Cheng Weikun, "Going Public Through Education: Female Reformers and Girls' Schools in Late Qing Beijing," *Late Imperial China* 21, no. 1 (June 2000): 117–18 for more detail on the Qing government's education policies for women.

83. Shen Zhi, "Xinhai geming shiqi de nü zhishi fenzi," *Shanghai shehui kexue yuan xueshu jikan*, no. 4 (1991): 60.

84. Cheng Weikun, "Going Public Through Education," 109.

85. Zhao Zhi, "Nüzi wu cai bian she de bo," *Zhongguo xin nüjie zazhi*, no. 3 (1907): 28.

86. Wang Zheng, *Women in the Chinese Enlightenment*, 125.

87. Ye Weili, "'Nü Liuxuesheng,'" 328.

88. Qian Nanxiu, "Revitalizing the Xianyuan (Worthy Ladies) Tradition," 406. The school was opened in 1898 in Shanghai.

89. Cheng Weikun, "Going Public Through Education," 107–44.

90. "Beiyang nüshifan xuetang xueye jicheng," *Dagong bao* (10 February 1908).

91. Sally Borthwick, "Changing Concepts of the Role of Women from the Late Qing to the May Fourth Period," in *Ideal and Reality: Social and Political Change in Modern China, 1860–1949*, ed. David Pong and Edmund S. K. Fung (Lanham, MD: University Press of America, 1985), 78.

92. Others saw education as a modernizing force through its ability to rid China of the scourge of superstition. An article in *Zhongguo ribao* of 1904 explained that religions in China hold back progressive thinking and that "northerners were more prone to superstition than southerners and women were more prone to superstition than men. . . . Because of superstition women's rights in China have not yet been revived . . . the level of women's knowledge is low and women's learning is not flourishing." "Nü gui," *Zhongguo ribao* (19 April 1904).

93. Qian Nanxiu, "Revitalizing the Xianyuan (Worthy Ladies) Tradition," 399.

94. "Xuejie yi su shefa yi baoquan nüxue zhi ming yu," *Zhongguo ribao* (10 October 1907).

95. Xing Long, "Xinhai geming qianxi de funü yundong," *Shanxi daxue xuebao: Zhe, she ban*, no. 3 (1988): 68. For the most comprehensive overview of Chinese women studying in Japan, see Xie Zhangfa, "Qingmo de liu Ri nü xuesheng ji huodong yu yingxiang," 63–86. A photo of Chinese women studying at the Aoyama Women's Vocational College is printed on the inside cover of *Nüzi shijie*, no. 11 (1904).

96. Chen Yan'an, "Quan nüzi liuxue shuo," *Jiangsu*, no. 3 (1903): 155–56.

97. "Gong ai hui tong ren quan liuxue qi," *Jiangsu*, no. 6 (1903): 159. Another women's rights journal published in Japan wrote in 1907, "if you educate women then the country really would produce women citizens." Lian Shi, "*Zhongguo xin nüjie zazhi* fakan ci," *Zhongguo xin nüjie zazhi*, no. 1 (1907): 2.

98. Lam Hok-chung, "Zhang Hanying," in *BDQP*, 289–93.

99. Zhou Yaping, "Lun Xinhai geming shiqi de funü canzheng yundong," *Lishi dang'an*, no. 2 (1993), 119.

100. Borthwick, "Changing Concepts of the Role of Women," 79.

101. Zhou Yaping, "Lun Xinhai geming shiqi de funü canzheng yundong," 121.

102. Wang Zheng notes that women ran the majority of the journals between 1897 and 1912. Wang Zheng, *Women in the Chinese Enlightenment*, 40. For a list of women's journals, see Ma Gengcun, *Zhongguo jindai funü shi*, 160–63.

103. See Mann, *Precious Records*, 49–50 for a discussion of segregation, women's writing, and its connection to virtue. For discussion of the early print media for women, see Barbara Mittler, *A Newspaper for China? Power, Identity, and Change in Shanghai's News Media, 1872–1912* (Cambridge, MA: Havard University Asia Center, 2004), 245–311.

104. "*Zhongguo xin nüjie zazhi* fakan ci," *Zhongguo xin nüjie zazhi*, no. 1 (1907): 2. Charlotte Beahan describes Luo Yanbin as a "compleat entrepreneur" since "shares in her paper sold briskly" and the monthly press run was a grand 7,000 copies. Few papers had larger print runs than this, and even fewer women's journals could equal this success. Beahan, "Feminism and Nationalism in the Chinese Women's Press," 405. For more discussion of this journal, see Li Yu-ning, "*Zhongguo xinnüjie* zazhi de chuangkan ji neihan," in *Zhongguo funü shi lunwenji*, ed. Li Yu-ning and Zhang Yufa (Taipei: Shangwuyin shuguan, 1981), 179–241. According to one contributor, the main goal of the journal was to pay full respect to the four characters comprising the words "Women Citizens" (*Nü zi guo min*). Lian Shi, "Ben bao duiyu nüzi guomin juan zhi yanshuo," *Zhongguo xin nüjie zazhi*, no. 1 (1907): 42.

105. The overwhelming majority of women's journals at this time were revolutionary in political persuasion. One exception to this general trend is Zhang Zhanyun's *Beijing Women's Paper* (*Beijing nübao*) published in 1905. This paper received funding from the empress dowager and included news designed for the court ladies. It focused on women's education as the key to the salvation of the nation. See Beahan, "Feminism and Nationalism in the Chinese Women's Press," 408–10.

106. Developing an independent spirit was sometimes linked directly to women's responsibilities. For example, Lian Shi wrote, "Women's responsibilities, women's rights derive from the fact that women are people and we have our own skills and talents . . . and abilities to strengthen our aspirations for independence." Lian Shi, "Ben bao wu da zhiyi yanshuo," *Zhongguo xin nüjie zazhi*, no. 3 (1907): 15.

107. Lian Shi, "Ben bao duiyu nüzi guomin juan zhi yanshuo," *Zhongguo xin nüjie zazhi*, no. 2 (1907): 23–24. The full article was printed over issues 1 and 2 of the magazine.

108. Chu Wo, "Nüzi jiating geming shuo," *Nüzi shijie*, no. 4 (1904): 2. *Women's World* was based in Shanghai and from 1904 published seventeen issues before closing in 1906. Ding Chuwo's name has variously been written as Ding Chucheng, Ding Chuwu. She published articles in her journal as Chu Wo. See Beahan, "Feminism and Nationalism in the Chinese Women's Press," 395–98. For an extensive essay on this journal, see the introduction in Xia Xiaohong, *"Nüzi shijie" wen xuan*, 1–52.

109. Ci Jian, "Nü guomin," *Zhongguo xin nüjie zazhi*, no. 5 (1907): 121.

110. Yan Bin, "Zhongguo liu Ri nü xuesheng hui chengli tonggao shu," *Zhongguo xin nüjie zazhi*, no. 2 (1907): 75.

111. Chen Xiefen, "Duli pian," *Nüxue bao* (1902 or 1903), cited in ZFYS, 43.

112. Jiu Si, "Lun zizhong," *Nüzi shijie*, no. 6 (1904): 9–11.

113. Yi Qin, "Lun Zhongguo nüzi zhi qiantu," *Jiangsu*, no. 4 (1903): 141–43 and no. 5 (1903): 129–31.

114. *Nü bao*, no. 2 (1902), cited in Zhou Yaping, "Lun Xinhai geming shiqi de funü canzheng yundong," 119.

115. *Liu Ri nüxuesheng zazhi*, no. 1 (1911), cited in Tang Rujin, "Shishu xinhai geming shiqi de funü yundong," *Shanghai shifan daxue xuebao: Zhe she ban*, no. 3 (1988): 39.

116. Pei Gong, "Nan nü pingdeng de biyao," *Zhongguo xin nüjie zazhi*, no. 2 (1907): 35–36. International comparisons were also used to shame women into action. Lian Shi described China as the most backward of all nations on its record of failure to promote women's rights, whereas the Europeans and Americans were the most advanced. Lian Shi, "Nüquan pingyi," *Zhongguo xin nüjie zazhi*, no. 1 (1907): 1–2.

117. "Liu Ri nüxuehui zazhi fakan ci," repr. in Tan Sheying, *Zhongguo funü yundong tongshi*, 21.

118. Yan Bin, "Zhongguo liu Ri nüxueshenghui chengli tonggao shu," 75–76.

119. Chu Wo, "Nüzi jiating geming shuo," 2.

120. Tang Qunying, Yan Bin, et al., "Qing gong juan nüjie," *Zhongguo xin nüjie zazhi*, no. 3 (1907): 101–6. This sentiment was echoed in the manifesto of the China Women's Association formed in Northern China in 1907. See "Zhongguo furen hui zhangcheng," *Zhongguo xin nüjie zazhi*, no. 3 (1907): 107–14.

121. Fo Zai, "Nü guomin," *Nüzi shijie* 6 (July 1907), repr. in Xia Xiaohong, ed., *"Nüzi shijie" wen xuan* (Guiyang: Guizhou jiaoyu chubanshe, 2003), 334–35.

122. Guo Yanli has noted she was born in 1877, see Guo Yanli, ed., *Qiu Jin shiwen xuan* (Beijing: Renmin wenxue chubanshe, 1982), 1. Chia-lin Pao Tao also reports 1877 as the birth year. Pao Tao, Chia-lin, "Ch'iu Chin's Revolutionary Career," *Chinese Studies in History* (Summer 1992): 10–24.

123. Qiu Jin's letter to her elder brother Qiu Yuzhang on 19 June 1905. See Qiu Jin, *Qiu Jin ji* (1960; repr., Shanghai: Shanghai guji chubanshe, 1979), 35.

124. On Ge Jianhao, see ZGNP, 139–40. Ge was frustrated with the domesticity of marriage and eventually left her husband. As an adult she attended school with her daughter, Cai Chang. The latter was to become prominent in the CCP.

125. Women such as Wu Zhiying (1862–1933) assisted Qiu Jin. Wu provided financial support for Qiu Jin, and after Qiu's departure for Japan, looked after her daughter. Wu Zhiying was active in the Revolutionary Alliance and joined the Shanghai Women's Northern Attack Brigade. See ZGNP, 139. She wrote an article on the Northern Attack Brigade for *Minli bao* describing the women's bravery and heroism. "Wu Zhiying fu nüzi Beifadui jun shu," *Minli bao* (17 January 1912). For an excellent discussion of the connections between Qiu and Wu, see Hu Ying, "Writing Qiu Jin's Life: Wu Zhiying and Her Family Learning," *Late Imperial China* 25, no. 4 (December 2004): 119–60.

126. Mary Backus Rankin, "The Emergence of Women at the End of the Ch'ing: The Case of Chiu Chin," in *Women in Chinese Society*, ed. Margery Wolf and Roxane Witke (Stanford, CA: Stanford University Press, 1975), 39–66.

127. This was a Japan branch of an organization by the same name that had formed in Shanghai in 1903 with the goal of reclaiming women's rights. See Han Xiaoping and Zhu Weibo, "Xinhai geming yu funü yundong," *Hebei shifan daxue xuebao: She ke ban*, no. 4 (1992): 59.

128. The Qing court pressured the Japanese government to promulgate a series of "Regulations Supervising Overseas Students from China" that aimed to curtail the students' political activities. In protest eight thousand students walked out of their schools in December 1905. Ono Kazuko, *Chinese Women in a Century of Revolution*, 61.

129. Qiu Jin, "*Zhongguo nübao fakan ci*," in *Qiu Jin shiwen xuan*, ed. Guo Yanli (Beijing: Renmin wenxue chubanshe, 1982), 3–5. For more information on Qiu Jin's journal, see Beahan, "Feminism and Nationalism in the Chinese Women's Press," 399–403.

130. Qiu Jin, "Mian nüquan," *Zhongguo nübao*, no. 2 (1907): 48.

131. Qiu Jin, "Jinggao yimeimen (jiexuan)," in *Qiu Jin shiwen xuan*, ed. Guo Yanli, 10–13 (Beijing: Renmin wenxue chubanshe, 1982).

132. For further detail on Qiu Jin's contribution to the Chinese revolution, see Jonathan Spence, *The Gate of Heavenly Peace* (London: Faber & Faber, 1982), 50–60. See also Amy D. Dooling and Kristina M. Torgeson, eds., *Writing Women in Modern China* (New York: Columbia University Press, 1998), 39–78 and Dorothea A. L. Martin, ed. "Qiu Jin: A Female Knight-Errant, a True Woman Warrior," special issue, *Chinese Studies in History* 34, no. 2 (Winter 2000–2001). Eileen J. Cheng provides an insightful discussion of Qiu Jin's legacy in her article "Gendered Spectacles: Lu Xun on Gazing at Women and Other Pleasures," *Modern Chinese Literature and Culture* 16, no. 1 (Spring 2004): 1–36.

133. Qiu Jin in Jonathan Spence, *The Gate of Heavenly Peace*, 57.

Chapter Three

1. Women battalions were still active into 1912, with bombing squads participating in suppressing the remnants of Qing loyalists. See "Beijing guanchang wen you nüzi jun," *Shenbao* (25 January 1912); "Minsheng xuesheng beifa jun chufa," *Shenbao* (29 January 1912). This article speaks of a women explosives team: "Yangzhou tongxin," *Shenbao* (31 January 1912). See also "Zhonghua nüzi guomin jun quandui," *Minli bao* (10 January 1912).

2. Ono Kazuko wrote of their sense of betrayal: "For the women who took part in the military arena, their demand for rights—for the franchise—as citizens of a republic, was something self-evident. For that reason the women's movement developed a suffrage movement after the establishment of the Republic of China. Women of the 1911 revolution sought equal treatment in the military as well as the right to vote, for these were important elements, they believed, in gender equality." Ono Kazuko, *Chinese Women in a Century of Revolution*, 80.

3. MSD, 52.

4. See Ernest P. Young, *The Presidency of Yuan Shi-k'ai: Liberalism and Dictatorship in Early Republic China* (Ann Arbor: University of Michigan Press, 1977), 79–80.

5. Xu Yu, *Zhonghua minguo zhengzhi zhidu shi* (Shanghai: Shanghai renmin chubanshe, 1992), 39.

6. Wang Jiajian, "Minchu de nüzi canzheng yundong," in *Zhongguo funü shi lunwenji*, ed. Li Yu-ning and Zhang Yufa (Taipei: Shangwuyin shuguan, 1981), 587.

7. John King Fairbank, *The Great Chinese Revolution, 1800–1985* (New York: Harper & Row, 1986), 172. Liu Wang Liming reprinted the electoral laws in her *Zhongguo funü yundong: Yi ce* (Shanghai: Shangwuyin shuguan, 1934), 25.

8. Fincher, *Chinese Democracy*, 223. See also W. L. Tung, *The Political Institutions of Modern China* (The Hague: Matinus Nijhoff, 1964), 45.

9. Jonathan Spence, *The Search for Modern China* (New York: Norton, 1999), 280.

10. Within this limited franchise the newly formed Nationalist Party won a majority of the seats in the new two-tiered parliament. The main organizer of the party, Song Jiaoren, hoped that this victory would enable the parliament to limit Yuan Shikai's power as president, by constitutional means. Zhao Suisheng has explained how constitutional debates at this time revealed the tension between advocates of a cabinet-style political system and those, including Yuan Shikai, who favored a presidential-style one. See Zhao Suisheng, *Power by Design*, 21–22.

11. The Chinese Socialist Party (*Zhongguo shehui dang*) was formed in Shanghai on 5 November 1911. Led by Jiang Kanghu, it disbanded under pressure from Yuan Shikai in August 1913. The simultaneous formation of the Women's Suffrage Alliance and the Socialist Party was detailed in "Shehui dang zhi jinxing," *Tianduo bao* (1 December 1911).

12. Lin Zongsu, "Nüzi canzheng tongzhi hui huiyuan Lin Zongsu xuan yuan," *Tianduo bao* (23–24 January 1912). See also "Nüzi canzheng tongmeng hui jianzhang," *Tianduo bao* (3 December 1911). For discussion, see Wang Jiajian, "Minchu de nüzi canzheng yundong," 582–83. The Women's Suffrage Comrades' Society appears to have used two names interchangeably: "tongzhi hui" (Comrades' Society) and "tongmeng hui" (Alliance). Here I have adopted the former when referring to Lin's organization in order to distinguish it from Tang Qunying's group, discussed later.

13. Louise Edwards, "Lin Zongsu," in *BDTC*, 347–50.

14. Lin Zongsu, "Lin Nüshi xu," in Jin Songcen, *Nüjie zhong*, 1–3.

15. ZGNP, 174.

16. This periodical lasted six years and published twenty-one issues.

17. FNCD, 95 and ZGNP, 174.

18. See, for example, Lu Shouzhen, "Lun nüzi yingyou xuanju quan," *Funü shibao*, no. 5 (1912): 13–14; Ha Sijing, "Meiguo funü zhi xuanju quan," *Funü shibao*, no. 7 (1912): 1–8. Some of these articles include photographs of women being arrested and conducting street parades.

19. The *People's Independence News* commenced publication in October of 1910 and included Revolutionary Alliance supporters such as Song Jiaoren in its string of editors. It was banned in September of 1913. MSD, 47–48.

20. "Shehui dang nü dangyuan Lin Zongsu," *Minli bao* (8 January 1912).

21. "Nanjing shehui dang dian," *Shenbao* (8 March 1912).

22. Sun Yat-sen and Lin Zongsu in "Nüzi jiangyou wanquan canzheng quan," *Shenbao* (8 January 1912).

23. See Lin Zongsu, "Nüzi canzheng tongzhi hui xuanyan shu," *Funü shibao*, no. 5 (1912): 17–19.

24. "Nüzi jiangyou wanquan canzheng quan."

25. Zhang Binglin in Shanghai shehui kexueyuan, ed., *Xinhai geming zai Shanghai shiliao xuanji* (Shanghai: Renmin chubanshe, 1981), 777. Translated in Li Yu-ning, "Sun Yat-sen and Women's Transformation," 63.

26. Sun Yat-sen in Shanghai shehui kexueyuan, ed., *Xinhai geming zai Shanghai shiliao xuanji*, 777. Translated in Li Yu-ning, "Sun Yat-sen and Women's Transformation," 63–64.

27. Lin Zongsu, "Nüzi canzheng tongzhi hui huiyuan Lin Zongsu xuan yuan."

28. See also "Nüzi tongmeng hui zhi zuzhi," *Shenbao* (22 February 1912).

29. "Nüzi canzheng tongmeng hui jian zhang cao an," *Nüzi baihua bao*, no. 3 (1912): 37.

30. Du Youdi, in a speech presented at the Women's Legal and Political University, emphasized the patriotic intent of the women's suffrage campaign to enhance its appeal to a broader audience. Du wrote that without equality between men and women national prosperity would be retarded. Du Youdi, "Nannü pingquan zuyi jiuguo," *Minli bao* (10 June 1912).

31. See Louise Edwards, "Tang Qunying," in *BDTC*, 504–9; Sheng Shusen, Tang Changchun, and Tao Zhisun, "Zhongguo nüquan yundong de xianqu, Tang Qunying," *Renwu*, no. 4 (1992): 82–90.

32. In 1935, Tang Qunying was invited to become an adviser to the Nationalist government. She died at the age of sixty-five in her home province.

33. See the regulations of the Women's Reinforcement Association, "Nüzi houyuan hui jianzhang," *Shibao* (7 December 1911). For a discussion of *Shibao* and its political importance, see Joan Judge, "The Factional Function of Print: Liang Qichao, *Shibao* and the Fissures in the Late Qing Reform Movement," *Late Imperial China* 16, no. 1 (June 1995): 120–40.

34. Shen Peizhen, "Chuangban nüzi shangwuhui xuyan," *Tianduo bao* (2 December 1911). The regulations for the Women's Society for the Respect of Military Affairs are in *Tianduo bao* (3–4 January 1912).

35. FNCD, 96.

36. See "Nüzi jingwu lianxi dui chengli," *Tianduo bao* (14 January 1912); "Nüzi jingwu lianxi dui," *Tianduo bao* (27 January 1912). See the Association's regulations in "Tongmeng nüzi jingwu lianxi dui jianzhang," *Minli bao* (13 February 1912).

37. Ma Gengcun, *Zhongguo jindai funü shi*, 221. Other than the women noted above, the leadership group of Tang's umbrella organization comprised an impressive array of prominent women from the anti-Qing movement—including Zhang Hanying, Cai Hui, and He Xiangning. It soon expanded into various regional areas, including a Hunan Branch at Changsha led by Ding Lan, a Hubei branch at Wuchang led by Lu Guoxiang and Wu Shuqing (circa 1892–?), a Jiangsu branch at Suzhou led by Jin Mingqing, and a Zhejiang branch based at Hangzhou led by Wu Meiwen. See Shen Zhi, "Xinhai geming shiqi de nü zhishi fenzi," 66.

38. Wu Mulan, "Tongmeng nüzi jingwu lianxi dui xuanyan shu," *Tianduo bao* (2 January 1912).

39. "Nü canzheng tuan yan shuo re," *Minli bao* (12 April 1912).

40. "Nüzi canzheng tongmeng hui jian zhang cao an," 37–38.

41. See Madeleine Yue Dong's discussion of the publication of unofficial satirical histories of the suffragist Shen Peizhen and the prostitute Xiaofengxian as "public women" in "Unofficial History and Gender Boundary Crossing in the Early Republic: Shen Peizhen and Xiaofengxian," in *Gender in Motion: Divisions of Labor and Cultural Change in Late Imperial and Modern China*, ed. Bryna Goodman and Wendy Larson (Lanham, MD: Rowman & Littlefield, 2005), 169–89.

42. "Shenzhou" is a utopian reference to China, and other women's publications made regular use of the term. See Xu Tianxiao, *Shenzhou nüzi xinshi* (1913; repr., Taipei: Daoxiang chubanshe, 1993).

43. Zhang's father, Zhang Tongdian, inspired her involvement in anti-Qing activities. Together they published the revolutionary *Great Han news* (*Da Han bao*) and as secret agents in the Jiangsu-Zhejiang region were instrumental in the overturning of Qing control of Suzhou. Zhang established the Shenzhou Women's United Assistance Society in Shanghai in early 1912, but soon revised the name (dropping the term "United") after the general meeting of 16 March 1912. Advertisements were placed in *Minli bao* over the week prior to the 16 March meeting (see the issues of 10, 12, and 13 March). An article outlining the meeting appeared as "Shenzhou nüjie gonghe xiejishe kaihui ji shi," *Shibao* (22 March 1912).

44. Switching to a monthly format under the editorship of Yang Jiwei and Tan Sheying, the *Shenzhou Women's News* was only able to produce four more issues before it ceased publication in mid-1913.

45. Jiang Zuobin, "Jinzhu *Shenzhou nübao*," *Shenzhou nübao*, no. 2 (1912): 1.

46. Ibid., 2.

47. Wu Tingfang served in Judicial Affairs and Foreign affairs. MSD, 783. He Miaoling was "daughter of a rather famous early convert to Christianity and wealthy businessman, Ho Fu-t'ang." Linda P. Shin, "Wu T'ing-fang: A Member of a Colonial Elite as Coastal Reformer," in *Reform in Nineteenth Century China*, ed. Paul A. Cohen and John E. Schrecker (Cambridge, MA: Harvard University Asia Center, 1976), 266. Song Qingling was also a member.

48. For a discussion of Sun's ambiguous attitude about the realization of women's suffrage, see Li Yuning, "Sun Yat-sen and Women's Transformation," 58–78.

49. "Nüjie canzheng zhi yaoqiu," *Minli bao* (3 March 1912). An earlier meeting had taken place between Sun and Zhang on 6 February 1912 with exactly the same results. Sun encouraged Zhang in her suffrage campaign but noted that education was crucial to women's access to political power. See *Linshi zhengfu gongbao*, no. 9 (6 February 1912): 6–8.

50. See the letter reprinted in Tan Sheying, *Zhongguo funü yundong tongshi*, 61–63. The Shenzhou Women's United Assistance Society cooperated occasionally with Tang's group. For example, together they raised funds to cover the costs of the war against the remnants of the Qing army. The women generated more that 15,000 yuan (in two batches of 5,000 and 10,000) and presented these to Sun Yat-sen on the 1st and 10th of February. "Da Zongtong duiyu xin nüjie zhi qiwang," *Shenbao* (10 February 1912).

51. Sun's letter was reprinted in Sun Yat-sen, "Sun Zhongshan xiansheng fu ben hui shu," *Shenzhou nübao*, no. 2 (1912): 1–2. The importance he placed on the correct preparation of women through expanding educational opportunities is further demonstrated in his speech to a school on 6 May 1912. He stresses the importance of sex equality to the new republic but states, "The education work has already begun, afterwards men and women can attain equal rights." "Sun xiansheng zai Guangdong nüzi shifan dier xiao yanshuo," *Minli bao* (13 May 1912).

52. Zhang Mojun married Sun Yat-sen's personal secretary, Shao Yuanzhong, in 1924 when she was forty-one. Her loyalty to the Nationalist Party was rewarded when she was the only woman elected to the Central Committee of the Nationalist Party in 1935. See Louise Edwards, "Zhang Mojun," in *BDQP*, 685–88. Wu Zhiying (1867–1934), longtime friend of Qiu Jin's, supported Zhang in her promotion of women's suffrage and women's education through the Shenzhou group. See Au Chi Kin, "Wu Zhiying," in *BDQP*, 236–38.

53. The entire petition appears in "Nüjie daibiao Zhang [*sic*] Qunying deng shang canyiyuan shu," repr. in Lin Zongsu's journal *Funü shibao*, no. 5 (1912): 21–22 and *Shenbao* (26 February 1912). A variation appeared as "Zhonghua minguo nüjie daibiao yaoqiu canzhengquan jiangyuan shu," *Shengjing shibao* (12 March 1912).

54. "Nüjie daibiao Zhang [*sic*] Qunying," *Shenbao* (29 February 1912). The Shenzhou Women's Assistance Society convened a meeting in Nanjing that over two hundred women attended. "Shenzhou nüjie canzheng tongmeng hui ji shi," *Shenbao* (2 March 1912).

55. Lin Zongsu, "Nüzi canzheng tongzhi hui xuanyan shu," 19. At the end of 1912, activists similarly spoke of encouragement that they received from the international women's suffrage movement and the importance of the visit to China of foreign suffragists. See "Nüzi canzheng tongmeng hui chengli zhisheng," 38, "Nanjing dian," and "Nüzi canzheng hui zhang" in *Shenbao* (10 September 1912); "Huanying nüzhengzhijia," *Shenbao* (5 September 1912).

56. "Nüzi canzheng hui shang Sun Zhongshan shu," *Shibao* (23 March 1912).

57. "Nüzi danao canyi yuan ji," *Shengjing shibao* (31 March 1912).

58. "Nüzi yaoqiu canzheng quan," *Minli bao* (23 March 1912). The women's petition to the president is also reprinted here.

59. See "Nüzi yaoqiu canzheng quan zhi baodong," *Dagong bao* (30 March 1912); "Nüzi danao canyi yuan ji."

60. "Yaoqiu nüzi canzheng quan zhi wuli," *Shibao* (23 March 1912).

61. Meng Huan, "Wen ping er," *Dagong bao* (1 April 1912).

62. On the British suffrage activists actions, see Kent, *Sex and Suffrage in Britain*, 200–201.

63. "Nüzi yi wuli yaoqiu canzheng quan," *Shenbao* (24 March 1912). On *Shenbao*, see Mittler, *A Newspaper for China*?

64. Wang Jiajian, "Minchu de nüzi canzheng yundong," 589.

65. "Nüzi yaoqiu canzheng quan."

66. See Shen Peizhen's telegram "Shen Peizhen nüshi dian," *Shenbao* (25 March 1912).

67. "You nüzi Tang Qunying," *Minli bao* (31 March 1912). See also "Nüzi canzheng tongmeng hui," *Shibao* (31 March 1912); "Canyi yuan yijue nüzi canzheng quan," *Shengjing shibao* (2 April 1912). This issue also reported on the failure of the British suffragists.

68. "Nüzi canzheng hui lai Beijing," *Aiguo bao* (14 April 1912).

69. "Nüzi canzheng hui shang Sun qianzongtong shu," *Shengjing shibao* (3 April 1912).

70. "Da Zongtong shenzhong nüzi canzheng wenti," *Dagong bao* (6 April 1912).

71. "Beijing dian: You nansheng lai jing," *Shenbao* (12 July 1912).

72. See the electoral laws in *Minli bao* (9, 10 August 1912); *Shenbao* (12, 13 August 1912).

73. "Beijing dian: Yuan Zongtong," *Shenbao* (10 August 1912).

74. "Nüzi canzheng tongmeng hui canzheng qingyuan shu" in Zhongguo di er lishi dang'anguan (National History Archives, no. 2). Cited in Xu Huiqi, "Tang Qunying yu 'Nüzi canzheng tongmeng hui—jianlun minchu funü canzheng huodong,'" *Guizhou shehui kexue*, no. 4 (1981): 31. *Aiguo bao* reports of a meeting between over two hundred women and Sun where the women asserted the adequacy of their political knowledge. "Nüjie huanying Sun, Huang, Chen jilüe," *Aiguo bao* (18 September 1912). See also "Wuhan nüjie qutan lu," *Shenbao* (14 October 1912).

75. "Canyiyuan yishi zhiyao," *Aiguo bao* (8 November 1912). In *Women's Vernacular News* a suffrage supporter by the pen name "Open Clouds" (Kai Yun) described how the men in the parliament demonstrated their continued inability to lead the nation and how they squander national funds on leisure pursuits and have completely ignored their responsibilities as policy makers. Kai Yun, "Canyi yuan zhi heian," *Nüzi baihua bao*, no. 3 (1912): 25. While in Beijing, Tang was active in a number of political initiatives. *Aiguo bao* reports that she attended a meeting of the Patriot Party (*Aiguo dang*). See "Aiguo dang kaihui jishi," *Aiguo bao* (1 October 1912).

76. Kai Yun, "Canyi yuan zhi heian." See also "Nüzi xuanju quan," *Shenbao* (8 November 1912); "Nüzi canzheng quan you li yi jie," *Shenbao* (13 November 1912).

77. Jiang Jilan, "Shuo nüzi canzheng zhi liyou," *Funü shibao*, no. 8 (1912): 1–2.

78. Ibid., 6.

79. Huai Bing, "Shuo nüzi canzheng zhi liyou," *Funü shibao*, no. 8 (1912): 43–44.

80. See the summary of the electoral laws in Chun Xiu, "Xuanju jianshuo," *Aiguo bao* (6, 7 December 1912).

81. For more on Wu Jinglian, see MSD, 852.

82. "Nüshi dama canyiyuan," *Aiguo bao* (11 December 1912).

83. Ibid. This event is reported in "Tang Qunying deng wu ren," *Shenbao* (11 December 1912).

84. "Shen Peizhen danao Yadong xinwenshe," *Shenbao* (19 December 1912).

85. Li San, "Xinzhi koukuai," *Shenbao* (18 October 1912). One response to reports of this speech is Si Yinglu, "Wen Shen nüshi yanshuo ganyan," *Shenbao* (23 October 1912).

86. The date directly referred to is 20 October 1911; however, I can find no evidence of their association being formed on that day. It appears that the Nanjing branch was established on this day but Lin Zongsu's Shanghai branch received more publicity. "Nüzi canzheng tongmeng hui chengli zhisheng," 35.

87. Ibid., 37.

88. Kai Yun, "Canyi yuan zhi heian." See also Chen Lingxia, "Nüzi canzheng zhi xiansheng," *Nüzi baihua bao*, no. 6 (1912): 27–30.

89. Kai Yun, "Canyi yuan zhi heian," 28–29.

90. ZFYS, 57.

91. The episode is reported over three days in "Tang Qunying da Changsha nao bao," *Minli bao* (28 February–2 March 1913).

92. Dong presents further evidence of the manner in which sexual morals were used to discredit suffragists. Shen Peizhen faced sexualized humiliation when she was charged with disorderly behavior after causing a ruckus in a restaurant. Media reports describe her real or imagined sexual behavior in salacious detail in a bid to discredit her. She was jailed for fifty days on a charge that normally would not incur such penalities. See Dong, "Unofficial History," 176–77.

93. For a discussion of Hu Hanmin's attitude about equality, see Chiang Yung-ching, "Hu Han-min's Ideas on Women's Rights and His Achievements," *Chinese Studies in History* (Summer 1977): 34–72.

94. Tan Sheying, *Fuyun sishinian* (Taibei, 1978), 65.

95. Ono Kazuko, *Chinese Women in a Century of Revolution*, 90 and Chiang Yung-ching, "Hu Hanmin's Ideas on Women's Rights," 48. See *Guangdong Xinhai geming shiliao*, ed. Zhongguo renmin zhengzhi xieshang huiyi Guangdong weiyuan hui wenshi ziliao yanjiu weiyuan hui (Guangzhou: Guangdong renmin chubanshe, 1981), 426–36 for further information on the women in Guangdong's parliament.

96. Tan Sheying, *Fuyun sishinian*, 65–66 includes a full list of participants.

97. With the collapse of the Guangdong parliament Deng went to Japan to study music. Nonetheless,

she was active during the anti-Japanese war in mobilizing the resistance around Guangdong. In 1948 she would join the Nationalist government as a member of its Control Yuan, and soon after this she left for Taiwan. See MSD, 739.

98. ZFYS, 58.

99. Tung, *Political Institutions*, 45.

100. "Nü canzheng zhi chengli," *Minli bao* (23 September 1912). See also "Yue sheng nü daiyishi lizheng nüzi can zheng quan," *Shenbao* (28 September 1912).

101. See "Yue nü daiyishi zhongzheng canzheng," *Shenbao* (10 October 1912); "Yue yihui foujue nüzi canzheng quan taidu," *Shenbao* (17 November 1912).

102. Mrs. Pankhurst, cited in Ono Kazuko, *Chinese Women in a Century of Revolution*, 89.

103. Mrs. Richard Wainwright, cited in Rheta Childe Dorr, "April 26th Hearing before the Senate Suffrage Committee," *Suffragist*, 28 April (1917): 9.

104. "Tongmeng hui nühuiyuan zhi fenji," *Dagong bao* (16 August 1912). See also "Hui dang zao dang zhi yijian," *Minli bao* (7 August 1912); "Tongmeng hui hebing gaizu jiwen," *Shenbao* (16 August 1912).

105. Cited in Xu Huiqi, "Tang Qunying yu 'Nüzi canzheng tongmeng hui,'" 32. A typical response to the women's demands was that they should establish schools in order to enhance women's virtue and knowledge. "Nüzi canzheng zhi sichao," *Minli bao* (10 August 1912).

106. "Nüzi daonao Tongmeng hui," *Minli bao* (18 August 1912); "Nühuiyuan dazhan weifeng," *Shenbao* (20 August 1912); "Tongmeng hui," *Shenbao* (23 August 1912); "Tongmeng hui gaizu," *Shenbao* (26 August 1912). The activists were aware of events in London where trials of the women's suffrage activists had resulted in a five-year jail term for two women. See "Canzheng zhi nüzi," *Minli bao* (9 August 1912); "Tichang funü canzhengquan," *Shengjing shibao* (4 April 1912); "Lundun dian," *Shenbao* (15 July 1912); "Yaoqiu canzheng zhi guaiju," *Shenbao* (1, 4 December 1912).

107. FNCD, 96. The Guangdong legislature of 1912 had not been popularly elected.

108. Ono Kazuko, *Chinese Women in a Century of Revolution*, 86–88. *Minli bao* noted that women in Australia and New Zealand were already voting and that Canada was heading in this direction. "Nüzi tuan zhi jinxing," *Minli bao* (30 August 1912).

109. "Sun Zhongshan xiansheng ru jing hou zhi di yi dahui," *Minli bao* (31 August 1912).

110. See "Nüzi canzheng tongmeng hui dian," *Minli bao* (31 August 1912); "Nüzi canzheng tongmeng hui," *Shenbao* (13 September 1912).

111. Sun Yat-sen, "Zai Guomindang chengli dahuishang de biaoshuo," *Minzhu bao* (26 August 1912), repr. in Sun Yat-sen, *Sun Zhongshan quanji: Di er juan*, 409. See also "Ershiwu ri zhi Huguang guan," *Shenbao* (31 August 1912); "Zhongguo Guomindang huiyi," *Shenbao* (9 September 1912).

112. "Sun Zhongshan xiansheng ru jing hou zhi di yi dahui." See also *Zhongguo ribao* (Beijing; 26 August 1912): 2, cited in David Strand, "Citizens in the Audience and at the Podium," in *Changing Meanings of Citizenship in Modern China*, ed. Merle Goldman and Elizabeth J. Perry (Cambridge, MA: Harvard University Press, 2002), 60; "Guomin dang ganshi xuanjuhui zhi guaiju," *Shenbao* (16 September 1912).

113. David Strand, "Citizens in the Audience and at the Podium." Cartoons at the time reveal that physical violence and chaos in parliament was not unthinkable. One in *Shenbao* (7 September 1912) shows an unruly scrum of parliamentarians fighting each other amidst upturned furniture. Other reports followed with a sardonic version of the men's humiliation at the hands of the women. "Xiao shuo," *Shenbao* (3 September 1912); "Ziyou tan," *Shenbao* (4 September 1912).

114. "Ershiwu ri zhi Huguang guan."

115. "Tang Shen liang nüshi zhi moyan," *Shenbao* (3 September 1912).

116. Sun Yat-sen, "Fu Nanjing canzheng tongmeng hui nü tongzhi han," in *Sun Zhongshan quanji*, 438. The cause was near its end by this stage, but the women filed another petition in November of 1912 only to have their party refuse to consider it.

117. See "Liu dang hebing kaihui ji," *Shenbao* (29 September 1912).

118. Kong Hai, "Duiyu nüzi canzheng quan zhi huaiyi," *Minli bao* (28 February 1912). Similar views were expressed in Gu Shen, "Nüzi canzheng wenti," *Shi bao* (24 March 1912).

119. Yang Jiwei, "Yang Jiwei nüshi lai han," *Minli bao* (5 March 1912). See also Qing Meng, "Duiyu nüzi canzheng zhi yanjiu," *Funü shibao*, no. 8 (1912): 7–8.

120. Kong Hai, "Fu Yang Jiwei nüshi han," *Minli bao* (5 March 1912).

121. Zhang Renlan, "Zhang Renlan nüshi lai han," *Minli bao* (9 March 1912). Two paragraphs of support by Kong Hai were appended to the letter.

122. "Nüzi canzheng tongzhi hui xuanyan shu," 19.

123. The letters not discussed include Yao Hui, "Nüzi canzheng zhi taolun—Yao Hui nüshi lai han," *Minli bao* (20 March 1912); Li Zhengfen, "Nüzi canzheng zhi taolun—Zhi Jiangnan Zhang Renlan tongzhi shu," *Minli bao* (24 March 1912); Chen Huangxing, "Nüzi canzheng zhi taolun—Chen Huanxing nüshi lai han," *Minli bao* (26 March 1912).

124. Zhu Lun, "Nüzi canzheng zhi taolun—Zhu Lun nüshi lai han," *Minli bao* (16 March 1912).

125. Zhang Xiaofen, "Nüzi canzheng zhi taolun—Zhang Xiaofen nüshi lai han," *Minli bao* (18 March 1912).

126. Zhang Hanying, "Nüzi canzheng zhi taolun—Fu Zhang Renlan nüshi lai shu," *Minli bao* (21 March 1912). For more discussion on Zhang Hanying, see FNCD, 95 and Lam Hok-chung, "Zhang Hanying," 289–93.

127. "Nüzi canzheng lun," *Dagong bao* (27, 28 March 1912).

128. "Nüzi yaoqiu canzheng quan zhi baodong." *Shengjing shibao* similarly gave space to the opponents to women's suffrage with an article declaring that women's nature, ability, education, and morality differed from men's. Only in morality were women better than men. According to this lead article, women's engagement with formal politics would bring no benefit to the nation or women. "Nüzi canzheng lun," *Shengjing shibao* (24, 26 March 1912).

129. Meng Huan, "Lun nüzi yaoqiu canzheng quan zhi guaixiang," *Dagong bao* (30 March 1912).

130. See "Ziyou tan," *Shenbao* (26 December 1912).

131. Ne Zhai, "Shi ke," *Shenbao* (26 March 1912). Debate resurfaced in *Shenbao* in September. See "Lun nüzi yi zhuzhong daode," *Shenbao* (5 September 1912); "Shiping san," *Shenbao* (6 September 1912).

132. Dun Gen, "Quan Shen Peizhen nüshi gaiming shuo," *Shenbao* (24 November 1912).

133. Dun Gen, "Bobo nüzi canzheng quan," *Shenbao* (18 March 1912).

134. Dun Gen, "Lixiang dianbao," *Shenbao* (16 October 1912).

135. "Canyiyuan jianfa wenti zhi da zhenglun," *Shenbao* (3 November 1912); "Xuanju quan ke yu bianfa xiguan xiang juezhan," *Shenbao* (4 November 1912).

136. Dun Gen, "Bianzi yu xuanju quan zhi guanxi," *Shenbao* (31 October 1912).

137. Du He, "Xining mo nüshi zhi ba da hutong jijieshu," *Shenbao* (22 November 1912).

138. "Nannü pingquan jianzhang," *Aiguo baihua bao* (17 September 1913), cited in Dong, "Unofficial History," 173.

139. Tao Hancui, *Minguo yanshi yanyi*, 8 vols. (Shanghai: Shihua shuju, 1936), 1:95–121, cited in Dong, "Unofficial History," 174.

140. See for example Ou Peifen "Jinggao zheng xuanju quan zhi nü huibao," *Minli bao* (7–8 June 1912). Peifen argues that discrepancies in educational opportunities must be rectified as well as calling for the prohibition of polygamy, liberation of female bondservants, and the prohibition of prostitution.

141. On chastity and female virtue in the mid-Qing, see Theiss, *Disgraceful Matters*.

142. Andrew Nathan, *Chinese Democracy* (New York: Knopf, 1985), 110.

143. "China to Vote on Monarchy," *Suffragist* 3, no. 42 (16 October 1915): 2.

144. The edict was titled "Edict on the law of the prohibited" (*Falu wu yunxu mingwen*). See Xu Huiqi, "Tang Qunying yu 'Nüzi canzheng tongmeng hui,'" 33.

145. "Shen Nüshi nanzheng zhi tanlun," *Minguo ribao* (15 August 1913).

146. "Yaoqiu nüzi canzheng quan zhi zhuanwen," *Shenbao* (24 May 1913).

147. "Zhian jingcha tiaoli," *Zhengfu gongbao*, no. 653 (3 March 1914). On the struggles to overturn the law in Japan, see Vera Mackie, *Creating Socialist Women in Japan: Gender, Labour and Activism, 1900–1937* (Cambridge, UK: Cambridge University Press, 1997), 35.

148. See Nathan, *Peking Politics*, pp. 93–113. He also includes numbers of registered voters by province (p. 94).

149. Spence, *The Search for Modern China*, 297.

Chapter Four

1. See Wang Zheng, *Women in the Chinese Enlightenment* and Vera Schwarcz, *The Chinese Enlightenment: Intellectuals and the Legacy of the May Fourth Movement of 1919* (Berkeley: University of California Press, 1986).

2. Some commentators praised the Qing, writing that Manchu women had more freedom than Han women. Ming Yang, "Wairen yanguang zhi Zhongguo funü gexin yundong," FNZZ 13, no. 12 (1927): 7.

3. For discussions of women in factory work, see Honig, *Sisters and Strangers* and Hershatter, *The Workers of Tianjin*.

4. See Tung, *Political Institutions*, 65–79.

5. Yan Shi, "Zuijin de nüquan yundong," FNZZ 8, no. 10 (1922): 61. FNZZ was the most important and long-running women's magazine this period. It ran from 1915 until 1931 and explored social, political, and educational issues as well as providing a forum for literary and artistic works. See Jacqueline Nivard, "Women and the Women's Press: The Case of *The Ladies' Journal* (*Funü zazhi*) 1915–1931," *Republican China* 10 (1984): 37–55.

6. See Fitzgerald, *Awakening China*.

7. See Feng Fei, *Nüxing lun* (Shanghai: Zhonghua shuju, 1923), 140; "Yichan zhidu he nannü ping-deng," *Shenbao* (5 March 1921); "Qing dajia kuaikuai quan nüzi jin xuexiao qu," *Shenbao* (May 7 1921); "Duoqi zhidu zhi guomin xing," *Shenbao* (9 May 1921).

8. Chow Tse-tsung, *The May Fourth Movement: Intellectual Revolution in Modern China* (Stanford, CA: Stanford University Press, 1960), 258.

9. Christina Gilmartin, "The Politics of Gender in the Making of the Party," in *New Perspectives on the Chinese Communist Revolution*, ed. Tony Saich and Hans van de Ven (Armonk, NY: M.E. Sharpe, 1995), 41.

10. For more detail, see Louise Edwards, "Opposition to Women's Suffrage in China: Confronting Modernity in Governance," in *Women in Republican China*, ed. Mechthild Leutner and Nicola Spakowski (Münster, Germany: LIT, 2004), 107–28.

11. Luo Jialun, "Funü jiefang," *Xin chao* 2, no. 1 (1919): 1–10.

12. Liang Qichao, "Renquan yu nüquan," *Chenbao fukan* (16 November 1922).

13. Zhang Peifen, *Funü wenti* (1922; repr., Shanghai: Shangwuyin shuguan, 1927), 64–65.

14. Li Hanjun, *Funü zhi guoqu yu jianglai* (Shanghai: Shangwuyin shuguan, 1921). This volume includes analysis of numerous matriarchal societies around the world. One commentator, Lao Zeren, was pessimistic in his/her assessment of the likelihood of quick success for suffrage in China. Lao compared China to Europe and America and noted China's backwardness in terms of women's education and independence. Lao Zeren, "Zhongguo funü yundong de jianglai," FNZZ 7, no. 9 (1921): 7–10. See also Ping Su, "Funü canzheng wenti," FNZZ 8, no. 11 (1922): 6–16. This issue of FNZZ was a special issue on women's suffrage.

15. See "Yingguo nannü zhi zhengquan," *Shenbao* (21 April 1921); You Tong, "Deguo zhi funü canzheng quan," FNZZ 8, no. 7 (1922): 33–40; "Yingguo guohui diyi nü yiyuan," *Shenbao* (1 February 1920).

16. Ze Min, "Shijie nüzi canzheng yundong kao," FNZZ 5, no. 12 (1919): 1.

17. Wu Yuxiu, "Nüzi yingyou canzheng quan de wojian," *Dagong bao* (25–27 May 1921).

18. For the Zhejiang women's actions, see "Zhejiang nüzi zheng canyu zhixian quan," *Shenbao* (22 August 1921). For Sichuan, see "Chuan sheng zhixian zhong zhi nüquan yundong," *Shenbao* (4 February 1923).

19. In the spring elections, UWA activist, Wang Bihua was elected to the provincial assembly of Zhejiang. The Jiangxi UWA's petition to the government on amending the constitution describes the trend toward women's suffrage internationally and nationally to be unstoppable. See Tan Sheying, *Zhongguo funü yundong tongshi*, 110. Wang Bihua, Chen Su, and Hou Ming led the Zhejiang group. Lü Meiyi and Zheng Yongfu, *Zhongguo funü yundong*, 341. For a copy of the Zhejiang, Hunan, and Guangdong provincial constitutions of 1921 and the 1923 Sichuan document, see Miao Quanji, ed., *Zhongguo zhixian shi ziliao huibian* (Taipei: Guoshi guan, 1989). Items relating to sex equality are found on pp. 695, 816, 838, and 855.

20. I cannot find restrictions on voting rights in the Guangdong provincial document, so there may have been no literacy requirement in Guangdong after 1921.

21. "Hunan sheng xianfa—Minguo shiyi nian yiyue yiri" (1 January 1922), repr. in Miao Quanji, ed., *Zhongguo zhixian shi ziliao huibian* (Taipei: Guoshi guan, 1989), 821.

22. "Zhejiang sheng xianfa shixing fa" (9 September 1921), repr. in Miao Quanji, ed., *Zhongguo zhixian shi ziliao huibian*, (Taipei: Guoshi guan, 1989), 724. The law allowed all eligible voters over twenty-five to stand for election except serving military personnel, government officials, or students.

23. "Sichuan sheng xianfa caoan," repr. in Miao Quanji, *Zhongguo zhixian shi ziliao huibian*, 856–57.

24. See the documents in Miao Quanji, *Zhongguo zhixian shi ziliao huibian*, 724, 821, 856.

25. "Quanzhe nüjie lianhe hui xuanyuan," repr. in Tan Sheying, *Zhongguo funü yundong tongshi*, 105–6.

26. "Guangdong nüjie lianhe hui zhangcheng," repr. in Tan Sheying, *Zhongguo funü yundong tongshi*, 97–104. For a CCP report on the Guangdong movement, see Zhongguo gongchandang funü bu (jielu), "Zhongguo gongchandang funübu guanyu Zhongguo funü yundong de baogao" (24 June 1924), repr. in ZFYLZ, 173.

27. Tan Sheying, *Zhongguo funü yundong tongshi*, 98.

28. "Guangdong nüjie lianhe hui zhangcheng," 97–104.

29. "Ji Guangdong nüzi guomin dahui," *Minguo ribao* (1 January 1920). See also "Yue nüjie er ci dahui ji," *Minguo ribao* (15 January 1920).

30. "Miss Wu Chih-mei," *Who's Who in China, 1918–1950*, vol. 3, 4th ed. (1950; repr., Hong Kong: Chinese Materials Centre, 1982), 225.

31. Wu Zhimei served on the provincial party executive committee in 1938 and later was active in China's wartime parliament. Her close ties to the Nationalist government continued when she was elected to the controversial National Assembly of 1947–48.

32. "Ji Guangdong nüzi guomin dahui."

33. See "Guangdong nüzi guomin dahui," *Shenbao* (1 January 1920). The manifesto is reprinted in Tan Sheying, *Zhongguo funü yundong tongshi*, 96. See also "Funü yaoqiu canzheng quan," *Chenbao* (6 January 1920).

34. "Yue nüjie er ci dahui ji.". See also "Guangdong nüjie er ci guominhui," *Shenbao* (5 January 1920).

35. "Yue nüjie lianhe hui zhi jinxing," *Minguo ribao* (27 January 1920); "Nüzi yaoqiu canzheng zhi shengyuan," *Minguo ribao* (28 January 1920). See also reports on the national push in *Shenbao* "Nüjie lianhe hui xiaoxi," *Shenbao* (18 January 1920).

36. "Yue nüjie zhi pai qie huiyi," *Minguo ribao* (31 January 1920).

37. "Nüzi xuanju yundong zhi shengli," *Guangdong qunbao* (20 February 1921).

38. "Zuori zhi sheng yi hui shiji," *Guangdong qunbao* (20 February 1921).

39. For the petition, see "Fu qing yuan shu," repr. in Guangdong Sheng funü yundong lishi ziliao bianxuan weiyuan hui, vol. 3, ed. *Guangdong funü yundong lishi ziliao* (Guangzhou: Guangdong sheng dang'an guan, 1991), 129.

40. *Labor and Women* was a left-wing weekly paper that began publication on 13 February 1921 and had prominent Communist men, including Chen Duxiu, on its editorial board. Based in Guangzhou, it ceased publication after only eleven issues. FNCD, 84.

41. "Guangzhou funü canzheng da huodong," *Laodong yu funü*, no. 8 (3 April 1921), repr. in Guangdong sheng funü yundong, ed. *Guangdong funü yundong lishi ziliao*, vol. 3, 127–29. For further descriptions of the events, see "Nüzi xuanju yundong zhi shengli," *Guangdong qunbao* (20 February 1921); "Zai xun sheng yiyuan oushang nüdaibiao an," *Laodong yu funü*, no. 11 (24 April 1921): 4; "Guangzhou nüzi zheng xuanquan xuwen," *Minguo ribao* (3 April 1921); "Nüzi yaoqiu xuanju quan fengchao," *Minguo ribao* (4 April 1921); "Nüzi canzheng yundong zhi yubo," *Minguo ribao* (11 April 1921); "Guangdong nüzi canzheng zhi da yundong," *Shenbao* (4 April 1921); "Xu ji Yuenüjie zhi canzheng yundong," *Shenbao* (5 April 1921); "Nüjie Deng Huifang," *Shenbao* (5 April 1921).

42. Huang Bihun, "Wo duiyu nüzi canzheng de ganxiang," *Laodong yu funü*, no. 11 (24 April 1921): 2.

43. "Huang Bihun gao quan guo funü," *Guangdong qunbao* (7 April 1921).

44. "Nüjie yundong xuanju dahuodong," *Guangdong qunbao* (30 March 1921). See also "Sheng hui duiyu nüzi canzheng an zhi xingshi," *Guangdong qunbao* (31 March 1921); "Nüzi lianhe hui wen sheng-hui," *Shenbao* (30 March 1921); "Guangdong zhi nüquan chao," *Shenbao* (March 31 1921); "Nüzi zheng xuanju quan," *Shenbao* (1 April 1921); "Nüjie zhi liang shi," *Shenbao* (1 April 1921); "Guangdong nüzi

canzheng zhi da yundong," *Shenbao* (4 April 1921); "Xuji Yue nüjie zhi canzheng yundong," *Shenbao* (5 April 1912); "Nüzi canzheng quan zhi wo jian," *Shenbao* (6 April 1912).

45. "Guangdong zhi nüzi canzheng yundong si fu," FNZZ 7, no. 7 (1921).

46. "Guangzhou funü canzheng da huodong," 129.

47. "Deng Huifang nüshi zhi tanhua," *Guangdong qunbao* (31 March 1921). See also "Nüzi canzheng an jing zao foujue," *Minguo ribao* (8 April 1921).

48. "Fou jue nüzi canzheng an zhi shezhan," *Guangdong qunbao* (2 April 1921).

49. "Nüjie lianhe hui zhi zhanlipin," *Guangdong qunbao* (29 April 1921).

50. "Liu Shaobi nüshi deng zhi Chen Shengzhang shu," *Guangdong qunbao* (8 April 1921); "Nüjie lianhe hui zhi yi an," *Guangdong qunbao* (25 April 1921).

51. "Yue nüzi canzheng yundong chenggong," *Dagong bao* (20 May 1921). The women continued to be active; see "Nüguomin dahui," *Guangdong qunbao* (2 July 1921).

52. For a discussion of *Minguo ribao,* see John Fitzgerald, "The Origins of the Illiberal Party Newspaper: Print Journalism in China's Nationalist Revolution," *Republican China* 21, no. 2 (April 1996): 1–22.

53. "Changsha nüjie lianhe hui cheng li xuanyan," in "Hunan nüzi zhi wuquan yundong," *Minguo ribao* (27 January 1921).

54. ZFYS, 125.

55. Tan Sheying, *Zhongguo funü yundong tongshi,* 107. See also "Xianfa taolun zhong zhi yi han," *Dagong bao* (5 May 1921).

56. "Quanti nüjie qingyuan shencha hui jishi," *Dagong bao* (17 May 1921). A follow-up report appeared on 19 May 1921.

57. "Hunan nüjie lianhe hui yijian shu," *Dagong bao* (6 May 1921).

58. Ibid., 7 May 1921. Further items on women's rights appeared on 14, 15, and 16 May.

59. Li Liuru, "Funü jiefang san da tiwen," *Dagong bao* (14–17 May 1921).

60. Cheng Xiluo, "Bu zuzhang nüzi canzheng," *Dagong bao* (16 May 1921).

61. Jiang Zhaoxiang, "Bo Cheng Xiluo jun de buzhang nü canzheng," *Dagong bao* (18–19 May 1921). The quotation comes from the 19 May 1921 section.

62. Class Seven of the No. 1 Girls' Normal School, "Zhi Cheng Xiluo shu," *Dagong bao* (18 May 1921). See also the discussion about protecting women from the polluting effects of politics in Jiang Shizhou, "Xue deng: Ping nüzi canzheng yundong," *Shishi xinbao* (15 August 1922).

63. Class Eight of the No. 1 Girls' Normal School, "Zhi shengxian shenchayuan Cheng Xiluo shu," *Dagong bao* (24–26, 28 May 1921).

64. Yi Chuheng, "He Cheng Xiluo xiansheng bu zhuzhang nüzi canzheng de shangliang," *Dagong bao* (30–31 May, 1–2 June 1921).

65. Pingzi, "Nüzi de yubei," *Dagong bao* (5 May 1921).

66. Pingzi, "Wo duiyu nüzi canzheng de xiwang," *Dagong bao* (3 June 1921).

67. "Nüjie huanying Xiong Zhuliang xiansheng jishi," *Dagong bao* (1 June 1921). See also "Nüzi yingdang chengshou yichan de liyou he duiyu fandui pai shencha yuan de zhonggao," *Dagong bao* (21 May 1921); Liu Qianhou, "Wo duiyu sheng xianfa de yijian," *Dagong bao* (22 May 1921).

68. Tan Sheying, *Zhongguo funü yundong tongshi,* 107–8; FNCD, 96–97.

69. Yan Shi, "Duiyu nüzi canzheng de xiwang," FNZZ 8, no. 7 (1922): 10–11.

70. "Changsha dian: Nüjie yin xianfa huiyi yiyuan . . . ," *Shenbao* (11 November 1924); "Changsha dian: Nüjie lizheng weichi nüquan," *Shenbao* (16 November 1924); "Changsha dian: Xian hui shan," *Shenbao* (17 November 1924).

71. "Changsha dian: Xianfa huiyi shiri kaihui," *Shenbao* (12 November 1924).

72. *Shenbao* reported on meetings prior to this merger. See "Ji Shanghai funü hui kai chengli da hui," *Shenbao* (1 January 1921); "Shanghai funü hui jinri kai tebie hui," *Shenbao* (11 March 1921); "Nüjie san tuanti huiyi," *Shenbao* (12 March 1921); "Shanghai funü hui kaihui ji," *Shenbao* (28 April 1921).

73. See Gilmartin, *Engendering the Chinese Revolution,* 62–64. Wang Huiwu was born in Zhejiang province and undertook her studies at women's colleges there. Her political activism started in the May Fourth Movement, and she became an outspoken proponent of women's rights. On shifting to Shanghai she joined the fledgling CCP and led its women's activities in the city during the 1920s including the running of the Pingmin Girls' School and the editing the *Women's Voice.* The journal appeared twice

NOTES TO PAGES 130–35

monthly from mid-December 1921 to autumn 1922. She remained in the PRC after 1949, where she held numerous posts in the central government. See Gilmartin, *Engendering the Chinese Revolution*, 230.

74. Cui Zhenhua was educated in one of the women's teachers colleges established in the last years of the Qing dynasty. She joined the Revolutionary Alliance in 1911 and in 1912 married prominent Alliance member, Zhang Ji. Zhang presided over the removal of sex equality from the Alliance program in 1912. Cui Zhenhua later went on to be a member of China's wartime parliament and in 1949 left the mainland for Taiwan. FNCD, 97.

75. See Li Dazhao's contribution in "Li Dazhao jun jiangyan nüquan yundong," repr. in ZFYLZ, 143–45. See also Chen Duxiu, "Funü wenti yu shehui zhuyi," *Guangdong qunbao* (30 January 1921), repr. in Zhonghua quanguo funü lianhe hui funü yundong lishi yanjiu, ed. *Wusi shiqi funü wenti wenxuan* (Hong Kong: Sanlian; Beijing: Shenghui dushu zhishi, 1981), 99–105. First published in *Guangdong qunbao* (30 January 1921). For English translation, see "The Woman Question and Socialism," *Chinese Studies in History* 31, no. 2 (Winter 1997–98): 90–94.

76. For a translation, see Pan Wei-tung, *The Chinese Constitution: A Study of Forty Years of Constitution-making in China* (Washington, DC: Institute of Chinese Culture, 1945), 179–90.

77. "The Constitution of the Republic of China, October 10, 1923," repr. in Ch'ien, *Government and Politics of China*, 436.

78. Translations of these documents are in Pan Wei-tung, *The Chinese Constitution*, 157–69 and 191–209.

79. Yan Shi, "Zuijin de nüquan yundong," 62.

80. Cai Yuanpei, "Ge tuanti qing feizhi zhian jingcha tiaoli," *Chenbao* (15 October 1922).

81. Gilmartin, *Engendering the Chinese Revolution*, 81.

82. Wang Xiaoying developed close ties with the Nationalist Party during these years and continued her involvement in women's education while holding positions in the Nationalist government. She was elected to the legislative assembly in 1936. In 1949 she left for Taiwan. FNCD, 105–6.

83. Tan Sheying, *Zhongguo funü yundong tongshi*, 114.

84. "Ben kan xuanyan," *Nüzi canzheng xiejin hui hui kan* 1 (10 December 1922): inside cover. This issue includes a photograph of members.

85. Shi Shuqing, "Women yundong de liyou he chuban de mudi," *Nüzi canzheng xiejin hui hui kan*, 1 (10 December 1922): 2.

86. Wan Pu, "Fandui nüzi canzheng lun de jieshi," *Nüzi canzheng xiejin hui hui kan*, 1 (10 December 1922): 4–6. She published a three-verse poem titled "Women's Political Rights" in this issue.

87. Ibid.

88. "Beijing nüzi canzheng xiejin hui qingyuan wen," repr. in Tan Sheying, *Zhongguo funü yundong tongshi*, 115–17.

89. Wang Liming was typical of the nonaligned democrat who comprised the Women's Suffrage Association. She was born in Anhui and gained a primary and secondary education in China before going to America to study at Northwestern University in 1916. She returned to China and established numerous schools for girls in Shanghai. Active in Protestant circles, Wang Liming was variously president of the WCTU, president of the Birth Control League, and founder of a refuge for beggar girls and slave girls in Shanghai. For more on Wang Liming/Liu Wang, see her role during the war against Japan later in Chapter 7. FNCD, 100; Liu Guanghua, "Wo de muqin Liu Wang Liming," *Renwu*, no. 6 (1981): 143–49; Wang Zheng, *Women in the Chinese Enlightenment*, 135–43; Louise Edwards, "Liu Wang Liming," in *BDTC*, 374–77. She is discussed as Mrs. Herman C. E. Liu in Helen Foster Snow's *Women in Modern China* (The Hague: Mouton, 1967), 79.

90. "Nüzi canzheng xiejin hui dahui ji," *Shenbao* (26 December 1922); Tan Sheying, *Zhongguo funü yundong tongshi*, 117.

91. On the links between the Women's Right's League and the CCP, see Gilmartin, *Engendering the Chinese Revolution*, 81–82.

92. See Liu Jucai, *Zhongguo jindai funü yundong shi*, 464–65. Miao Boying was from Hunan and attended the province's Girls' Normal School and Beijing's Women's Higher Normal School. She joined the CCP in 1921, and her activities in the Women's Rights League began a year later. Her Marxist training

had a substantial impact on the tenor of the manifesto. She died of illness in Shanghai at the age of thirty. See Beijing shi funü lianhe hui, ed., *Beijing nüjie* (Beijing: Beijing chubanshe, 1985), 113.

93. "Beijing nüquan yundong hui zhaodai bao xue jie," *Shenbao* (16 August 1922).

94. "Nüquan yundong hui xiang guohui qingyuan," *Shenbao* (8 September 1922).

95. Fei Juetian in *Chenbao* (30 July 1922), cited in Se Lu, "Duiyu nüzi canzheng yundong de yulun he wojian," FNZZ 8, no. 11 (1922): 3–4.

96. "Nüquan yundong tongmeng hui xiaoxi," *Shenbao* (4 February 1923).

97. "Shandong nüquan tongmeng hui chengli," *Shenbao* (26 December 1922).

98. "'Nü xing' xunkan fakan ci," *Nü xing*, no. 1 (25 April 1923): 1. I would like to thank Professor Hou Jie for assisting in locating copies of the *Women's Star*.

99. Xi Zu, "She ping," *Funü zhoubao* (29 October 1924).

100. Similarly, the Shandong group declares its aims to be "the extension of the legal and social rights and status of women." Tan Sheying, *Zhongguo funü yundong tongshi*, 130, 132.

101. Tan Sheying, *Zhongguo funü yundong tongshi*, 130, 132. Controlling prostitution was frequently linked to the advancement of women's rights. Li Zi wrote, "The first step in the liberation of women would be the abolition of the buying and selling of girls. This would then have the effect of reducing prostitution . . . if the right to sell girls was prohibited then this would show greater respect to human rights." Li Zi, "Nüzi jiefang," *Minguo ribao* (9 April 1919).

102. Tan Sheying, *Zhongguo funü yundong tongshi*, 121–24.

Chapter Five

1. Sheridan discusses Sun's promotion of this new notion of "nationalism" from the early 1920s. James Sheridan, *China in Disintegration: The Republican Era in Chinese History, 1912–1949* (New York: Free Press, 1975), 144.

2. Gilmartin, "The Politics of Gender in the Making of the Party," 33.

3. Lucien Bianco, "Peasant Responses to CCP Mobilization Politics, 1937–1945," in *New Perspectives on the Chinese Communist Revolution*, ed. Tony Saich and Hans van de Ven (Armonk, NY: M.E. Sharpe, 1995), 176.

4. For a gripping account of this period, see Harold R. Issacs, *The Tragedy of the Chinese Revolution*, 2nd rev. ed. (1938; repr., Stanford, CA: Stanford University Press, 1961).

5. The first national congress of the Nationalist Party was held on 20–30 January 1924.

6. "Manifesto of the First National Congress of the Kuomintang—January 30, 1924," repr. in Shieh, *The Kuomintang*, 84–85.

7. Tan Sheying, *Zhongguo funü yundong tongshi*, 144.

8. The best discussions of Xiang Jingyu's work are Gilmartin, *Engendering the Chinese Revolution*, 71–96 and Andrea McElderry, "Woman Revolutionary: Xiang Jingyu," *China Quarterly*, no. 105 (March 1986): 95–122.

9. Ibid., 113.

10. Christina K. Gilmartin, "Gender, Political Culture and Women's Mobilization in the Chinese Nationalist Revolution, 1924–1927," in *Engendering China: Women, Culture, and the State*, ed. Christina K. Gilmartin et al. (Cambridge, MA: Harvard University Press, 1994), 195–225.

11. Cai Chang was one of the few women to embark on the Long March in 1934 and remained loyal to the CCP. ZGNP, 78–79.

12. Yang left for the Soviet Union to study, returning to Shanghai in 1930 to assume positions on the Women's Bureau and the Central Committee. She continued her work for the CCP after 1949, assuming numerous positions in women's affairs as well as serving on the People's Congress. Yuan Shaoying and Yang Guizhen, eds., *Zhongguo funü mingren cidian*, 213–14; Gilmartin, *Engendering the Chinese Revolution*, 231–32. For biographies of Wang Yizhi and Cai Chang, see Gilmartin, *Engendering the Chinese Revolution*, 219, 230.

13. Li Dazhao, "The Postwar Woman Question," trans. H. R. Lan and V. Fong, *Chinese Studies in History* 31, no. 2 (Winter 1997–98): 17, 22. The original article appeared in *Xin qingnian* 6, no. 2 (15 February 1919): 141–47.

14. Chen Duxiu, "Chen Duxiu xiansheng zai nüjie lianhe hui yanci," *Guangdong qunbao* (31 January; 1 February 1921). All translations are from "The Woman Question and Socialism," in *Chinese Studies in History*, ed. H. R. Lan and Vanessa Fong, 31, no. 2 (Winter 1997–98): 90–94.

15. [Shen] Yanbing, "Zenyang fang neng shi funü yundong you shili," FNZZ 6, no. 6 (5 June 1920): 5–8. All translations are from "How Do We Make the Women's Movement Truly Powerful?" *Chinese Studies in History*, ed. H. R. Lan and V. Fong, 31, no. 2 (Winter 1997–98): 87. Yanbing also commented on the provincial constitutions. [Shen Yan] Bing, "Gao Zhejiang yaoqiu shengxian jiaru san tiaojian de nüzi," *Funü pinglun*, no. 4 (24 August 1921): 2–3.

16. "Zhongguo gongchangdang di er ci quanguo daibiao dahui guanyu funü yundong de jueyi" (23 July 1922), repr. in ZFYLZ, 30.

17. "Zhongguo gongchandang di san ci quanguo daibiao da hui guanyu funü yundong jueyi an" (June 1923), repr. in ZFYLZ, 68.

18. "Zhongguo gongchandang di sanci zhongyang kuoda zhexing weiyuan hui guanyu funü yundong yijue an" (September 1926), repr. in ZFYLZ, 476.

19. "Zhongguo gongchandang di si quanguo daibiao dahui duiyu funü yundong de yijue an" (1925), repr. in ZFYLZ, 281. Goodman notes the same techniques were used in mobilizing women from the general women's movement in the Shanxi region during the war against Japan. David S. G. Goodman, "Revolutionary Women and Women in the Revolution: The Chinese Communist Party and Women in the War of Resistance to Japan, 1937–1945," *China Quarterly*, no. 164 (2000): 915–42.

20. "Zhongguo gongchandang di sanci zhongyang kuoda," 475.

21. "Zhonggong zhongyang funü weiyuan hui gongzuo baogao (jielu)" (1927), repr. in ZFYLZ, 697.

22. Evans, *Comrades and Sisters*, 83.

23. [Xiang] Jingyu, "Zhongguo zuijin de funü yundong," *Qianfeng* 1, no. 1 (1 July 1923): 58–63.

24. Catherine Gipoulon, "Integrating the Feminist and Worker's Movement: The Case of Xiang Jingyu," *Republican China* 10 (November 1994): 29.

25. Gilmartin, *Engendering the Chinese Revolution*, 86.

26. [Xiang] Jingyu, "Duiyu wanguo nüquan tongmeng dahui de ganxiang," *Qianfeng* 1, no. 2 (1 December 1923): 48–50.

27. [Xiang] Jingyu, "Zhongguo funü yundong zaping," *Qianfeng* 1, no. 2 (1 December 1923): 51–56.

28. Xiang Jingyu, "Shanghai nüquan yundonghui jinhou ying zhuyi de san jian shi," *Funü zhoubao*, no. 12 (8 November 1923), repr. in Xiang Jingyu, *Xiang Jingyu wenji* (Changsha: Hunan renmin chubanshe, 1980), 111.

29. Xiang Jingyu, "Ping Wang Bihua de nüquan yundong tan," *Funü zhoubao*, no. 8 (10 October 1923), repr. in Xiang Jingyu, *Xiang Jingyu wenji* (Changsha: Hunan renmin chubanshe, 1980), 103–6.

30. (Xiang) Jingyu, "Zhongguo funü yundong zaping," 51–52. For an excellent discussion of the complexities of the term *ren'ge*, see Bryna Goodman, "The Vocational Woman and the Elusiveness of 'Personhood' in Early Republican China," in *Gender in Motion: Divisions of Labor and Cultural Change in Late Imperial and Modern China*, ed. Bryna Goodman and Wendy Larson (Lanham, MD: Rowman & Littlefield, 2005), 265–86.

31. Xiang Jingyu, "Jinhou Zhongguo funü de guomin geming yundong," FNZZ 10, no. 1 (1 January 1924): 28–32.

32. Xiang Jingyu, "Jinhou Zhongguo funü de guomin geming yundong," 29.

33. "Shanghai funü yundong weiyuan hui xuanyan," repr. in Tan Sheying, *Zhongguo funü yundong tongshi*, 145–46.

34. Xu Wentang, "Xiang Jingyu yu Zhonggong zaoqi funü yundong," *Jindai Zhongguo funü shi yanjiu*, no. 2 (June 1994): 75.

35. Yang Xianjiang, "Zhongguo de funü yundong," *Xin nüxing* 2, no. 1 (1927): 13.

36. "Nüjie guomin huiyi cucheng hui zhi faqi," *Shenbao* (5 December 1924).

37. Duan Qirui's Aftermath Conference convened between 13 February and 21 April 1925. It promulgated a number of laws about the national people's representative assembly and the formation of a committee on military and financial affairs. Li Chien-nung describes the regulations as follows: "All these regulations were enacted by the Executive Government on 24 April. But none of these regulations were more than paper. They were an effort to placate the people, but the Kuomintang objected to them,

and the warlords of course ignored them." Li Chien-nung, *The Political History of China, 1840–1928* (Princeton, NJ: Van Nostrand, 1956), 479.

38. "Shanghai mindang nü dangyuan zhi Zhongshan han," *Minguo ribao* (29 November 1924). *Minguo ribao* served as a major organ for the National Assembly movement and published a special column about it from 28 November 1924 through 28 May 1925.

39. "Nüjie guomin huiyi cucheng hui zhi faqi," *Shenbao* (5 December 1924). See also "Nüquan yundonghui zhuzhang jiaru guomin huiyi," *Minguo ribao* (4 December 1924); "Hu nüjie faqi guomin huiyi cucheng hui," *Minguo ribao* (5 December 1924).

40. Zhang Xichen, "Guomin huiyi yu nü guomin—zai Shanghai nü guomin dahui jiang," FNZZ 11, no. 5 (1925): 730.

41. "Nüzi canzheng hui zhi quanguo nüjie shu," *Minguo ribao* (18 December 1924). See also "Nüjie zhuzhang jiaru guomin huiyi zhi yifengxin," *Shenbao* (30 November 1924).

42. "Nüzi canzheng xiejin hui zhiyuan huiji," *Shenbao* (18 December 1924).

43. Xiang Jingyu, "Guomin huiyi yu funü," *Funü zhoubao* (14 December 1924), repr. in Xiang Jingyu, *Xiang Jingyu wenji* (Changsha: Hunan renmin chubanshe, 1980), 161–64.

44. Chen Wenqing, "Zhongguo zhengzhi yu nüzi canzheng," *Funü zhoubao* (28 May 1924).

45. "Nüjie bei canyu guomin huiyi," *Shenbao* (9 December 1924). See also "Nüjie guomin huiyi cucheng hui dian," *Shenbao* (14 December 1924).

46. "Nüjie guomin huiyi cucheng hui zhangcheng," *Shenbao* (21 December 1924). The founding constitution was reprinted with commentary in "Nüjie guomin huiyi cucheng hui choubei huiji," *Minguo ribao* (21 December 1924).

47. "Nüjie guomin huiyi cucheng hui choubeichu tongdian," *Shenbao* (13 December 1924); "Nüquan yundonghui zhi tongdian," *Shenbao* (4 December 1924).

48. "Nüjie canyu guominhuiyi zhi jinxing," *Shenbao* (11 December 1924).

49. "Nüjie guomin huiyi cucheng hui chengli ji," *Shenbao* (22 December 1924). See also "Nüjie guomin huiyi cucheng hui chengli ji," *Minguo ribao* (22 December 1924).

50. "Tianjin funü guomin huiyi cucheng hui chengli," *Minguo ribao* (31 December 1924). See also "Jin funü guomin huiyi cucheng hui chengli xuanyan ji jianzhang," in *Zhongguo funü yundong*, Liu Wang Liming (Shanghai: Shangwuyin shuguan, 1934), 37–39.

51. "Hu nüjie guomin huiyi cucheng hui tongdian," *Dagong bao* (1925), repr. in ZFYLZ, 434.

52. "Henan nüjie cucheng guomin huiyi zhi dianbao ji xuanyan," *Minguo ribao* (18 February 1925). The Tianjin group sent a similar message. "Tianjin funü guomin huiyi cucheng hui huiyuan dahui," *Minguo ribao* (25 February 1925).

53. Zhang Yangchen, "Guomin huiyi yu nü guomin," 730–31.

54. Song Yunkun, "Guomin huiyi yu funü xuanchuan," *Funü zhoubao* (16 February 1925).

55. "Nüjie guomin huiyi cucheng hui yizhou jishi," *Funü zhoubao* (16 February 1925).

56. See for example, "Nüjie guomin huiyi cucheng hui kaihui ji," *Shenbao* (11 May 1925).

57. "Hu nüjie dingqi kai nüjie guomin dahui," *Shenbao* (12 March 1925).

58. Xiang Jingyu, "Nü guomin huiyi de san da yiyi," *Funü zhoubao* (29 March 1925), repr. In Xiang Jingyu, *Xiang Jingyu wenji*, (Changsha: Hunan renmin chubanshe, 1980), 184.

59. See also Xiang Jingyu's "Ying lizheng funü tuanti canjia guomin huiyi," *Funü zhoubao* (13 April 1925), repr. in Xiang Jingyu, *Xiang Jingyu wenji* (Changsha: Hunan renmin chubanshe, 1980), 192–93.

60. Yang Xianjiang, "Zhongguo de funü yundong," 14.

61. "Guomin huiyi cucheng hui quanguo dahui baogao," *Minguo ribao* (28 May 1925).

62. Ibid.

63. Zhang Xichen, "Zuijin funü de yundong de shibai he jinhou yingqu de fangzhen," FNZZ 11, no. 7 (1925): 1124.

64. Zhang Xichen, "Guomin huiyi yu nü guomin," 731.

65. Zhe Sheng, "Faguo nüzi de canzheng guan," FNZZ 11, no. 1 (1925): 177–84; You Xiong, "Yingguo de funü zhengzhijia," FNZZ 11, no. 5 (1925): 801–4. A picture of Miss A. Pack, an American suffrage activist, features on the inside cover of FNZZ 12, no. 2 (1926).

66. Se Lu, "Zuijin shinian nei funüjie de huigu," FNZZ 10, no. 1 (1924): 16–22.

67. For further discussion, see Elizabeth J. Perry, *Shanghai on Strike: The Politics of Chinese Labor* (Stanford, CA: Stanford University Press, 1993).

68. Gilmartin, *Engendering the Chinese Revolution*, 132–33.

69. Ibid., 137.

70. "Shanghai gejie funü lianhe hui chengli," *Shenbao* (6 June 1925). See also, "Gejie funü lianhe hui xuanyan," repr. in Tan Sheying, *Zhongguo funü yundong tongshi*, 157–58.

71. Yang Xianjiang, "Zhongguo de funü yundong," 13–14.

72. "Guangdong funü jiefang xiehui xuanyan ji gangling" (1925), Guangdong Provincial Archives, repr. in ZFYLZ, 95–97.

73. "Nüzi canzheng xiehui tebie huiyi," *Shenbao* (6 June 1925). On the national products movement, see Gerth, *China Made*.

74. Tan Sheying, *Zhongguo funü yundong tongshi*, 159.

75. L. E. Collins, "The New Women: A Psychohistorical Study of the Chinese Feminist Movement from 1900 to the Present" (PhD diss., Yale University, 1976), 619-20.

76. For information on Zhang, see Yuan Shaoying and Yang Guizhen, eds., *Zhongguo funü mingren cidian*, 332–33; MSD, 880; FNCD, 98.

77. Gilmartin, *Engendering the Chinese Revolution*, 211.

78. Tan Sheying, *Zhongguo funü yundong tongshi*, 171–73. Tan includes a full name list of the twenty-two women involved in the original discussions.

79. Ibid., 174.

80. Ibid., 192–93.

81. Ibid., 206.

82. Chen Jiangtao, "Jinhou woguo funü yingyou zhi zhengfa quan," FNZZ 13, no. 10 (1927): 1–3.

83. Qian Di, *Nüxing yu shehui* (Shanghai: Guangming shuju, 1929), 6–7.

84. One example is Yang Dongchun, "Ping Zhongguo shijiu nianlai de funü yundong," FNZZ 17, no. 1 (1931): 7–16.

Chapter Six

1. The document was officially dated 12 April 1924. For a classic study of the Nanjing Decade, see Lloyd E. Eastman, *The Abortive Revolution: China under Nationalist Rule, 1927–1937* (Cambridge, MA: Harvard University Press, 1974).

2. Harold Issacs has described the tutelage period as follows: "Conceived by Sun as a kind of benevolent paternalism, this doctrine became in the hands of his heirs and successors a justification for the most despotic kind of tyranny." Issacs, *The Tragedy of the Chinese Revolution*, 57.

3. Edmund Fung, "Recent Scholarship on the Minor Parties and Groups in Republican China," *Modern China* 20, no. 4 (October 1994): 484–85.

4. See Strauss's assessment of institution building. Julia C. Strauss, *Strong Institutions in Weak Polities: State Building in Republican China, 1927–1940* (Oxford: Clarendon Press, 1998), 8.

5. See Gamble's discussion of the 5 June 1929 County Organization Act. Sidney Gamble, *North China Villages: Social, Political and Economic Activities before 1933* (Berkeley: University of California Press, 1963), 41–42, 151–52, 167–68, 267. However, he also provides evidence that at least one village included the requirement of "some literary knowledge" (p. 298). For the situation in the CCP areas, see Trygve Lötveit, *Chinese Communism, 1931–1934: Experience in Civil Government* (Lund: Scandinavian Institute of Asian Studies, Monograph no. 16, 1973), 16–18.

6. See Dikötter, *The Age of Openness*.

7. Gamble, *North China Villages*, 167, 267,

8. See Jan Kiely, "Third Force Periodicals in China, 1928–1949," *Republican China* 21, no. 1 (1995): 129–68.

9. Lawrence K. Rosinger, *China's Wartime Politics, 1937–1944* (Princeton, NJ: Princeton University Press, 1945), 56.

10. The problems and ambiguities in the document and in the Nationalist Party's implementation of its recommendations are discussed in Ch'ien, *Government and Politics of China*, 133–37.

11. In June 1927 the Nationalist government established a body charged with revising the nation's laws. It completed the task in October of 1928, but the Legislative Yuan was not yet established so the new laws were shelved. The civil code was eventually passed in a piecemeal fashion over the course of 1929 and 1931. See Bernice J. Lee, "The Change in the Legal Status of Chinese Women in Civil Matters from Traditional Law to the Republican Civil Code" (PhD diss., University of Sydney, 1975), 25–40.

12. See Qian Jianqiu, "Falü shang nannü pingdeng de yuanze," FNZZ 14, no. 4 (1928): 9–10.

13. Elisabeth Croll, *Feminism and Socialism in China* (London: Routledge & Kegan Paul, 1978), 155.

14. Ibid., 156.

15. Wang Zheng, *Women in the Chinese Enlightenment*, 24.

16. E. M. Pye, "The Women's Movement in China," *Asiatic Review* 25 (1929): 204–19, cited in Croll, *Feminism and Socialism in China*, 154.

17. Tao, "Jin ri funü zai zhengzhi shang de diwei," *Funü gongming*, no. 4 (1929): 13. This journal has no year of publication identified but notes that it publishes twice monthly. I have calculated the year according to this pattern and based on the evidence that its first issue appeared on 25 March 1929. From January 1932 the journal published only once per month. See FNCD, 86.

18. Li Zhishan, "'Sanyue bari' yu Zhongguo funü de yaoqiu," *Xin nüxing* 3, no. 1 (1928): 253–54. See also Zhou Yu, "Nannü pingdeng de xianjue tiaojian," FNZZ 15, no. 11 (1929): 17 and [Tan] Sheying, "Ruhe cuqi funü zhuyi zhengzhi zhi xingwei," *Funü gongming*, no. 7 (1929): 12–14.

19. Ye Zhijing, "Zhongguo funü de canzheng yundong," *Minguo ribao* (30 January 1931).

20. See "Juewu sanba jie tekan," *Minguo ribao* (8 March 1931); "Zhongguo funü yu guoji funü jie," *Minguo ribao* (9 March 1931).

21. Shanchuan jurong, "Shinian lai de funü canzheng quan," *Xin nüxing* 4 (October 1929): 1271–77; (November 1929): 1385–94.

22. Xu Yasheng, "Lun wo guo nüzi de canzheng wenti," FNZZ 15, no. 9 (1929): 2–3. Activists continued to press women to improve their political knowledge and maintain unity. See Huan Qi, "Funü canzheng zai Zhongguo bu fada de yuanyin," *Funü gongming*, no. 10 (1929): 5–8. Others traced the history of the suffrage movement from 1911 onward in order to construct a legitimizing narrative for the movement. See Fu Ping, "Zhongguo funü canzheng yundong zhi wojian," *Funü gongming*, no. 19 (1929–30?): 23–26; Jiang Xiaoguang, "Zhongguo funü yundong zhi shi zhi guancha," *Funü gongming*, no. 30 (1930): 23–26.

23. Zhong Tingxiu, "Shijie geguo funü canzheng yundong gaishu," FNZZ 15, no. 8 (1929): 13.

24. Liu Wang Liming, *Zhongguo funü yundong*, 21. For more international comparisons, see "Nüzi canzheng quan diaocha," *Minguo ribao* (15 June 1931).

25. Zi Ran, "Wanguo nüzi canzheng hui kaihui jilu," *Funü gongming*, no. 10 (1929): 40.

26. "Yingguo nüzi xuanju quan fada," *Funü gongming*, no. 6 (1929): 40.

27. The committee met from 9 March to 22 April 1931, and after six meetings it had completed a draft that was then approved by various central party committees and was ready to be referred to the convention due to commence only days later.

28. For a translation of the 1928 "Program of Political Tutelage" and the "Provisional Constitution of the Political Tutelage Period, 1 June 1931," see Pan Wei-tung, *The Chinese Constitution*, 239–40, 247–56.

29. The Nationalist Party dominated since not only did it have its own special category but it effectively controlled the other four groups as well. Ch'ien Tuan-sheng has described the convention as "a party convention." Ch'ien, *Government and Politics of China*, 137.

30. "Guomin huiyi yu funü daibiao wenti," *Minguo ribao* (22 March 1931).

31. Xu Yasheng, "Xunzheng yu funü," FNZZ 16, no. 5 (1930): 11–14. See also Se Lu's comment on the use of the "natural division of labor" in "Duiyu nüzi canzheng yundong de yulun he wojian," 3.

32. The groups that took part in this campaign came from as diverse provinces and municipalities as Nanjing, Guangdong, Tianjin, Shanghai, Kaifeng, and Sichuan. Newspapers reported on the bid for a women's quota. See "Funü tuanti canyu minhui," *Minguo ribao* (10 February 1931); "Funü yaoqiu canjia minhui wenti," *Minguo ribao* (21 April 1931); "Nüzi canzheng hui kaihui," *Minguo ribao* (28 April 1931); "Funü jie qing'e," *Minguo ribao* (7 May 1931).

33. Tan Sheying, *Zhongguo funü yundong tongshi*, 253. See also Tan Sheying, *Fuyun shishinian*, 31–36.

34. Some of the groups involved include the Women's Relief Association (*Funü jiuji hui*), the Women's Support Society (*Funü gongming she*), and Women's Youth League (*Nü qingnian hui*). See Tan Sheying, *Zhongguo funü yundong tongshi*, 253.

35. Jin Zhonghua, "Cong jiating dao zhengzhi," FNZZ 17, no. 5 (1931): 2–13. Her book from the early 1930s outlines the progress for women's suffrage internationally and the main arguments about suffrage. Jin Zhonghua, *Funü wenti* (Shanghai: Shangwuyin shuguan, 1933).

36. Tan Sheying, *Zhongguo funü yundong tongshi*, 254.

37. "Nüjie hanzhu: Minhui zhuxi Liu nüshi," *Minguo ribao* (12 May 1931).

38. Tan helped establish the Women's Support Society in 1928, and she assumed the task of editing its journal, *Women's Support* (*Funü gongming*), considered to be a Nationalist Party organ. Tan left for Taiwan with the retreating Nationalists in 1949. She wrote one of the earliest important surveys of the Chinese women's movement of the republican period, titled *A General History of the Chinese Women's Movement* (*Zhongguo funü yundong tongshi*) published in 1936. See also FNCD, 86.

39. Liu Chunyi studied in Japan from 1916 to 1921 and on her return to China became principal of Girls' Normal School in Xi'an. She was active in publishing women's journals and magazines in both Shanghai and Tianjin. By 1927 she was director of the Nationalist Party's women's bureau in Shanghai, and from this position won her place as a delegate to the convention. FNCD, 98, 107; H.G.W. Woodhead, *China Yearbook, 1939* (Shanghai: North China Daily News and Herald, 1939), 190. Li Zhishan was born in Yanshan, Hebei, and graduated from the Provincial Women's Normal College in 1918. She joined the Nationalist Party in 1923 and moved to Tianjin where she worked as a principal for a women's school and concurrently served as editor for the *Women's Star* and the Tianjin *Women's Daily* (*Funü ribao*). In 1929 she moved to Nanjing and assumed the position of secretary to the training department of the central Nationalist Party headquarters. *Who's Who in China*, 145.

40. Tao, "Jin ri funü zai zhengzhi shang de diwei," 14.

41. Liu Wang Liming, *Zhongguo funü yundong*, 24.

42. Lin Xi, "Guomin huiyi hou: Nüzi canzheng de zhunbei," *Minguo ribao* (25 May 1931).

43. Jinling nüzi daxue xuesheng, *Shijie funü de xiandao* (Shanghai: YWCA Publishing, 1934), 1.

44. Jin Shiyin, "Canzheng yundong shi funü jiefang de xianfeng," *Funü gongming*, no. 11 (1929): 10.

45. Yi Tao, "Xin minfa yu funü de guanxi," *Funü gongming*, no. 3 (1929): 6. See Xiao Ying, "Wo duiyu funü chengxu caichan de yijian," *Funü gongming*, no. 3 (1929): 6–8.

46. Lisa Tran, "Concubines under Modern Chinese Law" (PhD diss., University of California, Los Angeles, 2005), 71. I would like to express my gratitude to Lisa Tran and Kathryn Bernhardt for making this work available to me.

47. The "Book of Family" was promulgated on 26 December 1930 and effective from 5 May 1931. For the legal changes sought, see Tan Sheying, *Zhongguo funü yundong tongshi*, 256.

48. Lee, "Change in the Legal Status of Chinese Women," 43.

49. Ibid., 51.

50. Tran, "Concubines under Modern Chinese Law," 68. For a discussion of the broad changes in attitudes about families, see Susan Glosser, *Chinese Visions of Family and State, 1915–1953* (Berkeley: University of California Press, 2003).

51. For a full exploration of the evolution of the adultery laws, see Tran, "Concubines under Modern Chinese Law," chap. 3. See also Philip C. C. Huang, "Women's Choices under the Law: Marriage, Divorce and Illicit Sex in the Qing and Republic," *Modern China* 27, no. 1 (January 2001): 3–58.

52. See C.Y.W. Meng, "Fight for 'Sex Equality' in China," *China Weekly Review* (24 November 1934): 432.

53. Tran, "Concubines under Modern Chinese Law," 142.

54. See Lin Hao, "Zhongguo funü zhi jiefang yundong," *Nüzi yuekan* 1, no. 8 (1933): 14–17; Chen Yinxuan, "Nannü pingdeng yu fuqi caichan zhi de wenti," *Nüzi yuekan* 1, no. 6 (1933): 33–40.

55. Rubie S. Watson, "Women's Property in Republican China: Rights and Practice," *Republican China* 10, no. 1a (1994): 2.

56. For a detailed description of the various possible combinations of succession and inheritance rights for wives, see Lee, "The Change in the Legal Status of Chinese Women," 218.

57. Bernhardt, *Women and Property in China*, 133. Watson argued that the practical effects of these

laws were limited—most of rural China was unaware of the laws, and even in urban China they were rarely implemented. Watson, "Women's Property in Republican China," 2.

58. Bernhardt, *Women and Property in China*, 138–60.

59. Arif Dirlik, "The Ideological Foundations of the New Life Movement: A Study in Counterrevolution," *Journal of Asian Studies* 34, no. 4 (August 1975): 945–80.

60. *Who's Who in China*, 17.

61. Tan Sheying, *Zhongguo funü yundong tongshi*, 280–81.

62. Z. Y. Yu, "General Han Fu-chu's Drive against 'Modern Girls,'" *China Weekly Review* (31 October 1936): 322.

63. "Changsha Women Up in Arms Against Reactionary Police Head," *China Weekly Review* (22 August 1936): 432.

64. T. S. Young, "The Girl Guides," *China Weekly Review* (7 November 1936): 343.

65. Tang Guozhen, "Ruhe jiejue changji wenti," *Funü gongming* 1, nos. 3–4 (15 June 1932): 17–21, cited in Hershatter, *Dangerous Pleasures*, 260.

66. Hershatter, *Dangerous Pleasures*, 264–65.

67. Tan Sheying, *Zhongguo funü yundong tongshi*, 221. See her volume for manifestos and regulations of these organizations.

68. Ibid., 234–35.

69. Huang Jiade, *Xin nü xing* (Shanghai: Shanghai liangyou tushu, 1936), 3, 59.

70. "Zhonghua Suwei'ai gongheguo xuanfa dagang," cited in ZFYS, 297–98.

71. Lötveit, *Chinese Communism*, 16–18.

72. Ibid., 27.

73. Kay Ann Johnson, *Women, the Family and Peasant Revolution in China* (Chicago: University of Chicago Press, 1983), 53.

74. Matthew H. Sommer, "Making Sex Work: Polyandry as a Survival Strategy in Qing Dynasty China," in *Gender in Motion: Divisions of Labor and Cultural Change in Late Imperial and Modern China*, ed. Bryna Goodman and Wendy Larson (Lanham, MD: Rowman & Littlefield, 2005), 29–54.

75. ZFYS, 300–301.

76. Delia Davin, "Women in the Liberated Areas," in *Women in China: Studies in Social Change and Feminism*, ed. Marilyn B. Young (Ann Arbor: Center for Chinese Studies, University of Michigan, 1973), 75.

77. Johnson, *Women, the Family and Peasant Revolution*, 56–57. See also Hu Chi-hsi, "The Sexual Revolution in the Kiangsi Soviet," *China Quarterly*, no. 59 (1974): 477–90.

78. For more detail, see Lily Lee, *Women of the Long March* (Sydney: Allen & Unwin, 1999).

79. Christina K. Gilmartin, "Gender in the Formation of a Communist Body Politic," *Modern China* 19, no. 3 (July 1993), 317.

80. See Johnson, *Women, the Family and Peasant Revolution*, 51–54 for a discussion of the Jiangxi Soviet region.

81. "Funü yingdang zuo funü gongzuo," *Zhongguo funü* 1, no. 2 (1 July 1939): 19. For further discussion of the problems of "women's work," see Edwards, "Constraining Women's Political Work with 'Women's Work,'" 109–30.

82. For a copy of the "Revised Draft of Constitution—16 October 1934" see Pan Wei-tung, *Chinese Constitution*, 263–86. See also Mei Ju-ao, "On the Eve of Constitutional Government in China," *T'ien Hsia Monthly* 2, no. 5 (May 1936): 443–53.

83. Tung, *Political Institutions*, 137–38.

84. Rosinger, *China's Wartime Politics*, 70–85.

85. Ibid., 56.

86. "People's Assembly to Be Held on Nov. 12 as Scheduled," *China Weekly Review* (3 October 1936): 161.

87. ZFYS, 589.

88. Lü Yunzhang (1891–1974), a Shandong native, had been educated in Beijing at both the Women's Legal and Political College and the Women's Normal College. She joined the Nationalist Party in 1925 and, as editor of the party's women's organ, *Women's Friend* (*Funü zhi you*), became an active member of the party's

Women's Bureau. Lü published extensively on women's liberation, including two book-length works—*Collected Articles on the Women Question* (*Funü wenti lunwenji*) and *A History of the World Women's Movement* (*Shijie funü yundong shi*). After 1949 she left for Taiwan. FNCD, 98. For examples of Lü's analysis of problems facing the women's movement, see Edwards, "Policing the Modern Woman," 115–47. Wang Xiaoying was from Fujian province. She attended one of the new provincial Girls' Normal Schools and went on to study in Beijing at the Women's Normal College. She was principal of numerous schools around Fujian, Guangdong, and Shanghai. Her involvement in women's suffrage came in 1921 when she helped organize the Women's Suffrage Association in Beijing. While in Beijing she became involved in Nationalist Party politics and married senior party figure, Li Dachao. She was to continue her involvement in politics during the civil war period, serving in the Constituent National Assembly in 1946 and continuing as a member of the Legislative Yuan in 1947. FNCD, 105–6. Zhao Maohua (1898–?), originally from Sichuan, left for Germany in her youth and gained a PhD in Berlin. On her return to China she served in the Ministry of Education and on the National Defense Planning Committee. Woodhead, *China Yearbook, 1939*, 163.

Chapter Seven

1. Earlier versions of some parts of this chapter were published as "From Gender Equality to Gender Difference: Feminist Campaigns for Quotas for Women in Politics," *Twentieth Century China* 24, no. 2 (April 1999): 69–105.

2. Tan Sheying, *Zhongguo funü yundong tongshi*, 285. For the manifesto of the Women's Electoral Lobby, see pp. 288–89.

3. See articles 27.2 and 27.3. The details of the numbers within each category appear in the Law for the Election of Delegates to the National Assembly (*Guomindahui daibiao xuanju fa*) of 14 May 1936. This is found in Wu Jingxiong and Huang Gongjue, *Zhongguo zhixian shi* (Shanghai: Shangwuyin, 1937), repr. in *Minguo congshu* 27 (Shanghai: Shanghai shudian, 1989), 1006–47.

4. For more on liberal-democratic opposition groups, see Fung, *In Search of Chinese Democracy* and Mary G. Mazur, "Intellectual Activism in China during the 1940s: Wu Han in the United Front and the Democratic League," *China Quarterly*, no. 133 (March 1993): 27–55. The federation was a coalition of democratic parties that occupied the middle ground between the CCP and the Nationalist Party until 1947 when the Nationalist Party declared the federation illegal and ordered its disbandment.

5. Norma Diamond, "Women Under Kuomintang Rule: Variations on the Feminine Mystique," *Modern China* 1, no. 1 (January 1975): 9.

6. Chou Bih-er, Cal Clark, and Janet Clark, *Women in Taiwan Politics* (Boulder, CO: Lynne Rienner, 1990), 81.

7. Richard J. Evans, *The Feminists* (London: Croom Helm, 1977), 212.

8. See Richard J. Evans, *Comrades and Sisters: Feminism, Socialism and Pacifism in Europe, 1870–1945* (Sussex: Wheatsheaf Books; New York: St. Martin's Press, 1987), 66–92.

9. On the PPC, see Lawrence Nae-lih Shyu, "The People's Political Council and China's Wartime Problems, 1937–1945" (PhD diss., Columbia University, 1972); Fung, *In Search of Chinese Democracy*, 144–82.

10. For a summary of the dates and locations of the various meetings, see *Guomin canzheng hui shiliao* (Taipei: Yutai gongsi, 1962), 635. Ch'ien Tuan-sheng noted in 1942: "If the People's Political Council is to exercise its functions effectively, it should meet more often than hitherto." Ch'ien, "War-Time Government in China," *American Political Science Review*, no. 5 (October 1942): 858.

11. Tsao, *The Constitutional Structure of Modern China*, 108.

12. Ch'ien, *Government and Politics of China*, 281.

13. Gerry Groot, *Managing Transitions: The Chinese Communist Party, United Front Work, Corporatism and Hegemony* (London: Routledge, 2004), 6.

14. Fung, *In Search of Chinese Democracy*, 228.

15. ZFYS, 428. MacKinnon writes that this meeting was dominated by CCP members like Deng Yingchao and led by Song Qingling. Stephen MacKinnon, "Refugee Flight at the Outset of the Anti-Japanese War," in *Scars of War: The Impact of Warfare on Modern China*, ed. Diana Lary and Stephen MacKinnon (Vancouver: University of British Columbia Press, 2001), 131.

16. With the assassination of the poet Wen Yiduo in July of 1946, Liu Wang Liming took a leading role in the formation of the League for the Protection of Human Rights (*Zhongguo renquan baozheng weiyuan hui*). The Nationalist Party declared the league illegal in early 1947.

17. Zhonggong Shanghai shi weidang shi ziliao zhengji weiyuan hui, ed., *"Yi er. jiu" yihou Shanghai jiuguo hui shiliao xuanji* (Shanghai: Shanghai shehui kexue yuan, 1987), 312–13. See also Parks M. Coble, *Facing Japan: Chinese Politics and Japanese Imperialism, 1931–1937* (Cambridge, MA: Harvard University Asia Center, 1991), 335–42 and his "The National Salvation Association as a Political Party," in *Roads Not Taken: The Struggle of Opposition Parties in Twentieth-Century China*, ed. Roger B. Jeans (Boulder, CO: Westview, 1992), 135–47.

18. Unlike Liu, Shi Liang had not studied overseas. Her legal training was completed in 1923 at Shanghai Legal Studies University, and she practiced as a lawyer while maintaining her political activism. In 1927 she was imprisoned as a radical and with the help of Cai Yuanpei gained release. "Shi Liang tongzhi shengping," *Funü zuzhi yu huodong* 5 (1985): 42–43. See also "Shi Liang tongzhi yiti gaobie yishi zai Beijing juxing," *Renmin ribao* (12 September 1985).

19. See "China and India at San Francisco," *Amerasia* 4, no. 9 (May 1945): 136. W. Y. Tsao writes of Wu Yifang: "It is gratifying to mention that one of the five members of the Presidium was a lady whose name was Dr. Wu Yi-fang, president of the Ginling College for Women. Her election to the Presidium was a further testimony of the fact that in China today women have demonstrated their ability most splendidly to play their part in the sphere of social and political affairs. There were nine women councilors in the First Council and fifteen in the Second Council. All of them could well claim that they did in every way rival their fellow men members of the Council." W. Y. Tsao, *The Constitutional Structure of Modern China* (Carlton, Australia: Melbourne University Press, 1947), 111. Wu had graduated from the University of Michigan with a PhD and became president of Jinling College for Women in Nanjing while in her mid-thirties. See Edwards, "Wu Yifang," in *BDTC*, 561–64.

20. "Miss Wu Chih-mei," *Who's Who in China*, 225.

21. FNCD, 113.

22. ZGNP, 181–82.

23. Penny Summerfield, "Gender and War in the Twentieth Century," *International History Review* 19, no. 1 (February 1997): 4.

24. Arthur Marwick, *The Deluge: British Society and the First World War* (1965; repr., London: Macmillan, 1975), 95–105.

25. Evans, *The Feminists*, 222–26.

26. Ibid., 196.

27. ZFYS, 355.

28. "Madame Chiang Leads Women of China in Support of Defenders," *China Weekly Review* (7 August 1937): 371.

29. "Chinese Woman Lawyer Gives Statistics of Women's Activities," *China at War* 5, no. 3 (October 1940): 70.

30. Qin Jin, "Guomin dahui zhi fuxuan wenti," *Funü shenghuo* 3, no. 3 (August 1936): 5.

31. Ibid., 6.

32. Wang Ruqi, "Women yao canjia guomin dahui de zhixian," *Funü shenghuo* 4, no. 10 (1 June 1937): 2.

33. Ibid.

34. Ibid.

35. Ibid.

36. Ibid.

37. Articles in this special issue, *Funü shenghuo* 4, no. 11 (16 June 1937), that are not directly cited are Wen Yang, "Tan minzhu zhengzhi," 6–7; Mo Yan, "Jin ri Zhongguo de funü wenti yu minzhu zhuyi," 8–9; and Zi Jiu, "Women weishenme zhuzhang yao canjia guomin dahui," 10.

38. Wang Ruqi, "Women zenyang canjia guomin dahui de zhixian," *Funü shenghuo* 4, no. 11 (16 June 1937): 2.

39. Luo Qiong, "Canzheng yundong zai funü jiefang yundong zhong de diwei," *Funü shenghuo* 4, no. 11 (16 June 1937): 3–4.

40. Ji Hong, "Xin xianfa ying queding funü de quanli," *Funü shenghuo* 4, no. 11 (16 June 1937): 6.

41. Wang Ruqi, "Women zenyang canjia guomin dahui de zhixian," 1.

42. Qian Jianqiu eventually went to live in Taiwan and published on the women's movement. See her chapter, "Funü yundong," in *Zhonghua minguo kaiguo wushinian shilunji: Di er ce* (Taipei: Guofang, 1962).

43. Wang Ruqi, "Canjia quanguo funü daibiao dahui sanriji," *Funü shenghuo* 5, no. 1 (July 1937): 13–15.

44. *China Handbook, 1937–1945* (New York: Macmillan, 1947), 71.

45. For a list of the women in the first three councils, see Lü Fangshang, "Kangzhan shiqi Zhongguo de funü yundongzuo," in *Zhongguo funü shilun wenji*, ed. Li Youning and Zhang Yufa (Taipei: Shangwuyin shuguan, 1981), 410n42. My own count of women in the Fourth Council includes Wu Yifang, Tang Guozhen, Zhang Weizhen, Zhang Bangzhen, Tao Xuan, Wu Zhimei, Liu Hengjing, Liu Xianying, Chen Yiyun, Lü Yunzhang, Deng Yingchao, Xie Bingxin, Luo Heng, and Hu Mulan.

46. "Yan'an funüjie xianzheng cujin hui gao quanguo meimei shu," *Zhongguo funü* 1, no. 9 (8 March 1940): 11–12.

47. Minutes of the fifth session of the first council, cited in *Guomin canzheng hui shiliao* (Taipei: Yutai gongsi, 1962), 167–68. No similar time limits were placed upon the quotas recommended for overseas Chinese, minority groups, or employment groups.

48. Ibid., 177.

49. Wu Yifang, "The People's Political Council," *China at War* 6, no. 5 (May 1941): 86.

50. "Minutes of the Fifth Session of the First Council," 195.

51. "Minutes of the Third Session of the Third Council," *Guomin canzheng hui shiliao* (Taipei: Yutai gongsi, 1962), 438.

52. "Minutes of the First Session of the Fourth Council," *Guomin canzheng hui shiliao* (Taipei: Yutai gongsi, 1962), 477.

53. See also the CCP report on the PPC initiatives on women. Wang Ming, "Zhongguo funü yu xianzheng yundong," *Zhongguo funü* 1, no. 7 (20 December 1939): 2–3.

54. "San jie nü canzheng yuan de ming'e," *Funü yuekan* (1941).

55. "Minutes of the First Session of the First Council," 32–33.

56. "Minutes of the Fifth Session of First Council," 195–96.

57. "Women Postal Workers Can Marry," *China at War* 8, no. 4 (April 1942): 51–52.

58. "Minutes of the First Session of the Third Council," 333–34.

59. "International Women's Day," *China at War* 4, no. 4 (May 1940): 7.

60. "Yan'an funüjie xianzheng cujin hui gao quanguo meimei shu," 11–12; "Yan'an funüjie xianzheng cujin hui zhi Jiang Yizhang dian," *Zhongguo funü* 1, no. 9 (8 March 1940): 2; "Yan'an funüjie xianzheng cujin hui gao bianqu meimei shu," *Zhongguo funü* 1, no. 9 (8 March 1940): 12–13; "Yan'an funüjie xianzheng cujin hui zhi Song Qingling, He Xiangning xiansheng han," *Zhongguo funü* 1, no. 9 (8 March 1940): 13–14; "Yan'an funüjie xianzheng cujin hui zhi Song Meiling xiansheng han," *Zhongguo funü* 1, no. 9 (8 March 1940): 14–15.

61. MSD, 808.

62. ZFYS, 437–40.

63. The CCP women's journal *Women of China* published a history of the women's suffrage movement in China that suggested more sympathy for the movement than earlier CCP activists had. See Ya Su, "Zhongguo funü zai jindai shishang canzheng yundong de yantao (xu)," *Zhongguo funü* 1, no. 9 (8 March 1940): 18–26 and no. 10–11 (25 April 1940): 3, 44–46.

64. Ji Rong, ed., *Zhongguo funü yundong shi*, 121–22.

65. See *Guomin zhengfu yisong xianfa caoan zhi gonghan*, cited in Guo Wei, ed., *Zhonghua minguo xianfa shiliao*, repr. in Chen Yunlong, ed., *Jindai Zhongguo shiliao congkan: Di bashiba* (Taipei: Wenhai chubanshe, 1973), 154, 165, 173. Text reference is to the 1973 version.

66. Tsao, *The Constitutional Structure of Modern China*, 257. In the 1946 documents we also see the stipulation that women voters were required to identify themselves on their voter registration cards. The practice of inserting the character for "woman" after names of women politicians continues today in the PRC. Guo Wei, *Zhonghua minguo xianfa shiliao*, 173.

67. See "China and India at San Francisco," 132; "Declaration of the Democratic League of China," *Amerasia* (23 March 1945): 86–87.

68. "Chinese Communist Reaction to Chiang's Speech," *Amerasia* (6 April 1945): 105.

69. This 1946 document had no education or literacy requirements for voting. Only criminals were prohibited from voting. See Guo Wei, ed., *Zhonghua minguo xianfa shiliao*, 176.

70. Tan Sheying, *Fuyun sishinian*, 69.

71. "Guomin dahui daibiao xuanju bamian fa," in Guo Wei, *Zhonghua minguo xianfa shiliao*, 171. Other special groups were granted guaranteed representation as well—overseas Chinese were granted sixty-five seats; occupational groups, four hundred and fifty; Mongolians, fifty-seven; and Tibetans, forty.

72. "Lifayuan lifaweiyuan xuanju bamian fa," in Guo Wei, ed., *Zhonghua minguo xianfa shiliao*, 180.

73. Ch'ien, *Government and Politics of China*, 343.

74. Lin Wenqi, "Funü canzheng kaibuzou," FNZZ, no. 11 (1991): 120.

75. Chen Chih-mai, "The Post-War Government of China," *Journal of Politics* 9 (1947): 506.

76. ZFYS, 589. The women elected to the Legislative Yuan included familiar figures such as Wang Xiaoying, Wu Zhimei, Lu Yunzhang, Tang Guozhen, Zhou Min, and Chen Yiyun. The Control Yuan included women such as Deng Huifang and Cui Zhenhua. Tan Sheying, *Fuyun sishinian*, 72.

77. The ten groups included the China United Association (*Zhongguo funü lianyi hui*), China Women's Culture Society (*Zhongguo funü wenhua she*), the Women's Caucus of the Democratic Constitution Promotion Association (*Minzhu xianzheng cujin hui*), and the Modern Women's Society (*Xiandai funü she*). FNCD, 99, 100, 141.

78. Liu was born in Tianjin and had been active in both the 1911 revolution and the May Fourth Movement. Joining the CCP while studying in Paris in 1921, she also participated in the Nationalist Party's women's activities during the First United Front. She was expelled from the Nationalist Party in 1927 and also left the CCP. She avoided formal political alignment until the Japanese invasion of 1937, when she became active in numerous patriotic women's groups. In 1944 she joined the FCDP and was head of the women's bureau. Remaining in China after 1949 she rejoined the CCP in 1961. FNCD, 99.

79. Li Dequan was married to the northern warlord Feng Yuxiang, known as the "Christian general," in 1924. Feng was sympathetic to union activism and attempted to promote constitutional rule through his support of the Nationalist Party. His periods of control over Beijing in the 1920s enabled the CCP to develop its networks among the students and workers. Li Dequan and General Feng were forced to seek refuge in the Soviet Union in 1924 with the return to dominance in the north of the right-wing warlords Wu Peifu and Zhang Zuolin. On their return to China, Li Dequan was active in various patriotic organizations and with her husband made a trip to America in 1946 to garner support for those opposed to Chiang Kai-shek. In 1958 she joined the CCP. FNCD, 100. See also Snow, *Women in Modern China*, 85–85.

80. See "Guoda nüdaibiao jingxuan dongtai" and "Guanyu guoda ji guoda nüdaibiao" in *Xinhua ribao*'s supplement *Women's Road* (*Funü zhilu*), no. 129, cited in ZFYS, 590. *Women's Road* was a CCP paper edited by the women in the Southern Command. It commenced publication in May 1940 and published 149 issues before being banned by the Nationalist Party.

81. In 1926 Xu Guangping graduated as a teacher from Beijing Women's Normal College and moved to Guangzhou to teach in the Provincial Normal School. Her commitment to promoting political activism among her students is clear from an article published in the journal *New Femininity*, under the pen name Jing Song. She argued that few students cared about the Nationalist Party or the national government because these organs' attitude toward education was narrow and selfish. Jing Song "Xin Guangdong de xin nüxing," *Xin nüxing* 1, no. 12 (1926): 887. After 1949 she remained in China, serving in the PRC government and in the Women's Federation. Xu joined the CCP in 1960. Yuan Shaoying and Yang Guizhen, eds. *Zhongguo funü mingren cidian*, 152.

82. FNCD, 106.

83. Ibid., 109–110.

84. Liu Hengjing, *Funü wenti wenji, yi ce* (Nanjing: Funü yuekan she, 1947), 63.

85. For more on the sociopolitical trends, see Joseph W. Esherick, "War and Revolution: Chinese Society during the 1940s," *Twentieth Century China* 27, no. 1 (November 2001): 1–37; Suzanne Pepper, *Civil War in China: The Political Struggle, 1945–1949* (Berkeley: University of California Press, 1978).

86. "The Election Laws of the Shen-Kan-Ning Border Region, May 12, 1937," cited in Mark Selden, *The Yenan Way in Revolutionary China* (Cambridge, MA: Harvard University Press, 1971), 128.

87. Goodman notes that the high levels of illiteracy became a problem in the CCP areas because few cadres could perform the necessary administrative tasks. David Goodman, *Social and Political Change in Revolutionary China: The Taihang Base Area in the War of Resistance to Japan, 1937–1945* (Lanham, MD: Rowman & Littlefield, 2000), 115.

88. Selden, *The Yenan Way*, 128.

89. Goodman, *Social and Political Change*, 61.

90. "Fakan ci," *Zhongguo funü* 1, no. 1 (1 June 1939): 3.

91. Croll, *Feminism and Socialism in China*, 208.

92. Selden, *The Yenan Way*, 165.

93. Goodman, *Social and Political Change*, 61.

94. Ibid., 93. Ten Mile Village enfranchised all adults over the age of eighteen. Isobel and David Crook, *Revolution in a Chinese Village: Ten Mile Inn* (1959; repr., London: Routledge & Kegan Paul, 1979), 94.

95. William Hinton, *Fanshen: A Documentary of Revolution in a Chinese Village* (1966; repr., New York: Monthly Review Press, 1967), 330, 431.

96. Deng Yingchao, cited in Davin, "Women in the Liberated Areas," 86.

97. Hinton, *Fanshen*, 157–58.

98. Crook and Crook, *Revolution in a Chinese Village*, 106–7.

99. Ibid., 108.

100. Du Junhui, *Funü wenti jianghua* (Shanghai: Xin zhi shudian, 1936), 118–19.

101. Wang Ming, "Lun funü jiefang wenti," *Zhongguo funü* 1, no. 1 (1 June 1939): 4.

102. Zhang Pengzhou, "Funü shehui diwei zhi shide kaocha," *Nüsheng* 3, no. 20 (1935): 4.

103. Ding Ling, "Thoughts on March 8," in *I Myself Am a Woman: Selected Writings of Ding Ling*, ed. Tani E. Barlow with Gary J. Bjorge (Boston: Beacon Press, 1989), 316–21. The party leadership severely criticized Ding Ling for her "narrow" feminist vision, and their treatment of her served as a warning to women in Yan'an to avoid taint of "bourgeois feminism."

104. David S. G. Goodman, "Revolutionary Women and Women in the Revolution: The Chinese Communist Party and Women in the War of Resistance to Japan, 1937–1945," *China Quarterly*, no. 164 (December 2000): 919. He also notes that the Licheng Sixth Trigram movement of 1941, with its strong appeal to women, suggested that the problems for women were not being adequately addressed in the base areas. See his "Resistance and Revolution, Religion, and Rebellion: The Sixth Trigram Movement in Licheng, 1939–1942," in *North China at War: The Social Ecology of Revolution, 1937–1945*, ed. Feng Chongyi and David S. G. Goodman (Lanham, MD: Rowman & Littlefield, 2000), 148.

105. Johnson, *Women, the Family and Peasant Revolution*, 67.

106. Deng Yingchao, "Lüetan funü yu canzheng," *Funü xinyun* 5, no. 3 (1943), repr. in Zhonghua quanguo funü lianhe hui, ed., *Cai Chang, Deng Yingchao, Kang Keqing funü jiefang wenti wenxuan 1938–1987* (Bejing: Renmin chubanshe, 1988), 80–81.

107. Cai Chang, cited in Davin, "Women in the Liberated Areas," 76.

108. The constitution was adopted on 25 December 1946 by the National Constituent Assembly, promulgated by the National government on 1 January 1947, and made effective from 25 December 1947.

109. Xue Limin, *Taiwan diqu funü canzheng wenti zhi yanjiu* (Taipei: Tianyi chubanshe, 1977), 28. Xue cites Qian Jianqiu, "Funü yundong," 1143.

110. "Xin shidai, xin shiming, xin funü," *Xin funü* (March 1947): 4.

111. Li Luoxiao, "Funü yu xingxian," *Xin funü*, no. 13 (April 1948): 4.

112. Li Xueli, "Minzhu, ducai, fazhi, renzhi," *Xin funü*, no. 15 (June 1948): 4.

Chapter Eight

1. Lu Xun, "My Views on Chastity," trans. Yang Xianyi and Gladys Yang, 13–25, in *Lu Xun: Selected Works*, vol. 2 (1918; repr., Beijing: Foreign Languages Press, 1980).

2. I am grateful to Ellen Carol DuBois, Dick Cherny, and the participants in the American Historical

Association's panels on Women's Suffrage in the Pacific for the term "emblem of modernity." The conference was held in Hawaii during 1999, and a special journal issue resulted from the panels. See *Pacific Historical Review* 69, no. 4 (2000).

3. Francisco O. Ramirez, Yasemin Soysal, and Suzanne Shanahan, "The Changing Logic of Political Citizenship: Cross-national Acquisition of Women's Suffrage Rights, 1890 to 1990," *American Sociological Review* 62, no. 5 (October 1997): 735–45.

4. Lee Ann Banaszak, *Why Movements Succeed or Fail: Opportunity, Culture and the Struggle for Woman Suffrage* (Princeton, NJ: Princeton University Press, 1996).

Bibliography

Anonymous Sources

"Aiguo dang kaihui jishi" (Matters from the Patriot Party meeting). *Aiguo bao*
   (1 October 1912).
"Beijing dian: You nansheng lai jing" (Wire from Beijing: Southerners came to the
   capital). *Shenbao* (12 July 1912).
"Beijing dian: Yuan Zongtong" (Wire from Beijing: President Yuan). *Shenbao* (10
   August 1912).
"Beijing guanchang wen you nüzi jun" (Beijing Official circles has news of women's
   army). *Shenbao* (25 January 1912).
"Beijing nüquan yundong hui zhaodai bao xue jie" (Beijing women's rights move-
   ment hosts a study meeting). *Shenbao* (16 August 1922).
"Beiyang nüshifan xuetang xueye jicheng" (Report on the North Ocean Girls'
   Normal School promoting enterprise). *Dagong bao* (10 February 1908).
"Beijing nüzi canzheng xiejin hui qingyuan wen" (Petition from the Beijing's
   women's suffrage progress society). In *Zhongguo funü yundong tongshi* (A gen-
   eral history of the Chinese women's movement), edited by Tan Sheying, 115–17.
   Nanjing: Funü gongming she, 1936.
"Ben kan xuanyan" (Manifesto for this journal). *Nüzi canzheng xiejin hui hui kan*
   1 (10 December 1922), inside cover.

"Canyi yuan yijue nüzi canzheng quan" (Parliament rejects women's suffrage rights). *Shengjing shibao* (2 April 1912).

"Canyiyuan jianfa wenti zhi da zhenglun" (Huge debate on the question of hair cutting in the parliament). *Shenbao* (3 November 1912).

"Canyiyuan yishi zhiyao" (Parliamentary summary). *Aiguo bao* (8 November 1912).

"Canzheng zhi nüzi" (Women's suffragists). *Minli bao* (9 August 1912).

"Changsha dian: Nüjie lizheng weichi nüquan" (Telegram from Changsha: The women's movement vigorously argues to maintain women's rights). *Shenbao* (16 November 1924).

"Changsha dian: Nüjie yin xianfa huiyi yiyuan . . ." (Telegram from Changsha: As a result of the member of the constitutional meeting the women's movement . . .). *Shenbao* (11 November 1924).

"Changsha dian: Xian hui shan" (Telegram from Changsha: Constitution committee deletions). *Shenbao* (17 November 1924).

"Changsha dian: Xianfa huiyi shiri kaihui" (Telegram from Changsha: Ten-day meeting of the constitution meeting). *Shenbao* (12 November 1924).

"Changsha nüjie lianhe hui cheng li xuanyan" (Manifesto on the establishment of the Changsha UWA). Cited in "Hunan nüzi zhi wuquan yundong" (Hunan women's five rights movement), *Minguo ribao* (27 January 1921).

"Changsha Women up in Arms against Reactionary Police Head." *China Weekly Review* (22 August 1936): 432.

"China and India at San Francisco." *Amerasia* 4, no. 9 (May 1945): 131–42.

"China to Vote on Monarchy." *Suffragist* 3, no. 42 (16 October 1915): 2.

"Chinese Communist Reaction to Chiang's Speech." *Amerasia* (6 April 1945): 104–9.

"Chinese Woman Lawyer Gives Statistics of Women's Activities." *China at War* 5, no. 3 (October 1940): 70.

"Chuan sheng zhixian zhong zhi nüquan yundong" (Women's rights movement for writing the constitution in Sichuan). *Shenbao* (4 February 1923).

"Da Zongtong duiyu xin nüjie zhi qiwang" (The President's reaction to the hopes of the new women's groups). *Shenbao* (10 February 1912).

"Da Zongtong jingli nüxia" (The president salutes women warriors). *Minli bao* (19 January 1912).

"Da Zongtong shenzhong nüzi canzheng wenti" (The President deals discreetly with the question of women's suffrage). *Dagong bao* (6 April 1912).

"Declaration of the Democratic League of China." *Amerasia* (23 March 1945): 86–87.

"Deng Huifang nüshi zhi tanhua" (Discussion by Madame Deng Huifang). *Guangdong qunbao* (31 March 1921).

"Dongjing liu xuesheng jie de zhentan" (A spy among the students in Tokyo). *Zhongguo ribao* (13 March 1907).

"Duoqi zhidu zhi guomin xing" (National nature of polygamy). *Shenbao* (9 May 1921).

"Ershiwu ri zhi Huguang guan" (The 25th at Huguang hall). *Shenbao* (31 August 1912).

"Fakan ci" (Opening words). *Zhongguo funü* 1, no. 1 (1 June 1939): 3.

"Fou jue nüzi canzheng an zhi shezhan" (Women's suffrage bill voted down in a heated argument). *Guangdong qunbao* (2 April 1921).

"Fu qing yuan shu" (Petition from women). In *Guangdong funü yundong lishi ziliao* (Materials on the history of the women's movement in Guangdong), vol. 3, edited by Guangdong sheng funü yundong lishi ziliao bianzuan weiyuan hui. Guangzhou: Guangdong sheng dang'an guan, 1991.

"Funü jie qing'e" (The women's world requests a quota). *Minguo ribao* (7 May 1931).

"Funü tuanti canyu minhui" (Women's groups' participation in the citizens' convention). *Minguo ribao* (10 February 1931).

"Funü yaoqiu canjia minhui wenti" (The problem of women wanting to participate in the citizens' convention). *Minguo ribao* (21 April 1931).

"Funü yaoqiu canzhengquan" (Women demand suffrage rights). *Chenbao* (6 January 1920).

"Funü yingdang zuo funü gongzuo" (Women ought to do women's work). *Zhongguo funü* 1, no. 2 (1 July 1939): 19.

"Gejie funü lianhe hui xuanyan" (Manifesto of the All Women's Association). In *Zhongguo funü yundong tongshi* (A general history of the Chinese women's movement), edited by Tan Sheying, 157–58. Nanjing: Funü gongming she, 1936.

"Gong ai hui tong ren quan liuxue qi" (A letter from the members of the Gongai hui urging overseas study experience). *Jiangsu*, no. 6 (1903): 159.

"Guangdong funü jiefang xiehui xuanyan ji gangling" (The manifesto and central principles of the Guangdong Women's Emancipation Association; Guangdong Provincial Archives, 1925). In ZFYLZ, 95–97.

"Guangdong nüjie er ci guominhui" (Guangdong women's second citizens conference). *Shenbao* (5 January 1920).

"Guangdong nüjie lianhe hui zhangcheng" (Constitution of the Guangdong UWA). In *Zhongguo funü yundong tongshi* (A general history of the Chinese women's movement), edited by Tan Sheying, 97–104. Nanjing: Funü gongming she, 1936.

"Guangdong nüzi canzheng zhi da yundong" (Major action by the Cantonese women's suffrage movement). *Shenbao* (4 April 1921).

"Guangdong nüzi guomin dahui" (Reporting on the Cantonese women's people's assembly). *Shenbao* (1 January 1920).

"Guangdong zhi nü quan chao" (Guangdong tide of women's rights). *Shenbao* (31 March 1921).

"Guangdong zhi nüzi canzheng yundong si fu" (Four pictures of the Cantonese women's suffrage movement). FNZZ 7, no. 7 (1921).

"Guangzhou funü canzheng da huodong" (Cantonese women's suffrage actions). *Laodong yu funü*, no. 8 (3 April 1921). In *Guangdong funü yundong lishi ziliao*

(Materials on the history of the women's movement in Guangdong), edited by Guangdong sheng funü yundong lishi ziliao bianxuan Weiyuan Hui, 127–29. Guangzhou: Guangdong sheng dang'an guan, 1991.

"Guangzhou nüzi zheng xuanquan xuwen" (Continued report on the Cantonese women's struggle for voting rights). *Minguo ribao* (3 April 1921).

"Guizhou funü aiguo hui zhi daibiaotuan han" (Letter from the representatives of the Guizhou women's patriotic assocation). *Dagong bao* (2 September 1912).

"Guomin dang ganshi xuanjuhui zhi guaiju" (Strange performance at the National-ist Party elections). *Shenbao* (16 September 1912).

"Guomin huiyi cucheng hui quanguo dahui baogao" (Report on the National As-sembly Promotion general meeting). *Minguo ribao* (28 May 1925).

"Guomin huiyi yu funü daibiao wenti" (The citizens' convention and the problem of women's representatives). *Minguo ribao* (22 March 1931).

"Henan nüjie cucheng guomin huiyi zhi dianbao ji xuanyan" (The Henan WNA-PA's telegram and manifesto). *Minguo ribao* (18 February 1925).

"Hu nüjie dingqi kai nüjie guomin dahui" (Shanghai women fix a date to hold a women's national assembly). *Shenbao* (12 March 1925).

"Hu nüjie faqi guomin huiyi cucheng hui" (Shanghai women start an associa-tion for the promotion of the National Assembly), *Minguo ribao* (5 December 1924).

"Hu nüjie guomin huiyi cucheng hui tongdian" (Telegram from the Shanghai re-gion WNAPA). *Dagong bao* (1925). In ZFYLZ, 434.

"Huang Bihun gao quan guo funü" (Huang Bihun informs the nation's women). *Guangdong qunbao* (7 April 1921).

"Huanying nü canzheng huizhang" (Welcome to the women's suffrage leaders). *Minli bao* (10 September 1912).

"Huanying nüzhengzhijia" (Welcome to the women politicians). *Shenbao* (5 Sep-tember 1912).

"Hui dang zao dang zhi yijian" (Criticism on the destruction of a party and the formation of a party). *Minli bao* (7 August 1912).

"Hunan nüjie lianhe hui yijian shu" (Hunan UWA's letter of comment). *Dagong bao* (6–7 May 1921).

"Hunan sheng xianfa—Minguo shiyi nian yiyue yiri" (Constitution of Hunan Province; 1 January 1922). In *Zhongguo zhixian shi ziliao huibian* (Material on China's constitutional history), edited by Miao Quanji, 821. Taipei: Guoshi guan, 1989.

"In Heathen Lands." *Suffragist* 6, no. 47 (14 December 1918): 10.

"International Women's Day." *China at War* 4, no. 4 (May 1940): 5–7.

"Ji Guangdong nüzi guomin dahui" (Record of the Guangdong women citizens conference). *Minguo ribao* (1 January 1920).

"Ji Shanghai funü hui kai chengli da hui" (Report on Shanghai women's associa-tion convenes an establishing meeting). *Shenbao* (1 January 1921).

"Jin funü guomin huiyi cucheng hui chengli xuanyan ji jianzhang" (Tianjin WN-APA's manifesto and regulations). In *Zhongguo funü yundong: Yi ce* (China's

Women's Movement, Vol. 1), edited by Liu Wang Liming, 37–39. Shanghai: Shangwuyin shuguan, 1934.

"Juewu sanba jie tekan" (Special issue on consciousness-raising about International Women's Day). *Minguo ribao* (8 March 1931).

"Li Dazhao jun jiangyan nü quan yundong" (Li Dazhao's speech on the women's movement). In ZFYLZ, 143–45.

Linshi zhengfu gongbao (Provincial government public records), no. 9 (6 February 1912): 6–8.

"Liu dang hebing kaihui ji" (Record of the joint meeting of six parties). *Shenbao* (29 September 1912).

"Liu Ri nüxuehui zazhi fakan ci" (Introducing the *Journal of the Society for Women's Students in Japan*). In *Zhongguo funü yundong tongshi* (A general history of the Chinese women's movement), edited by Tan Sheying, 21. Nanjing: Funü gongming she, 1936.

"Liu Shaobi nüshi deng zhi Chen Shengzhang shu" (Letter from Ms. Liu Shaobi et al. to Provincial Governor Chen). *Guangdong qunbao* (8 April 1921).

"Lun nüzi yi zhuzhong daode" (Discussion on how women ought to pay attention to morality). *Shenbao* (5 September 1912).

"Lundun dian" (Telegram from London). *Shenbao* (15 July 1912).

"Madame Chiang Leads Women of China in Support of Defenders." *China Weekly Review* (7 August 1937): 371.

"Manifesto of the First National Congress of the Kuomintang: January 30, 1924." In *The Kuomintang: Historical Selected Documents, 1894–1969*, edited by Milton J. T. Shieh, 84–85. New York: St. John's University Press, 1970.

"Minsheng xuesheng beifa jun chufa" (Fujian province's student Northern Attack troops depart). *Shenbao* (29 January 1912).

"Miss Wu Chih-mei." In *Who's Who in China*. 4th ed., 3:225. 1950. Reprint, Hong Kong: Chinese Materials Centre, 1982.

"Nan nü bing zun lun" (On respecting both men and women). *Zhongguo xin nüjie zazhi,* no. 4 (1907): 1–6.

"Nanjing dian" (Telegram from Nanjing). *Shenbao* (10 September 1912).

"Nanjing shehui dang dian" (Telegram from the Socialist Party, Nanjing). *Shenbao* (8 March 1912).

"Nü canzheng tuan yan shuo re" (Women's suffrage groups debate and discuss). *Minli bao* (12 April 1912).

"Nü canzheng zhi chengli" (Precedent for women's participation in politics). *Minli bao* (23 September 1912).

"Nü gan si dui" (Women's dare to die brigade). *Tianduo bao* (14 December 1911).

"Nü gan si dui ru jing" (Women's dare to die brigade enters the capital). *Minli bao* (15 January 1912).

"Nü gui" (Women's ghosts). *Zhongguo ribao* (19–20 April 1904).

"'Nü xing' xunkan fakan ci" (Introducing *Women's Star*). *Nü xing*, no. 1 (25 April 1923): 1.

"Nüguomin dahui" (Women's citizens congress). *Guangdong qunbao* (2 July 1921).

"Nühuiyuan dazhan weifeng" (Women's party members' grand display of might). *Shenbao* (20 August 1912).

"Nüjie bei canyu guomin huiyi" (Women prepare to participate in the National Assembly). *Shenbao* (9 December 1924).

"Nüjie canyu guominhuiyi zhi jinxing" (Progress by WNAPA). *Shenbao* (11 December 1924).

"Nüjie canzheng zhi yaoqiu" (The demand by the women's world for participation in politics). *Minli bao* (3 March 1912).

"Nüjie daibiao Zhang [*sic*] Qunying" (Women's representative Zhang Qunying). *Shenbao* (29 February 1912).

"Nüjie daibiao Zhang [*sic*] Qunying deng shang canyiyuan shu" (The petition presented to parliament by Zhang Qunying). *Funü shibao*, no. 5 (1912): 21–22.

"Nüjie Deng Huifang" (The women's world's Deng Huifang). *Shenbao* (5 April 1921).

"Nüjie guomin huiyi cucheng hui chengli ji" (Report on the formation of WNAPA). *Minguo ribao* (22 December 1924).

"Nüjie guomin huiyi cucheng hui choubei huiji" (Record of the preparatory meeting of the WNAPA). *Minguo ribao* (21 December 1924).

"Nüjie guomin huiyi cucheng hui choubeichu tongdian" (Telegram on preparatory matters from WNAPA). *Shenbao* (13 December 1924).

"Nüjie guomin huiyi cucheng hui dian" (Telegram from WNAPA). *Shenbao* (14 December 1924).

"Nüjie guomin huiyi cucheng hui kaihui ji" (Report on the WNAPA meeting). *Shenbao* (11 May 1925).

"Nüjie guomin huiyi cucheng hui yizhou jishi" (Reporting on a week of WNAPA). *Funü zhoubao* (16 February 1925).

"Nüjie guomin huiyi cucheng hui zhangcheng" (WNAPA's constitution). *Shenbao* (21 December 1924).

"Nüjie guomin huiyi cucheng hui zhi faqi" (Advocacy of WNAPA). *Shenbao* (5 December 1924).

"Nüjie hanzhu: Minhui zhuxi Liu nüshi" (Women's world sends letter of respect: People's convention president Madame Liu). *Minguo ribao* (12 May 1931).

"Nüjie huanying Sun, Huang, Chen jilüe" (Brief report on the women's groups welcoming Sun, Huang, and Chen). *Aiguo bao* (18 September 1912).

"Nüjie huanying Xiong Zhuliang xiansheng jishi" (The women's movement welcomes Mr. Xiong Zhuliang). *Dagong bao* (1 June 1921).

"Nüjie lianhe hui xiaoxi" (News from the UWA). *Shenbao* (18 January 1920).

"Nüjie lianhe hui zhi yi an" (United Women's Association Proposal). *Guangdong qunbao* (25 April 1921).

"Nüjie lianhe hui zhi zhanlipin" (The spoils of war for the United Women's Association). *Guangdong qunbao* (29 April 1921).

"Nüjie san tuanti huiyi" (Joint meeting by three women's groups). *Shenbao* (12 March 1921).

"Nüjie yundong xuanju dahuodong" (Large scale activism by the women's movement on votes). *Guangdong qunbao* (30 March 1921).

"Nüjie zhi liang shi" (Two matters of the women's movement). *Shenbao* (1 April 1921).

"Nüjie zhuzhang jiaru guomin huiyi zhi yifengxin" (Letter from the women's movement promoting entrance to the National Assembly). *Shenbao* (30 November 1924).

"Nüquan da huodong" (Big activities for women's rights). *Minli bao* (5 September 1912).

"Nüquan yundong hui xiang guohui qingyuan" (Women's rights petition to the national assembly). *Shenbao* (8 September 1922).

"Nüquan yundong hui zhi tongdian" (Women's rights organizations send a telegram). *Shenbao* (4 December 1924).

"Nüquan yundong hui zhuzhang jiaru guomin huiyi" (The women's rights movement advocates to enter the citizens convention). *Minguo ribao* (4 December 1924).

"Nüquan yundong tongmeng hui xiaoxi" (News on the Women's Rights League). *Shenbao* (4 February 1923).

"Nüshi dama canyiyuan" (Ladies abuse legislators). *Aiguo bao* (11 December 1912).

"Nüzi canzheng an jing zao foujue" (Women's suffrage bill unexpectedly meets disaster and is vetoed). *Minguo ribao* (8 April 1921).

"Nüzi canzheng hui" (Women's suffrage meeting). *Minli bao* (27 September 1912).

"Nüzi canzheng hui kaihui" (Women's Suffrage Association holds a meeting). *Minguo ribao* (28 April 1931).

"Nüzi canzheng hui lai Beijing" (Women's Suffrage Association arrives in Beijing). *Aiguo bao* (14 April 1912).

"Nüzi canzheng hui shang Sun qianzongtong shu" (Message to former President Sun from the Women's Suffrage Association). *Shengjing shibao* (3 April 1912).

"Nüzi canzheng hui shang Sun Zhongshan shu" (Petition from the Women's Suffrage Alliance to Sun Yat-sen). *Shibao* (23 March 1912).

"Nüzi canzheng hui zhang" (Leader of the women's suffrage movement). *Shenbao* (10 September 1912).

"Nüzi canzheng hui zhi quanguo nüjie shu" (Message to the women of the nation from the Women's Suffrage Association). *Minguo ribao* (18 December 1924).

"Nüzi canzheng lun" (Discussion of women's suffrage). *Dagong bao* (27, 28 March 1912).

"Nüzi canzheng lun" (Discussion of women's suffrage). *Shengjing shibao* (24, 26 March 1912).

"Nüzi canzheng quan diaocha" (Investigation into women's suffrage rights). *Minguo ribao* (15 June 1931).

"Nüzi canzheng quan you li yi jie" (Women's suffrage rights suffer another defeat). *Shenbao* (13 November 1912).

"Nüzi canzheng quan zhi wo jian" (My view on women's suffrage rights). *Shenbao* (6 April 1912).

"Nüzi canzheng tongmeng hui" (Women's Suffrage Alliance). *Shenbao* (13 September 1912).

"Nüzi canzheng tongmeng hui" (Women's Suffrage Alliance). *Shibao* (31 March 1912).

"Nüzi canzheng tongmeng hui chengli zhisheng" (Glorious marker of the founding of the Women's Suffrage Alliance). *Nüzi baihua bao*, no. 2 (1912): 35–40.

"Nüzi canzheng tongmeng hui dian" (Telegram from the Women's Suffrage Alliance). *Minli bao* (31 August 1912).

"Nüzi canzheng tongmeng hui jianzhang" (Regulations of the Women's Suffrage Alliance). *Tianduo bao* (3 December 1911).

"Nüzi canzheng tongmeng hui jianzhang cao an" (Regulations of the Women's Suffrage Alliance). *Nüzi baihua bao*, no. 3 (1912): 37–38.

"Nüzi canzheng xiehui tebie huiyi" (Special meeting of the Women's Suffrage Association). *Shenbao* (6 June 1925).

"Nüzi canzheng xiejin hui dahui ji" (Report on the general meeting of the progressive association for women's participation in politics). *Shenbao* (26 December 1922).

"Nüzi canzheng xiejin hui zhiyuan huiji" (Members report on the women's suffrage progressive association meeting). *Shenbao* (18 December 1924).

"Nüzi canzheng yundong zhi yubo" (Repercussions of the women's suffrage movement). *Minguo ribao* (11 April 1921).

"Nüzi canzheng zhi sichao" (Trend of thought for women's suffrage). *Minli bao* (10 August 1912).

"Nüzi danao canyi yuan ji" (Report on women causing havoc in parliament). *Shengjing shibao* (31 March 1912).

"Nüzi danao Tongmeng hui" (Women disrupt the Revolutionary Alliance). *Minli bao* (18 August 1912).

"Nüzi houyuan hui beifa jun qiujidui jianzhang" (Regulations of the women's reinforcement northern attack relief brigade). *Minli bao* (4 February 1912).

"Nüzi houyuan hui jianzhang" (Regulations of the Women's Reinforcement Association). *Shibao* (7 December 1911).

"Nüzi jiangyou wanquan canzheng quan" (In the future women will have full political rights). *Shenbao* (8 January 1912).

"Nüzi jingwu lianxi dui" (Women's Training Troop). *Tianduo bao* (27 January 1912).

"Nüzi jingwu lianxi dui chengli" (The Women's Training Troop is established). *Tianduo bao* (14 January 1912).

"Nüzi lianhe hui wen shenghui" (UWA makes a request to the provincial parliament). *Shenbao* (30 March 1921).

"Nüzi tongmeng hui zhi zuzhi" (Formation of the Women's Alliance). *Shenbao* (22 February 1912).

"Nüzi tuan zhi jinxing" (Progress by women's groups). *Minli bao* (30 August 1912).

"Nüzi xuanju quan" (Women's electoral rights). *Shenbao* (8 November 1912).

"Nüzi xuanju yundong zhi shengli" (Victory in the women's voting movement). *Guangdong qunbao* (20 February 1921).

"Nüzi yaoqiu canzheng quan" (Women demand the right to participate in politics). *Minli bao* (23 March 1912).

"Nüzi yaoqiu canzheng quan zhi baodong" (Rebellious action by women demanding the right to participate in politics). *Dagong bao* (30 March 1912).

"Nüzi yaoqiu canzheng zhi shengyuan" (Support expressed for women's demand for suffrage). *Minguo ribao* (28 January 1920).

"Nüzi yaoqiu xuanju quan fengchao" (Current tide of women demand voting rights). *Minguo ribao* (4 April 1921).

"Nüzi yi wuli yaoqiu canzheng quan" (Women use military force to demand the right to participate in politics). *Shenbao* (24 March 1912).

"Nüzi yingdang chengshou yichan de liyou he duiyu fandui pai shencha yuan de zhonggao" (The reasons why women ought to have inheritance rights and a sincere message to the examiners who oppose this). *Dagong bao* (21 May 1921).

"Nüzi zheng xuanju quan" (Women vie for suffrage rights). *Shenbao* (1 April 1921).

"People's Assembly to Be Held on Nov. 12 as Scheduled." *China Weekly Review* (3 October 1936): 161.

"Qing dajia kuaikuai quan nüzi jin xuexiao qu" (Please everybody persuade girls to go to school). *Shenbao* (7 May 1921).

"Quanti nüjie qingyuan shencha hui jishi" (Investigative report on the request by the entire women's movement). *Dagong bao* (17 May 1921).

"Quanzhe nüjie lianhe hui xuanyuan" (Manifesto of the All Zhejiang UWA). In *Zhongguo funü yundong tongshi* (A general history of the Chinese women's movement), edited by Tan Sheying, 105–6. Nanjing: Funü gongming she, 1936.

"Riben liuxue nüxuesheng Gongai hui zhangcheng" (Women students in Japan and the constitution of the Mutual Love Society). *Jiangsu*, no. 2 (1903): 155–57.

"San jie nü canzheng yuan de ming'e" (Quotas for women in the third PPC). *Funü yuekan* (1941).

"Shandong nüquan tongmeng hui chengli" (Women's Rights Alliance established in Shandong). *Shenbao* (26 December 1922).

"Shanghai funü hui jinri kai tebie hui" (Shanghai Women's Association holds special meeting today). *Shenbao* (11 March 1921).

"Shanghai funü hui kaihui ji" (Report on the meeting of the Shanghai Women's Association). *Shenbao* (28 April 1921).

"Shanghai funü yundong weiyuan hui xuanyan" (Manifesto of the Shanghai Women's Movement Bureau). In *Zhongguo funü yundong tongshi* (A general history of the Chinese women's movement), edited by Tan Sheying, 145–46. Nanjing: Funü gongming she, 1936.

"Shanghai gejie funü lianhe hui chengli" (Meeting for the formation of SAWA). *Shenbao* (6 June 1925).

"Shanghai mindang nü dangyuan zhi Zhongshan han" (Women GMD party members send Sun Yat-sen a message). *Minguo ribao* (29 November 1924).

"Shehui dang nü dangyuan Lin Zongsu" (Women Socialist Party member, Lin Zongsu). *Minli bao* (8 January 1912).

"Shehui dang zhi jinxing" (The advance of the socialist party). *Tianduo bao* (1 December 1911).

"Shen Nüshi nanzheng zhi tanlun" (Madame Shen's presentation on the southern tour). *Minguo ribao* (15 August 1913).

"Shen Peizhen danao Yadong xinwenshe" (Shen Peizhen causes chaos in the East Asia News office). *Shenbao* (19 December 1912).

"Shen Peizhen nüshi dian" (Telegram from Madame Shen Peizhen), *Shenbao* (25 March 1912).

"Sheng hui duiyu nüzi canzheng an zhi xingshi" (The situation of the provincial parliament toward the women's suffrage bill). *Guangdong qunbao* (31 March 1921).

"Shenzhou nüjie canzheng tongmeng hui ji shi" (Report on Shenzhou Women's Association and Alliance for Women's Suffrage). *Shenbao* (2 March 1912).

"Shenzhou nüjie gonghe xiejishe kaihui ji shi" (Recent meetings of the Shenzhou Women's Assistance Society). *Shibao* (22 March 1912).

"Shi Liang tongzhi shengping" (The life story of comrade Shi Liang). *Funü zuzhi yu huodong* 5 (1985): 42–43.

"Shi Liang tongzhi yiti gaobie yishi zai Beijing juxing" (Farewell funeral for Comrade Shi Liang held in Beijing). *Renmin ribao* (12 September 1985).

"Shiping san" (Timely critiques). *Shenbao* (6 September 1912).

"Sichuan sheng xianfa caoan" (Draft constitution for Sichuan Province). In *Zhongguo zhixian shi ziliao huibian* (Material on China's constitutional history), edited by Miao Quanji, 856–57, Taipei: Guoshi guan, 1989.

"Sun xiansheng zai Guangdong nüzi shifan dier xiao yanshuo" (Mr. Sun's speech to the Guangdong Girls' No. 2 Normal School). *Minli bao* (13 May 1912).

"Sun Zhongshan xiansheng ru jing hou zhi di yi dahui" (Sun Yat-sen's first meeting after arriving in the capital). *Minli bao* (31 August 1912).

"Tang Qunying da Changsha nao bao" (Tang Qunying causes chaos at the Changsha news). *Minli bao* (28 February–2 March 1913).

"Tang Qunying deng wu ren" (Tang Qunying et al. 5 people). *Shenbao* (11 December 1912).

"Tang Shen liang nüshi zhi moyan" (Tang and Shen, the two ladies' black tears). *Shenbao* (3 September 1912).

"Tianjin funü guomin huiyi cucheng hui chengli" (The founding of the Tianjin WNAPA). *Minguo ribao* (31 December 1924).

"Tianjin funü guomin huiyi cucheng hui huiyuan dahui" (The general meeting of the Tianjin WNAPA). *Minguo ribao* (25 February 1925).

"Tichang funü canzhengquan" (Advocating women's suffrage). *Shengjing shibao* (4 April 1912).

"Tongmeng hui" (Revolutionary Alliance). *Shenbao* (23 August 1912).

"Tongmeng hui gaizu" (Reform of the Revolutionary Alliance). *Shenbao* (26 August 1912).

"Tongmeng hui hebing gaizu jiwen" (Report on the merger and reform of the Revolutionary Alliance). *Shenbao* (16 August 1912).

"Tongmeng hui nühuiyuan zhi fenji" (Anger erupts from the women Revolutionary Alliance members). *Dagong bao* (16 August 1912).

"Tongmeng nüzi jingwu lianxi dui jianzhang" (Regulations of the Alliance for the Women's Training Troop). *Minli bao* (13 February 1912).

"Wanguo nüzi canzheng tongmeng hui huizhang dao Hu" (International Women's Suffrage Alliance leaders arrive in Shanghai). *Minli bao* (2 September 1912).

"Womanhood Glorified." *Suffragist* 7, no. 30 (2 August 1919): 2.

"Women Postal Workers Can Marry." *China at War* 8, no. 4 (April 1942): 51–52.

Wu Zhiying. "Wu Zhiying fu nüzi Beifadui jun shu" (Wu Zhiying's letter on the Women's Northern Attack Brigade). *Minli bao* (17 January 1912).

"Wuhan nüjie qutan lu" (Record of the interesting discussions of the Wuhan women's world). *Shenbao* (14 October 1912).

"Xianfa taolun zhong zhi yi han" (A letter regarding the discussion of the constitution). *Dagong bao* (5 May 1921).

"Xiao shuo" (Speaking briefly). *Shenbao* (3 September 1912).

"Xin shidai, xin shiming, xin funü" (New times, new mission, new women). *Xin funü* (March 1947): 4.

"Xuanju quan ke yu bianfa xiguan xiang juezhan" (The vote and the custom of braids face a decisive battle). *Shenbao* (4 November 1912).

"Xu ji Yuenüjie zhi canzheng yundong" (Continued report on the Guangdong women's suffrage movement). *Shenbao* (5 April 1921).

"Xuejie yi su shefa yi baoquan nüxue zhi ming yu" (The education sector ought to think of a way to preserve the reputation of girls' schools). *Zhongguo ribao* (10 October 1907).

"Yan'an funüjie xianzheng cujin hui gao bianqu meimei shu" (Letter to the sisterhood of the border regions from YWAPC). *Zhongguo funü* 1, no. 9 (8 March 1940): 12–13.

"Yan'an funüjie xianzheng cujin hui gao quanguo meimei shu" (Letter to the sisterhood of the nation on the YWAPC). *Zhongguo funü* 1, no. 9 (8 March 1940): 11–12.

"Yan'an funüjie xianzheng cujin hui zhi Jiang Yizhang dian" (Telegram to Assembly Head Chiang from the YWAPC). *Zhongguo funü* 1, no. 9 (8 March 1940): 2.

"Yan'an funüjie xianzheng cujin hui zhi Song Meiling xiansheng han" (Letter to the esteemed Song Meiling from YWAPC). *Zhongguo funü* 1, no. 9 (8 March 1940): 14–15.

"Yan'an funüjie xianzheng cujin hui zhi Song Qingling, He Xiangning xiansheng han" (Letter to the esteemed Song Qingling and He Xiangning from YWAPC). *Zhongguo funü* 1, no. 9 (8 March 1940): 13–14.

"Yangzhou tongxin" (Communication from Yangzhou). *Shenbao* (31 January 1912).

"Yaoqiu canzheng zhi guaiju" (Strange theatrics in the demand for suffrage). *Shenbao* (1, 4 December 1912).

"Yaoqiu nüzi canzheng quan zhi wuli" (The military force of the demands for women's suffrage). *Shi bao* (23 March 1912).

"Yaoqiu nüzi canzheng quan zhi zhuanwen" (Propaganda materials of those demanding women's suffrage). *Shenbao* (24 May 1913).

"Yichan zhidu he nannü pingdeng" (Inheritance and sex equality). *Shenbao* (5 March 1921).

"Yingguo guohui diyi nü yiyuan" (England's first woman member in parliament). *Shenbao* (1 February 1920).

"Yingguo nannü zhi zhengquan" (Male and female political rights in England). *Shenbao* (21 April 1921).

"Yingguo nüzi xuanju quan fada" (Flourishing of voting among women in England). *Funü gongming*, no. 6 (1929): 40.

"You nüzi Tang Qunying" (A woman called Tang Quying). *Minli bao* (31 March 1912).

"Yue nü daiyishi zhongzheng canzheng" (Cantonese women parliamentarians fight for suffrage). *Shenbao* (10 October 1912).

"Yue nüjie er ci dahui ji" (Report on the second meeting of the Cantonese women's movement). *Minguo ribao* (15 January 1920).

"Yue nüjie lianhe hui zhi jinxing" (Progress for the Canton UWA). *Minguo ribao* (27 January 1920).

"Yue nüjie zhi pai qie huiyi" (Cantonese women's meeting to exclude concubines). *Minguo ribao* (31 January 1920).

"Yue nüzi canzheng yundong chenggong" (The Cantonese women's suffrage movement has success). *Dagong bao* (20 May 1921).

"Yue sheng nü daiyishi lizheng nüzi can zheng quan" (Women parliamentarians in Guangdong Province argue for women's suffrage rights). *Shenbao* (28 September 1912).

"Yue yihui foujue nüzi canzheng quan taidu" (Cantonese parliament position rejects women's suffrage rights). *Shenbao* (17 November 1912).

"Zai xun sheng yiyuan oushang nüdaibiao an" (Another request to the provincial parliamentarians on the case of the beating and wounding of the women representatives." *Laodong yu funü*, no. 11 (24 April 1921): 4.

"Zhejiang nüzi zheng canyu zhixian quan" (Zhejiang women vie for the right to participate in writing the constitution). *Shenbao* (22 August 1921).

"Zhejiang sheng xianfa shixing fa" (Executive law on the Zhejiang Province Constitution; 9 September 1921). In *Zhongguo zhixian shi ziliao huibian* (Material on China's constitutional history), edited by Miao Quanji, 724, Taipei: Guoshi guan, 1989.

"Zhi na nüzi zhi aiguo xin" (Building up patriotism among women). *Hubei xuesheng jie* (The Hubei students' world), no. 3 (March 1903): 65–67.

"Zhian jingcha tiaoli" (Police ordinances on public order). *Zhengfu gongbao* (Government public news), no. 653 (3 March 1914).

"Zhonggong zhongyang funü weiyuan hui gongzuo baogao (jielu)" (Report by the women's bureau for the central committee—excerpts; 1927). In ZFYLZ, 697.

"Zhongguo funü yu guoji funü jie" (Chinese women and International Women's Day). *Minguo ribao* (9 March 1931).

"Zhongguo furen hui zhangcheng" (Manifesto of the China Women's Association). *Zhongguo xin nüjie zazhi*, no. 3 (1907): 107–14.

"Zhongguo gongchangdang di er ci quanguo daibiao dahui guanyu funü yundong de jueyi" (Resolutions relating to the women's movement of the 2nd National People's Congress of the CCP; 23 July 1922). In ZFYLZ, 29–31.

"Zhongguo gongchandang di san ci quanguo daibiao da hui guanyu funü yundong jueyi an" (Draft resolutions relating to the women's movement of the 3rd National People's Congress of the CCP; June 1923). In ZFYLZ, 66–68.

"Zhongguo gongchandang di sanci zhongyang kuoda zhexing weiyuan hui guanyu funü yundong yijue an" (Draft resolutions relating to the women's movement of the third enlarged plenum of the CCP Executive Committee; September 1926). In ZFYLZ, 475–78.

"Zhongguo gongchandang di si quanguo daibiao dahui duiyu funü yundong de yijue an" (Draft resolutions relating to the women's movement of the 4th National Congress; 1925). In ZFYLZ, 281.

"Zhongguo gongchandang funübu guanyu Zhongguo funü yundong de baogao (jielu)" (Report on the Chinese women's movement by the CCP women's bureau—excerpts; 24 June 1924). In ZFYLZ, 168–86.

"Zhongguo guomindang huiyi" (China's Nationalist Party meeting). *Shenbao* (9 September 1912).

"Zhongguo liu Ri nüxuesheng hui zhangcheng" (Manifesto of the Society for Women Students in Japan). *Zhongguo xin nüjie zazhi*, no. 2 (1907): 76–81.

"*Zhongguo xin nüjie zazhi* fakan ci" (Introducing *China's New Women's World*). *Zhongguo xin nüjie zazhi*, no. 1 (1907): 2.

"Zhonghua minguo nüjie daibiao yaoqiu canzhengquan jiangyuan shu" (Memorial demanding women's suffrage by women representatives of the Republic of China). *Shengjing shibao* (12 March 1912).

"Zhonghua nüzi guomin jun faqi ren" (The initiator of the Chinese women's army). *Minli bao* (11 January 1912).

"Zhonghua nüzi guomin jun quandui" (Entire brigade of the Chinese women's army). *Minli bao* (10 January 1912).

"Ziyou tan" (Speaking freely). *Shenbao* (4 September 1912).

"Ziyou tan" (Speaking freely). *Shenbao* (26 December 1912).

"Zuori zhi sheng yi hui shiji" (Yesterday's events in the provincial parliament). *Guangdong qunbao* (20 February 1921).

Author-Identified Sources

Au Chi Kin. "Wu Zhiying." In *BDQP*, 236–38.

———. "Yan Bin." In *BDQP*, 258–61.

———. "Zhang Zhujun." In *BDQP*, 310–13.

Backus Rankin, Mary. "The Emergence of Women at the End of the Ch'ing: The

Case of Chiu Chin." In *Women in Chinese Society*, edited by Margery Wolf and Roxane Witke, 39–66. Stanford, CA: Stanford University Press, 1975.

Bailey, Paul J. *Gender and Education in China: Gender discourses and women's schooling in the early twentieth century*. London: Routledge, 2007.

Banaszak, Lee Ann. *Why Movements Succeed or Fail: Opportunity, Culture and the Struggle for Woman Suffrage*. Princeton, NJ: Princeton University Press, 1996.

Barlow, Tani. *The Question of Women in Chinese Feminism*. Durham, NC: Duke University Press, 2004.

———. "Theorizing Woman: Funü, Guojia, Jiating (Chinese women, Chinese state, Chinese family)." In *Feminism and History*, edited by Joan Wallach Scott, 48–75. Oxford: Oxford University Press, 1996.

Beahan, Charlotte, L. "Feminism and Nationalism in the Chinese Women's Press, 1902–1911." *Modern China* 1, no. 4 (October 1975): 379–416.

———. "The Women's Movement and Nationalism in Late Ch'ing China." PhD diss., Columbia University, 1976.

Beijing shi funü lianhe hui, ed. *Beijing nüjie* (Prominent Beijing women). Beijing: Beijing chubanshe, 1985.

Bernhardt, Kathryn. *Women and Property in China, 960–1949*. Stanford, CA: Stanford University Press, 1999.

Bianco, Lucien. "Peasant Responses to CCP Mobilization Politics, 1937–1945." In *New Perspectives on the Chinese Communist Revolution*, edited by Tony Saich and Hans van de Ven, 175–91. Armonk, NY: M.E. Sharpe, 1995.

Blackburn, Susan. "Winning the Vote for Women in Indonesia." *Australian Feminist Studies*, no. 14 (1999): 207–18.

———. "Women's Suffrage and Democracy in Indonesia." In *Women's Suffrage in Asia: Gender, Nationalism and Democracy*, edited by Louise Edwards and Mina Roces, 79–105. London: RoutledgeCurzon, 2004.

Bock, Gisela, and Susan James, eds. *Beyond Equality and Difference: Citizenship, Feminist Politics and Female Subjectivity*. London: Routledge, 1992.

Borthwick, Sally. "Changing Concepts of the Role of Women from the Late Qing to the May Fourth Period." In *Ideal and Reality: Social and Political Change in Modern China, 1860–1949*, edited by David Pong and Edmund S. K. Fung, 63–91. Lanham, MD: University Press of America, 1985.

Cai Yuanpei. "Ge tuanti qing feizhi zhian jingcha tiaoli" (Various groups request the abolition of the Police Ordinances on Public Order). *Chenbao* (15 October 1922).

Catt, Carrie Chapman. "The New China: She Sits in the Gallery and Looks Down on China's Ten Women Legislators, Who Had Been Called a Myth." *Woman's Journal* (5 October 1912): 314–15.

Chen Chih-mai. "The Post-War Government of China." *Journal of Politics* 9 (1947): 503–21.

Chen Duxiu. "Chen Duxiu xiansheng zai nüjie lianhe hui yanci" (Mr. Chen Duxiu's speech to the United Women's Association). *Guangdong qunbao* (31 January; 1 February 1921).

———. "Funü wenti yu shehui zhuyi" (The woman question and socialism). *Guangdong qunbao* (30 January 1921). In *Wusi shiqi funü wenti wenxuan* (Collected essays on the women problem in the May Fourth Movement), edited by Zhonghua quanguo funü lianhe hui funü yundong lishi yanjiu, 99–105. Hong Kong: Sanlian; Beijing: Shenghui dushu zhishi, 1981.

———. "The Woman Question and Socialism." *Chinese Studies in History* 31, no. 2 (Winter 1997–98): 90–93.

Chen Huangxing. "Nüzi canzheng zhi taolun—Chen Huanxing nüshi lai han" (Discussion on women's suffrage—Letter from Madame Chen Huanxing). *Minli bao* (26 March 1912).

Chen Jiangtao. "Jinhou woguo funü yingyou zhi zhengfa quan" (Women of my country ought to have political rights). FNZZ 13, no. 10 (1927): 1–3.

Chen Lingxia. "Nüzi canzheng zhi xiansheng" (First sounds of women's suffrage), *Nüzi baihua bao*, no. 6 (1912): 27–30.

Chen Wenqing. "Zhongguo zhengzhi yu nüzi canzheng" (Women's suffrage and China's politics). *Funü zhoubao* (28 May 1924).

Chen Xiefen. "Crisis in the Women's World." Translated by Jennifer Carpenter. In *Writing Women in Modern China: An Anthology of Women's Literature from the Early Twentieth Century*, edited by Amy D. Dooling and Kristina M. Torgeson, 83–86. New York: Columbia University Press, 1998.

———. "Duli pian" (On independence). *Nüxue bao* (1902 or 1903). In XMZS, 43.

———. "Nüjie kewei" (Dangers for the women's world). *Zhongguo ribao* 26 (27 April 1904).

Chen Yan'an. "Quan nüzi liuxue shuo" (Urging women to study overseas). *Jiangsu*, no. 3 (1903): 155–56.

Chen Yinxuan. "Nannü pingdeng yu fuqi caichan zhi de wenti" (Equality between men and women and the problem of the property system). *Nüzi yuekan* 1, no. 6 (1933): 33–40.

Cheng, Eileen J. "Gendered Spectacles: Lu Xun on Gazing at Women and Other Pleasures." *Modern Chinese Literature and Culture* 16, no. 1 (Spring 2004): 1–36.

Cheng Weikun. "Going Public Through Education: Female Reformers and Girls' Schools in Late Qing Beijing." *Late Imperial China* 21, no. 1 (June 2000): 107–44.

Cheng Xiluo. "Bu zuzhang nüzi canzheng" (Opposing women's participation in politics). *Dagong bao* (16 May 1921).

Chiang Yung-ching. "Hu Han-min's Ideas on Women's Rights and His Achievements." *Chinese Studies in History* (Summer 1977): 34–72.

Ch'ien Tuan-sheng. *The Government and Politics of China, 1912–1949*. 1950. Reprint, Stanford, CA: Stanford University Press, 1970.

———. "War-Time Government in China." *American Political Science Review*, no. 5 (October 1942): 850–72.

China Handbook, 1937–1945. New York: Macmillan, 1947.

Chou Bih-er, Cal Clark, and Janet Clark. *Women in Taiwan Politics*. Boulder, CO: Lynne Rienner, 1990.

Chow Kai Wing. "Chen Xiefen." In BDQP, 21–23.

Chow Tse-tsung. *The May Fourth Movement: Intellectual Revolution in Modern China*. Stanford, CA: Stanford University Press, 1960.

Chu Wo [Ding Chuwo]. "Nüzi jiating geming shuo" (On the women's family revolution). *Nüzi shijie*, no. 4 (1904): 2.

Chun Xiu. "Xuanju jianshuo" (Brief overview of the elections). *Aiguo bao* (6 and 7 December 1912).

Chuzo Ichiko. "Political and Institutional Reform, 1901–1911." In *The Cambridge History of China*. Vol. 11, edited by Denis Twitchett and John K. Fairbank, 375–415. Cambridge, UK: Cambridge University Press, 1980.

Ci Jian. "Nü guomin" (Women citizens). *Zhongguo xin nüjie zazhi*, no. 5 (1907): 121.

Class Eight of the No. 1 Girls' Normal School. "Zhi shengxian shenchayuan Cheng Xiluo shu" (Reply to examiner of the provincial constitution, Cheng Xiluo). *Dagong bao* (24–26, 28 May 1921).

Class Seven of the No. 1 Girls' Normal School. "Zhi Cheng Xiluo shu" (Reply to Cheng Xiluo). *Dagong bao* (18 May 1921).

Coble, Parks M. *Facing Japan: Chinese Politics and Japanese Imperialism, 1931–1937*. Cambridge, MA: Harvard University Asia Center, 1991.

———. "The National Salvation Association as a Political Party." In *Roads Not Taken: The Struggle of Opposition Parties in Twentieth-Century China*, edited by Roger B. Jeans, 135–47. Boulder, CO: Westview, 1992.

Collins, L. E. "The New Women: A Psychohistorical Study of the Chinese Feminist Movement from 1900 to the Present." PhD diss., Yale University, 1976.

Cott, Nancy F. "Early Twentieth-Century Feminism in Political Context: A Comparative Look at Germany and the United States." In *Suffrage and Beyond: International Feminist Perspectives*, edited by Caroline Daley and Melanie Nolan, 234–51. Auckland: Auckland University Press, 1994.

Croll, Elisabeth. *Changing Identities of Chinese Women: Rhetoric, Experience and Self-Perception in Twentieth Century China*. London: Zed Books, 1995.

———. *Feminism and Socialism in China*. London: Routledge & Kegan Paul, 1978.

Crook, Isobel, and David Crook. *Revolution in a Chinese Village: Ten Mile Inn*. 1959. Reprint, London: Routledge & Kegan Paul, 1979.

Davin, Delia. "Women in the Liberated Areas." In *Women in China: Studies in Social Change and Feminism*, edited by Marilyn B. Young, 73–91. Ann Arbor: Center for Chinese Studies, University of Michigan, 1973.

Deng Yingchao. "Lüetan funü yu canzheng" (Speaking briefly about women and political participation), *Funü xinyun* (The new women's movement) 5, no. 3 (1943). In *Cai Chang, Deng Yingchao, Kang Keqing funü jiefang wenti wenxuan, 1938–1987* (A collection of essays on women's liberation by Cai Chang, Deng Yingchao, and Kang Keqing, 1938–1987), edited by Zhonghua quanguo funü lianhe hui, 80–81. Bejing: Renmin chubanshe, 1988.

Diamond, Norma. "Women Under Kuomintang Rule: Variations on the Feminine Mystique." *Modern China* 1, no. 1 (January 1975): 3–45.

Dikötter, Frank. *The Age of Openness: China Before Mao*. Hong Kong: Hong Kong University Press, forthcoming.

Ding Chuwo [see Chu Wo].

Ding Ling. "Thoughts on March 8." In *I Myself Am a Woman: Selected Writings of Ding Ling*, edited by Tani E. Barlow with Gary J. Bjorge, 316–21. Boston: Beacon Press, 1989.

Dirlik, Arif. "The Ideological Foundations of the New Life Movement: A Study in Counterrevolution," *Journal of Asian Studies* 34, no. 4 (August 1975): 945–80.

Dong, Madeleine Yue. "Unofficial History and Gender Boundary Crossing in the Early Republic: Shen Peizhen and Xiaofengxian." In *Gender in Motion: Divisions of Labor and Cultural Change in Late Imperial and Modern China*, edited by Bryna Goodman and Wendy Larson, 169–89. Lanham, MD: Rowman & Littlefield, 2005.

Dooling, Amy D., and Kristina M. Torgeson, eds. *Writing Women in Modern China: An Anthology of Women's Literature from the Early Twentieth Century*. New York: Columbia University Press, 1998.

Dorr, Rheta Childe. "April 26th Hearing before the Senate Suffrage Committee." *Suffragist* (28 April 1917): 9.

Du He. "Xining mo nüshi zhi ba da hutong jijieshu" (An amusing proposal from Madam X to the prostitutes at Laneway no. 8). *Shenbao* (22 November 1912).

Du Junhui. *Funü wenti jianghua* (Talking on women's problems). Shanghai: Xin zhi shudian, 1936.

Du Qingchi. "Nan nü dou shi yiyang" (Men and women are all the same). *Nüzi shijie*, no. 6 (1904): 13.

Du Youdi. "Nannü pingquan zuyi jiuguo" (Gender equality and national salvation). *Minli bao* (10 June 1912).

DuBois, Ellen Carol. *Feminism and Suffrage: The Emergence of an Independent Women's Movement in America, 1848–1869*. 1978. Reprint, Ithaca, NY: Cornell University Press, 1980.

———. "Woman Suffrage Around the World: Three Phases of Suffragist Internationalism." In *Suffrage and Beyond: International Feminist Perspectives*, edited by Caroline Daley and Melanie Nolan, 252–76. Auckland: Auckland University Press, 1994.

———., and Robert Cherny, eds. *Woman Suffrage: The View from the Pacific*. Special issue, *Pacific Historical Review* 69, no. 4 (November 2000).

Dun Gen. "Bianzi yu xuanju quan zhi guanxi" (The connection between braids and voting rights). *Shenbao* (31 October 1912).

———. "Bobo nüzi canzheng quan" (Expressing my views on women's suffrage). *Shenbao* (18 March 1912).

———. "Lixiang dianbao" (Ideal telegrams). *Shenbao* (16 October 1912).

———. "Quan Shen Peizhen nüshi gaiming shuo" (Persuading Madame Shen Peizhen to change her name). *Shenbao* (24 November 1912).

Eastman, Lloyd E. *The Abortive Revolution: China under Nationalist Rule, 1927–1937*. Cambridge, MA: Harvard University Press, 1974.

Edwards, Louise. "Chin Sung-ts'en's *A Tocsin for Women*: The Dexterous Merger of Radicalism and Conservatism in Feminism of the Early Twentieth Century." *Jindai zhongguo funü shi yanjiu* (June 1994): 117–40.

———. "Chinese Women's Campaigns for Suffrage: Nationalism, Confucianism and Political Agency." In *Women's Suffrage in Asia: Gender, Nationalism, Democracy*, edited by Louise Edwards and Mina Roces, 59–78. London: Routledge-Curzon, 2004.

———. "Constraining Women's Political Work with 'Women's Work': The Chinese Communist Party and Women's Participation in Politics." In *Chinese Women: Living and Working*, edited by Anne E. McLaren, 109–30. London: RoutledgeCurzon, 2004.

———. "Co-opting the Chinese Women's Suffrage Movement for the Fifth Modernisation—Democracy." *Asian Studies Review* 26, no. 1 (September 2002): 285–307.

———. "Dressing for Power: Scholars' Robes, School Uniforms and Military Attire in China." In *The Politics of Dress in Asia and the Americas*, edited by Mina Roces and Louise Edwards. Eastbourne, UK: Sussex Academic, 2007.

———. "From Gender Equality to Gender Difference: Feminist Campaigns for Quotas for Women in Politics." *Twentieth Century China* 24, no. 2 (April 1999): 69–105.

———. "Hua Mulan." In *Biographical Dictionary of Chinese Women: Antiquity to the Sui Dynasty*, edited by Lily Lee. Armonk, NY: M.E. Sharpe, forthcoming.

———. "Lin Zongsu." In BDTC, 347–50.

———. "Liu Wang Liming." In BDTC, 374–77.

———. *Men and Women in Qing China: Gender in the Red Chamber Dream*. Leiden: E.J. Brill, 1988; Honolulu: University of Hawaii Press, 2001.

———. "Moving from the Vote into Citizenship: Crafting Chinese Women's Political Citizenship." *Berliner China-Hefte* 29 (2005): 5–17.

———. "Narratives of Race and Nation in China: Women's Suffrage in the Early Twentieth Century." *Women's Studies International Forum* 25, no. 6 (November–December 2002): 619–30.

———. "Opposition to Women's Suffrage in China: Confronting Modernity in Governance." In *Women in Republican China*, edited by Mechthild Leutner and Nicola Spakowski, 107–28. Münster, Germany: LIT, 2004.

———. "Policing the Modern Woman in Republican China." *Modern China* 26, no. 2 (April 2000): 115–47.

———. "Tang Qunying." In BDTC, 504–9.

———. "Women in the People's Republic of China: New Challenges to the Grand Gender Narrative." In *Women in Asia: Tradition, Modernity and Globalisation*, edited by Louise Edwards and Mina Roces, 59–82. Sydney and Ann Arbor: Allen & Unwin and University of Michigan Press, 2000.

———. "Women Warriors and Amazons of the mid Qing Texts *Jinghua yuan* and *Honglou meng*." *Modern Asian Studies* 29, no. 2 (1995), 225–55.

———. "Women's Suffrage in China: Challenging Scholarly Conventions." *Pacific Historical Review* 69, no. 4 (November 2000): 617–39.

———. "Wu Yifang." In BDTC, 561–64.

———. "Zhang Mojun." In BDTC, 685–88.

———. "Zhanzheng dui xiandai Zhongguo funü canzheng yundong de yinxiang: 'Weiji nüxing' de wenti" (The impact of war on women's suffrage in China: The problem of "crisis femininity"). In *Bainian Zhongguo nüquan sichao yanjiu* (Research on one hundred years of Chinese feminist thought), edited by Wang Zheng and Chen Yan, 220–26. Shanghai: Fudan University 2005.

———., and Mina Roces, eds., *Women's Suffrage in Asia: Gender, Nationalism and Democracy* (London: RoutledgeCurzon, 2004).

Elvin, Mark. "Female Virtue and the State." *Past and Present*, no. 104 (August 1984): 110–52.

Esherick, Joseph W. *Reform and Revolution in China: The 1911 Revolution in Hunan and Hubei.* Berkeley: University of California Press, 1976.

———. "War and Revolution: Chinese Society during the 1940s." *Twentieth Century China* 27, no. 1 (November 2001): 1–37.

Evans, Richard J. *Comrades and Sisters: Feminism, Socialism and Pacificism in Europe, 1870–1945.* Sussex: Wheatsheaf Books; New York: St. Martin's Press, 1987.

———. *The Feminists.* London: Croom Helm, 1977.

Fairbank, John King *The Great Chinese Revolution, 1800–1985.* New York: Harper & Row, 1986.

Fang Junji. "Yu nüxue yi fu nüquan shuo" (Using women's education to recover women's rights). *Jiangsu*, no. 3 (1903): 157.

Feng Fei. *Nüxing lun* (Discussing women). Shanghai: Zhonghua shuju, 1923.

Fincher, John. *Chinese Democracy: The Self-Government Movement in Local, Provincial and National Politics, 1905–1914.* London: Croom Helm; Canberra: Australian National University Press, 1981.

Finnane, Antonia. "What Should Chinese Women Wear? A National Problem." *Modern China* 22, no. 2 (April 1996): 99–131.

Fitzgerald, John. *Awakening China: Politics, Culture, and Class in the Nationalist Revolution.* Stanford, CA: Stanford University Press, 1996.

———. "The Origins of the Illiberal Party Newspaper: Print Journalism in China's Nationalist Revolution." *Republican China* 21, no. 2 (April 1996): 1–22.

Fletcher, Ian, Nym Mayhall, and Philippa Levine, eds. *Women's Suffrage in the British Empire.* London: Routledge, 2000.

Fo Zai. "Nü guomin" (Women citizens). *Nüzi shijie* 6 (July 1907). In *"Nüzi shijie" wen xuan* (Collected essays from *Women's World*), edited by Xia Xiaohong, 334–35. Guiyang: Guizhou jiaoyu chubanshe, 2003.

Fu Ping. "Zhongguo funü canzheng yundong zhi wojian" (My view of China's women's suffrage movement). *Funü gongming*, no. 19 (1929–30?): 23–26.

Fung, Edmund S. K. *The Military Dimension of the Chinese Revolution: The New Army and Its Role in the Revolution of 1911.* Canberra: Australian National University Press, 1980.

———. "Recent Scholarship on the Minor Parties and Groups in Republican China." *Modern China* 20, no. 4 (October 1994): 478–508.

———. *In Search of Chinese Democracy: Civil Opposition in Nationalist China, 1929–1949*. Cambridge, UK: Cambridge University Press, 2000.

Funü cidian bian xie zu, ed. (FNCD) *Funü cidian* (Dictionary of Women). Beijing: Qiushi chubanshe, 1990.

Gamble, Sidney. *North China Villages: Social, Political and Economic Activities before 1933*. Berkeley: University of California Press, 1963.

Gao Kuixiang and Shen Jianguo, eds. (ZGNP) *Zhonghua gujin nüjie pu* (Annals of ancient and modern women in China). Beijing: Zhonghua shehui chubanshe, 1991.

Gerth, Karl. *China Made: Consuming Culture and the Creation of a Nation*. Cambridge, MA: Harvard University Asia Center, 2003.

Gilmartin, Christina K. *Engendering the Chinese Revolution: Radical Women, Communist Politics and Mass Movements in the 1920s*. Berkeley: University of California Press, 1995.

———. "Gender in the Formation of a Communist Body Politic." *Modern China* 19, no. 3 (July 1993): 299–329.

———. "Gender, Political Culture, and Women's Mobilization in the Chinese Nationalist Revolution, 1924–1927." In *Engendering China: Women, Culture and the State*. Edited by Christina K. Gilmartin, Gail Hershatter, Lisa Rofel, and Tyrene White, 195–225. Cambridge, MA: Harvard University Press, 1994.

———. "The Politics of Gender in the Making of the Party." In *New Perspectives on the Chinese Communist Revolution*, edited by Tony Saich and Hans van de Ven, 33–55. Armonk, NY: M.E. Sharpe, 1995.

Gipoulon, Catherine. "The Emergence of Women in Politics in China, 1898–1927." *Chinese Studies in History* (Winter 1989–90): 46–67.

———. "Integrating the Feminist and Worker's Movement: The Case of Xiang Jingyu." *Republican China* 10 (November 1994): 29–41.

Glosser, Susan. *Chinese Visions of Family and State, 1915–1953*. Berkeley: University of California Press, 2003.

Goodman, Bryna. "The Vocational Woman and the Elusiveness of 'Personhood' in Early Republican China." In *Gender in Motion: Divisions of Labor and Cultural Change in Late Imperial and Modern China*, edited by Bryna Goodman and Wendy Larson, 265–86. Lanham, MD: Rowman & Littlefield, 2005.

Goodman, David S. G. "Resistance and Revolution, Religion, and Rebellion: The Sixth Trigram Movement in Licheng, 1939–1942." In *North China at War: The Social Ecology of Revolution, 1937–1945*, edited by Feng Chongyi and David S. G. Goodman, 131–54. Lanham, MD: Rowman & Littlefield, 2000.

———. "Revolutionary Women and Women in the Revolution: The Chinese Communist Party and Women in the War of Resistance to Japan, 1937–1945." *China Quarterly*, no. 164 (December 2000): 915–42.

———. *Social and Political Change in Revolutionary China: The Taihang Base Area in the War of Resistance to Japan, 1937–1945*. Lanham, MD: Rowman & Little-field, 2000.

Grimshaw, Patricia. "Gender, Citizenship and Race in the Women's Christian Temperance Union of Australia, 1890 to the 1930s." *Australian Feminist Studies* 13, no. 28 (1998): 199–214.

———. "Settler Anxieties, Indigenous Peoples and Women's Suffrage in the Colonies of Australia, New Zealand and Hawai'i, 1888–1902." *Pacific Historical Review* 69, no. 4 (November 2000): 553–72.

———. "A White Woman's Suffrage." In *A Woman's Constitution? Gender and History in the Australian Commonwealth*, edited by Helen Irving, 77–97. Sydney: Hale & Iremonger, 1998.

———. *Women's Suffrage in New Zealand*. 1972. Reprint, Auckland: Auckland University Press and Oxford University Press, 1987.

Groot, Gerry. *Managing Transitions: The Chinese Communist Party, United Front Work, Corporatism and Hegemony*. London: Routledge, 2004.

Guo Wei, ed. *Zhonghua minguo xianfa shiliao* (Historical materials on the constitutions of the Republic of China). In *Jindai Zhongguo shiliao congkan: Di bashiba* (Collected materials on modern China, vol. 88), edited by Chen Yunlong. 1947. Reprint, Taipei: Wenhai chubanshe, 1973.

Guo Yanli, ed., *Qiu Jin shiwen xuan* (Selected writings of Qiu Jin), 3–5. Beijing: Renmin wenxue chubanshe, 1982.

Guomin canzheng hui (Materials on the People's Political Council). Taipei: Yutai gongsi, 1962.

Gu Shen. "Nüzi canzheng wenti" (Problems in women's suffrage). *Shi bao* (24 March 1912).

Ha Sijing. "Meiguo funü zhi xuanju quan" (Voting rights for American women). *Funü shibao* no. 7 (1912): 1–8.

Hahner. J. E. *Emancipating the Female Sex: The Struggle for Women's Rights in Brazil*. Durham, NC: Duke University Press, 1990.

Han Xiaoping and Zhu Weibo. "Xinhai geming yu funü yundong" (The 1911 revolution and the women's movement). *Hebei shifan daxue xuebao: She ke ban* (Hebei Normal University journal: Social sciences edition), no. 4 (1992): 58–61, 66.

He Xiangning. "Jing gao wo tongbao jiemei" (A respectful note to my compatriot sisters). *Jiangsu*, no. 4 (1903): 144–45.

He Zhen [See Zhen Shu].

Hershatter, Gail. *Dangerous Pleasures: Prostitution and Modernity in Twentieth-Century Shanghai*. Berkeley: University of California Press, 1999.

———. *The Workers of Tianjin, 1900–1949*. Stanford, CA: Stanford University Press, 1986.

Hinton, William. *Fanshen: A Documentary of Revolution in a Chinese Village*. 1966. Reprint, New York: Monthly Review Press, 1967.

Ho, Clara Wing-chung, ed. (BDQP) *Biographical Dictionary of Chinese Women: The Qing Period, 1644–1911*. Armonk, NY: M.E. Sharpe, 1998.

Holton, Sandra Stanley. "The Making of Suffrage History." In *Votes for Women*, edited by June Purvis and Sandra Stanley Holton, 13–33. London: Routledge, 2000.

Honig, Emily. *Sisters and Strangers: Women in the Shanghai Cotton Mills, 1919–1949*. Stanford, CA: Stanford University Press, 1986.

Howell, Jude. "Women's Political Participation in China." *Parliamentary Affairs* 55 (2002): 43–56.

Hu Bin[xia]. "Lun Zhongguo zhi shuairuo nüzi bu de ci qi zui" (Women cannot avoid responsibility for the weakened state of China). *Jiangsu*, no. 3 (1903): 156–57.

Hu Binxia. "Zhu 'Gong ai hui' zhi qiantu" (To the future of the Mutual Love Society). *Jiangsu*, no. 6 (1903): 162–63.

Hu Chi-hsi. "The Sexual Revolution in the Kiangsi Soviet." *China Quarterly*, no. 59 (1974): 477–90.

Hu Ying. "Writing Qiu Jin's Life: Wu Zhiying and Her Family Learning." *Late Imperial China* 25, no. 4 (December 2004): 119–60.

Huai Bing. "Shuo nüzi canzheng zhi liyou" (Reasons for women's suffrage). *Funü shibao*, no. 8 (1912): 43–44.

Huan Qi. "Funü canzheng zai Zhongguo bu fada de yuanyin" (The reasons why women's suffrage fails to flourish in China). *Funü gongming*, no. 10 (1929): 5–8.

Huang, Philip C. C. "Women's Choices under the Law: Marriage, Divorce and Illicit Sex in the Qing and Republic." *Modern China* 27, no. 1 (January 2001): 3–58.

Huang Bihun. "Wo duiyu nüzi canzheng de ganxiang" (My feelings on women's suffrage). *Laodong yu funü*, no. 11 (April 24, 1921): 2.

Huang Jiade. *Xin nü xing* (New type of women). Shanghai: Shanghai liangyou tushu, 1936.

Issacs, Harold R. *The Tragedy of the Chinese Revolution*. 2nd rev. ed. 1938. Reprint, Stanford, CA: Stanford University Press, 1961.

Jayawardena, Kumari. *Feminism and Nationalism in the Third World*. London: Zed, 1985.

Ji Hong. "Xin xianfa ying queding funü de quanli" (The new constitution ought to guarantee women's rights). *Funü shenghuo* 4, no. 11 (16 June 1937): 5–6.

Ji Rong, ed. *Zhongguo funü yundong shi* (The history of the Chinese women's movement). Changsha: Hunan chubanshe, 1992.

Ji Xin. *Nüren yu zhengzhi: 90 niandai funü canzheng yundong* (Women and politics: The movement to participate in politics in the 1990s). Taibei: Nüshu wenshu shi, 2000.

Jiang Jilan. "Shuo nüzi canzheng zhi liyou" (Reasons for women's suffrage). *Funü shibao*, no. 8 (1912): 1–2.

Jiang Shizhou. "Xue deng: Ping nüzi canzheng yundong" (Study light: Critique of the women's suffrage movement). *Shishi xinbao* (15 August 1922).

Jiang Xiaoguang. "Zhongguo funü yundong zhi shi zhi guancha" (A historical survey of the women's movement in China). *Funü gongming*, no. 30 (1930): 23–26.

Jiang Zhaoxiang. "Bo Cheng Xiluo jun de buzhang nü canzheng" (Reply to Mr. Cheng Xiluo's opposing women's suffrage). *Dagong bao* (18–19 May 1921).

Jiang Zuobin. "Jinzhu Shenzhou nübao" (Sincerely offering best wishes to *Shenzhou nübao*). *Shenzhou nübao*, no. 2 (1912): 1–3.

Jin Shiyin. "Canzheng yundong shi funü jiefang de xianfeng" (Women's suffrage is the vanguard of women's liberation). *Funü gongming*, no. 11 (1929): 10.

Jin Songcen. *Nüjie zhong* (A Tocsin for Women). Shanghai: Datong shuju, 1903.

———. *Nüjie zhong* (A Tocsin for Women). Edited by Chen Yan. 1903. Reprint, Shanghai: Guji chubanshe, 2003.

Jin Yi [Jin Songcen]. *"Nüzi shijie* fakan ci" (Introducing *Women's World*), *Nüzi shijie* 1 (1904). In *"Nüzi shijie" wen xuan* (Collected essays from *Women's World*), edited by Xia Xiaohong, 55–56. Guiyang: Guizhou jiaoyu chubanshe, 2003.

Jin Zhonghua. "Cong jiating dao zhengzhi" (From the family to politics). FNZZ 17, no. 5 (1931): 2–13.

———. *Funü wenti* (The woman question). Shanghai: Shangwuyin shuguan, 1933.

Jing Song [Xu Guangping]. "Xin Guangdong de xin nüxing" (New women of new Guangdong). *Xin nüxing* 1, no. 12 (1926): 885–89.

Jingyu [see Xiang Jingyu].

Jinling nüzi daxue xuesheng. *Shijie funü de xiandao* (Stories of women pioneers). Shanghai: YWCA Publishing, 1934.

Jiu Si. "Lun zizhong" (On self-respect). *Nüzi shijie*, no. 6 (1904): 9–11.

Johnson, Kay Ann. *Women, the Family and Peasant Revolution in China*. Chicago: University of Chicago Press, 1983.

Judd, Ellen R. *The Chinese Women's Movement: Between State and Market*. Stanford, CA: Stanford University Press, 2002.

Judge, Joan. "Citizens or Mothers of Citizens? Gender and the Meaning of Modern Chinese Citizenship." In *Changing Meanings of Citizenship in Modern China*, edited by Merle Goldman and Elizabeth J. Perry, 23–43. Cambridge, MA: Harvard University Press, 2002.

———. "The Factional Function of Print: Liang Qichao, *Shibao* and the Fissures in the Late Qing Reform Movement." *Late Imperial China* 16, no. 1 (June 1995): 120–40.

———. "Talent, Virtue, and the Nation: Chinese Nationalisms and Female Subjectivities in the Early Twentieth Century." *American Historical Review* 106, no. 3 (2001): 765–803.

Kai Yun. "Canyi yuan zhi heian" (Darkness of the Parliament). *Nüzi baihua bao*, no. 3 (1912): 25–29.

Kent, Susan Kingsley. *Sex and Suffrage in Britain, 1860–1914*. Princeton, NJ: Princeton University Press, 1987.

Kiely, Jan. "Third Force Periodicals in China, 1928–1949." *Republican China* 21, no. 1 (1995): 129–68.

Ko, Dorothy. *Teachers of the Inner Chambers: Women and Culture in China, 1573–1722*. Stanford, CA: Stanford University Press, 1994.

Kong Hai. "Duiyu nüzi canzheng quan zhi huaiyi" (My concerns about women's participation in politics). *Minli bao* (28 February 1912).

———. "Fu Yang Jiwei nüshi han" (Reply to Madame Yang Jiwei's letter). *Minli bao* (5 March 1912).

Lam Hok-chung. "Zhang Hanying." In BDQP, 289–93.

Lao Zeren. "Zhongguo funü yundong de jianglai" (Future of the women's movement in China), FNZZ 7, no. 9 (1921): 7–10.

Larson, Wendy. *Women and Writing in Modern China.* Stanford, CA: Stanford University Press, 1998.

Lee, Bernice J. "The Change in the Legal Status of Chinese Women in Civil Matters from Traditional Law to the Republican Civil Code." PhD diss., University of Sydney, 1975.

Lee, Lily. *Women of the Long March.* Sydney: Allen & Unwin, 1999.

———., ed. (BDTC) *Biographical Dictionary of Chinese Women: The Twentieth Century, 1912–2000.* Armonk, NY: M.E. Sharpe, 2003.

———., ed. *Biographical Dictionary of Chinese Women: Antiquity to the Sui Dynasty.* Armonk, NY: M.E. Sharpe, forthcoming.

Lee Kam Keung. "Fang Junying." In BDQP, 34–37.

Li Chien-nung. *The Political History of China, 1840–1928.* Princeton, NJ: Van Nostrand, 1956.

Li Dazhao. "Li Dazhao jun jiangyan nü quan yundong" (Li Dazhao's speech on the women's movement). *Jiangsheng rikan* (5 February 1923). In ZFYLZ, 143–45.

———. "The Postwar Woman Question." Translated by H. R. Lan and V. Fong, *Chinese Studies in History* 31, no. 2 (Winter 1997–98): 17–23. First published as "Zhanhou zhi furen wenti." *Xin qingnian* 6, no. 2 (15 February 1919): 141–47.

Li Hanjun. *Funü zhi guoqu yu jianglai* (Women's past and future). Shanghai: Shangwuyin shuguan, 1921.

Li Liuru. "Funü jiefang san da tiwen" (Three important issues relating to women's liberation). *Dagong bao* (14–17 May 1921).

Li Luoxiao. "Funü yu xingxian" (Women and the passage of the constitution). *Xin funü,* no. 13 (April 1948): 4.

Li San. "Xinzhi koukuai" (Straight heart, fast mouth). *Shenbao* (18 October 1912).

Li Xiaojiang. "Economic Reform and the Awakening of Women's Consciousness." Translated by S. Katherine Campbell. In *Engendering China: Women, Culture and the State,* edited by Christina K. Gilmartin, Gail Hershatter, Lisa Rofel, and Tyrene White, 360–84. Cambridge, MA: Harvard University Press, 1994.

Li Xueli. "Minzhu, ducai, fazhi, renzhi" (Democracy, autocracy, rule of law, and rule by people). *Xin funü,* no. 15 (June 1948): 4.

Li Yu-ning. "Hsu Tsung-han: Tradition and Revolution." *Republican China* 10, no. 1a (November 1984): 13–27.

———. "Nüjie zhong yu Zhonghua nüxing de xiandai hua" (A Tocsin for Women and the modernization of China's women). In *Family Process and Political Process in Modern Chinese History: Part Two,* edited by Academia Sinica Modern History Institute, 1055–82. Taipei: Modern History Institute, 1992.

———. "Sun Yat-sen and Women's Transformation." *Chinese Studies in History* (Summer 1988): 58–78.

———. "*Zhongguo xinnüjie* zazhi de chuangkan ji neihan" (The founding and contents of the magazine *China's New Women's World*). In *Zhongguo funü shi lunwenji*, edited by Li Yu-ning and Zhang Yufa, 179–241. Taipei: Shangwuyin shuguan, 1981.

Li Zhengfen. "Nüzi canzheng zhi taolun—Zhi Jiangnan Zhang Renlan tongzhi shu" (Discussion on women's suffrage—Replying to the letter from Madame Zhang Renlan). *Minli bao* (24 March 1912).

Li Zhishan. "'Sanyue bari' yu Zhongguo funü de yaoqiu" (March 8th and China's women's demands). *Xin nüxing* 3, no. 1 (1928): 253–58.

Li Zi. "Nüzi jiefang" (Women's liberation). *Minguo ribao* (9 April 1919).

Li Ziyun. "Women's Consciousness and Women's Writing." In *Engendering China: Women, Culture and the State*, edited by Christina K. Gilmartin, Gail Hershatter, Lisa Rofel, and Tyrene White, 299–317. Cambridge, MA: Harvard University Press, 1994.

Lian Shi. "Ben bao duiyu nüzi guomin juan zhi yanshuo" (A speech on women citizens offered to this paper; parts 1 and 2). *Zhongguo xin nüjie zazhi*, no. 1 (1907): 41–50; no. 2 (1907): 21–26.

———. "Ben bao wu da zhiyi yanshuo" (This journal's five-great-ism speech). *Zhongguo xin nüjie zazhi*, no. 3 (1907): 15–26.

———. "Nüquan pingyi" (On the principle of equality and women's rights). *Zhongguo xin nüjie zazhi*, no. 1 (1907): 1–6.

———. "*Zhongguo xin nüjie zazhi* fakan ci" (Introducing *China's New Women's World*). *Zhongguo xin nüjie zazhi*, no. 1 (1907): 1–3.

Liang Qichao. "Renquan yu nüquan" (Human rights and women's rights). *Chenbao fukan* (16 November 1922).

Lin Hao. "Zhongguo funü zhi jiefang yundong" (China's women's liberation movement). *Nüzi yuekan* 1, no. 8 (1933): 14–17.

Lin Weihong. "Tongmeng hui shidai nü geming zhishi de huodong" (Activities of the noble women revolutionaries of the Revolutionary Alliance period). In *Zhongguo funü shilun wenji*, edited by Li Yu-ning and Zhang Yufa, 129–78. Taipei: Shangwuyin shuguan, 1981.

Lin Wenqi. "Funü canzheng kaibuzou" (March for women's participation in politics). FNZZ, no. 11 (1991): 118–29.

Lin Xi. "Guomin huiyi hou: Nüzi canzheng de zhunbei" (After the Citizens' Convention: Preparations for women's suffrage). *Minguo ribao* (25 May 1931).

Lin Zongsu. "Lin nüshi xu" (Preface by Madame Lin). In *Nüjie zhong* (A Tocsin for Women), Jin Songcen, 1–3. Shanghai: Datong shuju, 1903.

———. "Nüzi canzheng tongzhi hui huiyuan Lin Zongsu xuan yuan" (Declaration by the Women's Suffrage Comrades' Society member Lin Zongsu). *Tianduo bao* (23–24 January 1912).

———. "Nüzi canzheng tongzhi hui xuanyan shu" (Manifesto of the Women's Suffrage Comrades' Society). *Funü shibao*, no. 5 (1912): 17–19.

Liu Guanghua. "Wo de muqin Liu Wang Liming" (My mother Liu Wang Liming). *Renwu*, no. 6 (1981): 143–49.

Liu Hengjing. *Funü wenti wenji, yi ce* (Collected essays on the woman problem, Vol. one). Nanjing: Funü yuekan she, 1947.

Liu Jucai. *Zhongguo jindai funü yundong shi* (A history of the women's movement in Modern China). Beijing: Zhongguo funü chubanshe, 1989.

Liu Qianhou. "Wo duiyu sheng xianfa de yijian" (My comments on the provincial constitution). *Dagong bao* (22 May 1921).

Liu Wang Liming. *Zhongguo funü yundong: Yi ce* (China's Women's Movement, Vol. one). Shanghai: Shangwuyin shuguan, 1934.

Lötveit, Trygve. *Chinese Communism, 1931–1934: Experience in Civil Government.* Lund: Scandinavian Institute of Asian Studies, Monograph no. 16, 1973.

Louie, Kam. *Theorising Chinese Masculinity: Society and Gender in China.* Cambridge, UK: Cambridge University Press, 2002.

Lü Fangshang. "Kangzhan shiqi Zhongguo de funü yundongzuo" (China's women's movement in the war period). In *Zhongguo funü shi lun wenji (Collected works on Chinese Women's history)*, edited by Li Youning and Zhang Yufa, 378–412. Taipei: Shangwuyin shuguan, 1981.

Lü Meiyi and Zheng Yongfu. *Zhongguo funü yundong, 1840–1921* (The Chinese women's movement, 1840–1921). Zhengzhou: Henan renmin chubanshe, 1991.

Luan Xuefei. "He Xiangning yu Zhongguo gongchandang" (He Xiangning and the Chinese Communist Party). *Dongbei shida xuebao: Zhe, she ban* (Dongbei Normal University journal: Philosophy and social sciences edition), no. 4 (1992): 6–21.

Luo Jialun. "Funü jiefang" (The liberation of women). *Xin chao* 2, no. 1 (1919): 1–10.

Luo Qiong. "Canzheng yundong zai funü jiefang yundong zhong de diwei" (The place of the suffrage movement in the movement for women's liberation). *Funü shenghuo* 4, no. 11 (16 June 1937): 3–4.

Luo Yanbin [See Yan Bin].

Lu Shouzhen. "Lun nüzi yingyou xuanju quan" (Discussing the necessity for women to have voting rights). *Funü shibao*, no. 5 (1912): 13–14.

Lu Xun. "My Views on Chastity." Translated by Yang Xianyi and Gladys Yang. In *Lu Xun: Selected Works.* Vol. 2, 13–25. 1918. Reprint, Beijing: Foreign Languages Press, 1980.

Ma Gengcun. *Zhongguo jindai funü shi* (History of women in Modern China). Qingdao: Qingdao chubanshe, 1995.

Mackie, Vera. *Creating Socialist Women in Japan: Gender, Labour and Activism, 1900–1937.* Cambridge, UK: Cambridge University Press, 1997.

MacKinnon, Stephen. "Refugee Flight at the Outset of the Anti-Japanese War." In *Scars of War: The Impact of Warfare on Modern China*, edited by Diana Lary and Stephen MacKinnon, 118–35. Vancouver: University of British Columbia Press, 2001.

Mann, Susan. *Precious Records: Women in China's Long Eighteenth Century.* Stanford, CA: Stanford University Press, 1997.

———. "Widows in the Kinship, Class and Community structures of Qing Dynasty China." *Journal of Asian Studies* 46, no. 1 (1987): 37–55.

Mao Dun [see Shen Yanbing].

Martin, Dorothea A. L., ed. "Qiu Jin: A Female Knight-Errant, a True Woman Warrior." Special issue, *Chinese Studies in History* 34, no. 2 (Winter 2000–2001).

Marwick, Arthur. *The Deluge: British Society and the First World War.* 1965. Reprint, London: Macmillan, 1975.

Matsukawa, Yukiko, and Kaoru Tachi. "Women's Suffrage and Gender Politics in Japan." In *Suffrage and Beyond: International Feminist Perspectives*, edited by Caroline Daley and Melanie Nolan, 171–83. Auckland: Auckland University Press, 1994.

Mazur, Mary G. "Intellectual Activism in China during the 1940s: Wu Han in the United Front and the Democratic League." *China Quarterly*, no. 133 (March 1993): 27–55.

McElderry, Andrea. "Woman Revolutionary: Xiang Jingyu." *China Quarterly*, no. 105 (March 1986): 95–122.

Mei Ju-ao. "On the Eve of Constituional Government in China." *T'ien Hsia Monthly* 2, no. 5 (May 1936): 443–53.

Meng, C.Y.W. "Fight for 'Sex Equality' in China." *China Weekly Review* (24 November 1934): 432.

Meng Huan. "Lun nüzi yaoqiu canzheng quan zhi guaixiang" (On the strangeness of women wanting suffrage rights). *Dagong bao* (30 March 1912).

———. "Wen ping er" (Commentary two). *Dagong bao* (1 April 1912).

Miao Quanji, ed. *Zhongguo zhixian shi ziliao huibian* (Material on China's constitutional history). Taipei: Guoshi guan, 1989.

Mill, J.S. *On the Subjection of Women* (1869). Rpt. in Ann P. Robson and John M. Robson (eds), *Sexual equality: Writing by John Stuart Mill, Harriet Taylor Mill and Helen Taylor*, pp. 305-400. Toronto: Toronto University Press, 1994.

Min Jia-yin, et al., eds. *The Chalice and the Blade in Chinese Culture: Gender Relations and Social Models.* Beijing: China Social Sciences Publishing House, 1995.

Ming Yang. "Wairen yanguang zhi Zhongguo funü gexin yundong" (Outsiders' views of the innovations of China's women's movement). FNZZ 13, no. 12 (1927): 7–11.

Mittler, Barbara. *A Newspaper for China? Power, Identity, and Change in Shanghai's News Media, 1872–1912.* Cambridge, MA: Havard University Asia Center, 2004.

Molony, Barbara. "Citizenship and Suffrage in Interwar Japan." In *Women's Suffrage in Asia: Gender, Nationalism and Democracy*, edited by Louise Edwards and Mina Roces, 127–51. London: RoutledgeCurzon, 2004.

Mo Yan. "Jin ri Zhongguo de funü wenti yu minzhu zhuyi" (Democracy and the women question in current-day China). *Funü shenghuo* 4, no. 11 (16 June 1937): 8–9.

Nathan, Andrew J. *Chinese Democracy.* New York: Knopf, 1985.

———. *Peking Politics, 1918–1923.* Berkeley: University of California Press, 1976.

Ne Zhai. "Shi ke" (Ten *ke*'s). *Shenbao* (26 March 1912).

Nivard, Jacqueline. "Women and the Women's Press: The Case of *The Ladies' Journal* (*Funü zazhi*), 1915–1931." *Republican China* 10 (1984): 37–55.

Oldfield, Audrey. *Woman Suffrage in Australia: A Gift or a Struggle?* Cambridge and Melbourne: Cambridge University Press, 1992.

Ono Kazuko. *Chinese Women in a Century of Revolution, 1850–1950*, edited by Joshua A. Fogel. Stanford, CA: Stanford University Press, 1989.

Ou Peifen. "Jinggao zheng xuanju quan zhi nü huibao" (Respectful note to the women debating suffrage rights). *Minli bao* (7–8 June 1912).

Paisley, Fiona. "Cultivating Modernity: Culture and Internationalism in Australian Feminism's Pacific Age." *Journal of Women's History* 14, no. 3 (Autumn 2002): 105–32.

Pan Wei-tung. *The Chinese Constitution: A Study of Forty Years of Constitution-making in China*. Washington, DC: Institute of Chinese Culture, 1945.

Pao Tao, Chia-lin. "Ch'iu Chin's Revolutionary Career." *Chinese Studies in History* (Summer 1992): 10–24.

Pateman, Carole. "Three Questions about Womanhood Suffrage." In *Suffrage and Beyond: International Feminist Perspectives*, edited by Caroline Daley and Melanie Nolan, 331–48. Auckland: Auckland University Press, 1994.

Pearson, Gail. "Tradition, Law and the Female Suffrage Movement in India." In *Women's Suffrage in Asia: Gender, Nationalism and Democracy*, edited by Louise Edwards and Mina Roces, 195–219. London: RoutledgeCurzon, 2004.

Pei Gong. "Nan nü pingdeng de biyao" (The necessity for gender equality). *Zhongguo xin nüjie zazhi*, no. 2 (1907): 35–44.

Pepper, Suzanne. *Civil War in China: The Political Struggle, 1945–1949*. Berkeley: University of California Press, 1978.

Perry, Elizabeth J. *Shanghai on Strike: The Politics of Chinese Labor*. Stanford, CA: Stanford University Press, 1993.

Ping Su. "Funü canzheng wenti" (The question of women's suffrage). FNZZ 8, no. 11 (1922): 6–16.

Pingzi. "Nüzi de yubei" (Preparations by women). *Dagong bao* (5 May 1921).

———. "Wo duiyu nüzi canzheng de xiwang" (My hopes for women's participation in politics). *Dagong bao* (3 June 1921).

Purvis, June, and Sandra Stanley Holton. "Introduction: The Campaigns for Votes for Women." In *Votes for Women*, edited by June Purvis and Sandra Stanley Holton, 1–12. London: Routledge, 2000.

Pye, E. M. "The Women's Movement in China." *Asiatic Review* 25 (1929): 204–19, cited in Croll, *Feminism and Socialism in China*, London: Routledge & Kegan Paul, 1978.

Qian Di. *Nüxing yu shehui* (Women and society). Shanghai: Guangming shuju, 1929.

Qian Jianqiu. "Falü shang nannü pingdeng de yuanze" (The principle of sex equality in the law). FNZZ 14, no. 4 (1928): 9–10.

———. "Funü yundong" (The women's movement). In *Zhonghua minguo kaiguo wushinian shilunji: Di er ce* (The first fifty years of the Republic of China, Vol. 2). Taipei: Guofang, 1962.

Qian Nanxiu. "Revitalizing the Xianyuan (Worthy Ladies) Tradition: Women in the 1989 Reforms." *Modern China* 29, no. 4 (October 2003): 399–454.

Qin Jin. "Guomin dahui zhi fuxuan wenti" (The national assembly and the problem of the election of women). *Funü shenghuo* 3, no. 3 (August 1936): 4–6.

Qing Meng. "Duiyu nüzi canzheng zhi yanjiu" (On researching women's suffrage). *Funü shibao*, no. 8 (1912): 7–8.

Qiu Jin. "Jinggao yimeimen (jiexuan)" (A respectful announcement to my sisters [excerpts]). In *Qiu Jin shiwen xuan* (Selected writings of Qiu Jin), edited by Guo Yanli, 10–13. Beijing: Renmin wenxue chubanshe, 1982.

———. "Mian nüquan ge" (Ode on promoting women's rights). *Zhongguo nübao*, no. 2 (1907): 48.

———. *Qiu Jin ji (Collected Works of Qiu Jin)*. 1960. Reprint, Shanghai: Shanghai guji chubanshe, 1979.

———. "*Zhongguo nübao* fakan ci." (Introducing *China Women's News*). In *Qiu Jin shiwen xuan* (Selected writings of Qiu Jin), edited by Guo Yanli, 3–5. Beijing: Renmin wenxue chubanshe, 1982.

Ramirez, Francisco O., Yasemin Soysal, and Suzanne Shanahan. "The changing logic of political citizenship: Cross-national acquisition of women's suffrage rights, 1890 to 1990." *American Sociological Review* 62, no. 5 (October 1997): 735–45.

Rendall, Jane. "Citizenship, Culture and Civilisation: The Language of British Suffragists, 1866–1874." In *Suffrage and Beyond: International Feminist Perspectives*, edited by Caroline Daley and Melanie Nolan, 117–50. Auckland: Auckland University Press, 1994.

Roces, Mina. "Is the Suffragist an American Colonial Construct? Defining 'the Filipino Woman' in Colonial Philippines." In *Women's Suffrage in Asia: Gender, Nationalism and Democracy*, edited by Louise Edwards and Mina Roces, 24–59. London: RoutledgeCurzon, 2004.

Rosen, Stanley. "Women and Political Participation in China." *Pacific Affairs* 68, no. 3 (1995): 315–41.

Rosinger, Lawrence K. *China's Wartime Politics, 1937–1944*. Princeton, NJ: Princeton University Press, 1945.

Sapiro, Virginia. "When Are Interests Interesting? The Problem of Political Representation of Women." *American Political Science Review* 75, no. 3 (1981): 701–16.

Schwarcz, Vera. *The Chinese Englightenment: Intellectuals and the Legacy of the May Fourth Movement of 1919*. Berkeley: University of California Press, 1986.

Se Lu. "Duiyu nüzi canzheng yundong de yulun he wojian" (My appraisal of the public opinion on the women's suffrage movement), FNZZ 8, no. 11 (1922): 2–5.

———. "Zuijin shinian nei funüjie de huigu" (Review of the women's movement of the last decade), FNZZ 10, no. 1 (1924): 16–22.

Selden, Mark. *The Yenan Way in Revolutionary China.* Cambridge, MA: Harvard University Press, 1971.

Shanchuan jurong. "Shinian lai de funü canzheng quan" (Women's suffrage rights in the last ten years). *Xin nüxing* 4 (October 1929): 1271–77; (November 1929): 1385–94.

Shang Hai et al., ed. (MSD) *Minguo shi dacidian* (Big dictionary of the history of the republican period). Beijing: Zhongguo guangbo dianshi chubanshe, 1991.

Shang Mingxuan. *He Xiangning zhuan* (Biography of He Xiangning). Beijing: Beijing chubanshe, 1994.

Shanghai shehui kexue yuan, ed. *Xinhai geming zai Shanghai shiliao xuanji* (Selected historical materials on the 1911 revolution in Shanghai). Shanghai: Renmin chubanshe, 1981.

Shen Peizhen. "Chuangban nüzi shangwuhui xuyan" (Introduction to the Women's Society for the Respect of Military Affairs). *Tianduo bao* (2 December 1911).

[Shen Yan] Bing [Mao Dun]. "Gao Zhejiang yaoqiu shengxian jiaru san tiaojian de nüzi" (Advice to the women of Zhejiang who are demanding the inclusion of three articles in the Provincial Constitution). *Funü pinglun,* no. 4 (24 August 1921): 2–3.

———. "How Do We Make the Women's Movement Truly Powerful?" Translated by H. R. Lan and V. Fong. *Chinese Studies in History* 31, no. 2 (Winter 1997–98): 84–87.

———. "Zenyang fang neng shi funü yundong you shili" (How to make the women's movement strong), FNZZ 6, no. 6 (5 June 1920): 5–8.

Shen Zhi. "Xinhai geming shiqi de nü zhishi fenzi" (Women intellectuals in the 1911 revolution period). *Shanghai shehui kexue yuan xueshu jikan* (Shanghai social sciences academy journal), no. 4 (1991): 57–66.

Sheng Shusen, Tang Changchun, and Tao Zhisun. "Zhongguo nüquan yundong de xianqu, Tang Qunying" (The forerunner of the Chinese feminist movement, Tang Qunying). *Renwu,* no. 4 (1992): 82–90.

Sheridan, James. *China in Disintegration: The Republican Era in Chinese History, 1912–1949.* New York: Free Press, 1975.

Shieh, Milton J. T., ed. *The Kuomintang: Historical Selected Documents, 1894–1969.* New York: St. John's University Press, 1970.

Shi Shuqing. "Women yundong de liyou he chuban de mudi" (The rationale behind our movement and the objective of our publication). *Nüzi canzheng xiejin hui hui kan,* 1 (10 December 1922): 2–4.

Shin, Linda P. "Wu T'ing-fang: A Member of a Colonial Elite as Coastal Reformer." In *Reform in Nineteenth Century China,* edited by Paul A. Cohen and John E. Schrecker, 265–71. Cambridge, MA: East Asia Research Center, Harvard University Press, 1976.

Shyu, Lawrence Nae-lih. "The People's Political Council and China's Wartime Problems, 1937–1945." PhD diss., Columbia University, 1972.

Si Yinglu. "Wen Shen nüshi yanshuo ganyan" (Hearing of Madame Shen's speech). *Shenbao* (23 October 1912).

Snow, Helen Foster. *Women in Modern China*. The Hague: Mouton, 1967.

Sommer, Matthew H. "Making Sex Work: Polyandry as a Survival Strategy in Qing Dynasty China." In *Gender in Motion: Divisions of Labor and Cultural Change in Late Imperial and Modern China*, edited by Bryna Goodman and Wendy Larson, 29–54. Lanham, MD: Rowman & Littlefield, 2005.

Song Qingling. "Chinese Women's Fight for Freedom." In *Chinese Women through Chinese Eyes*, edited by Li Yu-ning, 87–101. Armonk, NY: M.E. Sharpe, 1992.

Song Yunkun. "Guomin huiyi yu funü xuanchuan" (The National Assembly and women's propaganda). *Funü zhoubao* (16 February 1925).

Spence, Jonathan. *The Gate of Heavenly Peace*. London: Faber & Faber, 1982.

———. *The Search for Modern China*. New York: Norton, 1999.

Spencer, Herbert. *Social Statistics, or the Conditions Essential to Human Happiness Specified; and the first of them developed*. New York: D. Appleton & Co., 1865.

Stanley Holton, Sandra. "The Making of Suffrage History." In *Votes for Women*, edited by June Purvis and Sandra Stanley Holton, 13–33. London: Routledge, 2000.

Strand, David. "Citizens in the Audience and at the Podium." In *Changing Meanings of Citizenship in Modern China*, edited by Merle Goldman and Elizabeth J. Perry, 44–69. Cambridge, MA: Harvard University Press, 2002.

Strauss, Julia C. *Strong Institutions in Weak Polities: State Building in Republican China, 1927–1940*. Oxford: Clarendon Press, 1998.

Summerfield, Penny. "Gender and War in the Twentieth Century." *International History Review* 19, no. 1 (February 1997): 3–15.

Sun Yat-sen. "Fu Nanjing canzheng tongmeng hui nü tongzhi han" (Correspondence to the women comrades of the Nanjing Women's Suffrage Alliance). In *Sun Zhongshan quanji*, edited by Zhongguo shehui kexueyuan, 438. Beijing: Zhonghua shuju, 1982.

———. "Sun Zhongshan xiansheng fu ben hui shu" (The letter from Mr. Sun Yat-sen that upset this Society). *Shenzhou nübao*, no. 2 (1912): 1–2.

———. "Zai Guomindang chengli dahuishang de biaoshuo" (Speech to the meeting establishing the Nationalist Party). *Minzhu bao* (26 August 1912). In *Sun Zhongshan quanji*, edited by Zhongguo shehui kexueyuan, 409. Beijing: Zhonghua shuju, 1982.

Tan Sheying. *Fuyun sishinian* (Forty years of the women's movement). Taibei, 1978.

———., ed. *Zhongguo funü yundong tongshi* (A general history of the Chinese women's movement). Nanjing: Funü gongming she, 1936.

[Tan] Sheying. "Ruhe cuqi funü zhuyi zhengzhi zhi xingwei" (How to encourage women's interest in politics). *Funü gongming*, no. 7 (1929): 12–14.

Tang Guozhen. "Ruhe jiejue changji wenti" (How to solve the prostitution problem). *Funü gongming* 1, nos. 3–4 (15 June 1932): 17–21. Cited in Gail Hershatter, *Dangerous Pleasures: Prostitution and Modernity in Twentieth-Century Shanghai*, 260. Berkeley: University of California Press, 1999.

Tang Qunying, Yan Bin, et al. "Qing gong juan nüjie" (An offering to the women's world). *Zhongguo xin nüjie zazhi*, no. 3 (1907): 101–6.

Tang Rujin. "Shishu Xinhai geming shiqi de funü yundong" (A tentative narrative of the women's movement of the 1911 revolution period). *Shanghai shifan daxue xuebao: Zhe she ban* (Shanghai Normal University journal: Philosophy and social sciences edition), no. 3 (1988): 39–40.

Tao. "Jin ri funü zai zhengzhi shang de diwei" (Women's current status in politics). *Funü gongming*, no. 4 (1929): 13–14.

Teng Ssu-yu and J. K. Fairbank. *China's Response to the West: A Documentary Survey, 1839–1923*. Cambridge, MA: Harvard University Press, 1961.

Theiss, Janet M. *Disgraceful Matters: The Politics of Chastity in Eighteenth-Century China*. Berkeley: University of California Press, 2004.

Thompson, Roger. *China's Local Councils in the Age of Constitutional Reform, 1898–1911*. Cambridge, MA: Harvard University Press, 1995.

Tien Ju-k'ang. *Male Anxiety and Female Chastity: A Comparative Study of Chinese Ethical Values in Ming-Ch'ing Times*. Leiden: E.J. Brill, 1988.

Tong, J. "The Gender Gap in Political Culture and Participation in China." *Communist and Post-Communist Studies* 36 (2003): 131–50.

Tran, Lisa. "Concubines under Modern Chinese Law." PhD diss., University of California, Los Angeles, 2005.

Tsao, W. Y. *The Constitutional Structure of Modern China*. Carlton, Australia: Melbourne University Press, 1947.

Tsu Jing. *Failure, Nationalism and Literature: The Making of Modern Chinese Identity, 1895–1937*. Stanford, CA: Stanford University Press, 2005.

Tung, W. L. *The Political Institutions of Modern China*. The Hague: Martinus Nijhoff, 1964.

Tyrell, Ian. *Woman's World Woman's Empire: The Women's Christian Temperance Union in International Perspective, 1880–1930*. Chapel Hill: University of North Carolina Press, 1991.

Waltner, Anne. "Widows and Remarriage in Ming and Early Qing China." *Historical Reflections* 8, no. 3 (1981): 129–46.

Wan Pu. "Fandui nüzi canzheng lun de jieshi" (Expounding on the opponents to women's suffrage). *Nüzi canzheng xiejin hui hui kan* 1 (10 December 1922): 4–6.

Wang Jiajian. "Minchu de nüzi canzheng yundong" (The women's suffrage movement of the start of the republican period). In *Zhongguo funü shi lunwenji*, edited by Li Yu-ning and Zhang Yufa, 577–608. Taipei: Shangwuyin shuguan, 1981.

Wang Liming [see Liu Wang Liming]

Wang Ming. "Lun funü jiefang wenti" (Discussing the question of women's liberation). *Zhongguo funü* 1, no. 1 (1 June 1939): 4.

———. "Zhongguo funü yu xianzheng yundong" (Chinese women and the constitution movement). *Zhongguo funü* 1, no. 7 (20 December 1939): 2–3.

Wang Ruqi. "Canjia quanguo funü daibiao dahui sanriji" (Three days participating in the national women's representatives meeting). *Funü shenghuo* 5, no. 1 (July 1937): 13–15.

———. "Women yao canjia guomin dahui de zhixian" (We want to participate in the drawing up of the constitution for the National Assembly). *Funü shenghuo* 4, no. 10 (1 June 1937): 1–2.

———. "Women zenyang canjia guomin dahui de zhixian" (How can we participate in the writing of the constitution in the National Assembly?). *Funü shenghuo* 4, no. 11 (16 June 1937): 2.

Wang Shuhuai. "Kang Youwei dui nüxing ji hunyin de taidu" (Kang Youwei's attitudes about women and marriage). *Jindai zhongguo funü shi yanjiu*, no. 2 (June 1994): 27–49.

Wang Xingjuan and Xu Xiuyu, eds. *Zhongguo funü canzheng de xingdong* (Women's involvement in politics in China in action). Beijing: Haitun chubanshe, 1995.

Wang Zheng. *Women in the Chinese Enlightenment: Oral and Textual Histories.* Berkeley: University of California Press, 1999.

Watson, Rubie S. "Women's Property in Republican China: Rights and Practice." *Republican China* 10, no. 1a (1994): 1–12.

Wen Yang. "Tan minzhu zhengzhi" (Speaking on democratic government). *Funü shenghuo* 4, no. 11 (16 June 1937): 6–7.

Who's Who in China. Vol. 3 (4th ed.). 1950. Reprint, Hong Kong, Chinese Materials Centre, 1982.

Witke, Roxanne. "Woman as Politician in China of the 1920s." In *Women in China: Studies in Social Change and Feminism*, edited by Marilyn Young, 33–45. Ann Arbor: Center for Chinese Studies, University of Michigan, 1973.

Woodhead, H.G.W. *China Yearbook 1939.* Shanghai: North China Daily News and Herald, 1939.

Wu Jingxiong and Huang Gongjue. *Zhongguo zhixian shi* (The history of constitution making in China). Shanghai: Shangwuyin, 1937. In *Minguo congshu* 27, 1006–47. Shanghai: Shanghai shudian, 1989.

Wu Mulan. "Tongmeng nüzi jingwu lianxi dui xuanyan shu" (Letter promoting the Women's Training Troop Alliance). *Tianduo bao* (2 January 1912).

Wu Shuzhen. "Zhongguo funü canzheng yundong de lishi kaocha" (Observations on the history of the Chinese women's suffrage movement). *Zhongshan daxue xuebao: She ke ban* (Zhongshan University journal: Social sciences edition) 2 (1990): 77–84.

Wu Yifang. "The People's Political Council." *China at War* 6, no. 5 (May 1941): 86.

Wu Yuxiu. "Nüzi yingyou canzheng quan de wojian" (My opinion on why women ought to have the right to participate in politics). *Dagong bao* (25–27 May 1921).

Xi Zu. "She ping" (Critique of society). *Funü zhoubao* (29 October 1924).

Xia Xiaohong, ed. *"Nüzi shijie" wen xuan* (Collected essays from *Women's World*). Guiyan: Guizhou jiaoyu chubanshe, 2003.

Xiang Jingyu. "Guomin huiyi yu funü" (The National Assembly and women). *Funü zhoubao* (14 December 1924). In *Xiang Jingyu wenji* (Collected works of Xiang Jingyu), 161–64. Changsha: Hunan renmin chubanshe, 1980.

———. "Jinhou Zhongguo funü de guomin geming yundong" (The state of the Chinese women's national revolution movement). FNZZ 10, no. 1 (1 January 1924): 28–32.

———. "Nü guomin huiyi de san da yiyi" (Three main significances of the women's national assembly). *Funü zhoubao* (29 March 1925). In *Xiang Jingyu wenji* (Collected works of Xiang Jingyu), 182–85. Changsha: Hunan renmin chubanshe, 1980.

———. "Ping Wang Bihua de nüquan yundong tan" (Critique of Wang Bihua on the women's movement). *Funü zhoubao*, no. 8 (10 October 1923). In *Xiang Jingyu wenji* (Collected works of Xiang Jingyu), 103–6. Changsha: Hunan renmin chubanshe, 1980.

———. "Shanghai nüquan yundong hui jinhou ying zhuyi de san jian shi" (Three points that the current Shanghai women's rights movement ought to notice). *Funü zhoubao*, no. 12 (8 November 1923). In *Xiang Jingyu wenji* (Collected works of Xiang Jingyu), 111–13. Changsha: Hunan renmin chubanshe, 1980.

———. *Xiang Jingyu wenji* (Collected works of Xiang Jingyu). Changsha: Hunan renmin chubanshe, 1980.

———. "Ying lizheng funü tuanti canjia guomin huiyi" (We ought to argue hard for the inclusion of women's associations in the national assembly). *Funü zhoubao* (13 April 1925). In *Xiang Jingyu wenji* (Collected works of Xiang Jingyu), 192–93. Changsha: Hunan renmin chubanshe, 1980.

[Xiang] Jingyu. "Duiyu wanguo nüquan tongmeng dahui de ganxiang" (Remarks on the Congress of International League for Women's Rights). *Qianfeng* 1, no. 2 (1 December 1923): 48–50.

———. "Zhongguo funü yundong zaping" (Notes on the Chinese Women's Movement). *Qianfeng* 1, no. 2 (1 December 1923): 51–56.

———. "Zhongguo zuijin de funü yundong" (The Chinese women's movement at the present moment). *Qianfeng* 1, no. 1 (1 July 1923): 58–63.

Xiao Ying. "Wo duiyu funü chengxu caichan de yijian" (My opinion on women's inheritance of property). *Funü gongming*, no. 3 (1929): 6–8.

Xie Zhangfa. "Qingmo de liu Ri nüxuesheng ji huodong yu yingxiang" (Women students studying in Japan at the end of the Qing—their activities and influences). *Jindai zhongguo funü shi yanjiu*, no. 4 (August 1996): 63–86.

Xing Long. "Xinhai geming qianxi de funü yundong" (The women's movement on the eve of the 1911 revolution). *Shanxi daxue xuebao: Zhe, she ban* (Shanxi University journal: Philosophy and social sciences edition), no. 3 (1988): 68–71.

Xiong Yuezhi. *Zhongguo jindai minzhu sixiang shi* (The history of modern democratic thought in China). Shanghai: Renmin chubanshe, 1986.

Xu Huiqi. "Tang Qunying yu 'Nüzi canzheng tongmeng hui'—jianlun minchu funü canzheng huodong" (Tang Qunying and the "Women's Suffrage Alliance"—a brief discussion on the women's suffrage movement at the start of the republican period). *Guizhou shehui kexue* (Guizhou social sciences), no. 4 (1981): 30–37.

Xu Tianxiao. *Shenzhou nüzi xinshi* (A new history of the women of Shenzhou). 1913. Reprint, Taipei: Daoxiang chubanshe, 1993.

Xu Wentang. "Xiang Jingyu yu Zhonggong zaoqi funü yundong" (Xiang Jingyu and the CCP's women's movement in the early period). *Jindai Zhongguo funü shi yanjiu*, no. 2 (June 1994): 65–80.

Xu Yasheng. "Lun wo guo nüzi de canzheng wenti" (Discussing the question of women's suffrage in our country). FNZZ 15, no. 9 (1929): 2–7.

———. "Xunzheng yu funü" (Tutelage government and women). FNZZ 16, no. 5 (1930): 11–14.

Xu Yu. *Zhonghua minguo zhengzhi zhidu shi* (The history of the political system of Republican China). Shanghai: Shanghai renmin chubanshe, 1992.

Xue Limin. *Taiwan diqu funü canzheng wenti zhi yanjiu* (Research on problems in the women's suffrage movement in Taiwan). Taipei: Tianyi chubanshe, 1977.

Ya Chi. "Lun zhuzao guomin mu" (On founding citizen mothers). *Nüzi shijie*, no. 7 (1904): 1–7.

Ya Su. "Zhongguo funü zai jindai shishang canzheng yundong de yantao (xu)" (Discussion of the Chinese women's suffrage movement through history, cont.). *Zhongguo funü* 1, no. 9 (8 March 1940): 18–26, and no. 10–11 (25 April 1940): 3, 44–46.

Yan Bin [Luo Yanbin]. "Zhongguo liu Ri nü xuesheng hui chengli tonggao shu" (Notice announcing the formation of the Society for Women Students in Japan). *Zhongguo xin nüjie zazhi*, no. 2 (1907): 75–76.

Yan Shi. "Duiyu nüzi canzheng de xiwang" (Regarding my hopes for women's suffrage). FNZZ 8, no. 7 (1922): 10–11.

———. "Zuijin de nüquan yundong" (The current women's movement). FNZZ 8, no. 10 (1922): 61–63.

Yang Dongchun. "Ping Zhongguo shijiu nianlai de funü yundong" (A critique of the women's movement of the last nineteen years). FNZZ 17, no. 1 (1931): 7–16.

Yang Jiwei. "Yang Jiwei nüshi lai han" (Letter from Madame Yang Jiwei). *Minli bao* (5 March 1912).

Yang Xianjiang. "Zhongguo de funü yundong" (China's women's movement). *Xin nüxing* 2, no. 1 (1927): 13–16.

Yao Hui. "Nüzi canzheng zhi taolun—Yao Hui nüshi lai han" (Discussion on women's suffrage—Letter from Madame Yao Hui). *Minli bao* (20 March 1912).

Ye Weili. "'Nü Liuxuesheng': The Story of American-Educated Chinese Women, 1880s–1920s." *Modern China* 20, no. 3 (July 1994): 315–46.

Ye Zhijing. "Zhongguo funü de canzheng yundong" (The Chinese women's suffrage movement). *Minguo ribao* (30 January 1931).

Yi Chuheng. "He Cheng Xiluo xiansheng bu zhuzhang nüzi canzheng de shangliang" (Joining the discussion about Mr. Cheng Xiluo's opposition to women's participation in politics). *Dagong bao* (30–31 May, 1–2 June 1921).

Yi Qin. "Lun Zhongguo nüzi zhi qiantu" (On the future of Chinese women). *Jiangsu*, no. 4 (1903): 141–43, and no. 5 (1903): 129–31.

Yi Tao. "Xin minfa yu funü de guanxi" (The new civil code and its connection to women). *Funü gongming*, no. 3 (1929): 3–6.

You Tong. "Deguo zhi funü canzheng quan" (Women's suffrage rights in Germany). FNZZ 8, no. 7 (1922): 33–40.

You Xiong. "Yingguo de funü zhengzhijia" (Women politicians in England). FNZZ 11, no. 5 (1925): 801–4.

Young, Ernest P. *The Presidency of Yuan Shi-k'ai: Liberalism and Dictatorship in Early Republic China.* Ann Arbor: University of Michigan Press, 1977.

Young, T. S. "The Girl Guides." *China Weekly Review* (7 November 1936): 343.

Yu, George T. *Party Politics in Republican China: The Kuomintang, 1912–1924.* Berkeley: University of California Press, 1966.

Yu, Z. Y. "General Han Fu-chu's Drive against 'Modern Girls.'" *China Weekly Review* (31 October 1936): 322.

Yuan Shaoying and Yang Guizhen, eds. *Zhongguo funü mingren cidian* (Dictionary of famous Chinese women). Changchun: Beifang funü ertong chubanshe, 1989.

Zarrow, Peter. "Citizenship in China and the West." In *Imagining the People: Chinese Intellectuals and the Concept of Citizenship, 1890–1920*, edited by Joshua A. Fogel and Peter G. Zarrow, 3–38. Armonk, NY: M.E. Sharpe, 1997.

———. "He Zhen and Anarcho-Feminism in China." *Journal of Asian Studies* 47, no. 4 (November 1988): 796–813.

Ze Min. "Shijie nüzi canzheng yundong kao" (Examination of the world women's suffrage movement). FNZZ 5, no. 12 (1919): 1–18.

Zhang Hanying. "Nüzi canzheng zhi taolun—Fu Zhang Renlan nüshi lai shu." (Discussion on women's suffrage—Letter replying to Madame Zhang Renlan's letter). *Minli bao* (21 March 1912).

Zhang Peifen. *Funü wenti* (The Problem of Women). 1922. Reprint, Shanghai: Shangwuyin shuguan, 1927.

Zhang Pengyuan. "Liang Qichao de liangxing guan" (Liang Qichao's view of the two sexes). *Jindai zhongguo funü shi yanjiu*, no. 2 (June 1994): 51–64.

Zhang Pengzhou. "Funü shehui diwei zhi shide kaocha" (Exploration of the history of women's status in society). *Nüsheng* 3, no. 20 (1935): 4–10.

Zhang Renlan. "Zhang Renlan nüshi lai han" (Letter from Madame Zhang Renlan). *Minli bao* (9 March 1912).

Zhang Xiaofen. "Nüzi canzheng zhi taolun—Zhang Xiaofen nüshi lai han" (Discussion on women's suffrage—Letter from Madame Zhang Xiaofen). *Minli bao* (18 March 1912).

Zhang Xichen. "Guomin huiyi yu nü guomin" (The national assembly and women citizens). FNZZ 11, no. 5 (1925): 730–31.

———. "Zuijin funü de yundong de shibai he jinhou yingqu de fangzhen" (The failure of the women's movement in recent times and the platform we should adopt into the future). FNZZ 11, no. 7 (1925): 1120–24.

Zhang Yangchen. "Guomin huiyi yu nü guomin—zai Shanghai nü guomin dahui jiang" (The National Assembly and women citizens—Speech given to the Shanghai women citizens meeting). FNZZ 11, no. 5 (1925): 730–31.

Zhang Yufa. "Women—A New Social Force." *Chinese Studies in History* (Winter 1977–78): 29–55.

Zhao Liancheng. "Tongmeng hui zai Gang Yue de huodong he Guangdong funü canjia geming de huiyi" (Reminiscences on the Revolutionary Alliance in Hong Kong and Macao and the participation of Cantonese women in the revolution). In *Guangdong Xinhai geming shiliao* (Materials on the 1911 revolution in

Guangdong), edited by Zhongguo renmin zhengzhi xieshang huiyi Guangdong weiyuan hui wenshi ziliao yanjiu weiyuan hui, 85–106. Guangzhou: Guangdong renmin chubanshe, 1981.

Zhao Suisheng. *Power by Design: Constitution-making in Nationalist China.* Honolulu: University of Hawaii Press, 1996.

Zhao Zhi. "Nüzi wu cai bian she de bo" (In opposition to the phrase "a women without talent is virtuous"). *Zhongguo xin nüjie zazhi*, no. 3 (1907): 27–29.

Zhao Zongpo. "Lun Xinhai geming shijian de funü aiguo huodong" (Discussion on the patriotic women's movements of the 1911 revolution period). *Shanghai shifan daxue xuebao: Zhe, she ban* (Shanghai Normal University journal: Philosophy and social sciences), no. 4 (1990): 60–65.

Zhe Sheng. "Faguo nüzi de canzheng guan" (French women's outlook on suffrage). FNZZ 11, no. 1 (1925): 177–84.

Zhejiang sheng Xinhai geming shi yanjiu hui, ed. *Xinhai geming Zhejiang shiliao xuanji* (Selections of the history of the 1911 revolution in Zhejiang). Hangzhou: Zhejiang renmin chubanshe, 1981.

Zhen Shu [He Zhen]. "Furen jiefang wenti" (The problem of women's liberation). *Tianyi* 8, 9, 10 (combined issue; 1907): 1–6.

———. "Nüzi fuchou lun" (Discussion on women's revenge). *Tianyi* 4 (1907): 1–6.

Zhong Tingxiu. "Shijie geguo funü canzheng yundong gaishu" (A brief account of the women's suffrage movement around the world). FNZZ 15, no. 8 (1929): 13–19.

Zhonggong Shanghai shi weidang shi ziliao zhengji weiyuan hui, ed. *"Yi er. jiu" yihou Shanghai jiuguo hui shiliao xuanji* (After one two nine: Selected materials on the Shanghai National Salvation Society). Shanghai: Shanghai shehui kexueyuan, 1987.

Zhonghua quanguo funü lianhe hui, ed. (ZFYLZ). *Zhongguo funü yundong lishi ziliao, 1921–1927* (Materials on the history of the Chinese women's movement, 1921–1927). Beijing: Renmin chubanshe, 1986.

———., ed. (XMZS) *Zhongguo funü yundong shi: Xin minzhu zhuyi shiqi* (The history of the Chinese women's movement: New democracy period). Beijing: Chunqiu chubanshe, 1989.

Zhou Huan. "Nüzi canzheng tan" (Speaking on women's suffrage). *Nüzi canzheng xiejinhui huikan* (Bulletin of the Women's Suffrage Association), no. 1 (10 December 1922): 6–14.

Zhou Yaping. "Lun Xinhai geming shiqi de funü canzheng yundong" (Discussing the women's suffrage movement of the 1911 revolution period). *Lishi dang'an* (Jing; Historical archives: Beijing), no. 2 (1993): 118–23, 125.

———. "Zhongguo funü canzheng de lishi guiji" (The historical locus of China's women's suffrage movement). *Jishou daxue xuebao: She ke ban* (Jishou University journal: Social sciences edition), no. 2 (1992): 74–78.

Zhou Yu. "Nannü pingdeng de xianjue tiaojian" (Prerequisite conditions for equality between men and women). FNZZ 15, no. 11 (1929): 17–19.

Zhu Lun. "Nüzi canzheng zhi taolun—Zhu Lun nüshi lai han" (Discussion on women's suffrage—Letter from Madame Zhu Lun). *Minli bao* (16 March 1912).

Zi Jiu. "Women weishenme zhuzhang yao canjia guomin dahui" (Why we lobby to participate in the National Assembly). *Funü shenghuo* 4, no. 11 (16 June 1937): 10.

Zi Ran. "Wanguo nüzi canzheng hui kaihui jilu" (Report on the IWSA meeting). *Funü gongming*, no. 10 (1929): 40.

Index

Page numbers in **bold type** refer to the most detailed discussion of a topic. Page numbers in *italic type* refer to illustrations.